SECURITIES LAW

Other books in the *Essentials of Canadian Law* Series

ESSENTIALS OF
CANADIAN LAW

SECURITIES
LAW

JEFFREY G. MACINTOSH

Faculty of Law
University of Toronto

and

CHRISTOPHER C. NICHOLLS

Faculty of Law
Dalhousie University

IRWIN
LAW

A Quicklaw Company

Published in 2002 by

Irwin Law
14 Duncan Street
Suite 206
Toronto, Ontario
M5H 3G8
www.irwinlaw.com

ISBN-10: 1-55221-020-0
ISBN-13: 978-1-55221-020-8

Library and Archives Canada Cataloguing in Publication

MacIntosh, Jeffrey G.
Securities law

(Essentials of Canadian law)
Includes bibliographical references and index.
ISBN 1-55221-020-0

1. Securities — Canada.   I. Nicholls, Christopher C.   II. Title.   III. Series.

KE1065.M32 2002   346.71'092   C2001-904065-2

The publisher acknowledges the financial support of the Government of Canada through the Book Publishing Industry Development Program (BPIDP) for its publishing activities.

We acknowledge the assistance of the OMDC Book Fund, an initiative of Ontario Media Development Corporation.

Printed and bound in Canada.

 2 3 4 5   07

With love to Susan, Devon, Katie, Robyn, and Will,
the anchor of my affections.

— J.G.M.

To Andrea, Robert, Diana, and Tori,
with great thanks and greater affection.

— C.C.N.

SUMMARY TABLE OF CONTENTS

DETAILED
TABLE OF CONTENTS

SELECTED LIST OF STATUTES, REGULATIONS, AND ABBREVIATIONS

STATUTES

CBCA   *Canada Business Corporations Act*, R.S.C. 1985, c. C-44

CFA   *Commodity Futures Act* (Ontario), R.S.O. 1990, c. C.20

OBCA   *Business Corporations Act* (Ontario), R.S.O. 1990, c. B.16

OSA   *Securities Act* (Ontario), R.S.O. 1990, c. S.5

REGULATIONS

CBCA Regulations   SOR/2001-512

OBCA Regulation   R.R.O. 1990, Reg. 62

OSA Regulation   R.R.O. 1990, Reg. 1015

OTHER ABBREVIATIONS

CDNX   Canadian Venture Exchange
(Now TSX Venture Exchange)

CSA   Canadian Securities Administrators

IDA   Investment Dealers Association

OSC   Ontario Securities Commission

OSCB   Ontario Securities Commission Bulletin

SEC   U.S. Securities and Exchange Commission

SEDAR   System for Electronic Document Analysis and Retrieval
(See National Instrument 13-101)

TSE   Toronto Stock Exchange

ary market trades necessitates ongoing public reporting requirements for securities issuers. In chapter 9, we look at the rules and policy relating to such "continuous disclosure" obligations.

As industry consolidation continues in Canada and abroad, take-over activity will continue apace in the coming months and years. Take-over bids are subject to a detailed regulatory regime in Canada, and we deal with that regime in chapter 10. In this chapter, we also canvass the securities law implications surrounding the related matter of corporate share repurchases or share buybacks, known more formally as issuer bids.

In chapter 11, we introduce the principal enforcement mechanisms available to Canada's securities regulators and consider the strengths and the limitations of those mechanisms.

Chapter 12 offers brief concluding remarks, and describes some of the recent developments that unfolded after the material in the earlier chapters of the book had been completed. But we do caution readers that there have been, and will be, many more changes than those mentioned in chapter 12. (The great pre-Socratic philosopher Heraclitus anticipated twenty-first century securities regulation when he declared "All is flux.") Among other things, we note that the Toronto Stock Exchange is now to be identified by the initials, "TSX" rather than TSE and its recently acquired affiliate, the CDNX, has lately been re-dubbed the "TSX Venture Exchange." These changes occurred very late in the book's production process, and so these new names have not been reflected throughout the text. A more significant (pending) development is the imminent completion of the first Five Year Review of Ontario securities law by the Securities Review Advisory Committee established under the chairmanship of Purdy Crawford. It is quite possible that by the time this is read, the committee's report will have been released. However, as our book goes to print, the report is not yet available and so we offer no comments upon it. We hasten to note, however, that although the report will no doubt contain important and useful recommendations for improvement to Ontario's securities laws, its publication will herald no immediate changes. Considerable discussion and debate of any new proposals will undoubtedly precede the launch of any major legislative initiatives prompted by the Crawford Committee's observations. In the meantime, the core features of securities regulation outlined in this book will remain as stable as can be expected in this world of Heraclitun flux.

We hope this book proves a useful resource and a helpful introduction.

In chapter 2, we begin our study of Canadian securities regulation with what might be regarded as a traditional introduction to a number of fundamental securities law concepts: "security," "trade," "distribution," and the "closed system." This chapter also introduces one of our fundamental themes: securities law, though characterized by a morass of technical detail, cannot be divorced from the broader public policy objectives it is intended to advance.

The critical importance of public policy is revealed again in chapter 3 in which we discuss something of the Canadian regulatory infrastructure and the key "players" within the system, especially Canada's provincial securities commissions, the securities exchanges, and other self-regulatory organizations (SROs). In this chapter, we also refer to the longstanding debate in Canada about the desirability and feasibility of establishing a national securities commission in place of the current regime of individual provincial and territorial regulation. It is here, too, that we outline the basic structural framework of Canadian securities regulation and the relationship between the legislation and the other regulatory and policy instruments through which securities law is administered.

The subject of chapter 4 is the regulation of industry professionals such as broker-dealers, advisers, and underwriters, and the electronic trading platforms or alternative trading systems (ATSs) that have had — and will continue to have — such an impact on the trading of securities.

Chapters 5, 6, and 7 deal with the principal transactional nexuses of securities regulation: public offerings, private placements, and a number of specific related topics such as rights offerings, the use of future-oriented financial information, alternative distribution methods, and the Canada-U.S. multijurisdictional disclosure system. We also include here a brief review of legal issues relating to mutual funds, those collective investment vehicles through which an increasing number of Canadians choose to invest.

One of the highest profile topics in securities law enforcement is insider trading liability; so we have devoted all of chapter 8 to that important and provocative subject. We try here to provide an introduction not only to the complex legal rules, but also to the economic and other policy arguments that have been made in support of those rules.

Traditionally, securities regulation has focused upon information disclosure to investors at the time of the initial sale of securities by issuers. Recently, however, regulators have increasingly directed their attention to sales in the secondary markets (e.g., purchases and sales through the facilities of a stock exchange.) An emphasis upon second-

PREFACE

In the final months of 2001, as we were completing the manuscript for this book, two events shook the North American capital markets. The first, of course, was the stunning terrorist attack of 11 September. The second was the December bankruptcy of Enron Corp. These two events, paradoxically, revealed at once both the fragility of the capital markets and their resilience.

They also demonstrated the close inter-relationship between the social, political and financial worlds. The financial markets are not a thing apart from ordinary human experience. They are very much a part of it. Yet, despite the importance of the capital markets to the Canadian economy — and so to the material well-being of all Canadians, and the political well-being of our country — there is very little general public awareness of how they function, let alone how they are regulated. Business students might encounter a few pages in a standard business law textbook outlining securities regulation in general terms; and law students at most — but not all — Canadian law schools might choose an upper year elective course in securities regulation. But we believe it would be of considerable benefit for more business managers, lawyers, public policy makers, and investors to be introduced to the fundamental principles and basic rules constituting modern securities regulation in Canada. This book is written in particular for law and business students. However, we hope that we have included sufficient detail that practising lawyers and business managers may also find it a useful source for preliminary reference and quick study.

The book contains discussion of most of the topics canvassed in an introductory law school course in securities regulation. In chapter 1, we offer a general overview of the Canadian capital markets, together with an introduction — at a conceptual, not a legal, level — to financial instruments and the markets in which they trade. We expect this opening chapter will be of most use to those readers approaching their study of securities law with little or no prior business background.

CANADIAN CAPITAL MARKETS AND INSTRUMENTS

A. INTRODUCTION

Securities law comprises a sophisticated body of statutory and policy instruments that regulate our capital markets. Before embarking upon a detailed review of the legislation and related policy instruments, it is useful, by way of background, to provide a brief sketch of some fundamental features of the Canadian capital markets and the financial instruments used for fund raising and investment purposes.

B. THE PURPOSE OF CAPITAL MARKETS

The Canadian economy is a mixed economy that consists of both the public and the private sectors. Capital markets perform an important function in relation to both of these economic sectors.

1) The Public Sector

The term "public sector" refers to the full range of activities carried on by governments. Governments, like private businesses, spend and raise money. Governments spend money on a wide range of public services, including social assistance programs (such as unemployment insurance and welfare); the building and maintenance of roads, bridges, and other infrastructure; the building and operation of schools and hospitals; and the operation of police forces, firefighting services, national parks, and national defence. To carry out these activities, governments raise money in two ways: (1) through the collection of taxes or other revenues, such as government licensing fees and administrative fees, lottery proceeds, and profits resulting from investments in Crown corporations; and (2) through the sale of government debt instruments, such as bonds. Through the latter type of fund raising, governments have become major participants in modern capital markets. Governments sell both short-term bonds, where the principal must be repaid in less than one year, and long-term bonds, where the principal must be repaid one year or more into the future.

2) The Private Sector

a) Profit and Not-for-profit Sectors

The private sector can be divided into the "for-profit" and the "not-for-profit" sectors. In the latter, private entities supply goods or services with a view to benefiting specific subgroups of the public, such as needy children, the homeless, and religious causes or community interests, such as the environment and educational causes. Private entities in the not-for-profit sector turn any surplus of revenue over expenses back into the operations of the non-profit enterprise. For-profit entities, by contrast, supply goods or services with a view to generating a profit for the owner(s) of the entities, who may be individuals, partners in a partnership, or shareholders of a corporation.

3) Net Savers and Net Users of Capital: Financial Investment and Real Investment

This book focuses mainly, although not exclusively, on the private for-profit sector, which forms the backbone of a predominantly capitalist economy such as Canada's. In this sector, capital markets play a vital role in transferring the savings of net savers of capital to net users of capital, and ultimately in financing various activities in the "real" economy.

By "net users of capital" we mean those enterprises — public or private — that need funds to carry on their operations. By "net savers of capital" we mean individuals or aggregations of individuals, such as corporations or partnerships, with a surplus of funds.

Net users of capital are the foundation of the real economy. The real economy consists of the aggregate of all the goods and services produced within a country. For example, activities such as constructing homes, making cars, conducting scientific research and development, running a travel agency, and offering legal services all constitute part of the real economy.

Capital markets transfer funds from net savers to net users, allowing real economic activity to take place. While a very few people, like the rattled hero of Stephen Leacock's "My Financial Career,"[1] might choose to hide their savings in a sock or under a mattress, most people invest their savings either through a financial intermediary, such as a bank or a mutual fund, or by purchasing investment products, such as stocks or bonds. In both cases, these financial investments support the real economy.

Suppose, for example, that you deposit your savings with a bank, a very important kind of financial intermediary. The bank keeps only a fraction of its deposits in liquid assets that can be returned to investors on demand. The bank lends out most of its deposit base in the form of mortgages and other loans. That money, in turn, is used to finance investments in the real economy, such as renovating a house or supplying a business with working capital.

Alternatively, you might choose to use your savings to purchase corporate stocks and bonds, either directly from their issuers (primary market purchases) or from other investors (secondary market purchases).

The funds from a primary market purchase turn into investment in the real economy, while the funds from a secondary market purchase might be channelled into the real economy, be invested in a financial intermediary, or be used for the purchase of other secondary market claims.

Capital markets, then, are the means whereby savings are spirited away from net savers to net users of capital, providing the link between financial and real assets. Consider the following example. Suppose Kim Sen accumulates $20,000 in savings. Tantalus Inc., a wholesale fruit seller, is looking for money to expand its business across Canada. Tantalus decides to raise funds through an offering of common shares to the public. If Kim invests $20,000 in the public offering, Tantalus will use Kim's savings to expand its business. Kim's investment in common shares is a *financial* investment. The use to which Tantalus puts the funds, however, represents a real investment — an investment in the real economy.

The financial economy consists of only financial claims, which come in many varieties. A deposit in a bank is a financial claim on the

---

1   *Literary Lapses* (Toronto: McClelland and Stewart Limited, 1971) at 1–4.

bank: you are entitled to withdraw your money at any time, subject to any agreement between you and the bank. If you invest in a guaranteed investment certificate (GIC), that, too, is a financial claim on the issuing institution. A life insurance policy with a cash-out value is also a financial claim. Shares in corporations are an important species of financial claim, as are corporate bonds or debentures. The rights associated with each type of financial claim vary. A bond, for example, usually entitles the holder to periodic payments of interest and to the ultimate repayment of the principal (i.e., the amount invested) on a named date. A share is a "perpetual" claim that remains outstanding forever, barring bankruptcy, winding-up, amalgamation, or other similar event of termination. The shareholder is entitled to participate in the payment of dividends if, and when, declared by the board of directors. The shareholder also has a residual claim on the corporation's assets (i.e., the right to receive the remaining assets of the corporation after all other claimants have been paid) should the corporation be wound up.

C. PRIMARY AND SECONDARY SECURITIES MARKETS

1) Primary Market Transactions

A corporation or other entity that sells or issues securities is typically referred to as a securities "issuer." When an issuer sells its own securities, that sale is a primary market transaction. Primary market transactions generally fall into one of three categories:

1. *Initial public offering*: The first time an issuer sells securities in itself to the public[2] is referred to as the "initial public offering," or the

---

2   The precise legal meaning of "the public" for securities law purposes was, at one time, extremely important in most Canadian jurisdictions for at least two reasons. First, the concept was relevant in determining when a prospectus would be needed to issue securities because the prospectus obligation was triggered by a distribution "to the public." However, with the adoption of the "closed system," in Ontario any "distribution" as defined in the *Securities Act* (Ontario), R.S.O. 1990, c. S.5 [*OSA*] gives rise to a prospectus requirement, making the concept of "the public" in this context no longer relevant. The second reason is that the concept of "the public" was important in determining whether an issuer was a "private company" or a "private issuer" for the purposes of certain exemptions from the prospectus requirement in the *OSA* and the rules. Briefly put, a private company or private issuer prohibits any invitations to "the public" to

"IPO." When such an offering is made, securities laws require that a comprehensive disclosure document known as a prospectus be prepared, filed with government regulators, and delivered to the purchasers of the securities. This initial offering of securities (especially common shares) to the public is often referred to as a "going-public" transaction. (The public offering process is discussed in chapter 6.)

2. *Subsequent (seasoned or follow-on) public offering*: Once the issuer has gone public, it may choose to raise money again from public investors through a public offering, requiring the issuer to produce a new prospectus.

3. *Private placement*: A private placement is a sale of securities effected by means of an exemption from the legal requirement to produce and deliver a prospectus. (Private placements are discussed in chapter 7.)

2) Secondary Market Transactions

Once issued, securities may be sold from one investor to another. Such sales are referred to as secondary market transactions. If the issuer is a private company (that is, a company that has never sold its securities to the public),[3] the terms of sale are usually negotiated between the seller and the buyer because no readily determined "market price" is available.

Once the corporation makes a public offering of securities by means of a prospectus, it becomes a "reporting issuer" under provincial securities legislation subject to specific, ongoing public reporting obligations, which are discussed in some detail in chapter 9.

The shares of reporting issuers are often traded through the facilities of stock exchanges or other organized securities markets. There are currently three stock exchanges in Canada: the Toronto Stock Exchange (TSE); the Bourse de Montreal (formerly the Montreal Exchange); and the Canadian Venture Exchange (CDNX), which the TSE acquired in 2001. Since 1999, each of these exchanges has specialized in specific types of securities trading. The TSE specializes in Canada's most senior equity issues (i.e., shares of the largest Canadian corporate and other issuers). The CDNX lists securities of smaller,

---

subscribe for its securities. (See, e.g., *OSA*, s. 1(1)). Recent changes in Ontario law, discussed in chapter 7, have removed these exemptions, but the "private company" exemption is still a feature of securities law in other Canadian jurisdictions.

3   The term "private company" has a more technical definition for securities law purposes, as discussed in chapter 7.

more junior companies. The Bourse de Montreal, which before 1999 competed with the TSE in the trading of senior securities, essentially has become an exchange over which derivative securities are traded.

Although the listing requirements of the CDNX are easier for smaller companies to satisfy than the listing requirements of the TSE, some firms that go public still do not meet the CDNX's listing standards. Prior to the 1999 realignment of Canada's stock exchanges, the shares of many such small companies were traded through the Canadian Dealing Network (CDN), which was a subsidiary of the TSE. The CDN consisted of two segments — the "quoted" and the "reporting" segments. In the quoted segment, dealers quoted prices at which they were willing to buy and sell the securities of the issuers. The reporting segment was, as the name suggests, merely a system for reporting trades in non-quoted issuers. The quoted segment consisted of about 340 issuers, and the reported segment consisted of several hundred more. As part of the exchange realignment process, the CDN was transferred to the jurisdiction of the CDNX. CDNX invited about 170 issuers whose securities had been quoted on the CDN system to transfer to a CDNX "Tier 3" listing in the fall of 2000. The remaining "unquoted" securities were moved to a new Web-based system known as the Canadian Unlisted Board Inc. (CUB), a subsidiary of the CDNX. The CUB market, in fact, is not really a "market" at all but rather is a trade-reporting system that records the price and volume of securities traded in unlisted securities. As a result of the exchange realignment process, about half of the CDN firms that had been quoted previously lost the benefit of dealer quotations and essentially lost their secondary market. In addition, the quoted firms that were invited to obtain a Tier 3 listing on the CDNX were subject to a "drop dead" date,[4] requiring them to qualify for a Tier 1 or a Tier 2 listing on or before a certain date.

The void created by the demise of CDN will be filled by a private corporation called the Canadian Trading and Quotation System (CNQ), which, at the date of writing is in the process of applying for recognition by the Ontario Securities Commission (OSC) as a quotation and trade-reporting system. The CNQ will allow reporting issuers in Ontario to apply for admission to the trading system, which will be a hybrid dealer and auction market.

---

4   The term "drop dead" date is a generic term used by securities lawyers to refer to any date by or before which something must be done.

D. TYPES OF FINANCIAL CLAIMS OR "SECURITIES"

1) Introduction

Because this is a book about securities regulation, it is important to provide a basic explanation of what we mean by the term "security." In this chapter only, the phrase "financial claim" will be used interchangeably with the term "security." (We want to emphasize that this chapter addresses only the *concept* of a security. The legal meaning is explored later in chapter 2.)

At the highest level of generality, a security, or financial claim, gives the holder a legal claim over the earnings of the issuer of the security and a further claim over the assets of the issuer, should the issuer be wound up. The security may also give the holder a variety of other rights, the most important of which is the entitlement to vote. The entitlement to vote typically includes both a right to vote for directors and a right to vote in respect of certain types of corporate transactions that are often referred to as fundamental changes, such as amalgamations, changes in the corporation's constitutional documents, and changes in the jurisdiction of incorporation. We begin by reviewing the attributes of the most common forms of securities issued by corporations.

2) Debtholders

A corporation may raise capital by issuing debt claims as corporate bonds or debentures. The terms "bond" and "debenture" are often used interchangeably[5] and refer to debt instruments issued under a contract with the corporation. The contract promises the debtholders interest payments on the principal amount of the debt and repayment of the principal due on the maturity date of the debt. The holders of the debt are referred to both as "debtholders" and as "creditors" of the corporation.

---

5   Occasionally distinctions are drawn between the term "bond" and the term "debenture" on the basis of whether (or how) the payment obligation represented by the instrument is secured. This distinction is frequently referred to in business school finance texts, for example, and also appears in the Canadian Securities Institute's *Canadian Securities Course*. (See *The Canadian Securities Course*, vol. 1 (Toronto: Canadian Securities Institute, 2001) at 5-2.) However, this usage does not appear to reflect universal Canadian convention, and, in any event, has no significance as a matter of law.

For example, a corporation might issue a $1000 bond on 2 January 2001, promising the purchasers that it will pay 10 percent interest per year for a total of ten years, with the bond maturing on 1 January 2011. Under this contract, the corporation must pay $100 interest each and every year until the bond matures. When the bond matures, the corporation must return the bondholder's $1000 investment.

The contract between the corporation and the bondholders is embodied in a document called a "trust indenture." This document indicates the issuer's obligations under the debt instruments, including, for example, what will happen if the issuer fails to meet various tests of financial health or fails to repay either the interest or the principal on the debt when it becomes due. The trust indenture is administered by an "indenture trustee" (usually a trust company) on behalf of the bondholders. Indeed, it is the indenture trustee, not the individual bondholders, that formally enters into the trust indenture with the issuer. The trust indenture typically allows the indenture trustee, in the event of payment default by the issuer, to take over the management of the issuer, appoint a receiver, or take other steps to secure repayment of the debt. It is, thus, critical to the survival of any company to ensure that it pays all of its debt claims in a timely manner. Trust indentures are typically subject to specific rules in corporate legislation (e.g., Part VIII of the *Canada Business Corporations Act*).[6]

a) Secured versus Unsecured Debt

Sometimes debt interests are secured on some or all of the assets of the issuer, creating "secured debt." When this is the case, the issuer's non-payment of interest or principal gives the debtholder a claim over the assets specifically secured under the instrument creating the debt. On the issuer's default, the creditor (subject to applicable provincial and federal laws) may enter the issuer's premises to seize and sell these assets to satisfy payment of the debt. A security interest gives the secured creditors priority in the secured assets over any others who claim that the issuer owes them money.

An issuer can have more than one class of secured creditor, and different classes of creditors may have co-equal or different priorities over the issuer's assets. Typically, banks insist on the highest priority of all those who lend money to a corporate issuer. Various classes of other lenders, such as bondholders, have progressively lower priorities over the assets (or, possibly, priorities over different corporate assets). Note,

---

6   *Canada Business Corporations Act*, R.S.C. 1985, c. C-44 [*CBCA*].

however, that all secured creditors retain a priority over all non-secured debtholders.

Debt may also be unsecured. With unsecured debt, the debtor is, of course, legally obliged to repay the debt plus the agreed-upon interest, but the creditor cannot look to any specific asset or assets of the debtor to secure this repayment. Any debtholder holding unsecured debt has a lower priority than the secured debtholders. Thus, in the liquidation of an issuer, if there is nothing left after the secured creditors have taken the assets to which they are entitled, the unsecured debtholders get nothing. All those holding unsecured debt have equal priority with one another (unless they have expressly agreed to subordinate their claims in favour of other creditors), and, so, share *pari passu* in respect of their claims after the issuer pays off the secured creditors. Unsecured creditors, however, have a higher priority claim than any class of shareholder.

There are various types of unsecured creditors. These include not only creditors holding unsecured bonds or debentures, but also trade creditors, employees, and anyone else to whom the corporation owes money.

Unlike holders of equity interests (i.e., shareholders), all creditors are "fixed claimants." No matter how profitable the debtor corporation becomes, the debentureholders' return on their investment remains limited to the amount of interest and the return of principal promised in the trust indenture. Similarly, whatever the corporation's profitability, trade creditors' claims are limited to the amount billed to the corporation plus any interest charged on the unpaid debt.

3) Shareholders (Holders of "Equity" Claims)

a) Common Shares

A corporation may raise money by issuing "equity" claims or shares. One type of equity claim is the common share. Common shares are distinguished by three important attributes: (1) the claim over the earnings stream, (2) the claim over assets on a winding-up, and (3) the right to vote. Each is discussed in turn below.

i) The Claim over the Earnings Stream

Each common shareholder is entitled to receive a *pro rata* share of any dividend declared by the corporation on the common shares. There is no legal obligation, however, for the corporation to pay any dividends whatsoever. The directors may decide to declare, or not to declare, dividends as they so choose.

Under what circumstances may the directors declare a dividend? The directors may declare a dividend on the common shares if (1) all fixed claimants (including preferred share claims, as discussed below) have been paid all amounts owing to them or (2) if the corporation has the financial resources to ensure that it can meet all of its obligations to the fixed claimants. The amount of any dividend declared by the directors is typically subject to express limitations under corporate law. For example, for corporations incorporated under the *Canada Business Corporations Act*, a dividend payment may not render the corporation unable to pay its liabilities as they become due.[7] The *CBCA* also requires that after the dividend payment, the realizable value of the corporation's assets must exceed the aggregate of its liabilities and stated capital of all classes of shares.[8] Thus, a shareholder's claim to dividends stands last in priority over the earnings stream. The corporation must make provision for all stakeholders with fixed claims, such as bondholders, preferred shareholders, and employees, before it can pay the shareholders anything. It is for this reason that the common shares are often referred to as a "residual" claim on earnings.

The fact that common shares represent a residual claim is both a burden and a boon for shareholders. There may not be sufficient funds in any given year after all the prior claimants have been paid to pay shareholders a dividend; however, should profits be spectacular, it is the common shareholders, not the fixed claimants, who become wealthy. After prior claims are paid, the remaining profits "belong" to the shareholders, in the sense that the directors may, if they wish, pay all remaining profits to the shareholders. If no dividends are declared, the value of the shares nonetheless will typically rise to reflect the increasing value of the residual assets of the corporation. The rising share value will, of course, represent a capital gain for shareholders.

ii) The Claim over Assets on a Winding-up
A corporation may voluntarily decide to wind up and distribute its assets or the proceeds from the sale of its assets. If it does, the common shareholders possess a "residual" claim over the assets or their proceeds, just as they possess a residual claim over earnings. Thus, upon a winding-up, all fixed claimants, including bondholders, trade creditors, employees owed back wages, and preferred shareholders, must be

---

7   See, e.g., *CBCA*, *ibid.* s. 42.
8   *Ibid.*

paid all amounts owed to them before any amounts may be distributed to the common shareholders. Again, however, once all fixed claimants are fully paid, the shareholders are entitled to the residue, that is, everything that is left over. Needless to say, if there are insufficient assets to satisfy the obligations owing to all of the fixed claimants, the common shareholders will receive nothing.

iii) The Right to Vote

Of the entire bundle of rights accorded shareholders, either by the express terms of the share conditions, the governing corporate law, the governing securities law, or otherwise, the most important is the right to vote. Shareholders are entitled to vote on the election of directors, the appointment of the corporation's auditors, and in respect of a variety of corporate "fundamental changes" such as amalgamations or major sales of assets. As we will see below, however, there may be one or more classes of shareholders whose shares do *not* entitle them to vote. Corporations are permitted to issue such non-voting shares if at least one class of shareholders has full voting rights.

b) Preferred Shares

Another type of equity claim is the preferred share. Although the term "preferred share" is not typically defined in corporate statutes, it has a generally accepted meaning in the financial community; namely, that a preferred share has some preference over the common shares in relation to the issuer's earnings and assets upon winding-up. Preferred shares are fundamentally different from common shares in that they typically represent fixed, rather than residual, equity claims.

i) The Claim over the Earnings Stream

Under the terms of issuance, preferred shareholders are usually entitled to a stated "preferred" dividend per annum. Such a dividend is "preferred" because it must be paid before any dividend can be paid to the common shareholders. However, as in the case of common shares, directors have no obligation to declare any dividends to the preferred shareholders, even when the preferred shares appear, on their face, to entitle holders to a stated annual dividend. Directors may declare dividends, if they so choose, provided that the applicable corporate law tests, as discussed above, are met.[9]

Preferred shares may be issued with "participation rights" that entitle holders not only to a fixed preferential dividend or return of capital

---

9   *Ibid.*

on a winding-up, but also to a right to participate, with the common shareholders, in any further dividends or distribution of residual value on a winding-up. Such participating shares represent residual, rather than fixed, claims.

As explained above, directors are not legally obliged to pay dividends to preferred shareholders, even when the shares carry a stated dividend rate. But, what happens if a preferred dividend is not paid in a given year? That depends on whether the preferred shares are "cumulative." If they are cumulative, any missed ("accrued") dividend(s) plus the dividend for the current year must be made good before any dividend can be paid to holders of lower ranking shares, such as common shares.

For example, suppose that a cumulative preferred share entitles holders to a $10 dividend per annum, and dividends have been missed in four different years (whether consecutive or not), including the current year. The non-paid dividends are referred to as "arrears" of dividends. If the directors wish to pay the common shareholders a dividend, the directors must first pay out all the accumulated arrears to the preferred shareholders. On the assumed facts, this means that $40 per preferred share must be paid to the preferred shareholders before any dividend may be paid to the common shareholders.

By contrast, if the shares in the above example were non-cumulative, the directors need pay only the current year's dividend ($10 per share) before declaring and paying a dividend in favour of the common shareholders. In today's marketplace, the issuance of non-cumulative preferred shares is quite rare.

ii) The Claim over Assets on a Winding-up
Preferred shareholders typically have a fixed claim over the assets of the corporation on a winding-up. This claim must be paid before the common shareholders receive any distribution of the corporation's assets. The amount of the preferred shareholders' claims on a winding-up is very often the amount paid for the shares when they were first issued, plus any accrued, but unpaid, dividends.

iii) No Voting Rights
Preferred shareholders are not usually given an express entitlement to vote for directors or in respect of fundamental corporate changes. Despite this, federal and provincial corporate laws frequently provide preferred shareholders with the right to vote on certain fundamental corporate changes to ensure that common shareholders do not use their voting power to engage in opportunistic redistribution of corporate entitlements in their favour at the expense of the preferred share-

holders.[10] Where non-voting shares have a residual right to share in an issuer's earnings and in its assets on winding-up, such shares may be listed on the TSE only if they are protected by so-called "coat-tail" provisions.[11] The purpose of such provisions is to ensure that a bidder for the issuer's voting shares cannot pay a premium to the voting shareholders in which the non-voting equity shareholders are not entitled to participate.

iv) Other Common Features

Preferred shares may be issued with any number of special features. For example, preferred shares may be "redeemable" or "retractable." Redeemable shares are subject to repurchase at the instance of the corporation at a specified price that is usually in excess of the issue price. If preferred shares are retractable, the holder may insist that the corporation repurchase the shares at a prespecified price. Retraction rights are often made contingent on the occurrence of an event.

If the shares are neither retractable nor redeemable, then, unlike debt, they are part of the "permanent" capital of the corporation and are never retired.[12]

4) Risk and Return of Different Types of Securities

To a financial economist, the two most important attributes of a security are its risk and its expected return. Risk is important because most people are risk averse — that is, risk is a cost. Given the choice between receiving a certain payoff of $100 and a 50 percent chance of a $0 payoff coupled with a 50 percent chance of receiving a $200 payoff, most people will choose the certain $100, even though the "expected value" of the alternative payoff (the sum of each dollar amount multiplied by the probability that it will be received) is equal to $100.

Because people are risk averse, investors must be compensated for bearing risk. All things equal, the greater the degree of risk associated with an investment instrument, the higher the expected return must be

---

10   See J.S. Ziegel et al., *Cases and Materials on Partnerships and Canadian Business Corporations*, 3d ed. (Toronto: Carswell, 1994) at 934–36.

11   *Toronto Stock Exchange Company Manual*, s. 699.4; Appendix E, "Policy Statement on Restricted Shares," s. 1.09, available online at <http://www.tse.ca/en/pdf/CompanyManual0202.pdf> (site accessed 2 May 2002).

12   This is subject to the possibility of a reduction of capital under applicable corporate legislation, or the launching of an "issuer bid" by the corporation to repurchase the shares on a voluntary basis. See, e.g., *CBCA*, above note 6, s. 38; and *OSA*, above note 2, Part XX. For a discussion of issuer bids, see chapter 10.

to induce investors to purchase the instrument. The expected return is typically expressed as a percentage return on the purchase price. Accordingly, once the expected *dollar value* of the return on any investment instrument has been determined, the expected *percentage* return on that instrument can be increased only by the issuer lowering the selling price. Thus, ignoring any impact that taxes may have, riskier instruments tend to command lower prices in the marketplace or, equivalently, require higher interest rates, higher dividend rates and/or expected capital gains.[13] This inverse correlation between risk and price (or positive correlation between risk and expected return) is the foundation of modern financial theory.

The various types of securities discussed above have quite different risk/return characteristics. Debt securities, having the highest priority in respect of both the earnings stream and the assets on a winding-up, have the lowest degree of risk (especially secured debt, which has the lowest risk of all). This is because the corporation makes contractual promises to pay interest in each period and to return the principal when the debt matures. Debtholders may sue the company if it defaults. An event of default may also result in effective control of the corporation being transferred to the debtholders; debtholders may appoint a "receiver" to run the corporation until the debt is paid. Default may also result in bankruptcy or similar statutory proceedings pursuant to which the common shareholders lose their entitlement to appoint the directors, the business of the corporation may be brought to an end, and the corporation's assets may be liquidated. In such proceedings, the debtholders have first priority over the assets of the corporation. Corporate debt, however, has a lower expected return than preferred or common shares issued by the same corporation because debt investments never yield more than the promised interest payments and return of principal.

Preferred shares are slightly riskier than debt securities. While preferred shares, like debt securities, represent fixed claims, preferred shareholders have no guarantee that the corporation will pay dividends in any given period. If dividends are not declared, preferred shareholders cannot sue to force payment and are not typically entitled to take over the management of the corporation. Indeed, there is no require-

---

13   A firm may attract investment even though there is little or no prospect of the payment of dividends, if it is expected that the firm will experience growth, and that this growth will result in an accumulation of assets or earning power. Such growth is reflected in the stock price, giving investors returns in the form of capital gains, rather than dividends.

ment that the corporation ever make good the missed dividends. Only if the preferred shares are cumulative and the directors wish to pay a dividend on the common shares, will the directors need to pay the arrears of dividends on the preferred shares.

Because of this added risk, preferred shares must have a higher after-tax expected return than debt to attract investors. Preferred shareholders expect their total return, which is a combination of dividends paid plus capital appreciation, to be higher than the return expected by debtholders.

Common shares are the most risky type of security because they represent a residual claim on both an issuer's earnings and assets. Investors purchase such securities only if their expected return (again, in the form of dividends plus capital appreciation) is greater than that of either the issuer's debt or preferred shares. The riskiness of the corporation's business and the terms of issuance of the common shares determine how much higher that expected return needs to be to attract investment.

5) Hybrid Securities

The terms "common share" and "preferred share" are not statutorily defined terms. In fact, corporate legislation typically provides few constraints on the types of securities that may be issued by a corporation. Thus, a corporation may issue hybrid shares that have characteristics of both preferred and common shares (or even debt-like features). The *CBCA*, subsection 24(3), for example, requires only that

> [w]here a corporation has only one class of shares, the rights of the holders thereof are equal in all respects and include the rights
>
> (a) to vote at any meeting of shareholders of the corporation;
>
> (b) to receive any dividend declared by the corporation; and
>
> (c) to receive the remaining property of the corporation on dissolution.

The *CBCA* also provides that a corporation may issue more than one class of shares, and, if this is done, "the rights set out in subsection (3) shall be attached to at least one class of shares but all such rights are not required to be attached to one class."[14]

Provided, in other words, that at least one class of shares is entitled to vote, at least one class is entitled to receive dividends, and at least

---

14   *CBCA*, above note 6, s. 24(4).

one class is entitled to receive any remaining property upon dissolution, no single class of shares needs to entitle its holders to all three of these fundamental rights.

At common law, however, there are restrictions on the types of securities that may be issued. The courts have made distinctions between a "debt" security and an "equity" claim.[15] The common law also establishes that the directors are under no obligation to pay dividends.[16] Thus, it does not appear possible to create a common share on which dividends *must* be paid, or debt that constitutes a residual claim on earnings. These problems are typically overcome in practice by issuing a *package* of securities with different attributes. An example is a convertible bond, which is a bond that may, at the instance of the holder, be converted at any time into a fixed number of common shares. Fixed interest payments must be paid on the bond, but if the share price appreciates, it may be worthwhile for the holder to convert the bond into common shares, thus becoming a residual claimant.

6) A Corporation's Share Capital: A Hypothetical Illustration

To help illustrate the flexibility of the share capital provisions of modern Canadian corporate and securities law, consider the following hypothetical share structure of ABC Corp., a corporation incorporated under the *CBCA* (or indeed under any similar provincial statute). ABC Corp.'s authorized capital consists of an unlimited number of Class A shares, an unlimited number of Class B shares, an unlimited number of Class C shares, and an unlimited number of Class D shares. The different classes of shares have rights as follows:

Class A Shares	Class B Shares
• Do not vote for directors	• Vote for directors
• Cannot receive dividends until the Class D and C shareholders are paid their preferential dividends	• Cannot receive dividends until the Class A, C, and D shareholders have received their preferential dividends

---

15   See, e.g., *Canada Deposit Insurance Corp. v. Canadian Commercial Bank*, [1992] 3 S.C.R. 558.

16   *Burland v. Earle* (1901), [1902] A.C. 83 (P.C.).

Class A Shares	Class B Shares
• Must be paid a dividend of $0.05 per annum before any dividends may be declared on the Class B shares	
• Share rateably with Class B shareholders in any further dividend	• Share rateably with Class A shareholders in any dividend declared after the Class D, C, and A preferential dividends have been paid
• Have a residual claim on assets ranking equally with the Class B shareholders' claim	• Have a residual claim on earnings and assets ranking equally with the Class A shareholders

Class C Shares	Class D Shares
• Do not vote for directors	• Do not vote for directors
• Cannot receive a dividend until the Class D shareholders have been paid their preferential dividend	
• Receive a preferential dividend of $5.00 per share before the Class A or B shareholders may be paid a dividend	• Receive a preferential dividend of $5.00 per share before the Class A, B, or C shareholders may be paid a dividend
• Have no residual claim on assets or earnings	• Have no residual claim on assets or earnings

In the above share structure, Class B shares are typical "common shares." They entitle their holders to all three of the fundamental rights described in subsection 24(3) of the *CBCA*. Class A shares are hybrids. They entitle their holders to a residual claim and resemble common shares; however, they are non-voting and entitle holders to a preferential dividend. This makes them look a bit like preferred shares. Hybrid securities of this type are often referred to as "non-voting common shares," and they typically have a trivial dividend preference over the voting common shares, given as a "sweetener" to attract purchasers. Under OSC Rule 56-501, these shares are considered "restricted shares," that is, equity shares other than common shares.[17]

---

17   OSC Rule 56-501 (1999), 22 OSCB 6761 at s. 1.1. See also above note 11.

We might have varied the Class B share conditions in our example above to provide that holders enjoy only partial voting rights, such as one vote for every ten shares held. Shares that have partial voting rights, but are otherwise participating shares, are referred to as "restricted-voting" shares.[18]

The Class C and D shares are both examples of classic preferred shares. The Class D shares, however, have a dividend preference even over the other class of preferred shares.

7) Options

a) Options Are Securities

An option is an instrument that gives the holder the right to buy or sell an underlying interest in respect of a named issuer at an agreed price, on or before an agreed date, but does not obligate the holder to do so. The underlying interest is often common shares of the named issuer. Options are "securities" within the meaning of Canadian securities legislation.[19]

b) Options Issued by a Corporation

A corporation may issue options that entitle holders to buy the issuer's own securities. A "right" is a common example of such an option. A right gives the holder the option to buy an additional share, or a fraction of an additional share, of a stated issuer at a stated price, on or before a stated date. For example, a right issued on 1 January 2001 might give the holder the right to buy one share of the corporation, on or before 15 February 2002 at a price of $50. In this case, the underlying interest of the option is the corporation's common shares, and the "exercise price" is $50.

Why would a corporation issue rights? Rights are sometimes issued to the existing shareholders of the corporation with an exercise price just below the existing market price. They are issued as an alternative financing technique to a straightforward issuance of shares. Such rights issues are discussed further in chapter 5. The purchase of rights gives the holders leveraged positions in the corporation, in the sense that an option to buy shares is always more risky than holding the shares themselves because option prices vary pronouncedly with changes in the underlying share price.

---

18   *Ibid.*

19   See, e.g., *OSA*, above note 2, s. 1(1) (definition of "security").

A "warrant" is essentially the same kind of option, although it may give the holder the right to exercise it over a longer period of time. Further, it will often be attached to the issuance of some other type of security, such as a bond.

c) In-the-Money, Out-of-the-Money, and At-the-Money Options

Suppose a right is issued to purchase a common share of a corporation at $40 when the market price of each common share is $50. In this case, we say that the option is "in the money." That means that the option, if exercised today, would yield a profit — in this case, $10 per common share purchased.

If the right were issued with an exercise price of $60, however, (assuming once again that the market price of each common share is $50) the option is "out of the money." No one, after all, would pay $60 for a share that can be purchased in the market for $50 because that is a money-losing proposition.

Finally, if the right is issued with an exercise price of exactly $50 when the market price for the shares is also $50, the option is said to be "at the money."

Note that even out-of-the-money share options have value, as long as there is time remaining before they expire, because the price of the corporation's shares may increase during the life of the option with the result that the options will be in the money.

d) Options Issued by Persons Other than the Corporation

Share options need not be issued by the corporation that is the issuer of the underlying shares. Other persons frequently issue options whose underlying interest is a security issued by a publicly traded corporation. The most common examples are put and call options.

A call option on a corporation's shares may be created by an option "writer" (i.e., a seller). The option writer sells the option to a purchaser for a price known as the option premium. The call option entitles the purchaser, if it so wishes, to force the writer to sell an outstanding share of a third-party corporation at a specified price (the exercise price) on or before a specified date. The corporation that originally issued this optioned share takes no part whatsoever in this transaction. Suppose, for example, that the price of an ABC Corp. common share is $25 on 1 March 2001. The writer (perhaps an investment banking firm) may create a call option with an exercise price of $30 to be exercised by the holder (if the holder so wishes) on or before 1 June 2001. The purchaser of the call option hopes that the price of ABC Corp.'s common shares will rise to more than $30 before 1 June. If it does not, the option will expire and be worthless. Obviously, the writer of the option hopes that the price of ABC's common shares will *not* rise to more than $30 on or before 1 June. In a sense, the writer and the purchaser of the option are making contrary "bets" on the future value of ABC stock. Once issued, call options may be traded in the secondary market.

A put option on corporate shares also may be created by an option writer; however, the purchaser of the option acquires the right to require the writer to purchase a corporate share from her at a stated price on or before a certain date. Using the example of ABC Corp. again, where the share price on 1 March is $25, the writer of a put option might sell the purchaser a put option, entitling the option purchaser to force the writer, on or before 1 June 2001, to buy from the purchaser a share of ABC Corp. at a price of $20. Note that at the time of issuance, the put option is "out of the money." If it expired on the date of issuance, its value would be zero. The purchaser hopes that the price of ABC will drop to an amount below $20 on or before 1 June.[20] If it drops to $15, for example, the purchaser can enter the market, buy a share of ABC at $15, immediately exercise the put option, and resell that same share to the writer for $20, for a $5 profit.

e) Options May Have a Variety of Underlying Interests

An option can be written against virtually any underlying interest, financial or otherwise, whose price is subject to variation. Options can be written, for example, against a stock index such as the S&P/TSX 60, the price of a precious metal, the price of an agricultural commodity, or an index of fine art values. Given that the price of every good whose price is determined in the market can vary, the number of different types of options that can be written is almost limitless.

f) Options Issued as a Compensation Device

Corporations frequently issue call options or other similar types of options as compensation for the services of senior executives and/or directors (referred to collectively below as "managers"). Options are a useful compensation device because, among other things, they give the managers more "leverage" than simply holding shares. In order to hold shares in the corporation, the manager must invest money. When options are granted, no investment takes place. The manager eventually

---

20   This example assumes that the buyer of the option is not already holding an ABC Corp. share and so has purchased the put option to speculate, rather than to hedge her exposure to changes in ABC Corp.'s share price.

profits to the extent that the share price rises above the exercise price of the options. Such options are thought to provide managers with a potent incentive to increase the value of the companies they manage, although critics sometimes see such options as little more than a subterfuge for transferring corporate value from shareholders to managers.

8) Futures

Futures (exchange-traded) and forwards (over-the-counter, or OTC) are contracts to sell a specified asset on a stated date in the future at a stated price. Like option contracts, futures contracts are written against a wide variety of underlying interests, the most common of which are currencies, commodities, indexes, and interest rates.

A hypothetical future example is a contract struck on 1 March 2001, in which the underlying interest is four litres of milk, the sale price is $10, and the settlement date is 1 June 2001. In this contract, the purchaser agrees to buy, and the seller agrees to sell, four litres of milk on 1 June for $10. Although the sale will not take place until 1 June, both parties are contractually committed to complete the transaction when that date arrives.

Futures contracts have long been used as a risk management tool. Farmers, for example, often sell futures contracts to purchasers of the commodities they produce, even before the crop or the animals have been raised. This transfers the risk of price fluctuations in the underlying interest to the purchasers.

Futures contracts are "securities" within the meaning of Canadian securities legislation[21] and thus fall within the domain of the securities regulators. However, commodity futures contracts that are publicly traded on a commodity futures exchange are excluded from the definition of "security" because they are separately regulated under special legislation dealing with commodities futures.[22] This legislation is nonetheless administered by the securities regulators.

9) Derivative Securities

The value of a "derivative security" depends on (or "derives" from) the value of another security, financial asset, or other reference value, which (as noted above) is referred to as the underlying interest. Rights

21   See above note 19.
22   In Ontario, this is the *Commodity Futures Act*, R.S.O. 1990, c. C.20 [*CFA*].

and warrants, as discussed above, are, thus, types of derivative securities, as are put and call options.

The term "derivative security" is also used to refer to futures and forward contracts. In fact, every derivative security, no matter how complex, can be characterized as either an option contract, a futures (or forward) contract, or a (frequently elaborate) combination of the two. The term derivative security is an umbrella term used to refer to a vast range of different types of financial instruments whose values vary with the underlying interests.

Derivative securities have exploded in popularity in the last decade, mainly as a result of an increased demand to hedge risk in volatile currency, interest rate, commodity, and stock markets. Although not all derivative instruments are "securities" within the meaning of provincial securities legislation,[23] the securities legislation of some provinces nonetheless gives the regulators the power to regulate such instruments.[24] Some of the securities regulatory issues surrounding derivatives are canvassed briefly in chapter 2.

E. CONCLUSION

An exhaustive review of Canada's financial system, markets, and institutions is beyond the scope of this book. We simply introduce in a very general way some of the basic attributes of Canadian capital markets, and the place the issuance and sale of securities occupies within them. The balance of this book focuses much more closely and rigorously on the details of securities laws as they relate to many of the matters mentioned in this chapter.

---

23   See above note 19.
24   See, e.g., *OSA*, above note 2, s. 143(1)35.

CHAPTER 2

FUNDAMENTAL SECURITIES LAW CONCEPTS

A. INTRODUCTION

In this chapter, we introduce some essential securities law terms and concepts. These include the three perhaps most foundational definitions in Canadian securities law: security, trade, and distribution.

B. WHAT IS A "SECURITY"?

1) Introduction

Thus far, we have considered, in *conceptual* terms, what constitutes a security and the basic characteristics of some common examples of securities. Now, we turn to a more detailed examination of the *legal* meaning of the term "security." The question of what constitutes a "security" is central to the application of securities legislation. The application of securities legislation depends on a finding that the transaction in question involves a security (although, as we shall see below, the securities regulators sometimes assume jurisdiction even when there is no security[1]). Many requirements of securities legislation are triggered when "securities" are involved, including the following:

---

1   See the discussion of derivatives in section B(12) below.

1. The requirement that an issuer prepare and distribute a prospectus depends on whether there is a distribution of "securities."[2]
2. The requirement that an issuer publicly disclose material changes in the life of the company (i.e., comply with continuous disclosure obligations) depends on whether it has issued securities (and whether these securities are publicly held, such that the company qualifies as a "reporting issuer").[3]
3. The criminal and civil prohibitions against insider trading are triggered only when someone with material non-public information trades in securities.[4]
4. The application of the take-over bid rules depends on whether there is a take-over bid to acquire the securities of an issuer.[5]
5. The registration requirements of the legislation come into play only when there is activity involving securities.[6]

What then is a security? Consider the following transactions:

- You buy shares or bonds of IBM through a broker.
- You buy shares or bonds in a small, private software company directly from the company.
- You buy a unit in a real estate limited partnership.
- You buy units in a mutual fund.
- You lend money to your aunt for the purpose of opening a commercial design studio.
- You buy an interest in a number of chinchillas, in return for a promise that you will share in any profits generated by the sale of the chinchillas.
- You open a bank account.
- You buy a life insurance policy.
- You buy an interest in a time-share condominium unit.

Which of these transactions involves a security? Most people would recognize that shares of a public company are securities. Most

---

2   *Securities Act* (Ontario), R.S.O. 1990, c. S.5 [*OSA*], ss. 1(1) (definition of "distribution") & 53.

3   *Ibid.* ss. 1(1) (definition of "reporting issuer," defined exclusively in terms of the trading status of the issuer's securities) & 75.

4   *Ibid.* ss. 76 & 130.

5   *Ibid.* s. 89(1) (definition of "take-over bid").

6   *Ibid.* ss. 1(1) (definitions of "underwriter" and "adviser") & 25 (when registration required).

people would likely recognize that bonds, or debentures,[7] or other similar debt instruments issued by a public company are also securities. It is likely that most people would similarly expect that shares or bonds in a *private* company are also securities. However, many would fail to recognize that every other transaction on this list may conceivably be characterized as a security, or *could* be so characterized, but for specific exclusions from the definition of security found in the securities legislation. This shows just how wide the legal definition of security cuts.

2) The *Securities Act* Definition

How is it possible that so many things can be classified as securities? The first place to look for an answer is the definitions section of the Act. In Ontario, "security" is defined as follows:

"security" includes,

(a) any document, instrument or writing commonly known as a security,

(b) any document constituting evidence of title to or interest in the capital, assets, property, profits, earnings or royalties of any person or company,

(c) any document constituting evidence of an interest in an association of legatees or heirs,

(d) any document constituting evidence of an option, subscription or other interest in or to a security,

(e) any bond, debenture, note or other evidence of indebtedness, share, stock, unit, unit certificate, participation certificate, certificate of share or interest, preorganization certificate or subscription other than a contract of insurance issued by an insurance company licensed under the *Insurance Act* and an evidence of deposit issued by a bank listed in Schedule I or II to the *Bank Act* (Canada), by a credit union or league to which the *Credit Unions and Caisses Populaires Act, 1994* applies or by a loan corporation or trust corporation registered under the *Loan and Trust Corporations Act*,

---

7   At one time, a bond represented secured debt, while a debenture represented unsecured debt — a distinction, as mentioned in chapter 1, that is still found in some finance texts. Today, however, the terms "bond" and "debenture" are often used interchangeably, although it would be unusual to use the term "debenture" to describe a debt instrument secured solely by a charge on a particular fixed asset.

(f) any agreement under which the interest of the purchaser is valued for purposes of conversion or surrender by reference to the value of a proportionate interest in a specified portfolio of assets, except a contract issued by an insurance company licensed under the *Insurance Act* which provides for payment at maturity of an amount not less than three quarters of the premiums paid by the purchaser for a benefit payable at maturity,

(g) any agreement providing that money received will be repaid or treated as a subscription to shares, stock, units or interests at the option of the recipient or of any person or company,

(h) any certificate of share or interest in a trust, estate or association,

(i) any profit-sharing agreement or certificate,

(j) any certificate of interest in an oil, natural gas or mining lease, claim or royalty voting trust certificate,

(k) any oil or natural gas royalties or leases or fractional or other interest therein,

(l) any collateral trust certificate,

(m) any income or annuity contract not issued by an insurance company,

(n) any investment contract,

(o) any document constituting evidence of an interest in a scholarship or educational plan or trust, and

(p) any commodity futures contract or any commodity futures option that is not traded on a commodity futures exchange registered with or recognized by the Commission under the *Commodity Futures Act* or the form of which is not accepted by the Director under that Act,

whether any of the foregoing relate to an issuer or proposed issuer; ("valeur mobilière").[8]

The first thing to note about this definition is that it states that the term security "*includes*" the various enumerations. The definition is not *exhaustive*: things other than those appearing on the list also may be found to be securities. It is unlikely that any court or securities regulator would have to venture outside of the list, however, because the

---

8   *OSA*, above note 2, s. 1(1).

various terms are "catchalls," designed to cast the net as wide as possible.[9] In fact, the definition of security is so wide that it can be reasonably asserted that only the common sense of securities regulators and the courts places limits on what will be regulated as a security.

3) A Summary of the Case Law

Before proceeding to a discussion of specific parts of the definition of security, we consider a summary of the main points to be gleaned from the cases in which the courts have interpreted the definition of "security."

a) Result-oriented Cases
The cases are profoundly result-oriented; that is, the result desired by the judge tends to drive the reasoning, rather than the reasoning driving the result.

b) Investor Protection
This result orientation derives from one of the fundamental policies underlying securities legislation, which is investor protection.[10] The legislation seeks to protect investors not only against fraud, but also against "the imposition of unsubstantial schemes"[11] foisted upon investors by overzealous promoters. Thus, if a court perceives that the purchaser of an interest is a person in need of the protection of the legislation, it is likely that the interest will be found to be a security. Conversely, if the purchaser is able to protect her own interests, or is protected under some other statutory scheme such as the *Condominium Act*,[12] the court is less likely to find the interest to be a security.

c) Expectation of Profit
In general, a security will be found when one person[13] secures the use of the money of another on the promise of profits. If the recipient of the money creates an expectation of profit over and above the return of

---

9   *Pacific Coast Coin Exchange of Canada* v. *Ontario (Securities Commission)* (1978), 80 D.L.R. (3d) 529 [*Pacific Coast*].

10   *OSA*, above note 2, s. 1.1(a).

11   *Hawaii* v. *Hawaii Market Center Inc.*, 485 P.2d 105 at 109 (Sup. Ct. 1971) [*Hawaii*].

12   *Condominium Act, 1998*, S.O. 1998, c. 19. See definition of "security," above, section (2), parts (e) and (f).

13   We use "person" here in the broad legal sense to include any natural person, corporation, or unincorporated entity, rather than in the somewhat narrower sense in which it is actually used in the *OSA*, where the term excludes corporations. See *OSA*, above note 2, s. 1(1) (definition of "person").

the initial value furnished by the purchaser, the courts tend to find that a security exists.

d) Risk Factor

A key factor is risk. To be characterized by the courts as a security, the investment need not be "speculative" in character (i.e., a high-risk investment). *Some* degree of risk is sufficient. Nonetheless, the riskier the transaction, the *more likely* it is that the court will find that the transaction involves the sale of a security. Again, it is the policy of investor protection that drives this result. The more risk the purchaser is exposed to, the more likely it is the court will find that she or he needs the protections furnished by the legislation.

e) Purchaser's Degree of Control

The degree of control exercised by the purchaser is also an important factor. The less ability an "investor" has to exercise control over the money spent, the more the investor must trust others to protect the investment. In such a case, the purchaser faces a greater risk and the court is more likely to find the interest to be a security.

f) Independent Value

Even if the subject matter of the contract has value independent of the success of the enterprise as a whole, the contract may still be characterized as a security. For example, in some circumstances, a contract for the sale of an interest in real estate has been characterized as a security.

g) Substance over Form

The courts have repeatedly stressed that substance guides them, not form. In practice, this means that arrangements that many people would not commonly regard as securities are often found to be securities. It also means that an interest created by a document that specifically denies that it creates a security may still be found, in substance, to constitute a security.

h) Overlap in Definition

The definition of security in the *OSA* includes "any investment contract." This is typically thought to be the widest part of the definition, and, indeed, more cases have been litigated under this part of the definition than under any other. However, the courts' reasoning used to define "investment contract" can easily be transposed to other parts of the definition of security, such as parts (b) and (i) of subsection 1(1) of the *OSA*. In short, there is considerable overlap in the nature of the specific enumerations in the definition of security.

i)   U.S. Cases

The Supreme Court of Canada has adopted the meaning of investment contract found in the leading U.S. cases. Canadian cases decided in lower courts and by securities administrators reflect this holding. Thus, while the statutory definitions of security in Canada and the United States differ slightly, the reach of the term is substantially the same in both countries. In practical terms, this means that U.S. cases may usefully be cited in Canada, both before the courts and the securities regulators, in arguing whether a particular interest is a security.

j)   Explicit Exclusions

The definition of security explicitly excludes a variety of interests, many of which would not commonly be thought of as securities. For example, part (e) of the definition in subsection 1(1) of the *OSA* excludes contracts of insurance, as well as evidence of a deposit issued by a bank (e.g., a bank book), a caisse populaire, a loan corporation or a trust corporation.[14] There are two reasons for these exclusions:

1. Without the exclusions, interests such as a contract of insurance and a bank book would very likely be found to be securities under at least one of the subparts of the definition.
2. There is no need to subject those who create these forms of "securities" to the regulation embodied in the *OSA* because their activities are regulated under other protective legislation, such as the federal *Bank Act*.

As noted in one recent case, "the cases have largely focused on the extended definitions."[15] Moreover, an examination of the "extended" or broad parts of the definition gives the greatest insight into what constitutes a security. Thus, in what follows, only the broadest parts of the specific enumerations found in the definition are canvassed. Readers may consult other sources for detailed discussions of each part of the definition.[16]

4) Shares and Debt Interests

Part (e) of the definition of securities in subsection 1(1) of the *OSA* includes "any bond, debenture, note or other evidence of indebtedness,

---

14   See also *OSA*, above note 2, s. 1(1) (f), (m), (n), & (p).
15   *R. v. Sisto Finance NV* (1994), 17 OSCB 2467 (Prov. Div.).
16   See, e.g., Victor P. Alboini, *Securities Law and Practice*, vol. 1 (Toronto: Carswell, looseleaf) at 29ff.

share, stock, unit, unit certificate, participation certificate, certificate of share or interest, preorganization certificate or subscription." This part of the definition makes it clear that shares (including common, preferred, and hybrid shares) are securities, as are bonds and debentures. Note that although many parts of the *OSA* are designed to apply only to public companies, shares and debt instruments in private companies are also securities.

Part (e) of the definition also includes "units," which includes interests in trusteed mutual funds, real estate investment trusts, and various forms of tax shelter instruments.

The balance of the definition in part (e) is extremely broad. Even a promissory note could be included in the phrase "note or other evidence of indebtedness." Whether a promissory note, in fact, would be found to be a security would depend, almost certainly, on the context of the transaction, and (as elaborated below) especially on whether the maker of the note was either able to protect her own interests or was adequately protected under another legislative scheme.

Note that we have now ascertained why the first five items in the list of transactions found at the beginning of section B(1) of this chapter either are securities or may, in some circumstances, be found to be securities. As will become apparent, there are other parts of the definition of security that also cover many, if not all, of these five items because of overlap in the parts of the definition.

5) Options

Part (d) of the definition of security in subsection 1(1) of the *OSA* includes "any document constituting evidence of an option, subscription or other interest in or to a security." This part of the definition sweeps in exchange-traded options issued by parties other than the issuer, such as put and call options traded through the facilities of the Canadian Derivatives Clearing Corporation. It also includes options issued directly by the issuer, such as rights and warrants (both of which are discussed above).

6) Other Instruments Commonly Known as Securities

Part (a) of the definition of securities in subsection 1(1) of the *OSA* includes as a security "any document, instrument or writing commonly known as a security." This part of the definition clearly overlaps with parts (d) and (e) of the definition (explored immediately above) in that most people regard common shares, preferred shares, bonds, debentures, and options as securities. Although part (a) of the definition appears to require that the interest in question be in writing, there is authority suggesting that this is not, in fact, the case.[17]

It is apparent from the jurisprudence that the courts are prepared to stretch part (a) of the definition well beyond what most people would commonly recognize as securities. For example, in *SEC v. C.M. Joiner Leasing Corp.*,[18] (discussed below under the heading "Investment Contracts"), the court found certain leasehold interests to be securities. In *SEC v. Glenn W. Turner Enterprises, Inc.*,[19] the court found that a pyramid sales scheme created an interest commonly known as a security. The court stated:

> The court doubts that Congress intended that in order to qualify under these general categories, a transaction must be commonly known to the man in the street as a security. Most securities are rather technical in nature and not likely to be understood except by the legal or financial community. It is sufficient that an offering be considered as a legal matter to be a security, regardless of the popular perception of it.

This case is important in defining the classes of persons whose views must be taken into account in order to qualify something as a security under part (a) of the definition. The instrument must be considered to be a security by "the legal or financial community," and not by the "[person] in the street." Given the average person's limited knowledge of financial instruments and the increasing complexity of financial transactions, the legal or financial community is the appropriate reference class of persons.

However, the last sentence of the above quote is tautological. The court tells us that something is a security if it can be "considered as a legal matter to be a security." But it is the court that defines what may be considered, as a legal matter, to be a security. The test is, thus, circular.

7) Interests in Property

Part (b) of the definition of securities in subsection 1(1) of the *OSA* includes "any document constituting evidence of title to or interest in the capital, assets, property, profits, earnings or royalties of any person

---

17   R. v. *McDonnell*, [1935] 1 W.W.R. 175 (Alta. C.A.).
18   320 U.S. 344 (1943) [*Joiner*].
19   348 F. Supp. 766 (D. Or. 1972).

or company." Perhaps the broadest part of this definition is "title to or interest in ... property ... of any person or company." The possible reach of this part of the definition is clear. If all that is required is a document constituting evidence of an interest in property, then a bill of sale is a security, as is a deed evidencing an interest in land, a mechanic's lien registered against a property, a mortgage, a vendor's interest in a vacuum cleaner bought on credit, and many other common types of interests in property. Thus, it would seem that something more than a simple property interest must be required to create a security. The following case, however, suggests that nothing more is required.

In *R. ex rel. Swain v. Boughner*,[20] Barbe purchased a half interest in a pair of royal chinchillas from Boughner. A bill of sale recorded the sale of the interest to Barbe, which transferred not only a property interest, but also "one-half the natural increase of said Chinchillas." A certificate was issued to Barbe that certified his ownership in the chinchillas and provided for the care of the animals and the disposition of the young.

The Crown contended that the certificate constituted a security under what is now part (b) of the definition in subsection 1(1) of the *OSA*. At the trial level, the magistrate held that no security existed because the words "of any person or company" (in part (b) of the definition of security, above) required Barbe to hold an *interest* in property belonging to *another* person, rather than actually owning the property (i.e., the chinchillas or a half interest in them) himself. On appeal, the Ontario High Court of Justice reversed this decision, holding that the "property" in question need not remain in another person or company, because the statute does not use the words "of 'another' person."[21]

On this reading of the statute, *any* document evidencing an interest in property is a security. It seems clear that the Ontario High Court of Justice erred on this specific point. On the court's reading of the statute, the definition of security becomes far wider than is necessary or desirable to carry out the purpose of the statute. Reading the statute as if it says "another person" better comports with the fundamental concept underlying the meaning of the term "security," which is the furnishing of risk capital by one person to another.

Nonetheless, the final outcome in *Boughner* is correct. As the discussion below makes clear, the interest (as evidenced by *both* documents furnished to Barbe) could, and should, have been characterized

---

20   [1948] O.W.N. 141 (H.C.J.) [*Boughner*].
21   *Ibid.* at 144.

as a security under the "investment contract" part of the definition of security. Although Barbe nominally purchased only chinchillas, the agreement obligated Boughner to care for, and ultimately dispose of, the animals in a manner that both parties hoped would generate a profit to be split between them. Thus, Barbe was clearly purchasing more than a simple property interest. He was led to expect that a profit over and above his initial stake would arise from his investment. The purchase of the chinchillas plus an interest in the profits bore little difference in substance from a purchase of shares in the chinchilla ranch.

Unfortunately, *Boughner* is not the only case to interpret this part of the definition in this overly broad manner. The Ontario Court of Appeal gave the section a similarly wide reading in *R. v. Dalley*,[22] stating:

> It was contended or suggested in argument for the appellant that the Court should not give the word "security" the broad and sweeping meaning I have just given to it. By so doing, it was urged, almost any agreement becomes a security since nearly every such document affords evidence of title to, or interest in, some property. But where the meaning of the statute is plain, as it appears to be here, the Court must give effect to it.

The Ontario Court of Appeal's holding implicitly acknowledges that "almost any agreement becomes a security" and gives this part of the definition a much wider meaning than the legislature surely intended.

A preferable interpretation may be found in *Ontario (Securities Commission) v. Brigadoon Scotch Distributor (Can.) Ltd.*[23] In *Brigadoon*, "warehouse receipts" were sold to a variety of purchasers. The receipts nominally evidenced only the passing of title in casks of whiskey. However, each cask remained in the possession of the vendor for the purpose of aging and eventual sale on behalf of the owner to a whisky blender. It was, no doubt, anticipated that this would generate a profit that would be distributed to the owners. It was alleged that the warehouse receipts constituted securities within the meaning of part (b) of the definition. In interpreting this provision, the court stated:

> The definition would not include documents of title which are bought and sold for purposes other than investment, for example, bills of lading and receipts for goods purchased for inventory or consumption purposes. Such an intention on the part of the Legislature

---

22   [1957] O.W.N. 123 (C.A.).
23   [1970] 3 O.R. 714 (H.C.) [*Brigadoon*].

can be inferred from the basic aim or purpose of the Securities Act, 1966, which is the protection of the investing public through full, true and plain disclosure of all material facts relating to securities being issued.[24]

Without further explanation, the court held that the warehouse receipts were securities under part (b).

The *Brigadoon* case emphasizes that, properly interpreted, part (b) of the definition of security adds nothing to the meaning of "investment contract" (discussed below). The court in *Brigadoon* was correct in holding that the warehouse receipts were securities. The purchasers in *Brigadoon* were led to believe that a profit would accrue over and above their initial investments. It is this element of investing for profit, and not merely an interest in property, that results in a characterization of the interest as a security.

Because of the potential for an overly ambitious interpretation by securities regulators and courts, it would perhaps be best if part (b) were removed from the definition of security.

8) Profit-sharing Agreements

Part (i) of the definition of securities in subsection 1(1) of the *OSA* includes "any profit-sharing agreement or certificate." Given its potential breadth, it is surprising that few cases have been litigated under this part of the definition.[25] However, in virtually every case in which it is alleged that there is a profit-sharing agreement, it is also alleged that the interest is a security by virtue of its being an investment contract. This is not surprising for two reasons. First, profit sharing is at the heart of the test for an investment contract. Second, the case law dealing with investment contracts is much more detailed than that dealing with profit-sharing agreements.[26] Again, therefore, in our view, little harm would be done by eliminating this part of the definition from the statute.

---

24   *Ibid.* at 717.

25   Some of the cases that have been the subject of judicial decisions are *R. v. Palomar Developments Corporation*, [1977] 2 W.W.R. 331 (Sask. Dist. Ct.); *Re Raymond Lee Organization of Canada*, [1978] OSCB 119; *R. v. Ausmus*, [1976] 5 W.W.R. 105 (Alta. Dist. Ct.); *Re Century 21 Real Estate Corporation* (1975), C.F.S.D.W.S. 1; *Ontario Securities Commission v. C & M Financial Consultants Limited* (1979), 23 O.R. (2d) 378 (H.C.J.).

26   See, e.g., *R. v. Ausmus*, above note 25.

9) Investment Contracts

a) Introduction

Part (n) of subsection 1(1) of the *OSA* includes in the definition of security "any investment contract." Many consider this phrase to be the
broadest part of the definition of security, although we have already seen
that there are other parts that are at least as wide. Part (n) is the most
litigated part of the definition. Perhaps most important, as the above
discussion makes clear, the courts' guidance under this part of the definition is transposable to other parts of the definition of security.

As we shall see below, the Canadian tests for determining when an
investment contract exists are the same as those adopted in the United
States. In what follows, we first canvass the leading U.S. cases and then
examine a selection of pertinent Canadian cases.

b) *SEC* v. *C.M. Joiner Leasing Corp.*

The first U.S. Supreme Court case interpreting "investment contract" is
SEC v. *C.M. Joiner Leasing Corp.*[27] The defendant, C.M. Joiner Leasing
(Joiner), purchased a number of leases of potentially oil-bearing property in Texas. These leases were conditional on Joiner drilling test
wells. To raise the money to conduct the drilling program, Joiner resold
some of its lease rights. Fifty purchasers bought parcels ranging in size
from 2.5 to 5 acres, at prices ranging from $5 to $15 per acre with most
purchases totalling no more than $25. The sales solicitation contained
the undertaking that Joiner would drill test wells to determine the
value of the properties.

The U.S. Supreme Court found that these interests constituted
securities within the meaning of the U.S. *Securities Act* of 1933. The
Joiner case is noteworthy in interpreting "investment contract" for a
number of reasons, which are discussed below.

i)   *The Importance of the Element of Economic Inducement,*
   or the Creation of an Expectation of Profit

The court recognized that Joiner was not merely selling leasehold interests. It was selling a hope of profit. As the court put it,

> [i]t is clear that an economic interest in the well-drilling undertaking
> was what brought into being the instruments that defendants were

---

27   *Joiner*, above note 18.

selling and gave to the instruments most of their value and all of their lure.[28]

ii) The Statutory Policy of Investor Protection

The court in *Joiner* held that

> courts will construe the details of an act in conformity with its dominating general purpose, will read text in the light of context and will interpret the text so far as the meaning of the words fairly permits so as to carry out in particular cases the general expressed legislative policy.
>
> In this case, the legislative policy is one of investor protection. Thus, the Act must be interpreted to further that policy.[29]

Note that this test is tautological. To define an interest as a security, the court in effect tells us that we must look to see if the person acquiring that interest is an investor. However, this merely pushes the inquiry back one step; we must then ask: "Who is an investor?" The test becomes circular because an investor is, after all, a person who buys a security.

References to the investor protection mandate of the statute are helpful only insofar as they emphasize that the interest in question must have an "investment" element to it. The investor must be led to expect that a return will accrue over and above her initial stake. Such references are also an indication of attitude: the courts are not timid in interpreting the statute.

iii) Substance Governs, Not Form

The defendant in *Joiner* argued that the interests could not be securities because, under Texas law, the lease assignments conveyed interests in real estate. It was argued, in other words, that something is *either* an interest in real estate *or* a security, but not both. The court rejected this reasoning, holding that the formal nature of the interest alleged to be a security is essentially irrelevant. The courts will be guided by substance, rather than form.

c) The *Howey* Test

The test for "investment contract" was further elaborated in *SEC* v. *W.J. Howey Co.*[30] Howey Co. raised money for the cultivation of citrus crops

---

28   *Ibid.* at 340.
29   *Ibid.* at 350.
30   328 U.S. 293 (1946) [*Howey*].

by selling some of its acreage. While Howey Co. was prepared to sell only land to purchasers, it urged potential buyers to enter into a service contract with Howey-in-the-Hills, a subsidiary company that cultivated, harvested, and marketed the citrus crop. Indeed, Howey Co. told purchasers that it was not feasible to invest in citrus groves without a service contract. Eighty-five percent of those who purchased land also entered into service contracts (mostly for ten-year terms) with Howey-in-the-Hills. The contracts gave Howey-in-the-Hills a leasehold interest with possession. Howey-in-the-Hills pooled the fruit, sold it, and allocated profits based on the output of each tract. The purchasers were mostly out-of-state residents who knew nothing about the citrus business.

In deciding that the *combination* of the land sales contract, the deed giving title to land, and the service contract was a security, the court in *Howey* reiterated those points from *Joiner* noted above.

The court in *Howey* also propounded perhaps the most widely used test for the existence of an investment contract:[31]

> [A]n investment contract for the purposes of the Securities Act means a contract, transaction or scheme, whereby a person invests his money in a common enterprise and is led to expect profits solely from the efforts of the promoter or a third party.

This test is essentially a reformulation of the "economic inducement" element that was pivotal in the *Joiner* decision. One difficulty in interpreting *Howey*, however, is what it means to have a "common enterprise." Another difficulty results from the use of the word "solely" in the above quotation. What if the "investor" also engages in efforts, however minimal, to produce a profit? These issues are dealt with further below.

On the facts of the *Howey* case, the court held that the test was met: the buyers were "attracted solely by the prospects of a return on their investment."[32] The sale of an "investment contract" was involved in the transaction, triggering the registration requirement of the *Securities Act* of 1933.

i) The Character of the Buyers

An important thread to the *Howey* decision is the buyers' inability to protect themselves. The court stressed that most of the buyers were

---

31   *Ibid.*
32   *Ibid.* at 300.

out-of-state residents who knew nothing about the citrus business. The court clearly felt that these buyers were in need of the "full and fair disclosure" that would be furnished by compliance with the *Securities Act*.

ii) Degree of Risk

The defendant in *Howey* argued that no security existed because the investment was not speculative or promotional in character. In other words, it was not high risk. In denying this defence, the court effectively held that only *some* risk is needed to create an investment contract.[33]

iii) Irrelevance of the Existence of Value Independent of the Success of the Enterprise

The defendant in *Howey* also argued that the land sales were not securities because the land had value independent of the success of the enterprise as a whole. Echoing *Joiner*, the court in *Howey* held that substance triumphs over form, and an interest may be a security even though it has value independent of the enterprise as a whole.

d) The *Hawaii* Test

The *Howey* test is one of the two most commonly used tests of what interests constitute investment contracts. The other commonly used test is found in *Hawaii v. Hawaii Market Center Inc.* decided by the Supreme Court of Hawaii.[34] The Hawaii Market Center (HMC) operated a retail store. To raise money to carry on business, HMC recruited "founder members," who were either "founder distributors" or "founder supervisors." A distributor purchased $70 worth of merchandise for $320. A supervisor purchased $140 worth of merchandise for $820. Both distributors and supervisors received "purchase authorization cards" that were distributed to potential shoppers. Only those with such cards were allowed to purchase merchandise at the store.[35]

Founder members could make money in two ways. First, if people to whom they had distributed purchase authorization cards bought merchandise, the members received a commission. Second, they could earn money by signing up others as founder members.

The defendant in the *Hawaii* case argued that the *Howey* test required purchasers to be "led to expect profits *solely* from the efforts of the promoter or a third party." However, founder members could

---

33   On the issue of risk, see also *Pacific Coast*, above note 9, and discussed in detail below in section (e) under Canadian Cases.

34   *Hawaii*, above note 11.

35   *Ibid.*

generate profits through their own efforts, and clearly did not rely *solely* on the efforts of a third party.

In finding that the interests were securities, the court in *Hawaii* was clearly motivated by the same concerns that underlie the tests in *Joiner* and *Howey*.[36] However, the court adopted a slightly more elaborate test[37] for the existence of an investment contract:

(1) An offeree furnishes initial value to an offeror, and

(2) a portion of this initial value is subjected to the risks of the enterprise, and

(3) the furnishing of the initial value is induced by the offeror's promises or representations which give rise to a reasonable understanding that a valuable benefit of some kind, over and above the initial value, will accrue to the offeree as a result of the operation of the enterprise, and

(4) the offeree does not receive the right to exercise practical and actual control over the managerial decisions of the enterprise.[38]

While consistent with *Joiner* and *Howey*, the *Hawaii* test makes it clear that not *all* of the "initial value" needs to be subjected to the risks of the enterprise.[39] It also sidesteps the problem created by *Howey's* requirement that the purchaser be led to expect profits "solely" from the efforts of a third party, by requiring only that the purchaser have no "practical and actual control" over management decisions.

e)   Canadian Cases

Pacific Coast Coin Exchange of Canada v. *Ontario (Securities Commission)*[40] is the leading Canadian case on the meaning of investment contract. Pacific Coast Coin Exchange (PCCE) sold silver on margin (i.e., on credit). Buyers were required to make a down payment of only 35 percent of the value of the purchase, and PCCE, in effect,

---

36   In particular, the court stated that an investment contract will be found when there is "the public solicitation of venture capital to be used in a business enterprise," and "the subjection of the investor's money to the risks of an enterprise over which he exercises no managerial control." *Hawaii*, above note 11 at 109.

37   This test is derived from Ronald John Coffey, "The Economic Realities of a 'Security': Is There a More Meaningful Formula?" (1967) 18 W. Res. L. Rev. 367, 412.

38   *Hawaii*, above note 11 at 651.

39   This is implicit in *Joiner*, above note 18, and *Howey*, above note 30.

40   *Pacific Coast*, above note 9.

loaned the rest of the purchase price. PCCE did not actually deliver the silver that was the subject of the contract. Indeed, at any given time, PCCE kept only a small quantity of silver on hand — far less than was necessary to make delivery to all buyers. What PCCE sold was a *contractual right* to receive silver. The buyer acquired the option to demand actual delivery of the silver on giving PCCE forty-eight hours' notice. Alternatively, the buyer could demand a notional "sale" of her silver, in which case the buyer would receive (or pay) the difference between the price of silver when the contract was entered into and the price of silver when the contract was liquidated. When a contract was closed out, PCCE would collect interest on the loaned portion of the purchase price, commissions, and "storage" charges. Eighty-five percent of PCCE's customers closed out their accounts without ever taking delivery of any silver.

This venture undoubtedly exposed PCCE to a non-trivial level of risk. If the price of silver rose, PCCE would be liable to pay any buyer who chose to liquidate the contract the difference between the contract price and the price of silver at the time of liquidation, or to enter the market, purchase the required quantity of silver, and deliver it to the buyer. Particularly if the price of silver rose dramatically, PCCE might easily find itself unable to meet all of its buyers' claims and, therefore, become insolvent.

To meet this risk, PCCE purchased silver futures. As explained in chapter 1, in a futures contract, the buyer agrees to pay a fixed price for a stated quantity of a good (in this case, silver) for delivery on a stated date in the future. These futures positions protected PCCE against a rise in the price of silver. If the price of silver rose, PCCE would still be able to take delivery of the specified quantity of silver at the fixed futures contract price. Furthermore, a futures contract may typically be resold to a third party, who then assumes the obligation to pay the price and receive the goods on the stated date. Thus, if the market price of silver rose, PCCE could at any time liquidate the futures contract by selling it at a premium to a third party (the premium reflecting the rise in the price of silver).

PCCE's exposure to the risk of changes in silver prices was therefore "hedged." If the price of silver rose, PCCE would lose money on the contracts it had made to sell silver to its purchasers, but it would make money on its futures contracts. Holding offsetting risks is the essence of a hedge.

To further its business, PCCE distributed promotional brochures that emphasized the value of silver not only as an investment, but also as a protection against inflation. The brochures predicted rampant inflation and even suggested the possible return of a major depression. PCCE, however, did not compile and distribute a prospectus to its buyers. As a consequence, the Ontario regulators issued a "cease trade" order, banning further trading activity by PCCE until such time as a prospectus was filed and distributed.

In appealing this ruling, PCCE argued that the contracts it sold did not constitute "securities" within the meaning of the Ontario legislation. If the interests were not securities, the prospectus requirement did not apply because it attached only to interests that are securities.

The *Pacific Coast* case turned on whether the interests sold by PCCE constituted "investment contracts." In finding that the interests were indeed investment contracts, the Supreme Court of Canada purported to adopt the *Howey* test. However, applying the *Howey* test literally would likely have resulted in the finding that there was no security. The buyers were clearly not led to expect profits "solely" from the efforts of PCCE; rather, the price of silver in international markets, over which PCCE had no control, was a key factor (indeed, perhaps *the* key factor) in the buyer's return. To get around this difficulty, the Supreme Court of Canada accepted a modification of the word "solely" in the *Howey* test, stating:

> The word "solely" in that test has been criticized and toned down by many jurisdictions in the United States. It is sufficient to refer to S.E.C. v. Koscot Interplanetary Inc. (1974), 497 F.2d. 473, and to S.E.C. v. Glen W. Turner Enterprises Inc. (1973), 474 F.2d. 476. As mentioned in the Turner case, to give a strict interpretation to the word "solely" (at p. 482) "would not serve the purpose of the legislation. Rather we adopt a more realistic test, whether the efforts made by those other than the investor are the *undeniably significant ones, those essential managerial efforts which affect the failure or success of the enterprise.*"[41]

On the facts of the *Pacific Coast* case, the court held that the essential managerial efforts were made by PCCE:

> The end result of the investment made by each customer is dependent upon the quality of the expertise brought to the administration of the funds obtained by appellant from its customers ... If Pacific does not properly invest the pooled deposit, the purchaser will obtain no return on his investment regardless of the prevailing value of silver; there is nothing that the customer can do to avoid that result.[42]

---

41   *Ibid.* at 539. [Emphasis added.]
42   *Ibid.* at 539–40.

Indeed, the court held that "the key to the success of the venture is the efforts of the promoter alone."[43]

The Supreme Court of Canada also accepted a refinement of the meaning of "common enterprise" in the *Howey* test:

> In the same case of *Turner*, the expression 'common enterprise' has been defined to mean (p. 482) 'one in which the fortunes of the investor are interwoven with and dependent upon the efforts and success of those seeking the investment or of third parties'... In my view, the test of common enterprise is met in the case at bar. I accept respondent's submission that such an enterprise exists when it is undertaken for the benefit of the supplier of capital (the investor) and of those who solicit the capital (the promoter). In this relationship, the investor's role is limited to the advancement of money, the managerial control over the success of the enterprise being that of the promoter; therein lies the community. In other words, the 'commonality' necessary for an investment contract is that between the investor and the promoter. There is no need for the enterprise to be common to the investors between themselves.[44]

Thus, the Supreme Court of Canada found that the *Howey* test applied and characterized the interests as investment contracts. The court in *Pacific Coast* held that the *Hawaii* risk capital test would lead to the same result.

The Supreme Court of Canada made a number of other important rulings in relation to what constitutes an investment contract:

1. In determining whether an interest is a security, U.S. cases on point are relevant because "the policy behind the legislation in the two countries is exactly the same."[45]
2. The definitions in the *OSA* are not mutually exclusive, but rather are "catchalls" to be given their widest meaning.
3. Securities legislation is "remedial legislation" to be "construed broadly."[46]
4. Substance, not form, governs the interpretation of what is a security.
5. The policy of securities legislation is "full and fair disclosure" with respect to those instruments commonly known as securities.

---

43   *Ibid.* at 540.
44   *Ibid.* at 539.
45   *Ibid.* at 538.
46   This statement, in fact, adds nothing to provincial and federal *Interpretation Acts*, which routinely provide that *all* legislation is remedial legislation to be given a broad and liberal construction.

In a strong dissent in *Pacific Coast*, Chief Justice Laskin would have held that the interests were *not* securities. According to Laskin C.J., the source of the buyers' risk was not the quality of the management brought to the project by PCCE, but the market risk inherent in the price of silver. The only difference between buying from PCCE and buying silver in the spot market was a concern over PCCE's solvency. Laskin C.J. would have held that a concern over the solvency of the enterprise is not enough to render the interests securities.

The *Pacific Coast* case illustrates just how broad the definition of security is. It is difficult to disagree with Laskin C.J.'s view that all that distinguished the scheme in question from a purchase of silver in the spot market was solvency risk. And, if solvency risk is enough to render an interest a security, it is difficult to know when to stop finding that particular interests are securities. A deposit in a bank or other financial institution would certainly be a security because there is always concern about the solvency of the institution. A life insurance policy, whether for term insurance or otherwise, would also constitute a security because of the concern about the solvency of the insurance company. Indeed, the purchase of *any* insurance contract would constitute a security for the same reason. For that matter, an agreement for the purchase of any valuable asset where payment is made in advance of delivery involves some risk that the seller may become insolvent and, so, unable to honour its delivery obligation. A purchase of a lottery ticket, a bet on a horse, a contribution of money to a hockey pool, a local bingo event, or a pyramid marketing scheme might also constitute purchases of securities. Perhaps even a loan of money to a friend would constitute a security because there is always a risk that the friend will become insolvent.

And yet, it seems certain that no court or administrator would hold an interest like the purchase of a lottery ticket to be a security. The degree of risk taken by the purchaser is small, and requiring a prospectus or a prospectus exemption would be extraordinarily costly relative to the benefit to be obtained. By contrast, in the *Pacific Coast* case, the sums of money involved and the risk taken by the purchasers were highly significant. In such a case, there is far greater call for the application of the securities legislation. Moreover, the promoters of the scheme in question attempted to induce investors to part with their money by making exaggerated and inflammatory, if not simply irresponsible, claims about the future of the financial markets.

This brings us back to the policy underlying the legislation: investor protection. The more a court or administrator perceives that capital contributors need protection, the more likely it is to find the interest to be a security. The amount of money involved, the degree of risk taken, and the likelihood that contributors of capital will be taken advantage of by promoters of the scheme all play a role in this regard. The *net* benefit to be achieved by applying the regulatory apparatus (i.e., the benefit less the cost) will also likely be a factor. While a court will rarely, if ever, make explicit reference to all, or indeed any, of these factors, it is beyond doubt that they will operate *sub rosa*, whether consciously or unconsciously.

Predicting whether an interest will be considered a security thus involves two levels of analysis. One is an avowedly legal analysis, which will be played out in the context of the tests that the courts have enunciated for the meaning of the term security. The other analysis takes place within the legal subtext, which includes those things that influence a judge to make a particular finding, but which are not explicitly referred to in the judgment.

Given the number of factors, both explicit and implicit, that enter into the determination of whether an interest is a security, it can be difficult to predict the outcome of particular cases. The Ontario Securities Commission's holding in *Re Sunfour Estates N.V.*[47] is illustrative. Sunfour Estates N.V. (Sunfour) was a corporation that owned land in Aruba, a small island off the coast of Venezuela. Local authorities approved the land for development. Sunfour wanted to sell undivided, co-tenancy interests in the land to various purchasers who would get the benefit of the planning approvals. The interests were to be sold in units of $10,000. The plan required each purchaser to sign a co-tenancy agreement, pursuant to which the owners were collectively entitled to select a management committee. The management committee, in turn, would select a manager (possibly Sunfour) to develop the property. Under the co-tenancy agreement, the owners were allowed to sell their interests, but only with the permission of a majority of the other owners.

Sunfour encountered difficulty in selling these interests to residents of Ontario because there was no prospectus exemption in the *OSA* that allowed Sunfour to sell the interests free of the prospectus requirement. Sunfour applied to the Ontario Securities Commission for a discretionary ruling[48] to permit the interests to be sold without compiling, filing, and distributing a prospectus.

---

47   (1992), 15 OSCB 269 [*Sunfour*].
48   Pursuant to s. 73, now s. 74 of the *OSA*, above note 2.

In negotiations with OSC staff prior to the hearing, Sunfour agreed to make certain concessions to secure the support of staff at the hearing. Sunfour agreed to change the co-tenancy agreement so that the property would be held only for resale. In the alternative, the property could be developed, but only with the approval of all the owners. Further, Sunfour agreed that units would be sold for $20,000 each.

In the *Sunfour* decision, the OSC held that the interests were not securities. Hence, the scheme required no exemption from the prospectus requirement. The OSC adopted the definition of investment contract reflected in the U.S. cases discussed above. The decision indicates that a sale of real estate may constitute a sale of a security if the buyer depends heavily on the "efforts and financial stability of the promoter."[49] However, the changes in the co-tenancy agreement indicated above gave the buyers some measure of control over the project. Thus, the Commission was persuaded that any risk inherent in the purchase of the units arose not from the efforts and stability of the promoter, but rather

> the success of the venture will depend on real estate values in Aruba, and nobody has much control over that ... [The buyers] are quite free to consult their own real estate agents in Aruba or otherwise if they want information or help in determining whether or when they should sell.[50]

A scrutiny of other cases defining investment contracts indicates that the *Sunfour* decision could easily have found that the interests were securities. The co-tenancy agreement contained "shotgun" clauses "which give an owner the right, on notice, to purchase another owner's interest or alternatively to be bought out by that owner at the same price."[51] An owner who refused to agree to develop the property would, almost certainly, be effectively forced out by an offer (or offers) from other owners under the shotgun clause. Perhaps more important, as a matter of business, the lure of the venture for prospective buyers lay not in holding undeveloped land for capital appreciation, but in developing the property for a profit. The normal expectation would be that all buyers would in fact agree to develop the property. Once this is done, each buyer is part of a collective enterprise over which he or she exercises little practical control, save to have his or her vote counted in determining the identity of the management committee. In net, one

---

49   *Sunfour*, above note 47 at 280 (citing OSC release (1988), 11 OSCB 4171).
50   *Ibid.* at 280 & 281.
51   *Ibid.* at 274.

would have thought that if the risk assumed by the buyers in *Pacific Coast* was sufficient to render the interest a security, then so the risk in *Sunfour* ought to have made the interest a security. In each case, risk external to the enterprise was a significant component of the risk facing the buyers. In fact, in *Sunfour*, the internal component of risk appears to have been at least as great as that in *Pacific Coast*.

Also of interest in *Sunfour* is the fact that both the OSC staff and the commissioners who decided the case were more willing to find that the interest was not a security when the minimum investment was raised to $20,000. There is little, if anything, in the jurisprudence that makes the minimum investment a relevant factor; however, it is easy to see why it is relevant having regard to the legal subtext. As pointed out above, the extent to which investors are thought to be in need of the protection of the *OSA* is an important factor in the determination of whether a particular interest is a security. The OSC staff's thinking was undoubtedly that raising the minimum investment would likely prevent less affluent buyers from investing, leaving only relatively well-heeled buyers with a comparatively greater ability to protect their own interests.[52]

Until very recent changes to the private placement rules in Ontario, discussed further in chapter 7, one of the most important exemptions from the prospectus requirement available under the *OSA* was found in clause 72(1)(d). This exemption permitted a distribution of securities without a prospectus where each purchaser of the securities invested at least $150,000.[53] The assumption underlying this exemption was that those who could afford to purchase $150,000 worth of securities would have the resources to protect their own interests. Although this logic has been questioned, it functioned for years as the basis for this commonly relied-upon prospectus exemption.

This demonstrates the close kinship between the prospectus exemptions and the determination of what constitutes a security. A finding that a particular interest is not a security accomplishes the same result (so far as the prospectus requirement is concerned) as an exemption from the prospectus requirement. A regulator who does not think that it is necessary to apply the prospectus requirement might *either* grant a prospectus exemption *or* find that an interest is not a

---

52   This logic can work rather perversely. If those less well-heeled investors who planned to invest are not discouraged by the higher minimum offering price, they end up being *more*, rather than *less*, at risk.

53   Although s. 72(1)(d) still appears in the *OSA*, recent revisions to OSC Rule 45-501 have effectively made it unavailable. See chapter 7.

security. In strict legal theory, the considerations that are used to determine whether an exemption ought to be granted are different from those used to determine whether something is a security. In practice, however, there is inevitably a considerable amount of overlap.

The *Sunfour* analysis was subsequently considered by the Ontario Court of Justice (General Division) (as it then was) in a 1995 decision, *Beer v. Towngate Ltd.*.[54] The plaintiffs in *Beer* argued, among other things, that certain agreements to purchase luxury condominiums (entered into at the peak of the residential real estate market in early 1989) were securities distributed by the developer in contravention of the *OSA* and were, therefore, void. The court rejected the characterization of these contracts as securities, noting that the purchasers were buying a "tangible asset,"[55] not a security. The developer's role in the project was not, in the court's view, "the kind of third party effort envisaged by *Howey*,"[56] but rather "the inherent value of the units is far more dependent upon market trends and prevailing economic conditions over which the promoter has no control."[57]

10)   Reprise

The *OSA* contains a long and comprehensive definition of security. Perhaps most important, the broadest parts of this definition, such as "interests in property," "profit-sharing agreements," and "investment contracts," are wide enough to embrace virtually any scheme in which one person[58] entrusts money to another. Only the common sense of the securities regulators and the courts draws a boundary between those instruments that will be characterized as securities and those that will not. This common sense is ultimately guided by the fundamental underlying policy of the *OSA* — investor protection. If an adjudicator is of the view that a particular scheme requires the protection of the legislation, it is very likely that the adjudicator will characterize the interest as a security. If that protection is not thought to be required, the interest is not likely to be characterized as a security.

In some situations the interest will be characterized as a security even though a buyer may not need the protection of the *OSA*. For example, it is abundantly clear that common shares are securities

---

54   [1995] O.J. No. 3009 (Gen. Div.) [*Beer*].
55   *Ibid.* at para 53.
56   *Ibid.*
57   *Ibid.*
58   By "person," we refer to a person in the broad legal sense that includes individuals and corporations. See above note 13.

under parts (a) and (e) of the *OSA* definition (if not under other parts). Because of this, no court or regulator would fail to characterize a common share interest as a security, even if the buyers were perfectly capable of protecting their own interests.

In short, an interest is a security if it clearly falls under one of the specific enumerations in the definition. If it does not, it might, nevertheless, be characterized as a security under one of the broad, open-ended parts of the definition, and policy considerations will govern.

Finally, some instruments that are securities are exempted from the coverage of the securities legislation because they are covered under other legislative schemes. A bank account, for example, is likely a security, but is exempted from the application of securities laws because bank deposits are protected by the comprehensive scheme of regulation contained in the *Bank Act*.[59]

11) What if There Is No "Security:" Does the *OSA* Apply?

At the outset, we indicated that the application of various provisions of the *OSA* turn on whether there is a security. In our view, this is entirely appropriate. The *OSA* was meant to deal with securities, not with consumer protection. This is apparent not only from the title of the legislation, but from its structure. As noted above, securities regulation covers five major areas: primary market offerings, secondary market trading, activities of market professionals, insider trading, and take-over bids. In respect of each of these, it is implicit that a condition precedent to the operation of the *OSA* is the presence of a security.

This is clearly true in relation to primary market offerings, as illustrated by the *Sunfour* case above. If what is being offered for sale is not a security, the prospectus requirement simply has no application. The presence of a security is also a condition precedent for the regulation of secondary trading. For example, only reporting issuers are subject to the continuous disclosure requirements of the *OSA*. A scrutiny of the definition of "reporting issuer"[60] makes it clear that reporting issuers are those companies that have issued *securities* to the public.

Similarly, the class of persons who must register under the *OSA* is limited to those who are engaged in *trading*.[61] An examination of the definition of "trading" indicates that trading activity necessarily involves the trading of a *security*.[62] In like manner, the Act's definitions

59   S.C. 1991, c. 46.
60   *OSA*, above note 2, s. 1(1).
61   *Ibid.* s. 25(1).
62   *Ibid.* s. 1(1).

make it clear that the application of the take-over bid[63] and insider-trading provisions[64] depends on the presence of a security.

The securities regulators, however, take the view that they have jurisdiction even in cases that do not involve a security. This jurisdiction is said to arise from the so-called "public interest" powers. This name derives from the fact that the legislation empowers the OSC to make a variety of orders "if in its opinion it is in the public interest to make the order or orders."[65] There are eight public interest powers enumerated in section 127 of the Act, which are discussed in detail in chapter 11.

A case in which one of the public interest powers was applied despite the absence of a security is *Re Albino*.[66] In *Albino*, Rio Algom Ltd. set up an incentive plan for its chief executive officer, George Albino. Under the plan, Albino was notionally, but not actually, "issued" a certain number of shares (commonly referred to as "phantom stock") of Rio Algom Ltd. Albino held an option to designate a date upon which the actual price of the company's stock would be compared to the price of the stock when the phantom stock units were issued. The difference was to be awarded to Albino in cash.

Albino appears to have possessed confidential information that would, when made public, impact negatively on the company's stock price. Albino delayed public disclosure of this information until after he was able to exercise his phantom stock options, apparently in order to enhance the value of the phantom stock units.

At a hearing before the Ontario Securities Commission, OSC staff asked the OSC to find that Albino had engaged in insider trading, contrary to the *OSA*. Commissioner Blain concluded that the insider-trading provisions had no application because the phantom stock units did not constitute securities. Commissioner Salter would have found that the units were securities. Commissioner Hansen declined to decide the issue of whether the phantom stock units were securities, although her

---

63   *Ibid.* s. 89(1) ("'take-over bid' means an offer to acquire [a certain percentage of] outstanding voting or equity *securities* ...") [emphasis added].

64   *Ibid.* s. 76(1) ("no person or company in a special relationship with a *reporting issuer* shall *purchase or sell* securities of the *reporting issuer*") [emphasis added]; s. 1(1) (definition of "reporting issuer"); *ibid.*, s. 76(2) ("no reporting issuer and no person or company in a special relationship with a *reporting issuer* shall inform ... another person or company of a material fact or material change with respect to the *reporting issuer* ...")[emphasis added]. See also *ibid.*, s. 134 (civil liability).

65   *Ibid.* s. 127(1).

66   (1991), 14 OSCB 365 [*Albino*].

reasons suggest that had she decided the issue, she would have sided with Commissioner Blain. Thus, only one of three commissioners was prepared to find that the interest in question was a security.

Nonetheless, two of the three commissioners (Hansen and Salter) took the view that the OSC had the jurisdiction to make an order denying Albino trading exemptions in Ontario (and ordered that such an order should issue). As articulated in the reasons of Commissioner Salter (adopted by Commissioner Hansen), the jurisdictional test for the issuance of a public interest order is not whether there is a security, but whether the transaction exhibits a significant connection to the capital markets of Ontario.

Although this appears to represent an overly broad view of the OSC's jurisdiction, it has found support in the courts. The regulators, supported by the courts, have long taken the view that the public interest powers may be invoked in the absence of a breach of any feature of the *OSA*, rules, regulations, policy statements, notices, documents, or expressed views of the OSC.[67] This by itself, however, does not resolve the *constitutional* issue of when the public interest powers may be invoked. This question was addressed by the Ontario Court of Appeal in *Quebec (Sa Majesté du Chef) v. Ontario Securities Commission*.[68] In *Asbestos*, the court ruled that not even a transactional nexus to Ontario is required to trigger Ontario's constitutional jurisdiction. All that is required to invoke the public interest powers, as a matter of constitutional law, is that the transaction have an *effect* on Ontario shareholders sufficient to prejudice the public interest.[69] This reasoning was subsequently endorsed by the Supreme Court of Canada in a subsequent case arising from the same set of facts.[70]

Although the correctness of this decision may be questioned,[71] it nonetheless represents the current state of the law. Combining *Albino* and *Asbestos*, it appears that the public interest sanctions in the *OSA* may be invoked even where there is no security, and even where the

---

67   See, e.g., *Re Canadian Tire Corp.* (1987), 10 OSCB 857, aff'd 59 O.R. (2d) 79 (Div. Ct.).

68   (1992), 10 O.R. (3d) 577 (C.A.) [*Asbestos*].

69   See also *Committee for Equal Treatment of Asbestos Minority Shareholders v. Ontario Securities Commission* (1997), 33 O.R. (3d) 651 (Div. Ct.). These cases are at odds with Justice Iacobucci's statement in *Pezim v. British Columbia (Superintendent of Brokers)*, [1994] 2 S.C.R. 557, rev'g (1992), 66 B.C.L.R. (2d) 257 (C.A.) that there is no independent public interest jurisdiction.

70   *Committee for Equal Treatment of Asbestos Minority Shareholders v. Ontario Securities Commission*, [2001] 2 S.C.R. 132.

71   See the discussion of the *Asbestos* decision in chapter 3.

transaction in question takes place outside the jurisdiction, so long as the transaction has a prejudicial impact on Ontario security holders.

12) Derivative Securities

Are derivative "securities" in fact securities within the meaning of the securities legislation? With the spectacular growth in markets for derivative securities in recent years, this is an important question.

Derivative securities usually consist of some permutation or combination of options and futures contracts. As explained earlier, an option contract is a contract that gives the holder a right to buy or to sell an underlying asset or interest that typically can be exercised either on or before a certain future date.[72] For example, a "put" option allows the holder to insist that another person purchase the optioned securities from the holder at a certain price (the "strike" or "exercise" price) on or before a certain date. Another commonly used option is a "right," which gives the holder the option of purchasing the securities of a particular corporation (directly from that corporation) on or before a certain date.

A futures contract, as discussed earlier, obligates one party to the contract to sell and the other party to buy a stated quantity of a good on a future date for a stated price.

The name "derivative" security originates from the fact that the value of the instrument is derivative of the value of something else, which is generally called the "underlying interest." For example, in the case of a silver futures contract, the underlying interest is silver. The value of the futures contract at any point in time depends on the price of silver when the time comes for delivery. Those who trade in silver futures contracts make forecasts of the future price of silver and adjust what they are willing to pay for the futures contract accordingly.

Some derivative instruments are clearly securities within the meaning of the securities legislation. For example, put options[73] and rights[74]

---

72 Such an option would be termed an "American" style option. By contrast, a "European" option gives the holder the right to exercise the option only on one specified date.

73 A put option gives the purchaser (or holder) the option of requiring the other party to the transaction (the seller, or "writer" of the option) to purchase from the holder a stated quantity of the securities of a particular issuer, at a stated price (the "strike price") on or before a certain date (the "expiry date").

74 A right is an option, usually issued to existing security holders of a particular issuer, enabling them to purchase additional securities in the issuer at a stated price. In some cases, rights will be sold to any willing purchaser, whether that purchaser is an existing security holder or not. Rights offerings are discussed further in chapter 5.

are both instruments commonly known as securities.[75] A right also confers an option to purchase other securities, which again qualifies it as a security under the *OSA*.[76] A call option is also clearly a security.[77]

Put and call options constitute the bulk of what are known as "exchange traded" derivative securities. They are typically traded over the Canadian Derivatives Clearing Corporation and are subject to regulation by both the securities regulators[78] and the exchange over which they trade. Because they are clearly securities, and because many of those who buy and sell such securities are comparatively unsophisticated retail traders, regulation of the trading of such securities has sparked little controversy.

Most of the controversy has arisen in relation to "over-the-counter" (OTC) derivative securities. OTC derivatives consist of privately negotiated contracts that are typically entered into between sophisticated parties such as financial institutions (banks, trust companies, insurance companies, pension funds, and mutual funds), securities dealers, large corporations, utilities, and governments. Although for the sake of convenience, the International Swaps and Derivatives Association (ISDA) has formulated standardized documentation for trades in OTC derivatives, the terms of OTC derivative transactions remain subject to individual negotiation.

Derivative contracts are most frequently entered into to hedge risk. For example, a corporation situated in Canada, but selling most of its product in the United States, is subject to exchange rate risk. If all its sales contracts require payment in U.S. dollars, the value of these contracts falls if the U.S. dollar falls relative to the Canadian dollar. The company may wish to hedge this risk by buying derivative products whose underlying interest is the value of the Canadian dollar vis-à-vis

---

75   See *OSA*, above note 2, s. 1(1)(a) (definition of "security"). Presumably, as derivative instruments become more commonplace, many will come within the definition of securities simply because they are commonly regarded as securities.

76   *Ibid.* s. 1(1)(d) (definition of "security,"). The *OSA* also specifically recognizes as securities "any commodity futures contract or any commodity futures option that is not traded on a commodity futures exchange registered with or recognized by the Commission under the *Commodity Futures Act* or the form of which is not accepted by the Director under that Act." (See *OSA*, s. 1(1)(p) (definition of "security")). This provision effectively makes the *Commodity Futures Act* the primary source of legislation governing futures contracts and options.

77   *Ibid*, s. 1(1)(a) & (d) (definition of "security").

78   For example, trading in put and call options is subject to the *OSA* rules relating to insider trading. See *OSA*, ss. 76 & 134.

the U.S. dollar, so that if the value of the U.S. dollar falls relative to the Canadian dollar, the value of the derivatives contract rises.

A swap contract is the most common form of OTC derivative. There are serious questions, however, about whether such interests constitute securities. For explanatory purposes, a swap arrangement may be described simply in this way (although, in practice, swaps are commonly entered into with financial intermediaries, rather than between two end-users). Company A has outstanding debt obligations with fixed interest payments. Company B has outstanding debt obligations with interest payments that float with the prime rate. Each contractually "swaps" its interest obligation with the other. Under this arrangement, each company will continue to pay the interest due on its own debt obligations; however, each is obliged to pay to the other any difference between its own interest obligation and the other's.

Assume, for example, that company A and company B are both obliged to pay their creditors $1,000 in interest per period when they enter the swap. Interest rates then fall such that in the next period, company B must pay its creditors only $500 in interest while company A, with fixed interest payments, remains obliged to pay $1,000. Company A pays its own creditors the $1,000 that it owes them, but is contractually entitled to collect $500 from company B. This is because, in the swap, company A agreed that it would *notionally* pay company B's creditors, and company B agreed that it would *notionally* pay company A's creditors. In each period, a "netting" or settling-up occurs between the two companies that puts each company in the same position it would have been in had the two companies *actually* paid the interest on each other's debt.

Is there a security in this transaction? None of the parts of the definition of securities in the *OSA*, including the broadest parts of the definition (e.g., an interest in property, an investment contract, or a profit-sharing agreement), appears to fit. This is not surprising. When the definition was formulated, few derivatives existed, and many derivatives, such as swaps, were unknown.

Moreover, applying the policy of the statute — the protection of investors — does not at first blush help to resolve the issue. In many cases, it is impossible to determine who is the vendor of the "security," and who is the "investor," in order to determine who needs the protection of the *OSA*. As noted above, the parties to a swap arrangement are typically financial institutions, corporations, and governments. All of these are sophisticated parties that generally do not require the protections furnished by securities legislation.

The OSC first tackled this problem in 1994,[79] by issuing a draft statement detailing how it proposed to regulate the OTC derivatives market. Following the receipt of comments from interested parties, the OSC issued a revised draft statement in November of 1996,[80] a revised proposed rule and companion policy in 1998,[81] a further revised version in January 2000,[82] and a "final" version in September 2000.[83] (The final version was, however, ultimately returned by the Minister of Finance for further consideration.) Although the details are complex, all these proposals seek to regulate transactions in derivatives on the basis of whether the parties to such transactions are in fact sophisticated traders capable of protecting their own interests or whether parties are in need of protection. For example, where both parties to the transaction are "qualified parties," neither the prospectus nor the registration requirements (nor any other part of the legislation) apply under the draft proposal.[84]

These OTC derivatives proposals properly reflect a purposive approach to securities regulation. They begin with the purpose of securities regulation — the protection of investors — and attempt to construct a regulatory structure that serves that overriding purpose. While many in the regulated community have disagreed with the details of the proposals, few have quarrelled with this basic, and sound, starting point.

For all its complexity, however, the proposal does not clearly resolve the issue of whether derivative instruments, such as swaps, are securities. The introduction to the proposal notes that amendments made to the *OSA* in 1994 (which gave the OSC the power to make rules)[85] conferred upon the OSC the power to make rules:

Regulating or varying this Act in respect of derivatives, including,

i.   providing exemptions from any requirement of this Act,

---

79   "Draft as Recommended by Staff — Over-the-Counter Derivative Transactions — Policy Statement: Interpretation of Transactions in OTC Derivatives" (1994), 17 OSCB 394.

80   "Notice of Proposed Rule and Proposed Policy Under the Securities Act: Over-the-Counter Derivatives" (1996), 19 OSCB 5929.

81   (1998), 21 OSCB 7755.

82   (2000), 23 OSCB 51.

83   (2000), 23 OSCB 6189.

84   For a detailed explanation of these proposals, see Christopher C. Nicholls, *Corporate Finance and Canadian Law* (Toronto: Carswell, 2000) at 220–25.

85   *An Act to Amend the Securities Act*, S.O. 1994, c. 33, s. 8. For a discussion of the OSC rule-making power, see chapter 3.

ii. prescribing disclosure requirements and requiring or prohibiting the use of particular forms or types of offering documents or other documents, and

iii. prescribing requirements that apply to mutual funds, non-redeemable investment funds, commodity pools or other issuers.[86]

The OSC's proposal suggests:

> The passing of [the above provision] permits the Commission to implement a regulatory regime for OTC derivatives that it considers appropriate, without regard for artificial distinctions as to whether particular derivatives transactions constitute trades in securities.[87]

The provision in question is drafted very broadly and appears to give the OSC carte blanche in regulating instruments that may be regarded "derivatives." The drafting is defective in at least two ways, however. First, the *OSA* does not define "derivatives." It is left to the OSC to determine what it shall regulate as derivative instruments. This cedes an overly broad discretion to the OSC. Second, and perhaps more serious, as noted earlier in this chapter, all the key provisions in the legislation apply only to instruments that are "securities." Thus, the application of existing securities law requirements to derivatives is left in doubt. Given the ever-increasing importance of derivative transactions to the economy, this uncertainty should be clarified by further legislative amendment.

C. WHAT IS A "TRADE"?

Although recent developments suggest that Canadian securities law is becoming more "issuer based," our current securities law regime is still primarily "transaction based." Securities laws focus on specific commercial transactions. The most fundamental of those transactions is a "trade" in securities.

The *OSA* defines the word "trade" very broadly. The words "trade" or "trading" are defined to include:

(a) any sale or disposition of a security for valuable consideration, whether the terms of payment be on margin, instalment or otherwise, but does not include a purchase of a security or, except as

---

86 *OSA*, above note 2, s. 143(1)35.
87 See above note 80

provided in clause (d), a transfer, pledge or encumbrance of securities for the purpose of giving collateral for a debt made in good faith,

(b) any participation as a trader in any transaction in a security through the facilities of any stock exchange or quotation and trade reporting system,

(c) any receipt by a registrant of an order to buy or sell a security,

(d) any transfer, pledge or encumbrancing of securities of an issuer from the holdings of any person or company or combination of persons or companies described in clause (c) of the definition of "distribution" for the purpose of giving collateral for a debt made in good faith, and

(e) any act, advertisement, solicitation, conduct or negotiation directly or indirectly in furtherance of any of the foregoing.[88]

1) Any Sale or Disposition for Valuable Consideration

The first paragraph of the trade definition indicates that the *OSA* regulates *sellers* of securities, not purchasers. By referring to dispositions "for valuable consideration," the paragraph also appears to exempt gifts or other gratuitous dispositions. Although the definition does not purport to be exhaustive (because it begins with the word "includes"), the exemption of gifts from the definition of trades is a sensible one. The reason for this can be traced back to the investor protection rationale of the legislation. If securities are being given, rather than sold, there is little or no danger that the donor will take advantage of the donee.[89]

Of course, it must be recalled that "valuable consideration" can take many forms. An issue or transfer of securities could constitute a trade even in cases where the recipient does not *appear* to be paying for the securities at the time of the transaction.

2) Excludes (Most) Share Pledges

Securities, such as shares in a corporation, are assets that can be used by owners as collateral for debt obligations. A common method of

---

88   *OSA*, above note 2, s. 1(1) (definition of "trade" or "trading").

89   There are, in fact, some contexts in which the giving of securities, without the exchange of valuable consideration, may present a danger to the donees. A noteworthy example is the "poison pill." This is discussed below in chapter 10.

granting a security interest in a share or other corporate security is a pledge. A pledge involves the transfer of the securities to the lender. When the loan is repaid, the securities are returned to the borrower. If the loan is not repaid, the lender is entitled to realize on its security. The transfer of a security from a borrower to a lender does not constitute a gratuitous disposition. Yet, the OSA was not intended to restrict the ability of securityholders to use the equity in their securities as loan collateral. Accordingly, pledges and other grants of a security interest in securities are excluded from the definition of "trading" except in two cases. First, the debt owed by the borrower to the lender must have been incurred "in good faith." It is not open for parties, in other words, to attempt to avoid the application of the OSA by disguising a sale transaction as a secured-lending transaction. Second, a pledge or other grant of security interest in a security constitutes a trade if the grantor is a "control person." The term "control person" is not defined in the OSA, although the term "control person distribution" is defined in Rule 14-501.[90] A "control person" refers to a person described in clause (c) of the definition of "distribution." The concept is discussed further below in connection with the meaning of "distribution." For the purposes of this section, it is sufficient to note that a control person is, generally speaking, a holder of a significant block of voting shares of an issuer. Special issues are raised when a control person pledges shares. The OSA tends to treat control persons as though they were the issuers of the securities because it is assumed generally that the people who control corporations or who have the power to materially influence control have special access to corporate information that is not available to smaller, public investors. Although the OSA is not intended to make it impossible or unduly burdensome for control persons to pledge or otherwise encumber their securities, such actions are kept within the definition of "trade" to ensure that they are subject to the Act's rules governing the use of material non-disclosed information.

3) Participation as a Trader: Receipt of an Order by a Registrant

"Trading" activity includes more than simply selling securities. For example, the Ontario definition includes "any participation as a trader in any transaction in a security through the facilities of any stock exchange or quotation and trade reporting system" and "any receipt by

---

90   (1997), 20 OSCB 2346, as am. (1999), 22 OSCB 1173.

a registrant of an order to buy or sell a security."[91] A "registrant" is a securities market professional. Such professionals must register with the securities regulators before they may ply their trade. Registrants and professional traders generally play only a facilitative role in consummating a purchase or sale of securities. Why, then, are such persons' activities defined as trades?

Again, the policy underlying the legislation sheds light. In order to adequately protect buyers of securities, it is insufficient to regulate only the actual sellers. Market professionals who advise sellers participate in negotiating, if not structuring, the terms of the sale. The activities of professional traders can have a critical impact on the functioning of the capital markets. Protection of buyers, and of the markets generally, requires that market professionals be regulated.

4) Acts in Furtherance of a Trade

Perhaps the most important part of the definition of trade is that it includes "any act, advertisement, solicitation, conduct or negotiation directly or indirectly in furtherance of" any of the other activities constituting a trade.[92] As soon as a prospective seller phones another person with a view to selling securities, for example, the prospective seller engages in trading, whether or not the phone call actually results in a sale.[93] The policy underlying the legislation accounts for the breadth of the definition. The legislation is not merely *curative* in nature, but also *prophylactic*. It seeks to allow the regulators to step in to prevent harm *before* it occurs, rather than waiting for the harm to crystallize.

5) Trades That Are *Not* Distributions

The regulation of primary market activity attaches only to a trade that constitutes a "distribution" of securities (the meaning of which is discussed below). However, a trade that is *not* a distribution is still subject to regulation. Any person engaged in trading must register with the securities regulators, either as a dealer (or a partner or person

---

91   *OSA*, above note 2, s. 1(1) (definition of "trading").

92   *Ibid.* (definition of "trade").

93   Drinkwater, Orr, and Sorell suggest that there must in fact be a completed sale before the initial solicitation can be characterized as a "trade." See D.W. Drinkwater, W.K. Orr, and R. Sorrell, *Private Placements of Securities* (Toronto: Carswell, 1985) at 31–33. This appears to be in error. The *OSA* makes it clear that soliciting a purchase prior to an actual sale is a trade: see, e.g., *OSA*, ss. 25(1)(c), 65(2), & 68.

employed by a dealer), or an adviser, unless an exemption from registration applies. (At one time, there was a separate registration requirement for underwriters, as well. However, that provision was changed in 1999.) The registration requirements, which are explored more fully in chapter 4, ensure that professionals engaged in securities market activities attain minimum standards of integrity, competence, and financial soundness. The exemptions from the registration requirement ensure that persons who are not securities market professionals need not register with the OSC.

D. WHAT IS A "DISTRIBUTION"?

The meaning of "distribution" follows from the policy of the *OSA*: protecting members of the investing public by ensuring that buyers receive full disclosure of all material facts relating to a given security before purchasing that security.[94] Distributions are trades in securities in which the information asymmetry between the buyer and the seller is likely to be at its greatest, with the buyers having the greatest risk of being taken advantage of. If a trade constitutes a distribution, the issuer is required to assemble, publicly file, and distribute to all buyers an informational document known as a prospectus.[95] Its purpose is to ensure that those who are asked to contribute capital to the corporation have sufficient information with which to make an informed investment decision. Prospectuses are long, typically ranging from about 30 to 150 pages. They are highly detailed and expensive to prepare.[96] The prospectus obligation applies to all issuers of securities, whether public or private, incorporated or unincorporated.[97] Details about the public offering process are canvassed in chapter 6.

The term "distribution" includes trades effected in three circumstances: (1) trades by issuers, (2) trades by control persons, and (3) sales of restricted securities held by exempt purchasers. Each of these is discussed below.

---

94 Even buyers with full information may overpay for securities. The *OSA* seeks to ensure only that buyers have all pertinent information in making a purchase decision so that any overpayment results from bad judgment or bad luck, rather than incomplete information.

95 *OSA*, above note 2, s. 53.

96 We refer here chiefly to traditional "long-form" prospectuses. It is now possible for larger issuers to distribute securities using more streamlined prospectuses. See Chapter 6 for details of these alternative prospectus regimes.

97 See, e.g., *OSA*, above note 2, s. 1(1) (definitions of "issuer" and "person"). By "public" or "private," we mean issuers in the public and private sectors.

1) Trades by Issuers

Issuers almost always have better information about the true value of the securities they sell than do the buyers. Thus, any sale by an issuer is a distribution to which the prospectus requirement attaches.[98]

2) Trades by Control Persons

Anyone who holds a sufficient number of securities to "affect materially the control of that issuer" is assumed potentially to have privileged access to information concerning the issuer of the securities.[99] People who fall within this part of the definition of distribution are "control persons."[100] A sale by a control person is deemed to be a distribution to which the prospectus requirement attaches.

Who is in a position to "materially affect the control of the issuer?" A control person does not require either legal (*de jure*) or practical (*de facto*) control. Legal control arises when a person, or a combination of persons acting together, hold or exercise voting control over shares entitled to elect a majority of directors. For example, in a corporation with one class of voting shares, legal control resides in the holder of 50.1 percent of the common shares.

Practical control may arise with holdings of less than 50 percent of the shares. The corporate law statutes define an ordinary resolution as a resolution passed by a majority of the shareholders *who actually vote*, whether in person or by proxy, rather than a resolution passed by a majority of *all shareholders*.[101] Not all shareholders of a public company typically exercise their voting entitlement. A shareholder or coalition of shareholders can thus be confident of securing the passage of an ordinary resolution (and thus electing all the directors) by holding shares carrying perhaps only 15 or 20 percent of the total votes. The number of shares required for any single blockholder to attain practical control will depend on how many shareholders typically vote their shares, as well as whether there are any other shareholders holding large share positions who might use their votes in opposition to that blockholder.

---

98 *Ibid.* ss. 1(1) & 53.

99 *Ibid.* s. 1(1) (definition of "distribution").

100 The term "control person" is not defined in the OSA. However, clause (c) of the definition of "distribution" in subsection 1(1) deems any trade in securities from the holdings of a person with these characteristics to be a "distribution." Moreover, OSC Rule 14-501 (1997), 20 OSCB 2690, defines the term "control person distribution" for the purposes of the Rules to mean "a trade described in clause (c) of the definition of distribution in subsection 1(1) of the Act."

101 See, e.g., *Canada Buisness Corporations Act*, R.S.C. 1985, c. C-44, s. 2(1) (definition of "ordinary resolution").

One might "materially affect the control" of an issuer without being able to exercise either legal or practical control. A blockholder with 5 percent of the common shares, but lacking legal or practical control, for example, may have sufficient power to exert influence over management on important issues. Such a blockholder is likely a "control person" within the meaning of securities legislation, and any sale of securities by that blockholder is a distribution requiring a prospectus.

Exemptions from the prospectus requirement are available for certain control-block distributions, and these are discussed in chapter 7.

1) Sales of Restricted Securities Held by Exempt Purchasers

a) Preventing a "Backdoor Underwriting"
Regulating primary market issuances of securities requires protection against the danger of a "backdoor underwriting" through the use of a prospectus exemption. Detailed discussion of sales of restricted securities held by exempt purchasers and how the danger of a backdoor distribution is addressed are deferred until further discussion of the exemptions from the prospectus requirement in chapter 7. However, the basic principles underlying the related distribution and exemption rules known as the "closed system" are introduced in the next section.

b) The "Closed System": A Brief Overview
Most Canadian provinces now have a "closed system" for regulating securities transactions.[102] In a closed system, any trade in securities that qualifies as a "distribution" requires a prospectus. The system is "closed" because there are a limited number of ways of escaping this prospectus requirement. As we shall see in chapter 7, the *OSA* and the related rules prescribe a number of specific exemptions from the prospectus requirement. Issuances of securities under the various prospectus exemptions are often referred to as "exempt market transactions," and the buyers of such securities are often referred to as "exempt purchasers." Purchasers of exempt securities are themselves subject to the prospectus requirement when they seek to resell the securities to others. Such a purchaser may escape this requirement by selling to another exempt purchaser (i.e., a person who qualifies under

---

102 Those that do not are Manitoba, New Brunswick, Prince Edward Island, and the Yukon Territory.

the applicable securities legislation to purchase securities in an exempt market transaction) or by holding the securities for a statutorily defined length of time (the so-called "restricted" or "hold" period) before attempting to resell.

It is important to understand that not just anyone can qualify as an exempt purchaser. Securities legislation specifically enumerates the categories of persons who can be exempt purchasers. These provisions are discussed in detail in chapter 7. At the highest level of generality, it may be said that a person may qualify as an exempt purchaser only where the protection afforded by a prospectus is not needed, such as where the buyer is sufficiently sophisticated to be able to protect her own interests when buying securities.[103]

E. CONCLUSION

In this chapter we surveyed some of the key definitional and interpretational issues that arise under the *OSA*. We have also emphasized the overarching role that policy plays in the application of our securities laws. Securities law is, in this regard, fundamentally different from, for example, income tax law where the Supreme Court of Canada has made clear in a series of recent decisions[104] that it is the precise wording of the *Income Tax Act*,[105] not the presumed underlying spirit or policy, of which the taxpayer must be mindful. In securities law, the underlying policy, for good or for ill, can sometimes trump the statutory text itself. This important feature of Canadian securities regulation should be kept in mind whenever one considers a securities law matter.

---

103 However, with the recent introduction of the "closely-held issuer" prospectus exemption, discussed further in chapter 7, exempt distributions may now be made on a limited basis to a much broader range of purchasers.

104 See *Neuman v. R.*, [1998] 1 S.C.R. 770; *Duha Printers (Western) Ltd. v. R.*, [1998] 1 S.C.R. 795; *Shell Canada Ltd. v. R.*, [1999] 3 S.C.R. 622.

105 R.S.C. 1985 (5th Supp.), c. 1.

CHAPTER 3

CANADIAN SECURITIES REGULATORS AND REGULATORY INSTRUMENTS

A. INTRODUCTION

Although the title of this book is *Securities Law*, it has become customary in both Canada and the United States to refer to the complex web of rules that govern our capital markets as "securities *regulation*." This phrase was coined by the late Professor Louis Loss in the title to his seminal book on the subject first published in 1951.[1] The term is an apt one because many of the most frequently encountered rules to which market participants are subject are not "laws" in the strictest sense, but nevertheless represent important regulatory initiatives. The focus of such industry regulation, as the Supreme Court of Canada has stated, "is on the protection of societal interests, not punishment of an individual's moral faults."[2]

This emphasis on societal protection, rather than individual punishment, also helps to explain the somewhat unique collaboration between securities regulators and those they regulate. Securities practitioners, for example, regularly spend time "on secondment" at the

---

1   *Anecdotes of a Securities Lawyer* (Boston: Little, Brown and Company, 1995) at 51. The Loss book evidently evolved from teaching materials he used in his pioneering course on the U.S. Securities and Exchange Commission, first taught at the Yale Law School in 1947. *Ibid.* at 48–51.

2   *Committee for Equal Treatment of Asbestos Minority Shareholders v. Ontario (Securities Commission)*, 2001 SCC 37 [*Asbestos Shareholders*].

OSC, serving in many capacities, frequently at the very highest levels. Moreover, there are formal and informal channels of communication between the regulators and the industry professionals intended to ensure that regulators understand the dynamic financial industry they govern and the effects, intended and unintended, of specific regulatory initiatives on the industry. For example, the OSC has established a special committee of practitioners — the Securities Advisory Committee to the OSC (currently ten Ontario securities lawyers and one U.S. securities lawyer) — to provide advice on regulatory policies and capital market issues.[3]

In this chapter, we sketch out the basic framework within which Canadian securities regulators operate, focusing on Canada's largest provincial regulator, the OSC. We also provide an overview of the sources of Canadian securities regulation.

B. THE CONSTITUTIONAL ISSUE

1) Division of Powers

No discussion of a branch of Canadian law is complete without some reference to the constitutional question of federal and provincial legislative authority. In the case of securities law, the constitutional question is of particular interest for the reasons explained briefly below.

Securities law in Canada, thus far, has been legislated exclusively at the provincial level. Unlike the United States, Canada has no federal securities legislation or federal securities regulator comparable to the U.S. Securities and Exchange Commission. There has never been any serious doubt cast on the general constitutional authority of provincial governments to pass legislation related to the trading of securities. That authority is found in subsection 92(13) of the *Constitution Act, 1867*,[4] which confers upon each provincial government the power to legislate with respect to property and civil rights in the province.

Corporations, the entities that issue most marketable securities, may be incorporated in Canada under either federal or provincial law. A constitutional question faced by the courts early in this century was whether provincial securities legislation applied to the issue and the sale of securities of federally incorporated companies. In 1929, it was

---

3   See OSC Commission Policy 11-601, "The Securities Advisory Committee to the OSC."

4   *Constitution Act, 1867* (U.K.), 30 & 31 Vict., c. 3.

successfully argued before the Privy Council that provincial securities legislation did not give provincial regulators power over the sale of securities of federally incorporated corporations where that legislation effectively "sterilized [the federal corporation] in all its functions and activities."[5] This apparent limitation on provincial securities regulators, however, was readily overcome. In a subsequent decision,[6] the Privy Council held that properly crafted provincial securities laws could indeed apply to federal companies. Specifically, such laws are valid as long as they do not require federal companies to register provincially before they can issue securities. The laws must permit federal companies either to be registered themselves *or* to sell their securities through a registered broker or salesperson. By allowing unregistered federal companies to sell securities through registrants, such laws, in the view of the Privy Council, do not create a "complete prohibition" on the issuance of capital by federally incorporated companies. Accordingly, provincial securities legislation in this form can validly apply to all companies operating within the province, including federal companies.[7]

As Canadian capital markets evolve, the efficacy of securities regulation at the provincial level is increasingly called into question. Securities transactions of any significant size are rarely conducted entirely within the borders of a single province. This fact gives rise to at least two regulatory issues. The first relates to jurisdictional questions that arise when an issuer has securityholders in a number of different provinces. To what extent should a securities regulator in any one of those provinces have jurisdiction to regulate the activities of that issuer? The second issue is the perennial question of whether Canada ought to replace its current regime of thirteen provincial and territorial regulatory agencies with a single, federal securities regulator.

2) Extraterritoriality

The potential "long arm" extraterritorial reach of provincial securities legislation was confronted in a 1992 Ontario Court of Appeal decision, *Quebec (Sa Majesté du Chef)* v. *Ontario Securities Commission.*[8] The *Asbestos* case involved a transaction by which the Quebec government attempted in the 1980s to "nationalize" Asbestos Corporation Limited

---

5   *In Re Sale of Shares Act and Municipal and Public Utility Board Act (Man.)*, [1929]
     1 W.W.R. 136 at 140 (P.C.).
6   *Mayland and Mercury Oils Limited v. Lymburn and Frawley*, [1932] 1 W.W.R. 578
     (P.C.).
7   *Ibid.*
8   (1992), 10 O.R. (3d) 577 (C.A.) [*Asbestos*].

(ACL), a publicly traded, TSE-listed company. Though a public company, ACL was controlled by a single shareholder, General Dynamics (Canada) Limited (GD Canada), which held almost 55 percent of ACL's shares. The Quebec government decided to purchase this 55 percent controlling interest. GD Canada was a wholly owned subsidiary of a U.S. corporation, General Dynamics Corporation (GD U.S.). For a variety of reasons, the Quebec government's transaction was not structured as a purchase of ACL shares from GD Canada, but rather as a purchase from GD U.S. of all the issued and outstanding shares it held in GD Canada. Because GD Canada's only asset was its 55 percent controlling interest in ACL, this purchase of GD Canada shares from its U.S. parent had the same economic effect as a purchase of ACL shares from GD Canada. However, although economically identical, the legal consequences of the two purchases were quite different. The purchase from GD U.S. did not involve a sale of any of the securities of the public company (that is, of ACL). Moreover, neither the purchaser of the securities (a Quebec Crown corporation) nor the seller of the securities (GD U.S.) was an Ontario entity. None of the sale negotiations were conducted in Ontario.

Once the purchase of the GD Canada shares was undertaken, the minority shareholders of ACL objected. They argued that if the transaction had been structured as a direct purchase of ACL shares, the purchaser would have been required by the take-over bid rules then in effect to make a similar offer (a follow-up offer[9]) to all of the remaining ACL shareholders. Because the purchaser made no such offer in this case, the minority shareholders complained to the OSC that the transaction constituted an illegal take-over bid and was abusive of their interests. The connection of the transaction to Ontario was rather tenuous, raising a threshold legal question concerning the OSC's jurisdiction in the matter. The Ontario Court of Appeal held that the *OSA* applied to the transaction, notwithstanding the consequential effects such an application might have on parties outside of Ontario. This

---

9   At the time of the purchase of the shares, the take-over bid rules of the Ontario *Securities Act* provided that when certain significant share acquisitions of reporting issuers were completed privately with a seller, the purchaser was then required, subject to certain exceptions, to make an offer on the same terms (a "follow-up offer") to the remaining shareholders. The *OSA* no longer includes such a "follow up-offer" requirement. For a discussion of the current take-over bid regime, see chapter 10.

decision, from which the Supreme Court of Canada denied leave to appeal, was the object of some criticism at the time, including from one of the authors of this book.[10] Briefly, critics were concerned that the court sanctioned the application of provincial securities laws to extraprovincial actions in circumstances where such actions had, at most, an indirect effect on Ontario residents (in this case, those minority shareholders of ACL who resided in Ontario). The problem with such an "effects" doctrine is twofold. First, it could seriously erode the traditional Canadian constitutional division of powers. Many undertakings and activities, after all, cross provincial borders. It is because of the interprovincial nature of such activities that our constitution provides that they are matters of federal, not provincial, legislative authority. Yet every such undertaking has, of necessity, some indirect effect on provincial residents. Thus, if indirect effects within a province are sufficient to justify provincial regulation, the delicate federal/provincial division of powers upon which the Canadian confederation is based will be undermined. Second, the same transaction may have indirect effects on the residents of several provinces, thus exposing market actors to several different, and perhaps contradictory, provincial regulatory schemes.

3) Lament for a National Canadian Securities Regulator

The possibilities of inconsistent or duplicative provincial regulation on the one hand and of regulatory lacuna on the other invite discussion of the long-debated question of whether Canada ought to have a single federal securities regulator. It may fairly be said that the quest for a national regulator is the most important ongoing and unresolved policy issue in Canadian securities regulation. It seems probable that the federal government has the constitutional authority to enter the securities law field unilaterally if it so chooses. In 1982, the Supreme Court of Canada made the following frequently cited comment on this issue:

> Parliament has not yet enacted any comprehensive scheme of securities legislation. To date the Canadian experience has been that the provinces have taken control of the marketing of securities, differing in this respect from the United States where the Securities and Exchange Commission has regulated trading and primary distribution of securities. I should not wish by anything said in this case to affect prejudicially the constitutional right of Parliament to enact a

---

10 See, e.g., Jeffrey G. MacIntosh, "A Supremely Bad Decision" *Financial Post* (26 June 1993) S4.

general scheme of securities legislation pursuant to its power to make laws in relation to interprovincial and export trade and commerce. This is of particular significance considering the interprovincial and indeed international character of the securities industry.[11]

Politically, however, it seems unlikely that the federal government would seek simply to usurp the role of provincial securities regulators. Past efforts aimed at forging a national regulator have involved significant federal-provincial negotiation. For a host of political, economic, and other reasons, however, the various attempts to create a national Canadian securities regulator have, thus far, all ended in failure.[12] Recently, it was suggested that many of the most vexing problems associated with provincial-level regulation have been abated somewhat by a series of interprovincial agreements and initiatives often touted by their supporters as having fostered a "virtual national securities commission."[13] These initiatives include efforts at an increased harmonization of securities law through the work of the Canadian Securities Administrators (CSA); a national online document filing system, called the System for Electronic Document Analysis and Retrieval (SEDAR);[14] the promulgation of national regulatory instruments, such as national instruments and national policy statements, discussed further below; and specific mutual recognition schemes, chiefly the Mutual Reliance Review System (MRRS) for prospectuses and annual information forms[15] as well as for exemptive relief applications.[16] All these advances are important and laudable, but many fundamental problems, particularly in the area of enforcement, are not likely to be fully addressed in the absence of a genuine national securities commission.

---

11   *Multiple Access Limited* v. *McCutcheon*, [1982] 2 S.C.R. 161 at 173–74, Dickson J. An influential treatment of this subject was written in 1978 by Philip Anisman and Peter Hogg as a background paper prepared in connection with the development by Consumer and Corporate Affairs Canada of its *Proposals for a Securities Market Law for Canada*. See Philip Anisman and Peter W. Hogg, "Constitutional Aspects of Federal Securities Legislation," in *Proposals for a Securities Market Law for Canada*, vol. 3 (Ottawa: Minister of Supply and Services Canada, 1979) at 135.

12   For an excellent synthesis of the issues surrounding the pursuit of federal securities legislation and a survey of the failed initiatives, see David Johnston and Kathleen Doyle Rockwell, *Canadian Securities Regulation*, 2d ed. (Toronto: Butterworths, 1998) at chapters 16–17.

13   See, e.g., "New Directions at the OSC — Remarks by David A. Brown, Q.C., Chair, November 3, 1998" (1998), 21 OSCB 6892.

14   National Instrument 13-101 (1996), 19 OSCB (Supp. 1).

15   National Policy No. 43-201 (1999), 22 OSCB 7308.

16   National Policy No. 12-201 (1999), 22 OSCB 7298.

In November 2001, the CSA announced the formation of a task force under the chairmanship of Stephen Sibold, chairman of the Alberta Securities Commission. The task force seeks to frame a model (or uniform) securities act that could be passed by the provincial legislators in every Canadian jurisdiction. Such a common statute, if one can be developed, could facilitate a proposed national (though not federal) "pan-Canadian" securities commission, exercising regulatory power delegated to it by each province if the provinces wished to participate in such an initiative. OSC Chairman David Brown outlined the goal of creating such a pan-Canadian commission in a speech delivered in Toronto on 20 November 2001.[17] The ultimate goal of forming such a regulator and the timetable for the preparation of a proposed model statute are both ambitious. Yet, even if these ambitious goals could be achieved, some argue that Canadian securities regulation will continue to be plagued by costly and inefficient duplication and inconsistency, unless the political will is found to introduce a workable federal securities law regime.

C. THE ONTARIO SECURITIES COMMISSION

1) Overview

The Ontario Securities Commission (OSC) is the administrative body responsible for regulating the Ontario securities industry. The OSC is an autonomous, self-funding Crown corporation. Its revenues come chiefly from the fees it charges in connection with activities subject to the *OSA*. For example, when reporting issuers distribute securities to the public or sell securities by way of private placement, they must pay the OSC a fee. When a take-over bid or a going-private transaction is completed, a fee must also be paid. Securities dealers and advisers must pay fees to become, and to remain, registered under the Act. There are even fees payable when reporting issuers file financial statements, material-change reports, or apply for exemptions from Ontario securi-

---

17   David Brown, "Dialogue with the OSC Keynote Address" (20 November 2001), available online at <http://www.osc.gov.on.ca> (site accessed 21 November 2001). The "model act" and "pan-Canadian" regulatory proposal have been briefly critiqued by one of the authors of this book. See Jeffrey MacIntosh, "Forget Quebec: The OSC's Plan for a Pan-Canadian Regulator Won't Work" *National Post* (30 November 2001). In March 2002, the CSA published additional information about the uniform securities legislation project. See CSA Notice 11-303, available online at <http://www.osc.gov.on.ca> (site accessed: 22 March 2002).

ties laws.[18] According to the OSC's 2001 annual report, the OSC's total revenue for the fiscal year ending 31 March 2001 was $83.8 million. Prospectus filing fees of all types accounted for 58.1 percent of the OSC's 2001 revenues, registration fees accounted for 26.6 percent, disclosure filing fees by reporting issuers constituted 10.7 percent, and fees for exemption applications made up about 1.4 percent.[19] In April 2001, the OSC proposed a new system of fees under which every reporting issuer, excluding mutual funds, would be required to pay an annual participation fee.[20] That proposal is pending at the date of writing.

The OSC comprises the commissioners of whom there must be at least nine and no more than fourteen.[21] (Currently, there are 10 commissioners.) Commissioners are appointed by the provincial cabinet for terms of not more than five years, but they may be reappointed.[22] These commissioners also act as the OSC's board of directors.[23] The extensive operations of the OSC are carried out by its large staff, numbering more than 300, including a considerable number of lawyers, accountants, and other professionals.[24]

The most senior-ranking OSC official is the chair of the OSC. The chair, who is also a commissioner, is appointed by the provincial cabinet for a term that must not exceed her or his term as a commissioner.[25] For many years the chair has been a senior member of the Ontario securities bar. Several former chairs returned to practice with their law firms when their terms as chair were completed. The current chair is David Brown, who practised with a major Toronto law firm before his appointment in 1998.[26]

As a general matter, the OSC is "responsible for the administration of the [*Securities Act*] and shall perform the duties assigned to it under [the *OSA*] and any other Act."[27] The two other statutes that are perhaps

---

18   The Schedule of fees is found in Schedule I to the *OSA Regulation*, R.R.O. 1990, Reg. 1015. Readers should note carefully s. 1.1 of the regulation, which provides for a 20 percent reduction in fees from the amounts stated throughout the Schedule.

19   Ontario Securities Commission, *Annual Report 2001*, available online at <http://www.osc.gov.on.ca>.

20   (2001), 242 OSCB 2108.

21   *Securities Act* (Ontario), R.S.O. 1990, c. S.5 [*OSA*], s. 3(2).

22   *Ibid.* s. 3(4).

23   *Ibid.* s. 3.1(1).

24   *Annual Report 2001*, above note 19. The OSC's statutory power to employ staff is found in *OSA*, above note 21, s. 3.6.

25   *OSA*, above note 21, s. 3(5) & (6).

26   *Annual Report 2001*, above note 19.

27   *OSA*, above note 21, s. 3.2(2).

most important in this regard are the Ontario *Business Corporations Act* and the Ontario *Commodity Futures Act*. The principal functions performed by the OSC include the following:

- Licensing securities industry professionals. The *OSA* refers to the requirement to be licensed as a "registration" requirement. Registration is discussed further in chapter 4.
- Reviewing prospectuses in connection with proposed public offerings of securities and, where appropriate, issuing receipts for them. As discussed further in chapter 6, subject to certain exemptions, securities may not be distributed in Ontario until the seller files a prospectus and obtains a receipt for it from the OSC.
- Promulgating Rules, policies and other instruments relating to the regulation of the securities industry.
- Providing exemptions from the requirements of Ontario securities law in appropriate cases.
- Enforcing Ontario's securities laws, including by sitting as a quasi-judicial tribunal in connection with administrative proceedings commenced pursuant to section 127 of the Act. The OSC's enforcement functions are discussed further in some detail in chapter 11.

The *OSA* confers upon the OSC the capacity and rights, powers, and privileges of a natural person,[28] and affords to the commissioners and staff immunity from any proceedings for "any act done in good faith in the performance or intended performance of any duty or in the exercise or the intended exercise of any power under Ontario securities law, or for any neglect or default in the performance or exercise in good faith of such duty or power."[29] The OSC is given broad powers, as discussed in chapter 11, both to enforce compliance with Ontario securities law and to grant exemptions from the provisions of the *OSA* where it is not prejudicial to the public interest to do so. Its exemption powers are found throughout the Act, and include the following:

- Power to approve an ownership interest in voting shares of The Toronto Stock Exchange Inc. in excess of the 5 percent restriction on

---

28   *Ibid.* s. 3.2(1).
29   *Ibid.* s. 141(1). In a recent decision, *Cooper v. Hobart* 2001 SCC 79 [*Hobart*], the Supreme Court of Canada held that a statutory regulator (in the specific case, the B.C. registrar of mortgage brokers) does not owe a duty of care to individual investors, but rather to the public as a whole. Accordingly, individual investors cannot sue such a regulator for negligence in failing to properly oversee the regulated entity. It seems clear that the reasoning in *Hobart* would apply equally to Canadian securities regulators.

TSE share ownership that otherwise applies and to waive voting restrictions that would otherwise apply to such large TSE shareholders, permitting a holder of more than 5 percent of such shares to vote those shares that represent a greater than 5 percent interest[30]

- Power to extend the time within which a renewal prospectus must be filed for continuously offered securities[31]
- Power to waive compliance with provisions of Part XV of the *OSA*, dealing with prospectus requirements in the case of secondary offerings. (Secondary offerings are distributions of previously issued securities of an issuer by someone other than the issuer itself.) Typically, such secondary offerings are made by "control persons," as discussed in more detail in chapter 6[32]
- Power to provide exemptions from the *OSA*'s registration and prospectus requirements[33]
- Power to exempt a reporting issuer from the continuous disclosure requirements in Part XVIII of the *OSA* and in the related regulations[34]
- Power to order that an issuer has ceased to be a reporting issuer[35]
- Power to deem that an issuer is a reporting issuer[36]
- Power to exempt a person or company from the requirements of the take-over and issuer bid provisions of the *OSA* and the *OSA Regulation*[37]
- Power to relieve a mutual fund or its management company from the prohibitions against making loans to, or other investments in, certain related parties in sections 111 and 112 of the *OSA*[38]
- Power to revoke or vary a previous decision of the OSC[39]
- Power to exempt persons or companies from any requirement of Ontario securities law in cases where there is no specific exemption procedure[40]

---

30   *OSA*, above note 21, s. 21.11(4).
31   *Ibid.* s. 62(5).
32   *Ibid.* s. 64(2).
33   *Ibid.* s. 74.
34   *Ibid.* s. 80.
35   *Ibid.* s. 83.
36   *Ibid.* s. 83.1.
37   *Ibid.* s. 104.
38   *Ibid.* s. 113.
39   *Ibid.* s. 144.
40   *Ibid.* s. 147.

2) The OSC as Administrative Tribunal and the Standard of Judicial Review

Decisions of the OSC may be appealed to the Ontario Divisional Court,[41] except orders granting exemption from registration or prospectus requirements under section 74 of the *OSA*, which are not appealable.[42] Appeals must be brought within thirty days after the OSC has either rendered its decision or released its reasons for the decision, if the reasons are issued later than the decision itself.

The courts have frequently considered the appropriate standard of judicial review to be applied to decisions of the OSC. The Supreme Court of Canada commented on this issue as recently as 2001. In *Committee for Equal Treatment of Asbestos Minority Shareholders v. Ontario (Securities Commission)*,[43] the Supreme Court of Canada upheld the OSC's decision not to make an order pursuant to its "public interest" jurisdiction under section 127 of the *OSA*.[44] The court held that, despite the fact that the *OSA* contained no "privative" clause shielding OSC decisions from judicial review, OSC decisions still should be accorded a "high degree of curial deference" because of the OSC's specialized expertise, the purpose of the statute, and the nature of the problem before the OSC.[45] The court noted that these factors must be balanced against the fact that the *OSA* grants an express right of appeal from OSC decisions. Accordingly, the court held that the appropriate standard of review was the "intermediate" standard of reasonableness: lying between the extreme standards of "correctness" on the one hand and "patently unreasonable" on the other. A reviewing court must uphold a decision of the OSC within the scope of its expertise, even if the court does not agree with the correctness of the decision, provided that the decision is found to be reasonable. It is not sufficient merely to demonstrate that the decision under review was not patently unreasonable.[46]

---

41   *Ibid.* s. 9(1).
42   *Ibid.* ss. 9(1) & 74(3)
43   *Asbestos Shareholders*, above note 2.
44   For a discussion of the OSC's powers under s. 127, see chapter 11.
45   The facts of the case are discussed further in chapter 11.
46   Other key cases considering the appropriate standard for judicial review include *Pezim v. British Columbia (Superintendent of Brokers)*, [1994] 2 S.C.R. 557; *Canada (Director of Investigation and Research) v. Southam Inc.*, [1997] 1 S.C.R. 748; and *Pushpanathan v. Canada (Minister of Citizenship and Immigration)*, [1998] 1 S.C.R. 982.

3) Proposed Merger of OSC and Financial Services Commission of Ontario

In its 2000 Budget, the Ontario government proposed to form a single provincial financial services regulator by merging the OSC and the Financial Services Commission of Ontario, which currently regulates provincially chartered insurance companies; mortgage, loan and trust companies, and other deposit-taking institutions; and pension plans. The stated rationale behind this proposed merger is that it would eliminate regulatory duplication and regulatory gaps.[47] This initiative appears to reflect an awareness of the increasing integration of financial services firms and the erosion of traditional distinctions between specific types of financial institutions. As economists such as Robert C. Merton have noted, institution-based regulation may need to give way in the modern financial services sector to what has been described as functional regulation.[48] In September 2000, the Ontario government issued a discussion paper outlining the proposed merger in some detail.[49] In April 2001, the government issued a consultation draft, soliciting comments on draft legislation intended to implement the merger.[50] At the date of writing, the Ontario government was still seeking comments on the consultation draft. If the merger proceeds, it would involve the incorporation of a new regulatory body, the Ontario Financial Services Commission, which would supervise the transition to a new integrated regulatory model, and would eventually be amalgamated with the OSC and the Financial Services Commission of Ontario. The amalgamated entity would be known as the Ontario Financial Services Commission. With respect to securities industry regulation, however, the new Ontario Financial Services Commission would exercise the same powers as the OSC. Accordingly, the regulatory principles and concepts discussed in this chapter are not likely to change materially in the new regime.

---

47   See, e.g., David A Brown, "Letter to Stakeholders Concerning Merger" (2000), 23 OSCB 3213.

48   See, e.g., Robert C. Merton, "The Financial System and Economic Performance" (1990) J. Fin. Serv. Research 263. For a discussion of the Merton functional vs. institutional approach in the Canadian financial services context, see Christopher C. Nicholls, "Financial Institution Reform: Functional Analysis and an Illustrative Look at Deposit Insurance" (1998) 13 Banking & Finance L. Rev. 235.

49   "Improving Ontario's Financial Services Regulation: Establishing a Single Financial Services Regulator" (2000), 23 OSCB 6346.

50   "Establishing a Single Financial Services Regulator: Consultation Draft" (12 April 2001), available online at <http://www.gov.on.ca/FIN> (site accessed: 31 August 2001). A similar regulatory consolidation has also been proposed in Quebec.

D. SECURITIES EXCHANGES AND SELF-REGULATORY ORGANIZATIONS (SROs)

1) Introduction

The securities industry has an interest in promoting high standards among its members and, in many instances, is in a better position to regulate the conduct of market professionals than government agencies. There are currently two types of self-regulatory organizations in Canada: securities exchanges and dealer organizations.

As a technical matter, under the *OSA*, these two types of organizations are treated separately. Section 21 provides that no stock exchange may carry on business in Ontario unless it is recognized by the OSC. Section 21.1 provides that self-regulatory organizations may apply to the OSC for such recognition. For the purposes of the *OSA*, the term "self-regulatory organization" effectively means a dealer organization, rather than an exchange. The term is defined in subsection 1(1) of the Act in this way:

> A person or company that represents registrants and is organized for the purpose of regulating the operations and the standards of practice and business conduct of its members and their representatives with a view to promoting the protection of investors and the public interest.[51]

At the date of writing, there are two "self-regulatory organizations" recognized under section 21.1: the Investment Dealers Association of Canada (IDA) and the Mutual Fund Dealers Association (MFDA). Both organizations operate under the auspices of the OSC, and association members remain subject to OSC disciplinary actions, notwithstanding the disciplinary powers the associations themselves may wield.

2) Exchanges

As explained above, only dealer organizations technically are referred to as "self-regulatory organizations" (SROs) within the *OSA*'s definition; however, securities exchanges, in common parlance, are regularly referred to as SROs as well. Indeed National Instrument 14-101 defines the initialism "SRO" to mean: "[a] self-regulatory organization, a self-regulatory body *or an exchange*."[52]

---

51   *OSA*, above note 21, s. 1(1) (definition of "self-regulatory organization").
52   National Instrument 14-101 (1997), 20 OSCB 1727, as amended at s. 1.1(1). [Emphasis added.]

Only the TSE is recognized by the OSC for the purposes of section 21.[53] The Canadian Venture Exchange was granted an exemption from the recognition requirement in December 2000.[54] The most recent version of the TSE recognition order was promulgated in January 2002, amending and restating the recognition order issued when the TSE demutualized in April 2000 (that is, converted from a member-owned organization to a for-profit business corporation). That recognition order, among other things, affirmed[55] an earlier 1997 protocol that provided for the OSC's oversight of the TSE rule proposals,[56] a practice that was reaffirmed in the 2002 recognition order. The principal development in 2002 was the formal separation of the TSE's exchange business and its regulatory function, with the recognition of a separate regulatory agency: Market Regulation Services Inc. (RS Inc.). The structure, role, and history of RS Inc. are discussed in chapter 4.

Moreover, since 1997, the TSE, in effect, has delegated regulation of its participating organizations (formerly TSE members) to other SROs, chiefly the IDA. The TSE has said that this delegation "has allowed the TSE to focus on market regulation and has reduced the duplication of efforts by consolidating the regulation of such activities within a smaller number of regulatory bodies."[57]

Accordingly, the disciplinary powers of the SROs have become an important part of the fabric of securities industry regulation. The IDA, through its district councils, has the authority to discipline IDA member firms and various employees of IDA member firms for breaches of securities law, breaches of the IDA's own rules and regulations, improper business conduct, and lack of qualifications. In the context of such discipline proceedings, the IDA has authority, among other things, to impose fines of up to $1 million per offence, or three times the amount of the pecuniary benefits gained by the offenders, to reprimand offenders, to suspend or revoke the "approval" of any person to work in an IDA member firm, and to expel a member from the IDA.[58]

---

53   *Re Securities Act and The Toronto Stock Exchange, Inc.* (2000), 23 OSCB 2495, amended and restated (2002), 25 OSCB 929.

54   *Re Securities Act and Canadian Venture Exchange, Inc.* (2000), 23 OSCB 8437.

55   *Re Securities Act*, above note 53, at Schedule "A," para. 8.

56   (1997), 20 OSCB 5682. Also note that under s. 21.7 of the *OSA*, the OSC has the power to review directions, decisions, orders or rulings of recognized exchanges or SROs.

57   See TSE website, at <http://www.tse.com> (site accessed: 5 September 2001).

58   By-law No. 20.10 of the Investment Dealers Association of Canada, available online at <http://www.ida.ca> (site accessed: 6 September 2001).

The MFDA, through its regional councils, has powers similar to those of the IDA to discipline MFDA members and "approved persons,"[59] that is, registrants who work with, or for, an MFDA member.[60]

E. SOURCES OF SECURITIES LAW AND POLICY

1) Introduction

There are many sources of securities law as well as "quasi-legal" pronouncements and communications from regulators that are of interest to capital market participants. The principal sources are listed below.

Sources of Law:

- The *Securities Act* (*OSA*)
- The *OSA Regulation*
- OSC Rules made under section 143 of the *OSA* (including blanket orders and rulings that were deemed rules pursuant to section 143.1 of the *OSA*)
- National Instruments
- Multilateral Instruments

It should be noted that subsection 1(1) of the *OSA* defines "Ontario securities law" to mean the *OSA*, the regulations (which means, according to the definition of "regulations" elsewhere in subsection 1(1), not only the *OSA Regulation*, but also, "unless the context otherwise indicates," the OSC Rules made under section 143 and deemed rules in the Schedule to the Act pursuant to section 143.1), and "in respect of a person or company, a decision of the Commission or a Director to which the person or company is subject."

Other Regulatory Instruments and Communications:

- National Policy Statements
- OSC Policy Statements
- Staff Notices
- Staff Accounting Communiqués

---

59 By-law No. 1, s. 25.1 of the Mutual Fund Dealers Association, available online at <http://www.mfda.ca> (site accessed: 6 September 2001).

60 *Ibid.* s. 1 (definition of "Approved Person").

2) Sources of Law

a) The *OSA*

The *OSA* provides the foundation upon which all of Ontario securities regulation is based. Since 1994,[61] the *OSA* has contained an express statement of purposes and fundamental principles. The two purposes of the statute are:

(a) to provide protection to investors from unfair, improper or fraudulent practices; and

(b) to foster fair and efficient capital markets and confidence in capital markets.[62]

These purposes are consistent with the objectives of securities regulation articulated by the International Organization of Securities Commissions (IOSCO), an international body to which major securities regulators throughout the world, including Canadian provincial regulators, belong.[63] It sometimes has been suggested that these two objectives are complementary rather than in competition with one another. On this view, the goal of fostering fair and efficient capital markets and confidence in those markets is achieved by vigilant investor protection. One need not balance the pursuit of one goal against the other.[64] Certainly, in a number of instances, this observation has validity. The regulatory approach concerning insider trading, discussed later in chapter 8, offers a convenient example. But, in many circumstances, it appears that relentless pursuit of investor protection could, indeed, come at the expense of market efficiency. The Supreme Court of Canada recently declared:

---

61   The 1994 amendment that introduced these provisions actually came into force on 1 January 1995.

62   *OSA*, above note 21, s. 1.1.

63   IOSCO has actually identified three basic objectives of securities regulation: "The protection of investors; Ensuring that markets are fair, efficient and transparent; The reduction of systemic risk." See IOSCO, *Objectives and Principles of Securities Regulation* (Feburary 2002), available online at <http://www.iosco.org> (site accessed: 12 March 2002).

64   The Kimber Committee, writing in 1965, noted that "[e]stablishment of conditions and practices in the capital market which best serve the investing public will normally be consistent with the best interests of the whole economy." *The Report of the Attorney General's Committee on Securities Legislation in Ontario* (Toronto: Queen's Printer, 1965) at para. 1.07.

[I]t is important to keep in mind that the OSC's public interest jurisdiction is animated in part by both of the purposes of the Act
described in s. 1.1, namely "to provide protection to investors from
unfair, improper or fraudulent practices" *and* "to foster fair and efficient capital markets and confidence in capital markets." Therefore in
considering an order in the public interest, it is an error to focus only
on the fair treatment of investors. The effect of an intervention in the
public interest on capital market efficiencies and public confidence in
the capital markets should also be considered.[65]

In the decision in which the above-quoted passage appeared, the OSC
explicitly found that certain actions taken by the Quebec government
were abusive of certain Ontario shareholders. Complaining shareholders sought a removal of exemptions otherwise available to Quebec under
the *OSA*. However, to grant such a remedy could, in fact, have damaged
Ontario's capital markets. The OSC was faced with a situation where the
twin purposes of the *OSA* were in conflict. The OSC may have regarded
the potential harm to the markets as outweighing whatever investor
protection benefits might have been derived from the order sought.

In addition to the two stated purposes, the *OSA* also sets out six
"fundamental principles" to which the OSC is to "have regard" as it
pursues the purposes of the statute. These principles fall roughly into
three groups: those that are self-evident, those that endorse current
practice, and those that signal a legislative preference for the future
direction of securities regulation. Little needs to be said of the self-
evident propositions. For example, it seems unlikely that the OSC
needs a statutory mandate to consider the fact that the importance of
the two purposes of the *OSA* must be balanced in specific cases[66] or that
effective securities regulation requires "timely, open and efficient
administration and enforcement of the Act."[67] (Would the regulators,
in the absence of this provision, staunchly advocate the advantages of
slow and inefficient administration?) As for the second group — principles that endorse current practice — perhaps the best example is the
articulation of the three primary means by which the purposes of the
OSA are to be achieved: mandatory disclosure rules, restrictions on
improper practices, and appropriate standards for registered market
participants.[68] The other principles that may be regarded as general
indications of legislative preference include the express endorsement of

---

65   *Asbestos Shareholders*, above note 2.
66   *OSA*, above note 21, s. 2.1(1).
67   *Ibid.* s. 2.1(3).
68   *Ibid.* s. 2.1(2).

the enforcement capabilities of self-regulatory organizations,[69] the promotion of harmonization of regulation,[70] and the principle that regulatory burdens ought to be proportionate to the significance of regulatory goals.[71]

b) The *OSA Regulation*

The Lieutenant Governor in Council (the legislative euphemism for the provincial cabinet) has a broad power to make regulations under the *OSA* in respect of a wide array of specifically enumerated matters,[72] as well as in respect of any other matter "advisable for carrying out the purposes of the Act."[73] The *OSA Regulation* was particularly important prior to 1994 because it was through the regulation that gaps or shortcomings in the statute could be addressed without the need for full-scale legislative amendment. Indeed, the *OSA Regulation* was somewhat unusual in this regard. Although they constituted subordinate legislation, according to the *OSA*, the regulations could, in effect, qualify provisions of the statute itself. Since the OSC was granted rule-making power in 1994, as discussed below, a number of regulations have been amended or revoked with new rules taking their places. The *OSA* provides that where an inconsistency exists between a regulation and a rule, the regulation prevails.[74] It is now possible, however, subject to ministerial approval, for the OSC to amend or revoke a regulation concurrently with making a rule.[75]

c) OSC Rules

i) Overview

An OSC rule is a legislative instrument made by the OSC following a statutorily prescribed publication, comment, and ministerial submission process. A rule is not subject to the *Regulations Act*,[76] and, as mentioned above, the *OSA Regulation* prevails over rules in the event of an inconsistency. But, in other respects, a rule "has the same force and effect as a regulation."[77]

---

69   *Ibid.* s. 2.1(4).
70   *Ibid.* s. 2.1(5).
71   *Ibid.* s. 2.1(6).
72   *Ibid.* s.143(1) & s. 143(2)(a).
73   *Ibid.* s. 143(2)(b).
74   *Ibid.* s. 143(13)
75   *Ibid.* s. 143(3).
76   *Ibid.* s. 143(11) and *Regulations Act*, R.S.O. 1990, c. R.21.
77   *Ibid.* s. 143(13).

The process for making a rule basically involves the following four steps:

1. *Notice*: The OSC publishes notice of the proposed rule in the OSCB.[78]

2. *Comment period*: Subject to certain exceptions, the OSC must give interested persons at least ninety days to comment on the proposed rule.[79]

3. *Republication (if necessary)*: If, following the original publication of the proposed rule, *material* changes to the rule are proposed, the amended rule must be published again,[80] and interested parties must be provided a length of time to comment "as the Commission considers appropriate."[81]

4. *Delivery to the Minister*: Once all necessary notice and comment periods expire, the OSC must deliver to the Ontario minister of finance a copy of the rule, together with copies of the notices, a summary of the representations and other documents received in respect of the proposed rule, and any other material information that the OSC considered.[82] The minister then has sixty days to approve the rule, reject the rule, or return the rule to the OSC for further consideration.[83] If the minister approves the rule, the rule comes into force fifteen days after the approval is granted (or at any later date specified in the rule.)[84] If the minister takes no steps during that sixty-day period, the rule comes into force automatically fifteen days later (i.e., on the seventy-fifth day after the rule was delivered to the minister) or a later date if the rule specified that it was to come into force on a later date.[85]

ii) Granting of Rule-making Authority (The Ainsley Decision)

The OSC was first granted rule-making authority by a 1994 amendment to the *OSA*, an amendment that actually became effective on 1 January 1995. The 1994 amendments were made in response to recommendations contained in the report of an OSC/Ministry of Finance Task Force, the Ontario Task Force on Securities Regulation, under the

---

78   *Ibid.* s. 143.2(1).
79   *Ibid.* s. 143.2(4).
80   *Ibid.* s. 143.2(7).
81   *Ibid.* s. 143.2(9).
82   *Ibid.* s. 143.3(1).
83   *Ibid.* s. 143.3(3).
84   *Ibid.* s. 143.4(1).
85   *Ibid.* s. 143.4(2).

chairmanship of Dean Ron Daniels.[86] The Task Force was struck in 1993 following the decision of the Ontario Court (General Division) in *Ainsley Financial Corp. v. Ontario (Securities Commission).*[87] The *Ainsley* case arose from a challenge launched by certain securities dealers known as "penny stock brokers"[88] against an attempt by the OSC to regulate their business operations with Policy Statement 1.10.[89] The trial court held, and the Ontario Court of Appeal subsequently confirmed, that the OSC did not have the legislative authority to promulgate this particular policy statement because many of its provisions constituted, in effect, legislation. The OSC argued that its U.S. federal counterpart, the Securities and Exchange Commission (SEC), frequently used this sort of regulatory initiative. The court noted, however, that the SEC, unlike the OSC, had been granted express "rule-making" power by its governing statute. The *Ainsley* decision raised serious concerns about the legitimacy of Policy 1.10 and a number of other OSC Policy Statements. In fact, some feared that the decision might generally impair the OSC's ability to discharge its statutory public interest mandate. Accordingly, one of the central questions upon which the Daniels Task Force focused was whether the OSC should be granted rule-making authority. Its answer was that the OSC should indeed be granted that authority.

iii) Deemed Rules

Once the *OSA* was amended to add the rule-making authority, as a transitional matter, a number of previously issued blanket orders or rulings became deemed rules. Blanket orders and rulings were a fairly common device previously used by the OSC to regulate interstitially. Blanket orders or rulings typically took the form of exemptions from some aspects of securities regulation in certain recurring situations. These blanket instruments offered a more efficient way to deal with such cases than the cumbersome alternative of issuing a large number of individual exemptions. Issuing blanket orders was also far speedier and more practical than attempting to initiate amendments to the *OSA* or

---

86   Ontario Task Force on Securities Regulation, *Responsibility and Responsiveness — Final Report of the Ontario Task Force on Securities Regulation* (1994), 17 OSCB 3208.

87   (1993), 14 O.R. (3d) 280 (Gen. Div.) [*Ainsley*], aff'd (1994), 21 O.R. (3d) 104 (C.A.).

88   "Penny stock" takes it name from stock with a per share trading price "in pennies" — i.e., a price of less than $1.00. However, Proposed OSC Policy 1.10, below note 89 at 1461-2, actually proposed a somewhat more technical definition, essentially intended to capture the most speculative, non-exchange traded securities, typically with a trading price of less than $5.00 each.

89   (1993), 16 OSCB 1459.

even to the *OSA Regulation* to deal with the circumstances that prompted the need for the exemptive relief. Some of the blanket orders and rulings that became deemed rules will be reformulated eventually as part of the policy reformulation process discussed in section 4 below. However, the legislators considered it inappropriate for the OSC to issue any new blanket rulings after the OSC rule-making powers were in place. After all, the purpose of granting the OSC rule-making authority was to provide the very sort of flexibility offered by blanket rulings, but with the additional transparency and procedural protections that accompany rule-making authority. Accordingly, section 143.11 of the *OSA* now prohibits the OSC from making any further blanket orders or rulings. This is not, however, quite the end of the story. The very frictions that the rule-making authority was intended to overcome, including the protracted process of attempting to have the *OSA* or the *OSA Regulation* amended, have also been encountered in the exercise of the rule-making procedure. This problem was recently alluded to by the Securities Review Advisory Committee formed to conduct the first five-year review of the *OSA*:

> [U]nder the Act, the Commission is required to republish for comment a proposed rule where the Commission proposes "material changes" to the original rule proposal that was published for comment. This requirement has often led to multiple republications of proposed rules and significant time delays.[90]

Thus, one might anticipate future proposals to amend the rule-making powers to reduce comment periods or perhaps to eliminate the second publication requirement.

d) National Instruments and Multilateral Instruments

National instruments[91] and multilateral instruments are a relatively new form of regulation that emerged following the granting of rule-making or regulation-making authority to some, but not all, provincial securities regulators. The use of these instruments reflects the continuing desire of provincial securities regulators to coordinate and harmonize their regulatory efforts in the new rule-making era. A national instrument is promulgated by the Canadian Securities Administrators (CSA),

---

90 Securities Review Advisory Committee, Issues List — Commentary and Additional Questions, (2000) 23 OSCB 3034 at 3044.

91 The description of national instruments in this section is based principally on information contained in OSC Notice, "Policy Reformulation Project" (1996), 19 OSCB 2310.

the umbrella organization that has no statutory basis, but to which all of Canada's provincial securities regulators belong. A national instrument is intended to be legislative in nature. Therefore, to have effect in a particular province, such an instrument normally must be adopted as a rule (or regulation) in that province. In order to ensure uniformity in every jurisdiction, national instruments are drafted "generically." For example, instead of referring to a specific provincial securities act, national instruments use the generic phrase "securities legislation" so that the instruments may be adopted unchanged in every provincial jurisdiction. Unfortunately, not every provincial regulator has been granted rule-making power. The status of national instruments in these provinces, where such instruments must be adopted as policies, remains somewhat unclear. Moreover, not all initiatives are adopted by every provincial regulator. Those instruments that have effect in some, but not all, provinces are designated "multilateral instruments" rather than "national instruments."

3) Other Regulatory Instruments and Communications

a) National and Local (OSC) Policy Statements
The *Ainsley* case was never intended to, and did not, end the use of policy statements by securities regulators. Indeed, the Ontario Court of Appeal expressly "recognized the Commission's authority to use non-statutory instruments to fulfil its mandate"[92] provided such instruments were not legislative in nature. The OSC and other Canadian securities regulators have long made use of policy statements to provide public guidance to issuers and market professionals with respect to the regulators' interpretation and proposed application of securities laws and with respect to the facts and circumstances that would most likely trigger regulatory intervention. Prior to 1994, there was no specific statutory basis for the promulgation of such statements, but, as commentators frequently observed, it was clear that regulators expected market participants to comply with these missives.

The *Ainsley* decision, however, confirmed what many commentators and practitioners had long suspected. Policy statements, though frequently very useful, occasionally amounted to unauthorized legislat-

---

92   *Ainsley*, above note 87 at 109 (C.A.).

ing by regulators.[93] When the *OSA* was amended in the wake of the *Ainsley* decision, specific statutory recognition of policy statements and a procedure for their promulgation were added. Section 143.8 now defines "policy" as

> a written statement of the Commission of,
>
> (a) principles, standards, criteria or factors that relate to a decision or exercise of a discretion by the Commission or the Director under this Act, the regulations or the rules;
>
> (b) the manner in which a provision of this Act, the regulations or the rules is interpreted or applied by the Commission or the Director;
>
> (c) the practices generally followed by the Commission or the Director in the performance of duties and responsibilities under this Act; and
>
> (d) something that is not of a legislative nature.[94]

Like rules, proposed policies must be published for comment.[95] However, unlike rules, policies are not required to be submitted to the minister of finance before they are finally adopted. The OSC has adopted a number of formal policy statements pursuant to the new procedure, many of which are discussed in this book. However, the broad statutory definition of "policy" leads to some question as to whether it might also sweep in other, less formal OSC staff communications, subjecting them to a publication and comment regime that could prove burdensome. This issue was specifically addressed by the OSC in a 1995 notice, discussed in section (b) below under the heading "Staff Notices and Accounting Communiqués."

There are two basic types of policy statements: local and national. National policy statements are issued by the CSA for adoption as policy statements in every province. Thus, for example, national policy statements are adopted in Ontario pursuant to section 143.8 of the *OSA*.[96] Local policy statements (in Ontario, OSC Policy Statements) are the initiatives of a provincial regulator only.

---

93 See, e.g., Philip Anisman, "Legitimating Lawmaking by the Ontario Securities Commission: Comments on the Final Report of the Ontario Task Force on Securities Regulation," in *Securities Regulation: Issues and Perspectives Papers Presented at the Queen's Annual Business Law Symposium 1994* (Toronto: Carswell, 1995) at 1.

94 *OSA*, above note 21, s. 143.8(1).

95 *Ibid.* s. 143.8(2)–(4). The comment period must be at least sixty days.

96 See "Policy Reformulation Project," above note 91 at 2310.

b) Staff Notices and Accounting Communiqués

The OSC staff also communicates with market participants through published statements that are not formally sanctioned by the OSC itself and are not subject to the lengthy notice and comment process required of policy statements. Such communications are typically of two sorts: staff notices and staff accounting communiqués.

In 1995, the OSC accepted a series of recommendations on staff communications that dealt with, among other things, the nature of, and the procedure for issuing, OSC staff notices.[97] One of the technical questions raised in this notice related to the difficulty encountered, following the 1994 *OSA* amendments, in drawing a clear distinction between "policies" (as defined in section 143.8) and mere staff notices. Drawing such a distinction is essential because policies are subject to a statutory notice procedure, but staff notices are not. In the 1995 notice, the OSC attempted to articulate a non-exhaustive and somewhat tentative list of criteria to be used to draw this important distinction. Essentially, under these criteria, an instrument is more likely to be considered a policy (as opposed to a mere staff notice) if it (a) reflects "crystallized" rather than developing views of the OSC; (b) relates to recurring matters of broad impact; (c) deals relatively less with strictly administrative or procedural matters; and/or (d) reflects significant involvement of the OSC, rather than only the OSC staff.[98]

Staff accounting communiqués were first issued in 1989 and were described, at that time, as publications "intended to assist reporting issuers and the financial community to understand more clearly staff's views on specific financial reporting issues."[99] Staff accounting communiqués tend to deal with rather technical accounting matters that go well beyond the scope of the issues dealt with in this book.

4) Policy Reformulation Project and Numbering System

Once the OSC received rule-making power, an important and ambitious process of reformulation began. The OSC was required to review all of its previous policy statements with a view to determining which parts of those policy statements were (or should be) legislative in nature and, therefore, embodied in rules rather than policy statements. This process was a substantial undertaking for several reasons, including the following:

---

97   See "Staff Notice — Recommendations of the Committee on Staff
     Communications" (1995), 18 OSCB 3617.
98   *Ibid.*
99   "Notice — Staff Accounting Communiqués" (1989), 12 OSCB 2457.

- Many policy statements combined both mandatory and non-mandatory features, making it impossible simply to "re-enact" policy statements as rules because their legislative and non-legislative features had to be separated and then reconstructed as rules and policies, respectively.
- Some, but not all, other Canadian jurisdictions eventually were granted rule-making (or regulation-making) power; so, Ontario's policy reformulation process had to be coordinated with other regulators to try to advance the goal of regulatory harmonization.
- The dynamic nature of securities practice meant that, even as the old policies were being reformulated, new developments also had to be addressed.

The OSC took the opportunity of the rule reformulation process to rationalize the structure of the rules and policies by introducing a five-digit numbering system based on subject-matter classification. Every instrument, rule, policy, and notice will have a unique five-digit number when the project is complete. The first digit indicates the general subject matter of the document, as follows:

1 — Procedure and Related Matters

2 — Certain Capital Market Participants

3 — Registration Requirements and Related Matters

4 — Distribution Requirements

5 — Ongoing Requirements for Issuers and Insiders

6 — Take-over Bids and Special Transactions

7 — Securities Transactions Outside the Jurisdiction

8 — Mutual Funds

9 — Derivatives[100]

The third number indicates the type of instrument. For example, the third digit of every national instrument is 1; of every national policy, 2; and of every OSC Rule and companion policy (i.e., a policy statement issued in conjunction with an OSC Rule), 5.

Consider the following example. Recently, OSC Policy 9.1, which dealt with insider bids, issuer bids, going-private transactions and related-party transactions, was reformulated. Those aspects of Policy

---

100 OSC Notice, "Numbering System for Policy Reformulation Project" (1996), 19 OSCB 4258.

9.1 that were legislative in nature were recast (with some substantive amendments) as a rule: Rule 61-501. The first number, "6," indicates that the subject matter of the new rule is "take-over bids and special transactions." The second number, "1," indicates a subject matter sub-category. The third number, "5," indicates that the instrument is a local (i.e., OSC rather than national) rule. The final two numbers, "01," indicate that this is the first such local rule made by the OSC within this particular subject-matter category and subcategory. The OSC also issued a new companion policy to Rule 61-501. The companion policy was designated "61-501 CP." It bears the same category and subcategory numbers as the rule ("61"). The third number is a "5" to indicate the link between this companion policy and the rule in respect of which the policy provides specific guidance. (The third number of an OSC policy, other than a companion policy, is "6.") The tag letters "CP" distinguish the companion policy from the rule.

Just as the transition in Canada from imperial to metric measure posed some adjustment difficulties for those who had become accustomed to the older, less methodical system, the OSC's new rational numbering system has taken experienced practitioners some getting used to. However, it seems clear that when the reformulation process is complete, practitioners at every level of experience will find it much easier to navigate the complex system of legislative and quasi-legislative instruments that have now assumed far greater importance in many respects[101] than the *OSA*.

F. SUMMARY AND CONCLUSION

The goals of investor protection and enhancing market efficiency are easily stated as general principles, but the mechanics of pursuing these goals, particularly in an increasingly complex financial marketplace, are necessarily complicated. The dynamics of financial markets call for constant regulatory updating and fine-tuning and, indeed, reveal one of the enduring difficulties in this area of regulation. On the one hand, market participants have a right to demand transparency and certainty. On the other hand, the complexity of the markets and financial instruments with which the OSC must contend are daunting. The attempt to

---

101 For an excellent summary of the policy reformulation project from the regulators' perspective, see "Staff Notice Re Rule-Making in Ontario" (1995), 18 OSCB 4939.

reduce regulation to writing is admirable, but regulating dynamic markets with static written instruments is unwieldy. The attempt to do so has led to a proliferation of rules and policies that seem to constitute an ever-unfinished work with no page limit and no due date. Ultimately, however, the health of Canadian capital markets cannot depend upon the volume of new regulation, but rather increasingly must look to the good faith and integrity of informed, responsible, and honest market participants.

CHAPTER 4

SECURITIES DEALERS, OTHER REGISTRANTS, AND ALTERNATIVE TRADING SYSTEMS (ATSs)

A. INTRODUCTION

Securities regulation, traditionally, has focused on the activities of two groups of market participants: securities issuers and securities market professionals, such as brokers and dealers.

In this chapter, we discuss the regulation of securities market professionals, the stock exchanges, and other organizations (such as self-regulatory organizations, or SROs) to which such professionals belong. We also touch briefly upon the recent challenges and opportunities offered by computerized alternative trading systems.

B. SECURITIES FIRMS: OVERVIEW

Like the sale of many consumer goods, the sale of securities to the public requires sophisticated distribution channels. Automobile manufacturers, for example, do not typically sell their products directly to consumers. Instead, they sell their products to dealers at wholesale, and those dealers then resell the products at a profit to retail buyers. In the securities industry, these two functions — buying from the producer (or issuer) at "wholesale" and subsequently reselling to the public — also are performed by firms known as dealers, although when dealers initially purchase securities from the issuer, they are described as underwriters.

The term "underwriting" in the securities industry means something quite different from underwriting in the insurance industry, but both sorts of "underwriting" share a common element. Historically, when firms made certain financial commitments in writing, they indicated that commitment by *writing* the firm name *under* the terms of the commitment in the document. In modern securities industry parlance, underwriting refers to the business of raising money for firms by purchasing their securities (essentially at wholesale prices) with a view to reselling them at a profit. It is the underwriter, not the issuer, who bears the risk of resale. Thus, from the issuer's point of view, the underwriter commits itself to provide financing. As discussed further in chapters 5 and 6, the *OSA* actually extends the definition of underwriting to include the sale of securities by financial firms even when those firms do not make such a firm contractual commitment, but merely act as agents of the issuer in a distribution.[1] In other words, whenever a securities firm assists a company by distributing its shares or other securities to investors for a fee, the securities firm will be deemed an underwriter for purposes of the *OSA*. That legal characterization does not change even if the firm has not literally underwritten the issue by committing itself to buy the issuer's securities with a view to reselling them.

Securities firms that carry on the business of underwriting are often referred to as investment banks. In Canada, in a process that began with changes to financial institutions legislation in 1987, the largest investment banks have become subsidiaries of the largest Canadian chartered banks. But, investment banks need not be affiliated with such commercial or retail banks, and some of the world's largest investment banks, such as Goldman Sachs, are not so affiliated.[2]

---

1   *Securities Act* (Ontario), R.S.O. 1990, c. S.5 [*OSA*], s. 1(1).

2   It has occasionally been suggested that there are increasing commercial pressures on investment banks to have commercial bank affiliations. It has been reported that some large securities issuers demand access to low interest commercial loans as a condition for awarding lucrative underwriting engagements. Investment banks affiliated with large commercial banks able to make such loans are, accordingly, frequently in a better position to win such engagements than independent securities firms. See, e.g., Andrew Willis, "Is a Bank Loan Better than Good Analyst Coverage?" *Globe and Mail* (30 August 2001) B13.

Underwriting firms, of course, do much more than simply purchase securities for resale. They also provide advice to issuers about, among other things, how to structure financings and how to design and price securities to be issued. Securities firms are well equipped to provide such advice. They are in constant touch with the markets and have developed special systems and expertise enabling them not only to evaluate what features securities ought to have to make them attractive to investors, but also how to price the most complex and innovative of securities. Moreover, because underwriting is a competitive business, firms have significant incentives to develop new financial products to meet the needs of both issuers and investors so that the firms may win new underwriting engagements.

Traditionally, when securities firms purchased shares for their own account, as principals and not merely as agents for their clients, they were said to be engaged in securities "dealing." When they purchased and sold shares as intermediaries or agents for others, they were said to be acting as "brokers." This distinction between the terms "dealer" and "broker" is still important in some contexts, but, for purposes of Ontario securities law, the meaning of the two terms is modified, as discussed further below.

Finally, some securities industry professionals act neither as dealers nor brokers, but rather (or perhaps additionally) hold themselves out as investment advisers whose investment advice may be obtained for a fee.

What should be clear, however, is that both issuers and investors rely on securities firms for their integrity and expertise, whether the firms engage in underwriting, broker-dealer activities, or advising activities. It is well known that in markets for many tangible consumer goods, unscrupulous sales people often prey upon vulnerable or gullible consumers by using high-pressure tactics and grandiose, unsubstantiated claims. In the case of the sale of intangible assets, such as securities, these risks are magnified. Even the most educated consumer, after all, cannot "kick the tires" of an original issue, high-yield bond. Securities fraud is, sadly, all too easy to perpetrate. And honest but incompetent securities dealers and advisers can also lead investors to their financial ruin.

History, ancient and modern, is filled with stories of securities scams and debacles. Securities regulators hope that similar disasters can be avoided in the future by imposing strict rules upon firms whose business turns on the buying and selling of securities — firms that are thought to act as the securities market's "gatekeepers."

C. REGISTRANTS

1) Section 25 of the *OSA*

An examination of the regulation of securities industry professionals must begin with the basic registration requirement in section 25 of the *OSA*. Section 25 provides that no person or company shall

(a) trade in a security or act as an underwriter unless the person or company is registered as a dealer, or is registered as a salesperson or as a partner or as an officer of a registered dealer and is acting on behalf of the dealer; or,

...

(c) act as an adviser unless the person or company is registered as an adviser or is registered as a representative or as a partner or as an officer of a registered adviser or is acting on behalf of an adviser

and the registration has been made in accordance with Ontario securities law and the person or company has received written notice of the registration from the Director and, where the registration is subject to terms and conditions, the person or company complies with such terms and conditions.[3]

The term "registration," in this context, essentially refers to a licensing requirement. The Ontario Securities Commission (OSC) regulates securities firms through this mandatory licensing requirement with a view to ensuring the following:

- Securities dealers and other securities professionals satisfy at least certain minimum standards of training and proficiency.
- Securities industry professionals act with integrity.
- Securities firms are adequately capitalized, minimizing the risk of their becoming insolvent (and thereby jeopardizing investors and others).

2) Categories of Registration

a) General Categories: Dealers and Advisers
Section 25 of the *OSA* requires that dealers, advisers, and underwriters (and their salespeople, partners, officers, or representatives) must be registered under the *OSA* before they may lawfully trade in securities.

---

3   *OSA*, above note 1, s. 25(1). (Clause (b) of this subsection was repealed in 1999.)

Owing to the broad definition of trading, discussed in chapter 2, failure to register makes it impossible for such firms to carry on business. Since 1999, there has been no separate registration requirement for underwriters. Instead, a firm that engages in securities underwriting must be registered as a dealer, under the category of dealer registration appropriate for the particular underwriting functions carried out by that firm.[4] The two general categories for registration are, then, dealer and adviser registration.

b) Registration Subcategories
The *OSA Regulation* provides for ten specific subcategories of dealer registration and five specific subcategories of adviser registration.

i)   Dealer Subcategories
The dealer registration categories are as follows:

- Broker
- Financial intermediary dealer
- Foreign dealer
- International dealer
- Investment dealer
- Limited market dealer
- Mutual fund dealer
- Scholarship plan dealer
- Securities dealer
- Securities issuer[5]

ii) Adviser Subcategories
The specific adviser registration categories are as follows:

- Financial adviser
- Investment counsel
- Portfolio manager
- Securities adviser
- International adviser[6]

---

4   See *OSA Regulation*, R.R.O. 1990, Reg. 1015 [*OSA Regulation*[, s. 100.

5   *Ibid.* s. 98.

6   *Ibid.* s. 99.

c) Application for Registration

Applications for registration are made to the OSC on forms prescribed by regulation[7] in accordance with OSC Rule 31-504,[8] and subject to the conditions of registration set out in OSC Rule 31-505.[9] Since 1 March 2001, all securities dealers and brokers are required to be members of a self-regulatory organization (SRO) recognized by the OSC.[10] (SROs are discussed in more detail later in this chapter.)

Currently, registrants are required to renew their registrations annually,[11] but at the date of writing a proposal is pending for the introduction of a permanent registration system.[12] Under such a system, registrants would be required to pay annual fees, but would no longer be obliged to seek yearly renewals of their registrations. Needless to say, the OSC would continue to have the power to suspend or revoke the registration of a wayward registrant under section 127 of the *OSA*, as discussed in chapter 11, if the circumstances warranted such action. The Canadian Securities Regulators, at the date of writing, are also in the process of developing a national registration database (NRD) although this is not expected to be operational until late in 2002.[13]

3) Capital Requirements

a) Overview

The *OSA Regulation* imposes upon securities dealers a series of capital requirements. These requirements are similar in structure to the capital adequacy rules to which banks and other financial institutions are subject,[14] and they have the same objective of reducing the risk of firm insolvency. In other non-financial industries, individual firms may determine for themselves how much financial risk they wish to take. It is understood that any business venture involves risk and that business managers are generally better able than governments or regulators to assess what level of risk is most appropriate. It is also understood that

---

7 *Ibid.* s. 129; Forms 3 and 4.

8 (1997), 20 OSCB 4534.

9 (1999), 22 OSCB 731.

10 OSC Rule 31-507 (2000), 23 OSCB 5657.

11 *OSA Regulation*, above note 4, s. 130.

12 "Notice of Proposed Multilateral Instrument 33-108, Permanent Registration" (2001), 24 OSCB 4514.

13 OSC Staff Notice 33-719 (2001), 24 OSCB 1671.

14 For a discussion of capital adequacy rules applicable to Canadian banks, see Christopher C. Nicholls, *Corporate Finance and Canadian Law* (Toronto: Carswell, 2000) at chapter 7.

insolvency or bankruptcy, although unfortunate, cannot be prevented without imposing constraints that would impair necessary risk-taking and economic growth. In the securities industry, however, as in the banking sector, the collapse of firms can have far-reaching effects on consumers (who may maintain accounts with dealers representing significant portions of their life savings) and even on the financial system itself. Accordingly, minimum capital rules are imposed on such firms, notwithstanding that such rules may very well keep some prospective entrants out of the market, and may occasionally constrain profitable business ventures.

The two concepts that are essential to understanding the capital requirements for securities dealers are minimum free capital and net free capital. Each is discussed in turn below.

b) Minimum Free Capital

Minimum free capital (MFC) is an amount of capital that securities dealers are required to maintain as a kind of cushion against unforeseen, adverse financial circumstances. The amount of MFC required of any particular dealer varies depending upon (a) the amount of any insurance deductible in that dealer's mandatory bonding or insurance policies, and (b) the dealer's liabilities (adjusted in accordance with special rules set out in the *OSA Regulation*).[15] Not surprisingly, the higher the dealer's insurance deductible and liabilities are, the higher the amount of MFC the dealer is required to maintain. The basic formula for calculating the MFC for a dealer (other than a dealer who is also a futures commission merchant) is as follows:

MFC = (Insurance Deductible)

+ $25,000 of **net free capital**[16] (or, if the dealer is a mutual fund dealer or scholarship plan dealer, of **working capital**)[17]

+ (.10 × first $2.5 million of adjusted liabilities) + (.08 × next $2.5 million of adjusted liabilities) + (.07 × next $2.5 million of adjusted liabilities) + (.06 × next $2.5 million of adjusted liabilities) + (.05 × amount of all remaining adjusted liabilities)

---

15   *OSA Regulation*, above note 4, ss. 96 & 107.
16   See discussion in section (c) below.
17   "Working capital" for this purpose means the dealer's current assets minus its current liabilities, as these amounts appear on the dealer's balance sheet. (See *OSA Regulation*, above note 4, s. 96.)

Where the dealer is an underwriter, it must maintain an MFC equal to the amount of any mandatory insurance deductible plus $10,000 of net free capital.[18]

c) Net Free Capital

Because minimum free capital includes a minimum of $25,000 of net free capital for most securities dealers, it is important to understand, at least in a basic way, the meaning of net free capital. As the name suggests, net free capital is intended, in theory, to represent the firm's unencumbered net liquid assets (i.e., assets that can be turned to cash readily and are not required by the dealer to satisfy any known firm obligation at the date of calculation). However, the regulations do not leave it to each dealer to use its own formula to determine the extent of such unencumbered liquid assets. Instead, the definition of net free capital[19] and Form 9[20] provide a specific detailed method of determining net free capital.

d) Minimum Free Capital Rules for Advisers

Advisers may also be subject to minimum free capital requirements if they exercise control over their clients' funds or securities, or if they provide investment advice "tailored to the needs of specific requirements."[21] However, even where advisers are subject to such rules, the requirements are considerably less onerous than the dealer and underwriter requirements because the financial failure of an adviser likely poses fewer systemic risks (i.e., the failure of one adviser is not as likely to trigger defaults by other industry players). Thus, advisers are generally required to maintain MFC in an amount equal to the amount of any mandatory insurance deductible plus $5000 of working capital.[22]

4) Margin Requirements

Securities firms routinely lend money to their clients to assist them to buy securities. The securities purchased with such loans are held in the clients' accounts maintained with the firm, which become, in effect, security for the loans. There are specific rules in place, however, aimed at ensuring that loans of this sort do not become dangerously underse-

---

18   *OSA Regulation*, above note 4, s. 107(5).
19   *Ibid.* s. 96.
20   *Ibid.* s. 107(6)(b), 107(5), and Form 9.
21   *Ibid.* s. 107(3).
22   *Ibid.* For the meaning of "working capital" for this purpose, see above note 17.

cured and so risk the financial health of the securities firms. These rules require the client of a securities firm to provide at least part of the price of the proposed trade whenever the client wishes to borrow money from the firm to complete a trade. That portion (or percentage) of the price that must be provided by the client is referred to as the "margin requirement."

Margin requirements specified by securities industry rules are lowest for the least risky securities (like government bonds) and highest for the most speculative equity securities. Indeed, some securities are considered so risky that they cannot be bought or sold on margin at all. When brokers buy such risky securities on behalf of clients, the clients must provide all the necessary funds by the trade settlement date. To illustrate how margin requirements operate, consider the following simple example. The margin requirement for a five-year Government of Canada bond is 2 percent of market value.[23] Thus, an investor wishing to purchase such a bond at a current market price of $1000 needs to have $20 in his or her margin account and may borrow the balance of the purchase price from the securities dealer. Naturally, the dealer charges the client interest on this loan while any amounts are outstanding. If, on the other hand, the investor wishes to purchase $1000 worth of shares in a particular TSE-listed company, where each share is trading at $1.70, the investor would be required to have no less than $800 in her or his margin account because such shares have a margin requirement of 80 percent of their market value.[24]

Once securities are purchased on margin, of course, their market value might very well fluctuate. In particular, if the market value of securities held in a margin account declines, the amount of the loan the dealer is permitted to extend to the client also declines. For example, if a client purchases 100 shares when such shares are trading at $1.70 per share, the securities firm may lend that customer up to $340 to finance the purchase (i.e., because such shares have a margin requirement of 80 percent, the securities firm is permitted to loan the investor up to 20 percent of the total purchase price: 20 percent of $1700 is $340). However, if the market price of the purchased shares later falls to $1.50 each (or $1500 in total), the firm would be permitted to have an outstanding debt to its client in respect of those shares of only $300 (i.e., 20 percent of $1500, the new (lower) market value of the shares). Therefore, the dealer must take steps to ensure that the loan to its

---

23   Investment Dealers Association of Canada, Regulation 100.2(a)(i).
24   *Ibid.* 100.2(f)(i).

client is reduced, or that the client places sufficient cash or financial assets into the account to bring the account back into line with the margin requirements. The requirement to make such an adjustment is known as a "margin call." Typically, the dealer will communicate such a call to the investor before taking any other steps. However, if the client fails to deposit additional cash or securities in response to a margin call, the dealer can, and will, sell sufficient securities in the investor's account to satisfy the margin call.

In *Varcoe v. Sterling*[25] the court found that the broker's failure to communicate a margin call to an investor before taking action with the investor's account to deal with the problem was a violation of an industry standard. The court held that such failure, together with other shortcomings, constituted a breach of the broker's duty to its client.

However, failure to successfully communicate margin calls before taking further action is not invariably improper. In *Janic v. TD Waterhouse Investor Services (Canada) Inc.*,[26] a brokerage client was out of the country, and essentially unreachable, at the time his broker made a margin call. After attempting to reach the client at his Canadian address by sending a letter and placing two telephone calls, the broker sold all of the securities in the client's account. The securities had fallen so far in value that even liquidation of the entire account was insufficient to satisfy the debt owing to the broker, and, so, the account was left in a deficit position. The client brought an action against the broker for negligence and breach of contract in connection with the sale. The client testified that he was unaware of the brokerage firm's power to sell the securities in his account to maintain margin. The court expressed "surprise" over this lack of awareness, given the sophisticated nature of the client's trading activities, endorsed the action taken by the firm, and dismissed the client's claim.

5) Proficiency Requirements

In addition to imposing capital requirements aimed at forestalling the insolvency of securities firms, securities regulators establish minimum standards of dealer training and proficiency to protect the investing public. The basic proficiency requirements are found in OSC Rule 31-502.[27] It is here that one finds, among other things, the requirements

---

25 (1992), 7 O.R. (3d) 204 (Gen. Div.), aff'd (1992), 10 O.R. (3d) 574 (C.A.), leave to appeal to S.C.C. refused [*Varcoe*].

26 [2001] O.J. No. 1476 (S.C.J.).

27 (2000), 23 OSCB 5658.

for dealers to complete certain prescribed courses and to satisfy other licensing (i.e., registration) requirements.

6) "Know-Your-Client" and Suitability Rules

When an investor first opens up an account with a broker, the investor is required to answer a series of questions about the investor's financial situation and investment objectives. Novice investors may find some of these questions rather intrusive. But brokers are, in fact, required to obtain such information from their clients in order to comply with the "know-your-client" and suitability rules.[28] The purpose of such rules is twofold: to protect the markets and to protect investors. The "know-your-client" rules derive, in part, from the view that securities dealers are gatekeepers who screen out people of dubious reputation whose illicit trading activities might damage the capital markets. However, until recently, this aspect of the "know-your-client" rule has received little prominence. Indeed, a recent IDA proposal relating to changes in the know-your-client rules states that the rule "was primarily developed to ensure that registrants had sufficient knowledge of clients' affairs to determine if investments were suitable to their particular circumstances as well as assess their creditworthiness."[29] However, a recent decision of the British Columbia Securities Commission[30] and the anti-terrorist initiatives undertaken in the aftermath of the 11

---

28 It is not uncommon for both sorts of rules to be referred to simply as the "know-your-client" rules, a usage that appears to be found in some of judicial decisions relating to dealers' obligations to ensure the suitability of investments sold to their clients. This usage, as explained below, is logical since the suitability rules depend upon the "know-your-client" rules.

29 Investment Dealers Association of Canada, "revisions to Regulation 1300, Part I: Know Your Client Requirements and Corporate Accounts" (17 October 2001), available online at <http://www.ida.ca> (site accessed: 12 March 2002).

30 *In the Matter of the Securities Act*, R.S.B.C. 1996, c. 418, and *In the Matter of Jean-Claude Hauchecorne* and *In the Matter of the Vancouver Stock Exchange* (indexed as *Hauchecorne, Re*), British Columbia Securities Commission, Weekly Summary, Edition 99:51 (24 December 1999) at 69. The B.C. Securities Commission stated in this decision that the know-your-client rule "requires the broker to learn the identity of the client and ... look behind any corporate veil to determine who has a financial interest in the account."

September 2001 terrorist attacks[31] have renewed interest in the use of the "know-your-client" rules as a tool to weed out undesirable market participants. The suitability rules are based on the notion that dealers must use their professional expertise to protect each individual client from making investments that are inappropriate for her or him.

There is a vast array of financial products available to investors, and each exposes an investor to a unique level and type of risk. Currency futures or hedge funds might be appropriate investments for the sophisticated individual with a high net-worth who looks for a chance to earn a high return on the speculative portion of her or his portfolio. But, such investments could prove disastrous for the conservative investor of limited means who perhaps relies on more modest investments to provide a stable retirement income or to finance a child's university education. Yet, the very investors who are the most vulnerable — the smaller, retail investors — are also, typically, the investors with the least financial sophistication. As the court in *Varcoe*[32] explained, "'[s]uitability' is governed by the amount that the client can afford to lose in a risky business without doing significant harm to financial obligations or lifestyle."

Accordingly, securities law imposes upon dealers, advisers, and salespersons an obligation to make inquiries about their clients to "ascertain the general investment needs and objectives of the client and the suitability of a proposed purchase or sale of a security for the client."[33] The Investment Dealers Association of Canada (IDA), the

---

31 In the aftermath of the 11 September 2001 terrorist attacks in the United States, the significance of the "know-your-client" rules have assumed somewhat greater prominence amid the concern to identify financing activities of terrorist organizations. A former U.S. treasury official was recently quoted in the context of the banking industry as saying, "the occasionally controversial doctrine of 'knowing one's customer' ... will have to be expanded." See Paul Beckett and Glenn R. Simpson, "Suspect Network Used Major U.S. Banks to Make Wire Transfers" *Wall Street Journal* (9 November 2001) A4, quoting Patrick Jost. The International Organization of Securities Commissions (IOSCO) announced the formation in October 2001 of a "Project Team" headed by Michel Prada to consider appropriate securities regulatory reform in light of September 11, including client identification issues. See IOSCO, Press Release, "Creation of a Special Project Team" (12 October 2001), available online at <http://www.iosco.org> (site accessed: 11 March 2002). The Investment Dealers Association of Canada also recently proposed changes to know-your-client rules dealing with offshore accounts. According to news reports, the OSC did not believe such proposals went far enough. See Richard Blackwell, "IDA Targets Offshore Accounts" *Globe and Mail* (7 March 2002) B1.

32 *Varcoe*, above note 25.

33 OSC Rule 31-505, s. 1.5.

securities dealers' self-regulatory organization, also has its own suitability requirements to which its members are subject.[34] Where IDA members comply with the IDA rule, they are exempt from the OSC rules on the subject.[35]

The advent of discount brokerages, for some time, has forced regulators, investors, and courts to be flexible in their approaches to the suitability rules. More recently, the rationale underlying such rules has been challenged especially by advances in communication and trading technology. Today, investors can obtain significant information about investment opportunities at a very low cost (for example, through the Internet) and can trade securities without using the traditional services of a broker (again, typically, though not exclusively, via online trading services). Regulators recognize that many investors wish to take advantage of these opportunities and that the suitability rules could severely constrain them. For example, a client who wants to execute online trades without delay would be constrained from so doing by the suitability rule, which requires all trades to be vetted by a broker before they can be inputted into the trading system.

A number of regulatory initiatives point toward relaxing these rules in appropriate cases. For example, on 10 April 2000, the CSA published a notice indicating that dealers who provide only trade execution services to their clients may apply for, and, in appropriate circumstances will be granted, relief from the suitability rules.[36] The issue of possibly relaxing the rules in our modern information age was also broached by the Securities Review Advisory Committee in the issues list it released in connection with the five-year review of Ontario securities legislation.[37] More recently, the OSC adverted to advances in information and trading technologies that seem to argue for changes in the suitability rules in its notice of a proposed rule dealing with direct purchase plans, referred to in chapter 5. In that notice, the OSC noted, among other things, that "individual investors now have access to more information concerning issuers than analysts had only a few years ago."[38]

---

34   IDA Regulation 1300.1(b), 1800.5(b), and 1900.4.

35   OSC Rule 31-505, s. 1.1.

36   "CSA Provides Relief from Suitability Obligations" (2000), 23 OSCB 2683. For an example of an order granting such relief, see *Versus Brokerage Services Inc.* — *MRRS Decision* (2000), 23 OSCB 6392, order varied (2001), 24 OSCB 1615.

37   Securities Review Advisory Committee, "Issues List" (2000), 23 OSCB 3034 at 3036 (para. 12 b).

38   "Notice of Proposed Rule Under the *Securities Act*, Proposed Rule 32-501, Direct Purchase Plans," (2000), 23 OSCB 7867 at 7868.

Moreover, the Investment Dealers Association of Canada, in September 2001, adopted amendments to its suitability rules that would permit IDA members to apply to the IDA for an effective exemption from the suitability rules where the member does not provide recommendations to its clients.[39]

The future direction of the "know-your-client" and suitability rules and the consequent role of dealers and advisers in the modern Canadian securities markets are in a period of important and substantial transition.

7) Broker Liability

Consideration of the suitability rules is important not only in the specific context of dealer regulation, but also in the more general discussion of potential broker-dealer liability to clients.

As a general matter, the level of a broker's responsibility and his or her potential liability to clients, depends upon the functions the broker undertakes for the client. The Supreme Court of Canada has said:

> The relationship of an investor to his or her discount broker will not likely give rise to a fiduciary duty, where the broker is simply a conduit of information and an order taker.[40]

Failure to comply with the suitability rules can also form the foundation of a tort claim. As stated in a recent Ontario decision[41] interpreting the earlier holding in *Varcoe v. Sterling*,[42] "statutes, regulations, and by-laws enacted to control commodity futures trading 'informed' the duty of care imposed upon brokers to their clients."[43]

Plaintiffs have even attempted to assert claims of personal liability against individuals within brokerage firms who had compliance responsibilities, but with whom the plaintiffs had no personal dealings.

---

39 See IDA Bulletin 2885, "Amendments to Regulation 1300, 1800.5, and 1900.4 Policy 9" (6 September 2001), available online at <http://www.ida.ca> (site accessed: 12 March 2002).

40 *Hodgkinson v. Simms*, [1994] 3 S.C.R. 377. See also *Laflamme v. Prudential-Bache Commodities Canada Ltd.*, [2000] 1 S.C.R. 638; *Varcoe*, above note 25 at 234–35 (Gen. Div.): "The relationship of broker and client is not per se a fiduciary relationship ... The circumstances can cover the whole spectrum from total reliance to total independence"; *Maghun v. Richardson Securities of Canada Ltd.* (1986), 58 O.R. (2d) 1; *Lockwood v. Nesbitt Burns Inc.*, [2000] O.J. No. 2857 (S.C.J.); and *Turcotte v. Global Securities Corp.*, [2000] B.C.J. No. 1667 (S.C.).

41 *Zraik v. Levesque Securities*, [1999] O.J. No. 2263, varied (only on quantum of damages) [2001] O.J. No. 5083 (C.A.) [*Zraik*].

42 *Varcoe*, above note 25.

43 *Zraik*, above note 41 at para. 93.

At least one action based on such a claim recently survived a motion to strike when the matter came before the Ontario Court of Appeal.[44] Finally, the courts have recently been called upon to interpret traditional legal rules in the context not only of human error, but also of computer system error[45] and perhaps of simultaneous human and computer error.

8) Compensation Fund

The *OSA Regulation* requires that every dealer participate in a compensation fund.[46] The purpose of a dealer compensation fund is similar to that of deposit insurance in the case of banks and other deposit-taking institutions. Unlike bank deposit insurance, however, the dealer compensation fund is not government guaranteed. If a dealer becomes insolvent, clients of the dealer can seek compensation for losses against the fund. The compensation fund in which Canadian dealers participate is known as the Canadian Investor Protection Fund (CIPF). The CIPF is an industry-funded trust that provides coverage for losses incurred by clients of insolvent dealers of up to $1 million each.[47]

9) Universal Registration

Part XI of the *OSA Regulation* contains the "universal registration" rules. The purpose of the universal registration rules is to prevent securities firms from evading regulatory scrutiny and capital and proficiency requirements by strategically limiting their activities strictly to types of securities trading for which statutory registration exemptions are available. The rules achieve their objective by denying the registration exemptions to securities industry professionals. Thus, the regulations do not permit "market intermediaries" (a specially defined term, as explained below) to rely upon the registration exemptions in subsections 35(1) and (2) of the *OSA* except in limited circumstances.[48] The rules define a "market intermediary" as any "person or company that engages or holds himself, herself or itself out as engaging in Ontario in the business of trading in securities as principal or agent, other than trading in securities purchased by the person or company for his, her

---

44   *Anger v. Berkshire Investment Group Inc.* (2000), 141 O.A.C. 301 (C.A.).
45   See, e.g., *Robet v. Versus Brokerage Services Inc.*, [2001] O.J. No. 1341 (Sup. Ct.).
46   *OSA Regulation*, above note 4, s. 110.
47   Available online at <http://www.cipf.ca> (site accessed: 19 March 2002).
48   *OSA Regulation*, above note 4, s. 206.

or its own account for investment only and not with a view to resale or distribution."[49]

Market intermediaries must seek and obtain registration from the OSC if they wish to participate in trading activities, including those that would be exempt from the registration requirements if they were carried on by anyone other than a market intermediary. Additional registration exemptions added by OSC Rule 45-501 were also made subject to similar universal registration restrictions.[50]

10) Dealer Conflicts of Interest and Networking Arrangements

a) Introduction

Clients of securities dealers typically rely on those dealers for securities-trading services and for financial advice. In addition, when securities dealers perform the underwriting function, the clients implicitly rely on the dealers to ensure that securities are priced fairly, prospectus disclosure is complete and reliable, and adequate due diligence investigations have been undertaken. Dealers can find themselves in situations where their financial interests (or the financial interests of affiliated companies or companies otherwise connected to the dealers) could be in conflict with their duties to perform their underwriting obligations vigilantly and to provide their clients with sound, disinterested advice. The potential for such conflicts, or apparent conflicts, is particularly great in Canada where major securities dealers are subsidiaries of the largest chartered banks. Regulators, therefore, have developed a series of rules and principles aimed at addressing the problems that could arise from such conflicts.

The dealer conflict rules basically address two situations:

- Underwriting conflicts: These occur where a registrant underwrites the securities of an issuer that is somehow related or otherwise connected to the registrant or, indeed, is the registrant itself.
- Dealer conflicts: These occur where a registrant provides advice or recommendations relating to the purchase or sale of securities of itself, a related party, or a connected issuer, and where a registrant enters into various cross-selling or other arrangements with a financial intermediary (such as a bank).

---

49   *Ibid.* s. 204(1).
50   OSC Rule 45-501 (2001), 24 OSCB 5549, s. 3.4.

A related conflict issue, which was recently the focus of a Canadian industry report, arises in connection with the work of securities industry analysts.[51]

b) Underwriting Conflicts

The underwriting conflict rules have been the subject of recent changes that came into force on 3 January 2002. These rules represent the culmination of a regulatory process that has unfolded over the past fifteen years. The *OSA Regulation* formerly contained a series of "connected issuer" and "related issuer" rules that were amended when the new regime came into effect. These rules were introduced in 1987 when legislative changes permitted financial institutions to acquire securities firms. The rules were, in effect, modified by a 1992 blanket order of the OSC that subsequently became a deemed rule.[52] That deemed rule lapsed in December 2000. In the meantime, in 1998, the CSA promulgated proposed "multijurisdictional instrument" 33-105.[53] Although that instrument was never finally approved, it became the *de facto* rule on the subject.[54] Then, in June 2001, a revised version of Multilateral Instrument 33-105 was published for comment.[55] The comment period ended on 22 August 2001, and on 19 October 2001, an amended version of National Instrument 33-105 was delivered to the minister of finance and was approved in December 2001.[56] The underwriting conflict rules prescribed by NI 33-105[57] are briefly summarized below.

---

51   Securities Industry Committee on Analyst Standards, *Setting Analyst Standards: Recommendations for the Supervision and Practice of Canadian Securities Industry Analysts* (October 2001).

52   *Re Limitations on a Registrant Underwriting Securities of a Related Issuer or Connected Issuer of the Registrant* (1997), 20 OSCB 1217.

53   Multijurisdictional Instrument 33-105 (1998), 21 OSCB 781. The instrument was issued before the term "multilateral instrument" had become settled as the standard term to describe instruments to which some, but not all, members of the CSA agreed.

54   See, e.g., Torys, "Draft Rule on Underwriting Conflicts Republished for Comment": "Even though it was not formally adopted, the 1998 draft rule has essentially been implemented." (29 June 2001) available online at <http://www.torys.com> at "Publications."

55   (2001), 24 OSCB 3805.

56   (2001), 24 OSCB 6452 [NI 33-105]. Note that the final version is a *national*, and not merely a *multilateral*, instrument. This change was made possible by a decision taken by the Quebec Securities Commission to adopt the final version of the instrument in Quebec. When the National Instrument came into effect, corresponding changes were also made to the *OSA Regulation*. See O. Reg. 504/00.

57   *Ibid.* s. 6.1.

i)   When Will Special Conflict Rules Apply?

The rules come into play when a registrant acts as an underwriter in connection with a distribution by itself (either as an issuer or a selling securityholder) or by an issuer that is a "connected issuer" or a "related issuer" of the registrant. The two key defined terms in the rule, therefore, are "connected issuer" and "related issuer." The distinction between these two terms is crucial because, as discussed further below, when a "connected issuer" is involved, NI 33-105 imposes only a disclosure obligation. However, when a "related issuer" is involved, the instrument not only requires specific disclosure of the relationship, but also may require that another *independent* underwriter participate in the transaction.

ii)   When Is an Issuer a "Related Issuer"?

Subsection 1.2(2) of National Instrument 33-105 defines a person or company to be a "related issuer" of another person or company where

(a)   the person or company is an influential securityholder of the other person or company,

(b)   the other person or company is an influential securityholder of the person or company, or

(c)   each of them is a related issuer of the same third person or company.

The definition of "influential securityholder," upon which the concept of "related issuer" depends, is complicated. The definition sets out four separate categories of influential securityholders. At the highest level of generality, an influential securityholder of an issuer is a securityholder with a significant equity interest (more than 20 percent) in that issuer or a securityholder with a lower equity interest (more than 10 percent) when combined with direct or indirect representation on the issuer's board of directors. To ensure that the definition catches all firms that have such close relationships, the definition sweeps in indirect equity holdings, includes interests held by related issuers, and applies not only when a person or company has an equity interest and board representation in the issuer, but also when the issuer has such an interest in the person or company said to be the "influential securityholder."

Looking somewhat more closely at the four categories set out in the definition, perhaps the most straightforward is the one found in part (a) of the definition. This category defines an "influential securityholder" of an issuer as any person, company, or professional group that has ownership of, or power to direct the voting of, more than 20 percent of the issuer's voting securities. The definition also includes any person, company, or professional group that owns or has the power to direct the voting of securities that entitle the holder to receive more than 20 percent of the distributions made on the equity securities of the issuer, whether as dividends, on a winding-up, or otherwise (distribution entitlement). Any person, company, or professional group that controls, or is a general partner of, the issuer, if the issuer is a general or limited partnership, is also covered by the definition.

The remaining three categories bring the following within the definition:

1. Persons, companies, or professional groups with lower voting or distribution entitlements (i.e., more than 10 percent rather than 20 percent) in cases where (a) such persons, companies, or professional groups have a right (together with related issuers) to nominate 20 percent of the directors of the issuer (or a related issuer of the issuer), or have officers or directors that constitute at least 20 percent of the directors of the issuer or a related issuer of the issuer; or (b) the issuer (together with its related issuers) has 20 percent board representation or a right to nominate 20 percent of the board of the person, company, or a related issuer of the person or company.

2. Persons or companies in respect of which the issuer has a 10 percent voting or distribution entitlement in cases where either (a) the issuer (and its related issuers) also have 20 percent board representation or the right to nominate 20 percent of the directors to the board of the person or company (or a related issuer of the person or company); or (b) the person or company (together with its related issuers) has 20 percent board representation or the right to nominate 20 percent of the directors to the board of the issuer (or a related issuer of the issuer).

3. The registrant of any professional group[58] that comes within paragraphs (a) or (b) of the definition of "influential securityholder."

iii) When Is an Issuer a "Connected Issuer"?

A connected issuer is an entity that has a more tenuous connection with the registrant than does a "related issuer." In the past, the concept included entities that were indebted to the registrant or a related issuer

---

58   A "professional group" is defined in s. 1.1. of NI 33-105 as a group that consists of

    (a)   any employee of the registrant,

    (b)   any partner, officer or director of the registrant,

    (c)   any affiliate of the registrant,

    (d)   any associated party of any person or company described in paragraphs (a) through (c) or of the registrant.

of the registrant. Under NI 33-105, the test is a subjective one. An issuer or selling securityholder is a connected issuer of a registrant where there is a relationship between: that issuer or selling security-holder (or a related issuer of either), on the one hand, and the regis-trant, related issuers of the registrant; or any director, officer, or partner of the registrant or of a related issuer of the registrant, on the other hand. This relationship must be such that it "may lead a reasonable prospective purchaser of the securities [being distributed] to question if the registrant and the issuer [or the selling securityholder, as the case may be] are independent of each other."[59]

The CSA provides charts in the appendices to Companion Policy 33-105 CP illustrating the detailed analytical steps required to deter-mine whether, and how, NI 33-105 will apply.

iv) What Are the Special Rules?

The rules are not intended to prohibit dealers (i.e., registrants) from acting as underwriters for issuers or selling securityholders to whom the dealers are related or connected. The rules do, however, impose three sorts of requirements aimed at reducing the potential harm that might arise where such conflicts of interest exist. Each is discussed below.

aa) Disclosure

Specific disclosure rules are mandated in the case of potential conflicts and include the specific information to be set out in the prospectus or other document used in connection with any distribution in which such issues arise.[60] Three points about this disclosure obligation bear emphasis here. First, the disclosure obligation applies when the issuer or selling securityholder is *either* a related issuer *or* a connected issuer. Second, the required disclosure is specifically prescribed in Appendix C to NI 33-105. Third, the disclosure obligation applies not only to public offerings, but also to private placement disclosure documents.[61]

---

59   NI 33-105, above note 56, s. 1.1 (definition of "connected issuer").

60   Concurrently with the coming into force of the instrument, the *OSA Regulation* was amended. These amendments include the revocation of *OSA Regulation*, s. 224, which currently includes disclosure requirements. See also Form 41-501F1, Item 24; Form 44-101F3, Item 14; and National Instrument 44-102, s. 6.5. (See above note 56.)

61   This conclusion is clear from the reference in NI 33-105, above note 56, s. 2.1(1), to "a prospectus *or another document*."[Emphasis added.] Moreover, the fact that the disclosure obligation applies to both public offerings and private placements is expressly confirmed in Companion Policy 33-105 CP (2001), 24 OSCB 7687, s. 2.3(1).

bb) Independent Underwriters

The rules impose requirements, in some cases, for the participation of other arm's-length registrants as underwriters. Specifically, NI 33-105 requires an underwriter that is independent of the issuer or selling securityholder to participate in any of the following transactions: a prospectus offering of any type of securities, or a distribution (i.e., an exempt distribution, or private placement) of special warrants when (1) a registrant acts as an underwriter (in connection with its own distribution of securities whether as an issuer or as a selling securityholder), or (2) a registrant acts as a "direct underwriter"[62] in connection with such a distribution by a related issuer.[63] To understand why an exempt distribution of special warrants is included here, it is important to understand the basic structure of a special warrant transaction. Special warrants typically are distributed by way of private placement. The warrants entitle the purchasers, at their option, to exercise the warrants and to receive in exchange for them other securities (the "underlying securities") of the issuer without paying any additional consideration. The issuer, in turn, agrees to file a prospectus in respect of the underlying securities, so that they will become freely tradeable. Thus, a special warrant deal offers the speed of a private placement, but provides investors with freely tradeable securities. However, the purchasers' investment decisions are made at the time of purchase of the warrants, not at the time the purchasers exercise the special warrants and obtain the underlying securities pursuant to the prospectus. Accordingly, the underwriters' due diligence and pricing work must be undertaken before the exempt distribution of the special warrants. Although the sale of the special warrants is, in form, a private placement, that placement invariably will be followed by a distribution under a prospectus, but the pricing of that "public" offering will have been completed at the time of the earlier warrant private placement.[64]

cc) Role of Independent Underwriter

In those instances where an independent underwriter is required, NI 33-105 imposes two sorts of requirements to assure that the role of such independent underwriters is meaningful. First, an independent

---

62 A "direct underwriter" is an underwriter in a contractual relationship with the seller or, when the distribution is a rights offering, a dealer-manager. See NI 33-105, above note 56, s. 1.1 (definition of "direct underwriter").

63 NI 33-105, above note 56, s. 2.1.

64 For a general discussion of special warrant transactions, see OSC Staff Notice 46-701 (1989), 12 OSCB 2163.

underwriter must underwrite either 20 percent of the offering or an amount equal to the largest portion of the distribution underwritten by a non-independent underwriter, whichever is less. (If the transaction is a "best efforts agency" deal rather than a firm commitment underwriting, the independent underwriter must receive 20 percent of the agents' total fees or an amount equal to the largest amount received by a non-independent underwriter, whichever is less.) Second, the identity of the independent underwriter and the role played by that underwriter in conducting due diligence and in structuring and pricing the offering must be disclosed in the prospectus or other document relating to the special warrants, as the case may be.[65]

c) Dealer Conflicts

Conflicts and potential conflicts also arise in contexts other than those in which dealers underwrite securities. These potential (non-underwriting) conflicts are of four principal sorts:

* Trading in, or providing advice to investors in respect of, the securities of the registrant itself or a related issuer of the registrant
* Providing recommendations to investors with respect to investment in securities of the registrant or a related issuer of the registrant
* Entering into cross-selling, networking, or other arrangements with a related financial institution
* Acting as directors of issuers

The first two of these matters are dealt with in the *OSA Regulation*, which provides, in essence, that (a) if a registrant trades in its own securities or those of a related issuer, the registrant, subject to certain exceptions, must disclose to the other party to the trade the nature of the registrant's relationship to the issuer,[66] and (b) registrants may not advise or make recommendations with respect to their own securities or securities of related issuers unless full and proper disclosure of the potential conflict is made and, in certain cases, consent of the client is obtained.[67]

Regulatory response to conflicts of the third type have evolved considerably during the past few years. Until very recently, a combination

---

65   NI 33-105, above note 56, s. 2.1(3).

66   *OSA Regulation*, above note 4, s. 225.

67   *Ibid*, ss. 227 & 228. Following the January 2002 amendments to the *OSA Regulation*, the definition of "related issuer" in s. 219(1) now incorporates by reference the meaning of that term in s. 1.1 of NI 33-105, as discussed above.

of regulations,[68] "Principles of Regulation"[69] issued by the CSA, and a "Distribution Structures Position Paper"[70] attempted to provide a scheme within which securities dealers affiliated with financial institutions (mainly banks) could operate within bank branches and enter into cross-selling or other so-called "networking arrangements."[71] The term "networking arrangement" was, prior to 1 August 2001, a term defined in the *OSA Regulation* and readers may encounter the term in older discussions of Ontario securities law. These regulations and principles of regulation were revoked or rescinded as of 1 August 2001, and the regulatory concerns with which they had intended to deal are now the subject of a new national instrument, National Instrument 33-102, and a Companion Policy, 33-102 CP.[72]

The new regime adopts a fairly flexible approach to issues of potential conflict where a registrant is affiliated with a financial institution. Among other things, registrants are prohibited from engaging in tied selling[73] and from requiring that clients settle their transactions with the registrant through an account at a Canadian financial institution.[74] Where registrants carry on a securities business within an office or a branch of a financial institution, the registrant is obliged to make specific disclosure to retail clients to ensure that such clients understand the distinction between investing in risky securities and investing in government-insured bank deposit instruments.[75]

With respect to the fourth area of potential conflict, where registrants act as directors of reporting issuers, the CSA offers some regulatory guidance in Multilateral Policy 34-202.[76] The regulators' principal concern is that a registrant not make use of information obtained in the registrant's capacity as a director to benefit the registrant's clients before such information is publicly disclosed.

---

68   *Ibid.* s. 229.
69   "Principle of Regulation 1 — Re: Distribution of Mutual Funds by Financial Institutions" (1988), 11 OSCB 4436; "Principle of Regulation 2 — Re: Full Service and Discount Brokerage Activities of Securities Dealers in Branches of Related Financial Institutions" (1988), 11 OSCB 4640; "Principle of Regulation 3 — Re: Activities of Registrants Related to Financial Institutions" (1990), 13 OSCB 1779.
70   See OSC Staff Notice 33-718, "Networking Applications" (2000), 22 OSCB 245.
71   *OSA Regulation*, above note 4, s. 219(1).
72   (2001), 24 OSCB 3030.
73   National Instrument 33-102, *ibid.* s. 5.1.
74   *Ibid.* s. 4.1.
75   *Ibid.* Part 6.
76   (1998), 21 OSCB 6608.

d) Analysts' Standards

Investment banking firms typically employ securities analysts to research securities issuers and to provide valuation advice and recommendations as to whether a particular security ought to be bought, sold, or held. Analysts performing this role, however, may find themselves in a position of conflict because their employers' revenues depend upon securing investment banking engagements. Needless to say, when an issuer hires a firm to underwrite its securities, it will be dismayed if the securities analysts employed by that firm do not provide supportive reports and recommendations. Moreover, significant conflicts may also arise when the analyst's employer has a long, or a short, position in securities covered by the analyst. These and many other issues were recently surveyed by the Securities Industry Committee on Analyst Standards, which released its final report in October 2001.[77] The committee's report contained thirty-three recommendations dealing with improved disclosure, improved standards for research reports, analyst registration and supervision, corporate governance and independence, and investor education.[78] The issue of sell-side analysts' conflicts also became the subject of considerable media attention following the bankruptcy of Enron Corporation in December 2001 and has prompted the promulgation of new SEC rules on the subject as well as recent IDA proposals.

11) International Issues

As the securities industry has become increasingly international in scope, regulators have had to contend with a number of cross-border issues. A few such issues are canvassed here for illustrative purposes.

a) Residency Requirements

Section 213 of the *OSA Regulation* provides that a registered dealer, other than an individual or an international dealer or issuer, must be a Canadian company or other Canadian entity. At one time, similar residency rules also applied to advisers, but these rules were revoked in 1987, as a matter of law, and changed as a matter of administrative practice beginning in 1994.[79] Accordingly, it is now possible, under certain conditions, for non-residents to be granted registration in the adviser and international adviser categories.[80]

---

77   See above note 51.

78   *Ibid.* at 11.

79   See OSC Notice "Residency Requirements for Advisers and Their Partners and Officers" (1994), 17 OSCB 4206.

80   International advisers are subject to the rules in OSC Rule 35-502 (2000), 23 OSCB 7989. See *OSA Regulation*, above note 4, s. 99(5).

b) Breach of Requirements of Other Jurisdictions

In a world where the cross-border trading of securities can be accomplished simply by clicking a computer mouse, Canadian registrants may occasionally be drawn into situations where their activities stray across provincial or national borders. Even though Canadian investors and markets are not directly at risk from any of those activities, the CSA has warned that violation by a registrant from one jurisdiction of the rules of any other provincial or foreign jurisdiction may be grounds for disciplinary action against that registrant.[81]

c) Exemptions for U.S. Broker-Dealers and Agents

It is common for U.S. companies with Canadian subsidiaries or operations to post American employees in those Canadian operations, often for significant periods of time. As well, some Americans choose to spend their retirement in Canada for all or part of the year, just as many retired Canadians (including those dubbed "snowbirds" by the Canadian popular media) prefer warmer American locations, at least during the most severe Canadian winter months. Americans who are temporarily in Canada, however, very likely maintain their investments in the United States. And if, from time to time, they wish to make additional trades of non-Canadian securities in their U.S. investment accounts, they will need to use the services of their U.S. broker-dealers. If their contact with those U.S. broker-dealers occurs while they are in Canada, the broker-dealers could be said to be trading in Canada. If those broker-dealers are not registered in accordance with Canadian securities laws, such trading by the brokers is illegal. The CSA has determined, however, that there is no compelling policy reason to prevent Americans temporarily resident in Canada from dealing with their U.S. brokers, or to hinder any former American residents from seeking the assistance of U.S. brokers in dealing with investments held in tax-advantaged retirement plans (such as "Individual Retirement Accounts" — a U.S. concept similar to Canadian Registered Retirement Savings Plans). Accordingly, National Instrument 35-101[82] provides a conditional exemption from the registration requirements for U.S. broker-dealers dealing with American residents or former American residents living in Canada. In the case of Americans who are only temporarily resident in Canada, the U.S. broker-dealer must have had a previous client relationship with the individual before she or he left the United States. No such restriction applies in the case of an

---

81   National Policy 34-201 (1998), 21 OSCB 6607.
82   (2000), 23 OSCB 8511.

American in Canada dealing with his or her American retirement plan. There are a number of other technical rules with which the U.S. broker-dealer must comply, including the important limitation that the exemption applies only in respect of trades in foreign (i.e., non-Canadian) securities. (It is also worth noting that in June 2000, the SEC adopted a rule that permits Canadians living in the United States to manage investments in their RRSPs, RRIFs, and other retirement accounts without requiring that any securities sold to those accounts be registered under U.S. federal securities laws.)[83]

d) Recent Settlements with Foreign Web-based Trading Firms

It is implicit in the conditional exemption rules described above that, where a U.S. firm trading in securities in Canada does not satisfy the specific conditions referred to, no exemption is available. Accordingly, any firm that trades securities in a Canadian jurisdiction without satisfying the provincial registration requirements violates Canadian law. Modern Internet technology, however, has made it remarkably simple for Canadians to execute securities trades through U.S. brokers online. The fact that such brokers violate Canadian law by dealing with Canadian clients may very well come as a surprise to some of those brokers as well as to those Canadian clients who are often attracted by lower fees than are available from Canadian-based competitors. In June 2001, several Canadian securities regulators concluded settlement agreements with three Web-based American brokerage firms that had been dealing with Canadian residents. Each firm agreed to pay a monetary penalty, to comply with applicable Canadian securities legislation in the future, and to seek registration in the Canadian jurisdictions in which it has clients.[84]

---

83 See Security and Exchange Commission Release Notice 2000 WL 739244 (SEC) Release Nos. 33-7860, 34-42905, and IC 24491.

84 *Re Securities Legislation of British Columbia, Alberta, Saskatchewan, Manitoba, Ontario, Quebec, Nova Scotia, New Brunswick, Newfoundland and Yukon and Re Ameritrade, Inc.; Re Securities Legislation of British Columbia, Alberta, Saskatchewan, Manitoba, Ontario, Quebec, Nova Scotia, New Brunswick, Newfoundland and Yukon and Re Datek Online Brokerage Services, LLC; Re Securities Legislation of British Columbia, Alberta, Saskatchewan, Manitoba, Ontario, Quebec, Nova Scotia, New Brunswick, Newfoundland and Yukon and Re TD Waterhouse Investor Services, Inc.*

D. ALTERNATIVE TRADING SYSTEMS

1) Introduction

The intersection of the twin purposes of securities regulation — investor protection and enhancing capital market efficiency and investor confidence — is rarely observed so clearly as in the recent regulatory response to alternative trading systems. Alternative trading systems (ATSs), generally speaking, are computer-based systems that automate the process of trading in securities in whole or in part.[85]

These systems provide methods for trading securities that offer useful alternatives to older, manual trading systems. For example, in traditional open outcry equity exchanges, of which the New York Stock Exchange remains the last important example, floor traders seeking to fill market orders on behalf of clients to buy or sell securities of an issuer must walk to a particular trading post located on the exchange floor. There a kind of "mini auction" may take place involving the "specialist" assigned by the exchange to that particular stock and other traders at the post. Alternative trading systems eliminate the need for any such face-to-face bargaining. Instead, prospective buyers and sellers do not "meet" on a particular section of an exchange trading floor, but "meet" virtually in cyberspace. Prospective buyers and sellers may enter their orders into a computer system where a sophisticated computer algorithm, rather than a specialist, helps them to facilitate a trade.

Of course, securities exchanges throughout the world have used computer-based trading systems for many years.[86] (Even on the New York Stock Exchange, many aspects of the trading process are computerized, including the routing of all smaller retail orders.) But, it is the advent of new proprietary, computer-based trading systems developed and promoted by private firms that has prompted regulatory and industry scrutiny and wariness. Regulators, industry professionals, and

---

85 We use the term "alternative trading system" in this sentence in a general sense, rather than as a specifically defined term. As explained below in section (2), National Instrument 21-101 now includes a definition of an alternative trading system for the purposes of that instrument that is considerably narrower than our general definition suggests.

86 Over twenty years ago, the TSE was already experimenting with a computer-based trading system, CATS. For a discussion of these early initiatives, which is particularly interesting for a twenty-first century reader, see Hugh J. Cleland, "Applications of Automation in the Canadian Securities Industry: Present and Projected," in *Proposals for a Securities Market Law for Canada*, vol. 3 (Ottawa: Minister of Supply and Services Canada, 1979) at 947.

the public appreciate the advantages that computers offer, whether in terms of speed, reliability, or otherwise; however, the use of alternative trading systems in Canada also raises concerns of market fragmentation. Market fragmentation refers to the effect that occurs when the same security may be traded on multiple markets. The problems created by market fragmentation are many. Among other things, if markets are fragmented, some of their most important functions are compromised. For example, fragmented markets are less liquid and do not offer a useful price discovery function. Fragmented markets may even lead to unfairness because buyers and sellers are not assured that they are obtaining the best price available at any given time.[87] As a result, the regulatory approach to permitting the operation of alternative trading systems in Canada reflects an attempt to balance the benefits that such systems may provide against the potential harm to the markets that could inadvertently result from an uncoordinated expansion of new ATSs.

The history of the foray (or attempted foray) of ATSs into Canada has been reviewed in some detail elsewhere.[88] The regulatory consideration of the issues raised by the operation of ATSs culminated in the promulgation of National Instrument 21-101, Companion Policy 21-101 CP, and National Instrument 23-101, all of which came into force on 1 December 2001.[89]

2) National Instrument 21-101

a) ATS Choice of Regulation
National Instrument 21-101 essentially permits ATSs to elect how they wish to be regulated, except in cases where the ATS performs certain "exchange-type" functions. Those ATSs are required to seek and obtain recognition from the securities regulatory authorities to operate as exchanges. (As a technical matter, as explained below, a system performing such exchange-type functions is not considered an ATS.)

The regulatory options available to an ATS are (i) to function as an exchange, (ii) to become a member of an exchange, and (iii) to be reg-

---

87   For a discussion of market fragmentation in the context of the ATS Proposal, see (1999), 22 OSCB (ATS Supp.) 29.

88   See, e.g., Christopher C. Nicholls, *Corporate Finance and Canadian Law* (Toronto: Carswell, 2000) at 290ff. See also "Notice of Proposed National Instrument 21-101 Marketplace Operation" (1999), 22 OSCB (ATS Supp.) Appendix "A," "Regulation of Alternative Trading Systems in Canada," s. 2.1.

89   (2001), 24 OSCB 10.

istered as a dealer and become a member of a self-regulatory entity. Each of these options is discussed below.

i)   To Function as an Exchange

Technically, an ATS that becomes recognized as an exchange ceases to be an ATS as defined in National Instrument 21-101. Moreover, in some cases this "choice" is of the Hobson's variety. An ATS that performs any of the four traditional exchange functions[90] is required, as a condition of operation, to become recognized as an exchange.[91]

ii)   To Become a Member of an Exchange

An ATS that chooses to become an exchange member (the method of operation used prior to the new rules) is exempt, as a technical matter, from National Instrument 21-101, and instead is subject to the rules governing exchange members generally.[92]

iii) To Be Registered as a Dealer and Become a Member
of a Self-regulatory Entity[93]

Currently, the only self-regulatory entity to which an ATS could belong for this purpose is the IDA.[94] An ATS that chooses to register as a dealer is required also to enter into a written agreement with a regulation services provider that will perform market regulation with respect to trading on the ATS.[95] The rationale underlying the requirement that

---

90   The four exchange functions identified in the instrument are providing listing requirements, guaranteeing a two-sided market, setting requirements for the conduct of subscribers, and disciplining subscribers. National Instrument 21-101, above note 89, s. 1.1. definition of "alternative trading system," Companion Policy 21-101 CP, above note 89, s. 3.1(2).
91   Companion Policy 21-101, above note 89, s. 3.3(3).
92   National Instrument 21-101, above note 89, s. 2.1.
93   *Ibid.* s. 6.1.
94   *Ibid.*; Companion Policy 21-101 CP, above note 89, s. 3.4(5).
95   National Instrument 21-101, above note 89, s. 8.3. "Regulation services provider" is defined in the instrument to mean a "person or company that provides regulation services and is (a) a recognized exchange, (b) a recognized quotation and trade reporting system, or (c) a recognized self-regulatory entity." (*Ibid.* s. 1.1). On 28 September 2001, the TSE and the IDA filed an application on behalf of Market Regulation Services Inc. (RS Inc.) seeking recognition of RS Inc. — which is jointly owned by the TSE and the IDA — as a self-regulatory organization with a view to having RS Inc. serve as a regulation services provider. The application was filed with securities regulators in Alberta, British Columbia, Ontario, and Quebec. On 29 January 2002, the OSC recognized RS Inc. as a self-regulatory organization: (2002), 25 OSCB 891. (RS Inc. was also recognized in Alberta, British Columbia, Manitoba, and Quebec.) The recognizing

ATSs not only belong to an SRO, but also engage the services of a regulation services provider was set out in a 1999 CSA paper that was an appendix to the original 1999 ATS regulatory proposal.[96] That paper notes the important distinction between SRO *member* regulation (as performed by exchanges and SROs) and *market* regulation — a function performed by Canadian exchanges, but *not* carried out by the IDA or other organizations independent of the exchanges. Market regulation includes imposing trading rules and engaging in surveillance and enforcement activities. Market regulation is essential to ensure the integrity of a securities marketplace. Yet, as the CSA notes, it would be anomalous to compel ATSs that intend to compete with traditional exchanges to submit to market regulation carried out by those very exchanges. Thus, the CSA concluded in 1999 as follows:

> To deal with competitive issues ... ATSs will be permitted to choose the SRO that will perform their market regulation function. Allowing ATSs the opportunity to choose also gives the exchanges an opportunity to compete based on services and to recapture some of the costs they incur as self-regulatory organizations.[97]

b) Securities Permitted to Be Traded on an ATS
An ATS is not permitted to function as a marketplace for all types of securities. Only the following four types of securities may be traded on an ATS:[98]

- Securities listed on a recognized Canadian exchange or quoted on a recognized quotation and trade-reporting system
- Corporate debt securities
- Government debt securities

---

regulators also approved the Universal Market Integrity Rules (published at (2002), 25 OSCB 1006). The TSE has retained RS Inc. as a regulation services provider (2002), 25 OSCB 891, pursuant to a Regulation Services Agreement (2002), 25 OSCB 932. RS Inc. will, accordingly, provide market regulation services to the TSE. For brief background information on the new TSE/RS Inc. relationship, see "TSE and Market Regulation Services Inc. (RS) — A Backgrounder," available online at <http://www.tse.com> (site accessed: 12 March 2002).

96   "Notice of Proposed National Instrument 21-101 Marketplace Operation" (1999), 22 OSCB (ATS Supp.), Appendix "A," "Regulation of Alternative Trading Systems in Canada."

97   *Ibid.* at 30.

98   National Instrument 21-101, above note 89, s. 6.3.

- Securities listed on an exchange or quoted on a quotation system that is regulated by an ordinary member of the International Organization of Securities Commissions (IOSCO).

c) Market Integration

The new ATS regime seeks to avoid the potential problems posed by market fragmentation through a scheme of mandatory marketplace integration. The central idea behind market integration is straightforward. If every marketplace (i.e., every exchange, quotation and trade-reporting system, and ATS) is linked electronically, there will be not only increased transparency and reliable price discovery, but also price protection for buyers and sellers of securities.

National Instrument 21-101 anticipates a two-step "phased approach" to market integration.[99] In Phase 1, which will apply until 1 January 2004, each new marketplace trading in securities will be required to establish an electronic connection to the "principal market" for those securities. The determination of which market is the "principal market" for any particular security will be based on the trading volumes for the previous calendar year.

After 1 January 2004, Phase 2 integration begins. The goal of Phase 2 is the full integration of all marketplaces "in order to ensure that there will be price protection for all orders between all competing marketplaces."[100] Phase 2 integration will be achieved in one of two ways: (1) through the interposition of a "market integrator" to which each marketplace will be connected, or (2) through a requirement that every marketplace be linked to every other marketplace.[101] A clear aim of the regulators is to provide each participant with equivalent trading access to all the marketplaces to which the ATS of which he or she is a subscriber is linked.[102]

3) National Instrument 23-101 Trading Rules

In tandem with the new ATS rules, the CSA also has promulgated National Instrument 23-101,[103] which sets out common trading rules to be observed by all Canadian securities marketplaces. In the CSA Notice accompanying the original proposed version of National Instrument

---

99 Companion Policy 21-101 CP, above note 89, s. 11.1(1).
100 *Ibid.* s.11.1(5).
101 *Ibid.* s. 11.1(1).
102 National Instrument 21-101, above note 89, s. 9.4.
103 (2001), 24 OSCB 55.

23-101 in 1999, the CSA explains that common trading rules are necessary because it is essential that ATSs be subject to appropriate market rules, yet, unless such rules are put forward by the regulators (as opposed to the exchanges), the ATSs might be compelled to submit to market rules framed by the very exchanges with whom they are in competition.[104]

4) Summary

A comprehensive discussion of the complex new ATS rules is beyond the scope of this book. However, it is hoped that this summary of some of the highlights of the new regime illustrates how the introduction of new technology into the Canadian securities marketplace has helped to challenge and refine traditional regulatory objectives and approaches.

E. CONCLUSION

In this chapter we have tried to provide an introduction to some of the key regulatory issues related to registrants — those individuals and firms whose livelihoods depend upon trading in securities. In many ways, it is through the registration requirement and the overseeing of registrants by regulators and SROs that securities laws may be expected to have their strongest influence and impact.

---

104 (1999), 22 OSCB (ATS Supp.). It might be noted here that the TSE took issue with the notion that Canadian ATSs ought never to be subject to regulation by their competitors. The TSE argued that this position appeared to derive from a misunderstanding of the U.S. ATS regulatory regime. Under that regime, the TSE argued, contrary to the perception of many Canadian regulators, ATSs are not wholly free from regulation by their competitors. In fact, ATSs trading Nasdaq securities have been subject to Nasdaq rules notwithstanding that Nasdaq is regarded as an ATS competitor. See letter from Barbara Stymiest to British Columbia Securities Commission, (19 October, 2000), available online at <http://www.osc.gov.on.ca/en/Regulation/Rulemaking/Rules/ats_com_001019_bgstymiest.pdf> (site accessed: 2 April 2002).

CHAPTER 5

THE ISSUANCE OF SECURITIES: SELECTED ISSUES

A. INTRODUCTION

Business enterprises, such as corporations, partnerships, and limited partnerships, raise capital through a variety of means. In particular, they borrow money from banks or other lending institutions, or they sell securities. If a corporation chooses to raise capital through the issuance of any type of security, its capital-raising activities are governed by securities legislation. Because of the broad definition of "security" canvassed in chapter 2, securities legislation covers almost all types of capital raising, except borrowing funds from banks or other similar kinds of lenders.

It is conventional to divide the discussion of securities issuances into the two broad categories of public offerings and private placements (or exempt distributions). We follow that convention with our review of these subjects in chapters 6 and 7, respectively. But, there are a number of important topics surrounding the sale of securities by issuers and the purchase of securities by investors that are not necessarily confined to either of these categories. Those matters are the subject of this chapter, in which we canvass a number of legal issues and regulatory initiatives relating to the following:

- Rights offerings
- Future-Oriented Financial Information (FOFI)

- Alternative distribution methods (including direct purchase plans and sales to shareholders holding small blocks of shares)
- The Multijurisdictional Disclosure System
- Mutual funds (investment vehicles that, as issuers themselves, raise unique policy concerns from the public-offering perspective, and provide to investors an alternative to direct investment in traditional securities issued by industrial corporations)

B. RIGHTS OFFERINGS

1) Introduction

A rights offering refers to a distribution by an issuer to its own securityholders of rights to acquire additional securities of the issuer at a price stated in the offering document. The advantage of a rights offering from the issuer's perspective is that the offerees (i.e., the prospective purchasers of the securities) are already familiar with the issuer because they have previously chosen to purchase its securities. The advantage of a rights offering from the perspective of securityholders, particularly when the offering involves rights to acquire common shares, is that the securityholders may, if they wish, maintain their proportionate interest in the issuer.

Consider the following example. A corporation, Rightsco Ltd., has a total of ten common shareholders, each holding exactly ten Rightsco shares (i.e., each shareholder has a 10 percent equity interest in the firm). Rightsco needs to raise capital by issuing an additional 100 shares. Rightsco can either offer these shares to new investors or it may, by way of a rights offering, offer to sell the new shares to its existing shareholders. If Rightsco chooses to conduct a rights offering, each of the ten current shareholders is granted, free of charge, the basic right to subscribe for (i.e., to purchase from the issuer) up to ten of the new shares. It must be emphasized that it is only the *right* to purchase shares that is distributed free of charge, *not* the shares themselves, which will be issued only to shareholders who choose to exercise their rights, and who pay the share subscription price. Thus, if every shareholder chooses to take full advantage of his or her rights, then when the transaction is over, Rightsco will have 200 shares outstanding, and each of its ten shareholders will own twenty (or 10 percent) of those shares. Each shareholder's proportionate stake in Rightsco shares, in other words, remains unchanged. However, some shareholders might

choose not to exercise their rights. After all, although the rights themselves are granted to the shareholders free of charge, to *exercise* a right,
a shareholder must pay Rightsco the subscription price of any shares
purchased. Some shareholders might not wish to, or be able to, make
such an additional investment in Rightsco shares. In that case, any
unsubscribed-for shares would then be offered, *pro rata*, to the remaining shareholders. This process of making subsequent offers of unsubscribed-for shares continues until either all 100 shares are sold or there
are no Rightsco shareholders left who are willing to buy any unsold
shares. If some shares remain unsold, they could, perhaps, be taken up
by an underwriter pursuant to a standby commitment entered into
before the rights offering began. (A standby commitment is a contractual obligation of an underwriter to purchase any securities not purchased by those to whom the rights offering was initially made.)

Some financial economists suggest that rights offerings appear,
generally speaking, to be cheaper than traditional securities offerings.
They note that "the arguments that firms make for avoiding rights
issues don't make sense,"[1] and suggest that it is something of "an
anomaly in the finance profession"[2] that rights offerings are not more
common. We say no more about that theoretical controversy here.
Rather, we confine our discussion to an exploration of the securities
law issues raised by rights offerings.

2) *OSA*, Clause 72(1)(h), and National Instrument 45-101

When an issuer distributes to its own securityholders rights to purchase additional securities, that distribution may be exempt from the
prospectus requirement pursuant to clause 72(1)(h) of the *OSA*. The
rights-offering exemption is based upon the assumption that existing
securityholders of an issuer already know about the issuer — indeed
have previously made an investment decision to acquire the issuer's
securities — and, therefore, do not require the information disclosed in
a prospectus. The OSC has, however, confined the exemption within
strictly defined limits. The exemption under clause 72(1)(h) stipulates
that a proposed rights offering is exempt from the prospectus requirement only if the issuer provides the OSC with advance notice of the

---

1   Richard A. Brealey and Stewart C. Myers, *Principles of Corporate Finance*, 5th ed.
    (Toronto: McGraw-Hill, 1996) at 405.
2   Stephen A. Ross, Randolph W. Westerfield, and Jeffrey Jaffe, *Corporate Finance*,
    4th ed. (Toronto: Irwin, 1996) at 537. For a recent empirical test of one finan-
    cial economic theory explaining rights offerings, see Ajai K. Singh, "Layoffs and
    Underwritten Rights Offers" (1997) 43 J. Fin. Econ. 105.

proposed offering, and the OSC does not, within ten days, give notice of any objection. The issuer must also satisfy any request made by the OSC for additional information. In addition, the exemption is available only if the issuer complies with the requirements of National Instrument 45-101,[3] which are discussed further below. Moreover, the exemption is never available for rights offerings by a reporting issuer that would result in more than a 25 percent increase in the number of the issuer's outstanding securities or, if the securities are debt instruments, in more than a 25 percent increase in the outstanding principal amount of indebtedness,[4] including amounts raised in other rights offerings completed within the previous twelve months. This quantitative restriction is consistent with the long-held view of the regulators that major financings ought to be made pursuant to a prospectus, and not in reliance upon the rights-offering exemption.[5] National Instrument 45-101 and Companion Policy 45-101 CP[6] provide a number of other examples of situations in which the rights-offering exemption is not available.[7]

3) Rights-Offering Circular

Although a rights offering made in compliance with National Instrument 45-101 is exempt from the prospectus requirement, the issuer is nonetheless required to produce an alternative disclosure document: a rights-offering circular. The information required to be included in a rights-offering circular is set out in Form 45-101 F. The rights-offering circular must be filed with the OSC in both draft and final form, and, provided the OSC either accepts or does not object to the circular, the issuer must also send the circular to every securityholder who will receive rights under the offering.[8]

4) Basic and Additional Subscription Rights

A rights offering provides an issuer's existing securityholders with the opportunity to maintain their proportionate stake in the issuer's securities by purchasing securities upon the exercise of the rights distrib-

---

3   (2001), 24 OSCB 4397 [NI 45-101].
4   *Ibid.* s. 2.2(1).
5   See, e.g., former OSC Policy 6.2 at III, 3.
6   (2001), 24 OSCB 4405 [CP 45-101].
7   NI 45-101, above note 3, s. 2.2; CP 45-101, *Ibid.* s. 1.2.
8   NI 45-101, *Ibid.* s. 3.2.

uted to the securityholders. However, some securityholders (the declining securityholders) may not wish to invest additional funds in the issuing company and so would prefer not to exercise their rights. Accordingly, to ensure that the issuer raises all the capital it requires, the issuer will make provision in the rights offering to allow others to purchase the securities to which the declining securityholders were originally entitled. To ensure that such additional subscription privileges are not used to favour some securityholders over others, National Instrument 45-101 mandates that if an additional subscription right is provided to *any* securityholder, the same right must be provided to *every* securityholder. The right must enable each securityholder to purchase additional securities proportional to the number of rights exercised by that securityholder under the basic subscription right.[9]

5) Standby Commitment

As indicated in the introduction to this section, an issuer frequently ensures the success of a rights offering by obtaining, in advance, from a third-party financier that is typically, though not necessarily, an investment bank, a commitment to purchase any securities not taken up by the securityholders pursuant to the exercise of their rights. National Instrument 45-101 requires that, if the issuer has arranged for a standby commitment prior to commencing a rights offering, the issuer must disclose the details of the commitment in the rights-offering circular,[10] provide the regulators with evidence that the person or company furnishing the commitment has the financial capacity to honour it,[11] and provide all of the securityholders with the sort of additional subscription rights described in section 4 above to prevent such commitments from being used to dilute the ownership stake of any current shareholders.[12] Existing shareholders, in other words, must be given the opportunity to purchase all shares *pro rata* before any securities are acquired by "outsiders" pursuant to a standby commitment.

---

9   *Ibid.* Part 7.
10   *Ibid.* at Form 45-101 F, Item 9.
11   *Ibid.* s. 6.1.
12   *Ibid.* s. 7.2.

6) Rights-Offering Prospectus

An issuer might prefer to complete a rights offering pursuant to a prospectus. Among other things, this ensures that the rights are freely tradeable and do not require the holder to adhere to any resale restrictions of the sort discussed in some detail in chapter 7. National Instrument 45-101 permits an issuer to distribute rights under a prospectus only if the prospectus qualifies not only the rights themselves but also the securities of the issuer to be issued when the rights are actually exercised.[13] The reason for this restriction is readily explained. If only the rights were qualified for sale under a prospectus, a rightsholder could sell his or her rights to a third-party purchaser. That third party, presumably, would pay the exercise price, exercise the right, and receive the underlying security from the issuer. However, suppose the rights-offering prospectus — the only prospectus prepared in connection with the distribution — contained a misrepresentation. The purchaser of the underlying security would have no recourse against the issuer under section 130 of the *OSA*, which provides investors with a special statutory civil remedy in the case of prospectus misrepresentations (discussed in more detail in chapter 6). This would be anomalous because the original rights holder would have received his or her rights without charge, and yet, even though he or she risked no money and made no investment decision, that original rightsholder nevertheless *did* receive a prospectus. Yet, any transferee of that right, who pays to exercise the right and purchase the underlying security from the issuer, receives none of the protections to which he or she would have been entitled had the issuance occurred without the intermediate step of a rights offering. This rationale for the prospectus restriction is made explicit in Companion Policy 45-101 CP.[14]

C. FUTURE-ORIENTED FINANCIAL INFORMATION (FOFI)

When investors buy securities, they are implicitly making judgments about the future financial performance of the firm that issued those securities. Yet, investors can never be in quite as good a position as the managers of the company itself to project how the company might per-

---

13   *Ibid.* s. 4.2.
14   Above note 6, s. 2.2.

form in the future. It is the managers' job, after all, to be familiar with the business prospects of their employer. In an ideal world, investors would benefit significantly if they had access to a firm's internal business forecasts and projections — the view of the company's future held by those best equipped to formulate such a view. Ours, however, is not an ideal world. The great securities debacles of the past almost invariably have involved speculative bubbles inflated by lavish and unfounded promises of future financial gains. The very sort of information that would, in theory, be of most benefit to investors has been, in practice, the chief source of mischief in our markets. For some time, the fear of new "securities bubbles" overshadowed the legitimate desire for disclosure of future-oriented information, and securities law generally discouraged the use of forward-looking statements. But, recently, efforts have been made to increase the availability and scope of meaningful future-oriented information. As we see in chapter 9, this new approach is reflected in the rules regarding management discussion and analysis (MD&A) and the annual information form (AIF). It is also seen in National Policy No. 48,[15] which deals with the use of future-oriented financial information (FOFI) in various disclosure documents, including prospectuses, offering memoranda, rights-offering circulars, and take-over bid circulars.

National Policy No. 48 divides FOFI into two categories: forecasts and projections. Forecasts are less speculative than projections because they are based upon "[a]ssumptions all of which reflect the [issuer's] planned courses of action for the period covered given management's judgment as to the most probable set of economic conditions."[16] Projections differ from forecasts in that projections may incorporate one or more "hypotheses." Hypotheses are defined in the Policy Statement to mean, "[a]ssumptions that assume a set of economic conditions or courses of actions that are consistent with the issuer's intended course of action and represent plausible circumstances."[17] Thus, hypotheses must represent "plausible" circumstances, but not necessarily "the most probable" outcomes.

Because they are more speculative than forecasts, projections are subject to greater restrictions. First, as a general matter, if an issuer chooses to include FOFI in a disclosure document, it must be in the form of a forecast (rather than a projection), unless the issuer has oper-

---

15   (1992), 15 OSCB 5978, as am. by (1993), 16 OSCB 194. In 1997, a proposed
      national instrument was introduced to replace National Policy No. 48. See
      National Instrument 52-101(1997), 20 OSCB 3749. However, at the date of
      writing, National Instrument 52-101 has not been finalized or adopted.
16   National Policy No. 48, *ibid.* at Part 2 (definition of "forecast").
17   *Ibid.* (definition of "Hypotheses").

ated for less than twenty-four months. It is presumably thought that an issuer with less than twenty-four months of operating history does not have sufficient data or operating experience to provide meaningful FOFI without incorporating certain hypotheses. Second, when a projection is published in documents such as prospectuses and offering memoranda, it must be accompanied by a bold-faced note, warning the reader that actual results could vary materially from projected results.[18] The use of hypotheses is also subject to some constraints.[19] All FOFI, whether in the form of a forecast or a projection, must be prepared in accordance with the Canadian Institute of Chartered Accountants handbook,[20] and normally may not extend to a date more than two years in the future.[21] Estimating results more than two years in the future is thought to be, in most cases, unreasonable.

Perhaps the three most significant requirements contained in the policy statement for the use of FOFI are the obligations: (1) to update FOFI if changes occur,[22] (2) to compare FOFI to actual results each time the issuer files its financial statements,[23] and (3) to ensure that the issuer's outside auditors are involved in the preparation of FOFI and deliver an unqualified auditors' report thereon.[24]

It should be noted that National Policy No. 48 is a policy statement, not a local rule or national instrument. You will recall from Chapter 3 that mandatory, legislative-like provisions should not be included in policy statements. At the date of writing, National Policy No. 48 was in the process of being reformulated as National Instrument 52-101. Until that instrument is finalized and adopted, the status of certain aspects of the FOFI regime prescribed in National Policy 48 remains somewhat ambiguous.

In a recent decision, the Ontario Superior Court refused to strike out a claim seeking damages pursuant to section 130 of the *OSA* in respect of a misrepresentation arising from FOFI contained in a prospectus. The defendants argued that, because FOFI was forward-looking, it could not constitute a statement of material fact. Cumming J. disagreed and dismissed the defendants' motion to strike the plaintiffs' pleadings.[25]

---

18   *Ibid.* s. 5.1.
19   *Ibid.* s. 5.2.
20   *Ibid.* s. 3.2(1).
21   *Ibid.* s. 4.2.
22   *Ibid.* Part 7.
23   *Ibid.* s. 6.1.
24   *Ibid.* Part 9.
25   See *Kerr v. Danier Leather Inc.*, [2001] O.J. No. 950 (Sup. Ct.).

D. ALTERNATIVE DISTRIBUTION METHODS

1) Direct Purchase Plans and Use of the Internet

It has become increasingly common in the United States for issuers to sell their securities directly to investors without the involvement of a licensed securities dealer.[26] Not surprisingly, the Internet has facilitated this type of direct purchase plan. In response to this growing trend south of the border, in 2001, the OSC adopted Rule 32-501[27] to permit issuers to institute direct purchase plans that would be exempt from the *OSA's* registration requirement. In other words, issuers can sell securities in certain circumstances, directly to investors, rather than through a registered securities dealer. The rule requires, among other things, that purchasers receive not only a prospectus relating to the plan, but also a specifically prescribed disclosure statement that flags for the investor the fact that he or she is making the purchase without the advice of an investment professional. Rule 32-501 came into force on 4 October 2001.[28]

Closely related to the expansion of direct purchase plans is the increased use of the Internet for securities-trading activities. In 2000, the CSA adopted National Policy 47-201,[29] which canvasses a number of Internet-related securities issues. One of the most important challenges posed by the new electronic media is that messages can be seamlessly and instantaneously transmitted to a global audience, making traditional border-bound securities regulation particularly difficult. National Policy 47-201 sets out the position of Canada's securities regulators on this jurisdictional issue. As a general rule, a person or company that "posts on the Internet a document that offers or solicits trades of securities ... [that is] accessible to persons or companies in [a]

---

26   See Notice of Proposed Rule 32-501 (2000), 23 OSCB 7867, in which the OSC states that "there are over 1600 plans listed on www.netstockdirect.com, a major U.S. website that provides information about, and permits on-line investment in direct purchase plans in the U.S."

27   (2001), 24 OSCB 4743.

28   Online at <http://www.osc.gov.on.ca/en/Regulation/Rulemaking/Rules/011005 _notice_final_rule_32-501.html> (site accessed: 20 February 2002). Recent media reports indicate, however, that before direct purchase plans become significant in Canada, rules similar to OSC Rule 32-501 will need to be adopted nationally. See Rob Carrick, "Direct Purchase Plans Allow You to Bypass Brokers," *Globe and Mail* (30 October 2001) B18.

29   (1999), 22 OSCB 8170.

local jurisdiction" will be considered to be trading in securities in that jurisdiction,[30] unless the document has an appropriate disclaimer and the seller takes "reasonable precautions" not to sell or offer securities to anyone in that local jurisdiction.[31] Moreover, a person or company located in certain provinces (Alberta, British Columbia, and Quebec) is considered to be trading in those provinces if that person or company distributes securities through the Internet, even where those distributions are made entirely to residents of other jurisdictions.[32] The policy also requires those who distribute securities by way of an Internet-accessible prospectus, to record the names and addresses of all recipients of a preliminary prospectus, even in cases where the recipients "merely view a preliminary prospectus by electronic means."[33] This recording requirement is not really new. It is, rather, the regulators' interpretation of provisions of provincial securities acts, such as section 67 of the *OSA*, in the context of an Internet offering.[34]

2) Sales to Securityholders Holding Small Blocks of Securities

Finally, we note that National Instrument 32-101[35] allows for the sale of securities of stock exchange-listed companies to securityholders holding small blocks of securities to take place in certain cases without the participation of a registrant. For companies listed on the Toronto Stock Exchange (TSE), such sales must be made in accordance with the TSE's "Policy Statement on Small Shareholder Selling and Purchase Arrangements."[36]

---

30 *Ibid.* s. 2.2(1).

31 *Ibid.* s. 2.2(2).

32 *Ibid.* s. 2.3. In this regard, the recently proposed Multilateral Instrument 72-101, "Distribution Outside of the Local Jurisdiction" (2000), 23 OSCB 6260, is also noteworthy. However, in March 2002 the CSA staff indicated that it would not be proceeding with this initiative. See chapter 7, note 65 below.

33 National Policy 47-201, above note 29, s. 2.5(3).

34 For a discussion of Internet offerings in the context of the financing of small and medium-sized businesses, see Stéphane Rousseau, "Internet-based Securities Offerings by Small and Medium-Sized Enterprises: Attractions and Challenges" (2001) 35 Can. Bus. L.J. 226. For a detailed review of the use of the Internet for securities trading, see IOSCO, "Report on Securities Activity on the Internet II" (IOSCO, June 2001), available online at <http://www.iosco.org> (site accessed: 12 March 2002).

35 (1997), 20 OSCB 5435.

36 *Toronto Stock Exchange, Company Manual*, Appendix D, para. 830-085, available online at <http://www.tse.ca/en/pdf/CompanyManual0202.pdf> (site accessed: 21 March 2002).

E. MULTIJURISDICTIONAL DISCLOSURE SYSTEM

One recent international regulatory initiative that also deserves mention is the Canada/U.S. Multijurisdictional Disclosure System (MJDS) first instituted in 1991. The details of the MJDS are found in National Instrument 71-101,[37] Companion Policy 71-101 CP,[38] and OSC Rule 71-801.[39] Reciprocal rules have been promulgated in the United States by the Securities and Exchange Commission (SEC). The SEC, some time ago, however, indicated a desire to end the multijurisdictional disclosure system, favouring, instead, a move toward more multilateral (rather than merely bilateral) international initiatives. At the date of writing, no definitive formal statement has been issued with respect to the future of the multijurisdictional disclosure system.

The basic theory underlying the MJDS is that the securities laws and the standards of securities regulation in Canada and the United States are not substantially different. For certain issuers, and under certain circumstances, it is more efficient in cross-border transactions if disclosure documents prepared for use in one jurisdiction, can also be used (with minor variation) in the other. Also, regulatory review in one jurisdiction might obviate the need for such review in the other. Thus, an MJDS-eligible U.S. issuer completing a public offering of securities in Canada could use U.S.-style disclosure documents (with a few additions) and be subject to review by the SEC, rather than by the Canadian provincial securities regulators. Similarly, MJDS-eligible Canadian issuers could distribute securities in the United States using modified Canadian disclosure documents subject to Canadian regulatory review. Indeed, the system is not confined to securities offerings. It also facilitates cross-border take-over bids, issuer bids, and other business combinations as well as compliance with proxy and other continuous disclosure obligations.

To be eligible to use the MJDS system to access the Canadian markets, a U.S. issuer must meet eligibility requirements aimed at ensuring that such an issuer is of significant size and has had a significant reporting history. There are three basic eligibility categories, described below.

---

37   (1998), 21 OSCB 5104.
38   (1998), 21 OSCB 5089.
39   (1998), 21 OSCB6919.

1) Investment Grade Debt or Preferred Shares

In this eligibility category the issuer must, in effect, have been a reporting issuer not in default under the U.S. *Securities Exchange Act of 1934* (*1934 Act*) for at least twelve calendar months. The issuer must not be an investment company or a commodity pool issuer. The securities issued must be either non-convertible or not convertible for at least one year. If the securities are convertible into equity securities, those securities must have a public float of at least U.S. $75 million prior to the filing of the MJDS prospectus.

2) Rights Issue

The issuer must have a thirty-six month *1934 Act* reporting history, but must not be an investment company or a commodity pool issuer. The issuer must have a class of its securities listed on the NYSE, the American Stock Exchange, or the Nasdaq National Market for at least twelve months. The rights themselves must satisfy certain requirements relating to their terms, exercise, and transferability.

3) Other Cases

In this category, in addition to the twelve-month reporting requirement and the investment company and commodity pool issuer restrictions, the issuer's equity shares must have a public float of not less than U.S. $75 million.[40]

F. MUTUAL FUNDS

1) Overview

A mutual fund is a type of pooled investment vehicle that is organized as a corporation or, more commonly in Canada, as a trust.[41] Individual investors buy securities issued by the mutual fund. Those securities are in the form of shares, if the mutual fund is organized as a corporation,

---

40   National Instrument 71-101, above note 37, s. 3.1.

41   The fact that most Canadian mutual funds are organized as trusts prompted the CSA to commission a background paper in relation to its recent mutual fund concept proposal discussed further below. See David Stevens, "Trust Law Implications of Proposed Regulatory Reform of Mutual Fund Governance Structures," available online at <http://www.osc.gov.on.ca> (site accessed: 12 March 2002).

or in the form of mutual fund "units," if the fund is a trust. The mutual fund, with the advice of its expert asset managers, then uses the money acquired from the sale of its own securities to purchase securities issued by other businesses. The defining characteristic of a mutual fund, for the purposes of the *OSA*, is that the value of the mutual fund's own investments (adjusted by the fees the fund must pay to its managers and advisers) is reflected in the value of the mutual fund shares or units held by the fund's investors. There are two basic types of mutual funds: closed-end and opened-end. A closed-end fund sells a specific number of shares or units and invests the proceeds from the sale of those units. Unitholders who no longer wish to invest in the mutual fund must dispose of their investment by selling their units to other investors. The mutual fund itself will not generally redeem or repurchase outstanding units. Opened-end funds, which appear to be the more common type of mutual fund in Canada, offer their shares or units to the public continuously, pursuant to special securities-offering rules. The shares or units sold by opened-end funds typically entitle the holder to redeem at any time on relatively short notice. Holders who no longer wish to invest in an opened-end fund need not find another investor who is willing to buy their units because the mutual fund itself will buy back the units at a price based upon the net asset value of the fund. Investment by Canadians in mutual funds is significant. According to a CSA Concept Proposal released in March 2002, as of 31 January 2002, $427 billions were invested in more than 2,500 Canadian mutual funds.[42]

2) The Benefits of Mutual Funds

The advantages of mutual funds, especially for smaller "retail" investors, are many and are usually thought to include the following:

- Persons investing small amounts can gain the benefits of portfolio diversification without high transaction costs (especially trade execution).
- Persons investing small amounts can benefit from professional portfolio management that is usually available, on a personal basis, only to investors with a high net worth (i.e., wealthy investors). This facilitates, among other things, investment in equity as opposed to debt securities, which is particularly important for long-term investment because equity offers greater opportunities for long-term capital appreciation.

---

42 See CSA Concept Proposal 81-402, "Striking a New Balance: A Framework for Regulating Mutual Funds and Their Managers" (1 March 2002), available online at <http://www.osc.gov.on.ca> (site accessed: 12 March 2002).

- Investors in some mutual funds, such as money market mutual funds, can bypass financial intermediaries, such as banks, and so earn higher returns on their shorter-term savings.

3) Regulatory Concerns Raised by Mutual Funds

Investors, fund promoters, and regulators recognize the potential benefits of mutual funds. However, the same attributes that make mutual funds attractive to small retail investors may also lead to potential abuses and thus raise regulatory concerns. Among those regulatory concerns are the following:

- *Investors' Disclosure Needs*: Mutual funds are often sold to the least sophisticated investors whose need to receive clear and plain financial disclosure may be different from that of the average equity investor. Such investors in mutual funds might be expected to respond differently in the event of sharp, unexpected changes in securities markets than more sophisticated investors.
- *Calculation of Fund's Net Asset Value*: Because (opened-end) mutual funds entitle investors to redeem their mutual fund units for cash, based on their proportionate share of the fund's net asset value (NAV), it is crucial that the calculation of NAV be accurate.
- *Disclosure of Potential Investment Risk*: Mutual funds are often marketed to customers of financial institutions who may purchase them as a substitute for insured fixed-income investments. This possibility raises concerns as to the adequacy of disclosure of potential investment risk.
- *Meaningful Comparison of Funds*: Investors may select a mutual fund based upon that fund's historical performance or "track record." As the number of funds available in the market increases, competition for the investors' funds has escalated, making it critical for fund performance figures to be reported reliably and in a form that permits investors to compare funds meaningfully.
- *Management Expense Ratio (MER)*: Mutual fund returns to investors depend not only on the success of asset managers in choosing securities, but also on the level of fees that are charged to the fund for such portfolio management, investment, investment advice, and other administrative services. The mutual fund's pre-tax expenses, expressed as a percentage of a fund's average net asset value, is known as the management expense ratio (MER). To ensure that investors can properly compare the MER of one fund to the MER of other funds, there must be rules in place to ensure that MER is calculated and disclosed in the same way by all funds.

- *Duties of Mutual Fund Managers*: The very structure of mutual funds makes certain conflicts almost inevitable. Mutual funds are typically created by mutual fund companies that make profits by providing administrative management and, in particular, asset management services to the funds. The trustees of each mutual fund trust or the directors of each mutual fund corporation are actually under a duty to act in the best interests of their investors, not the company that may have created those funds. Yet, if an asset manager affiliated with the original fund promoter is underperforming, concerns may arise as to how easy it may be for the fund to dismiss the manager or otherwise to deal with the problem.
- *Effect of Sales Commissions on Mutual Fund Managers*: Because mutual funds are typically sold on commission, the incentives of mutual fund sales people may not always be aligned with the objectives of their customers.
- *Use of High-risk Investment Strategies*: As the mutual fund business has become more competitive, pressures upon mutual fund managers to produce high short-term returns may lead to high-risk investment strategies and the use of highly leveraged products, which might not be understood fully by the small retail purchasers of the mutual fund units.

Although the regulatory initiatives relating to mutual funds are complex and detailed, they may, for the most part, be understood as attempts to deal with many of the above issues. Canadian regulators have commissioned a number of studies on the Canadian mutual fund industry in the past several years that have identified these and other concerns.[43]

The *OSA* and the *OSA Regulation*[44] both have provisions dealing specifically with mutual funds. The most recent major regulatory instruments that have been introduced in the mutual fund area are as follows:

---

43   Three of the most important of these studies are Glorianne Stromberg, *Regulatory Strategies for the Mid-'90s — Recommendations for Regulating Investment Funds in Canada* (Canadian Securities Administrators, 1995); Glorianne Stromberg, *Investment Funds in Canada and Consumer Protection: Strategies for the Millennium* (Ottawa: Office of Consumer Affairs, Industry Canada, 1998); Stephen I. Erlichman, *Making it Mutual: Aligning the Interests of Investors and Managers — Recommendations for a Mutual Fund Governance Regime for Canada* (Canadian Securities Administrators, 2000). A fourth study was prepared by staff of the Ontario Securities Commission in connection with the CSA's 2002 mutual fund concept proposal. See "The Canadian Mutual Fund Industry: Its Experience with and Attitudes toward Mutual Fund Regulation: A Background Research Paper to Concept Proposal 81-402 of the Canadian Securities Administrators" (March 2002), above note 42.

44   *OSA Regulation*, R.R.O. 1990, Reg. 1015, Part IV.

- National Instrument 81-101 and Companion Policy 81-101 CP,[45] which concern primarily the prospectus requirements for mutual fund distributions, including Form 81-101 F1 (the form of the mutual fund simplified prospectus) and Form 81-101 F2 (prescribing the contents of a mutual fund annual information form).
- National Instrument 81-102 and Companion Policy 81-102 CP,[46] which are concerned principally with regulation of the mutual funds themselves, including, among other things, provisions relating to investment restrictions, conflict of interest, method of mutual fund sales, calculation of NAV, calculation of MER, sales communications, and prohibited representations.
- National Instrument 81-105 and Companion Policy 81-105 CP[47] which regulate mutual fund sales practices.
- CSA Concept Proposal 81-402, "Striking a New Balance: A Framework for Regulating Mutual Funds and Their Managers" (1 March 2002),[48] proposing a new regulatory framework based upon "five pillars": registration for mutual fund managers, mutual fund governance, product regulation, disclosure and investor rights, and regulatory presence. One of the most significant proposals in this document involves the suggestion that a so-called "governance agency," a body independent of the mutual fund manager, be establised to oversee each manager's management of mutual funds. The majority of the members of such "agencies" would be independent of the fund manager and would have the authority to call a meeting of unitholders, where necessary, to seek the ouster of the wayward fund manager.

G. CONCLUSION

In this chapter we have touched briefly upon several matters generally relevant to the issuance of securities. In the following two chapters, we discuss the process of issuing securities in a compartmentalized fashion, focusing on public offerings in chapter 6 and exempt offerings (or private placements) in chapter 7. After considering the securities law implications of public and private offerings, the reader might find it useful to revisit the subjects discussed in this chapter.

---

45   (2000), 23 OSCB (Supp.) 3.
46   (2000), 23 OSCB (Supp.) 59.
47   (1998), 21 OSCB 2713.
48   Available online, see above note 42.

THE PROSPECTUS PROCESS

A. INTRODUCTION

1) The Cost of Assembling a Prospectus

When an issuer makes a public offering of its securities, it must prepare a prospectus. A prospectus is a lengthy, detailed disclosure document containing information about the company issuing the securities. In theory, the purpose of the prospectus is to provide prospective investors with all the information they need to make informed investment decisions. In practice, however, it is often suggested that the length and complexity of prospectuses make them virtually inaccessible to anyone other than financial analysts and their lawyers. In any event, assembling a prospectus is expensive. The average costs incurred by an issuer for a multi-province offering of approximately $20 million have been estimated at about $400,000.[1] These expenses include

1. the cost of hiring lawyers, underwriters, accountants, and in some cases other professionals, such as mining engineers or appraisers, to assemble the prospectus or to contribute expert reports to be included in the prospectus;

---

1   Paul E.C. Benson, "The Going Public Decision," *Insight*, June 1993.

2. the costs of a "roadshow," which is the promotional tour undertaken by the issuer and its investment bankers to sell the offering to the public;
3. the cost of printing the prospectus;
4. the cost of translating the prospectus into French, if the offering is to be made in Quebec; and
5. the listing fees required by stock exchanges.[2]

In addition, the underwriter(s), typically an investment banking firm or consortium of firms, must be compensated. The underwriter's sales fee is calculated as a percentage of the total value of the offering. Although such fees can range widely, they average about 4 to 7 percent of the offering price. In net, the entire cost of selling a $20 million issue through a prospectus could easily reach or exceed $1.5 million.

Costs are not strictly proportional to the size of the issue. As a general rule, the costs of assembling a prospectus are relatively fixed. Thus, the aggregate cost of floating a $10 million issue through a prospectus is not significantly less than for a $20 million issue. Indeed, underwriting fees tend to rise as the offering gets smaller. Moreover, it is more difficult, and hence more costly, for small issuers to assemble the information required to be put in a prospectus. Thus, the aggregate issue costs, as a proportion of offering proceeds, tend to rise, often dramatically, for smaller offerings.

2) The Prospectus Process

A private placement of securities via one of the prospectus exemptions greatly reduces the costs of financing and, in particular, the legal and other costs described above associated with assembling and filing a prospectus. However, very often an issuer will wish to tap a larger number of potential buyers than is available through a private placement. A public offering, via prospectus, gives an issuer access to the broadest possible market for its securities. This chapter explores the process leading up to, and culminating in, an issuance of securities under a prospectus. We also discuss the four fundamental types of prospectus offerings:

---

2   Note that the issuer need not list on a stock exchange in connection with a public offering of securities, but most public offerings will be accompanied by a stock exchange listing to facilitate secondary market liquidity.

- Long-form prospectus
- Short-form prospectus (formerly referred to as prompt offering prospectus (POP))
- Shelf prospectus
- Post-receipt pricing prospectus (PREP)

B. PRIMARY AND SECONDARY OFFERINGS

There are essentially two types of distribution that require the use of a prospectus: a primary offering and a secondary offering. A primary offering refers to a distribution of securities by the issuer of those securities. A secondary offering refers to a sale of previously issued securities of an issuer, not by the issuer itself, but by a control person (i.e., a person referred to in clause (c) of the definition of "distribution" in subsection 1(1) of the *OSA*). As discussed in chapter 7, sales of securities by control persons may often be completed without a prospectus in reliance upon an appropriate exemption. Where no such exemption is available, or where the selling securityholder wishes to obtain the benefits of selling freely tradeable shares, a prospectus is required. In the case of such a secondary offering, the issuer, its directors, and its officers still need to furnish the same information and certificates even though the securities are being sold by a holder and not by the issuer itself. The issuer, its directors, and its officers are exposed to the same liabilities as in the case of a primary offering by the issuer itself. The Director has authority under the *OSA* to order the issuer, in such cases, to provide the necessary information and material,[3] and to waive compliance with certain provisions where the issuer has not participated, provided that all reasonable efforts have been made to comply with the relevant securities laws and that such a waiver is not otherwise likely to prejudice any person or company.[4]

In the interest of simplicity, however, for the balance of this chapter we focus on prospectus offerings made by the issuer of the securities rather than on prospectus offerings made by a selling securityholder.

---

3   *Securities Act* (Ontario), R.S.O. 1990, c. S.5 [*OSA*], s. 64(1).
4   *Ibid*. s. 64(2).

C. THE UNDERWRITER'S ROLE

1) Introduction

Public offerings of securities invariably involve the participation of one or more investment banking firms performing the role of underwriter, as discussed generally in chapter 4. The underwriter sells the issuer's securities. Although there is no legal requirement to employ an underwriter to effect an offering, practical business reasons compel almost all issuers to do so. The underwriter's expertise is extensive and includes assessing market demand for an issuer's securities; setting the terms of the offering (e.g., the nature of the securities offered); providing advice with respect to changes to the business, management, or ownership structure to make the offering more attractive; and pricing and marketing the offering. Few, if any, issuers can replicate these skills.

In respect of the marketing function, the underwriter will have developed contacts over a period of years with potential buyers of the issuer's securities, including institutional and retail buyers. Primary market offerings, however, are still sold overwhelmingly to institutions such as pension and other funds. These contacts allow the underwriter to sell securities much more expeditiously than the issuer can by itself.

2) Types of Underwritings

There are generally four different types of underwritings:

- Best efforts
- Firm commitment
- Bought deal
- Standby underwriting (standby underwritings are discussed together with rights offerings in chapter 5 and are not discussed in this chapter)

a) Best Efforts

In a best-efforts underwriting, the underwriter acts as a sales agent, promising to use reasonable efforts to sell as much of the issue as it is able. In this type of "underwriting," the contract between the issuer and the underwriter is styled, revealingly, as an "Agency Agreement," rather than an "Underwriting Agreement." The underwriter collects a commission on only those securities that it actually sells to third-party purchasers.

b) Firm Commitment

In a firm-commitment underwriting, the underwriter agrees to purchase the entire issue of securities. If the underwriter is unable to resell
the securities to its various clients, it cannot return the unsold securities to the issuer. The underwriter's compensation is, in effect, the difference between the price at which it buys the securities and the price
at which it resells them to the public. However, in the case of a sale of
equities, the underwriting agreement between the issuer and the
underwriters typically provides that the underwriters purchase the
securities from the issuer at the issue price (i.e., the same price at
which they are sold to purchasers pursuant to the prospectus), and
then receive from the issuer an underwriting fee based on a percentage
of that price. At the closing, payment of the underwriting fee might be
satisfied in one of two ways, depending upon the terms of the underwriting agreement. The issuer might deliver a separate cheque to the
underwriter or, alternatively, the underwriter might deduct the fee in
calculating the amount that must be paid to the issuer to purchase the
offered securities. Because the prospectus under which the securities
are lawfully distributed specifies the price of those securities, the
underwriters must sell the securities in the distribution at that price. In
the case of certain "hot issues" (i.e., offerings that are perceived by
investors to be especially attractively priced and therefore expected to
experience significant gains in the secondary markets), it would
undoubtedly be possible for underwriters distributing the offering to
find buyers for underwritten securities willing to pay prices higher
than the prospectus price. However, underwriters are expressly forbidden, by IDA By-law No. 29, from selling securities in the course of a
distribution at any such higher price.[5]

The usual firm-commitment underwriting begins with the issuer
approaching the underwriter to assist in an issuance of securities. The
underwriter assembles a team of employees and/or outside consultants
with the various types of expertise described earlier in section (1). The
underwriter plays a key role in assembling the preliminary and final
prospectuses, determining the terms of the offering, and pricing the
offering. Although underwriters are retained and paid by the issuer,
they also indirectly represent the interests of the ultimate purchasers of
the securities. This delicate balancing of roles is especially obvious in

---

5   Investment Dealers Association of Canada, By-law 29.2, available online at
    <http://www.ida.ca/Files/Regulation/RuleBook/RuleBook_en.pdf> (site accessed:
    8 April 2002).

the case of public debt offerings. The underwriters must seek from the issuer the same kinds of assurances, security, and covenants that a lender normally seeks from a borrower, notwithstanding that the underwriters do not expect to hold a significant part of the issuer's debt once the distribution process is complete.

c)   Bought Deal

The bought deal is really a species or subcategory of the firm-commitment underwriting. In Canada, the key distinction between the bought deal and the more conventional (sometimes called "marketed") deal is that the underwriter's contractual obligation to purchase the issuer's securities occurs earlier in the process. In a traditional marketed deal, the underwriter is under no obligation to purchase securities from the issuer until the underwriting agreement is signed, which is typically immediately before the final prospectus is filed and receipted. In a bought deal, however, the underwriting agreement is signed earlier, typically at the time of the preliminary prospectus.[6] The bought deal imposes additional risk upon underwriting firms and is subject to slightly different pre-marketing rules, as discussed further below. What should also be clear is that a bought deal is only possible in circumstances where a prospectus can be filed quickly. Accordingly, bought deals occur only in the context of short-form prospectus offerings, as discussed later in this chapter.

d)   Structure of an Underwriting Agreement

An underwriting agreement between an issuer of securities and an underwriting firm (or firms) typically deals with the following five fundamental matters.

i)   Issuer's Corporate Representations and Warranties

The issuer typically provides an extensive series of representations and warranties relating to, among other things, its legal status and the due authorization and issuance of the securities to be sold.

---

6   The phrase "bought deal" is not defined in securities laws, but is defined by the Investment Dealers Association of Canada, *Ibid.* By-law 29.13, to mean: "a transaction pursuant to an agreement under which an underwriter, as principal, agrees to purchase securities from an issuer or selling security-holder with a view to a distribution of such securities pursuant to the POP System ... or comparable system in any Canadian province and such agreement is entered into prior to or contemporaneously with the filing of the preliminary short-form prospectus." For a detailed discussion of bought deals, see Gordon du Val, "The Bought Deal in Canada" (1996) 26 Can. Bus. L.J. 358.

ii) Issuer's Transaction Obligations

The issuer agrees to take a number of specific steps (including completing the prospectus and providing any necessary amendments) to facilitate the successful filing of the prospectus and the subsequent completion of the offering. The issuer's obligations also include payment of the underwriters' fees and observing a "blackout" period during which the issuer agrees not to issue any other securities of the same type as those to be sold under the prospectus.

iii) Underwriters' Transaction Obligations (and "Market-out" and "Disaster-out" Clauses)

In a firm-commitment underwriting, the underwriters' primary obligation, of course, is to purchase the securities from the issuer at the time of closing. That obligation is typically subject to one or both of two sorts of limitations: a "market-out" clause and a "disaster-out" clause. A "market-out" provision in the underwriting agreement permits the underwriters to terminate their obligations if the state of the financial markets is such that the underwriters, acting reasonably, determine that the securities cannot be marketed profitably. A "disaster-out" clause permits underwriters to terminate their obligations if a significant event affects financial markets or the issuer's business. The distinction between "market-out" and "disaster-out" clauses is especially important in the context of margin requirements, discussed in chapter 4. Where an underwriting agreement includes only a disaster-out clause, the margin requirement for the distributed securities is 50 percent of the normal margin from the date of commitment until the settlement date or expiry of the clause. Where the agreement contains a market-out clause, however, there are no margin requirements in respect of the underwritten securities until the expiry of the clause or the settlement date. If the underwriting agreement contains neither clause, normal margin is required from the date of the commitment. Where margin is required, the requirement may be further reduced where a chartered bank has provided an underwriting loan facility.[7]

In *Retrieve Resources Ltd.* v. *Canaccord Capital Corp.*,[8] the British Columbia Supreme Court considered the meaning of the phrase "the state of the financial markets" in a market-out clause upon which a securities firm sought to rely in terminating an agency agreement. The key interpretive question was whether the phrase referred to financial markets *in general* (requiring the agent to demonstrate some general down-

---

7   Investment Dealers Association of Canada, *Ibid.* Rule 100.5.
8   [1994] B.C.J. No. 1897 (S.C.)

turn) or merely to the market for that particular issuer's shares. The court preferred the latter interpretation, holding that the "only sensible interpretation is that the clause is intended to afford protection to the placee in reference to the specific shares to be placed."[9] It should be noted that the facts in this case were rather unusual. The agreement in which the market-out clause appeared was a best-efforts agency agreement, not a firm-commitment underwriting. Moreover, the significance of the termination of the agency agreement was not simply that the securities firm's obligations ended. Instead, a previously arranged sale of the issuer's securities — which had been subject to the agency agreement remaining in force — was terminated when the agent purported to exercise the market-out clause. Nevertheless, *Retrieve Resources* remains one of the few Canadian authorities on the interpretation of the market-out clause.

iv) Prospectus Filing and Securities Sale Closing Conditions
The agreement specifies the steps to be taken and the documents to be delivered at the time of filing the final prospectus and, later, at the time of the actual closing of the transaction, when the securities are delivered to the underwriters against payment by the underwriters of the sale proceeds.

v) Issuer's Indemnity of the Underwriters
It is a standard feature of underwriting agreements to include an indemnity given by the issuer in favour of the underwriters, the underwriters' agents, and the underwriters' employees for any losses that may be incurred by them on the issuer's account.

D. BASIC STAGES OF A PUBLIC OFFERING

In the discussion that follows, it is important to keep in mind the basic steps involved in a public offering. At the most fundamental level, a public offering consists of five stages:

- The initial discussions/negotiations between the issuer and the underwriter
- The drafting and filing of a preliminary prospectus
- The drafting and filing of a final prospectus
- The closing of the transaction for the purchase and sale of the offered securities

9   *Ibid.* at para. 53.

• The end of the distribution period

We will consider some of the important legal issues encountered during each of these critical stages.

E. WHAT CAN BE DONE BEFORE THE PRELIMINARY PROSPECTUS IS FILED?

1) Limitations on Testing the Waters

Before going to the trouble and expense of preparing a prospectus, as described in the introduction to this chapter, management of the issuer often determines whether there is a market for the securities of the firm. Or perhaps the issuer has gone to an underwriter to raise money in the public market, and the underwriter wants to determine the demand for the firm's securities. Can this be done?

Amazingly enough, the answer is that the law allows very little "testing the waters" to determine market demand, by either the issuer, or an agent, such as an underwriter, acting on its behalf. This is because of the definitions of "trade" and "distribution" in the *OSA*. A "trade" is defined to include "any act, advertisement, solicitation, conduct or negotiation directly or indirectly in furtherance of [a sale by the issuer]."[10] Testing the waters to determine market demand is commonly thought to be an act in furtherance of a sale (i.e., the ultimate sale of the issuer's securities). In the United States, when such activities are undertaken before a registration statement is filed with the SEC and becomes effective, it is sometimes referred to as "gun jumping."[11]

These broad definitions have two consequences. First, once an act is a trade, the registration requirement comes into play.[12] Although an issuer might register itself as a "security issuer,"[13] the requirements are onerous, and few issuers wish to go this route. Second, because the trade relates to a primary market issuance of the issuer's securities, it is also a "distribution," and every non-exempt distribution requires a prospectus.[14] The net result is that — subject to very limited exceptions — the issuer must file a preliminary prospectus before it or the under-

---

10   *OSA*, above note 3, s.1(1) (definition of "trade).

11   See, e.g., Louis Loss and Joel Seligman, *Securities Regulation*, 3d ed., vol. 1 (Frederick, MD: Aspen Law & Business, 1998) at 442–63.

12   See, e.g., *OSA*, above note 3, s. 25.

13   See, e.g., *OSA Regulation*, R.R.O. 1990, Reg. 1015, s. 98.10.

14   *OSA*, above note 3, s. 53(1).

writer can start testing the waters. As detailed further below, a preliminary prospectus is a draft of the issuer's prospectus that is filed with the securities authorities.

There are two rationales behind forbidding issuers and their agents from testing the waters. One is the danger of insider trading. An issue of new securities by a firm that is already public (or, more technically, is a reporting issuer) very often affects the price at which the issuer's outstanding securities trade. For example, on average, common shares drop in price by about 1 to 2 percent on the announcement of a new issue.[15] If testing the waters were permitted, it would involve the communication of privileged information (i.e., the information that the firm expects to make a public offering of securities) to a select few (those canvassed to determine market demand). This creates a danger that those who are canvassed will misuse the information to sell their existing holdings of the issuer's securities to avoid a loss (i.e., that they will engage in insider trading, as discussed in more detail in chapter 8).

The second rationale behind the broad definition of trade is to enable securities regulators to step in at an early stage — before there is a consummated sale — to prevent wrongdoing, such as high-pressure sales tactics or other exploitation of prospective investors who received inadequate information about the securities they are being tempted to purchase. The danger of this sort of abuse associated with testing the market, however, is minimal. Testing the market involves information gathering, rather than high-pressure sales tactics (although, there is some danger that the issuer or its agent may misrepresent the firm's prospects in order to pump up the potential market for the firm's securities). The insider-trading rationale likely plays a larger role in the policy against testing the waters than does the prevention-of-abuse rationale.

It is important to recognize, however, that sensible limits must be placed on the meaning of "any act ... in furtherance of [a sale]." Read with literal strictness, a trade and a distribution occur because the trade relates to a primary market issuance when the issuer approaches an underwriter with a view to making a primary offering of securities. This activity, therefore, ought to be forbidden until the preliminary

---

15   This is commonly thought to be due to a "signalling effect." The signal arises from the fact that management will be more likely to effect a new issuance of securities when it has private information (i.e., information not reflected in the trading price) that the firm's securities are overvalued. That way, it can use a market price that is "too high" to sell new claims at a price that is very advantageous for the existing shareholders.

prospectus is filed.[16] However, it is virtually unheard of for an issuer to file a preliminary prospectus before contacting an underwriter. The common practice is for the issuer to have discussions with the underwriter well before the preliminary prospectus is filed. Perhaps most important, from a policy perspective, there is no reason why issuers should *not* be able to do this. In this case, the number of people receiving inside information is small, and insider trading by members of the underwriting team would severely damage the underwriter's reputation. For this reason, underwriters strictly police their employees to ensure that they do not engage in insider trading. More fundamentally, underwriters could not perform the role expected of them by the financial community and, indeed, by securities regulators if the *OSA* were read in this fashion. Thus, no court or administrative tribunal would interpret the legislation in such a restrictive way. This is a good illustration of how, and why, the policy underlying securities legislation must be used to interpret the statute sensibly.

The primary rationale against testing the waters — the prevention of insider trading — does not apply in the case of a private company that is "going public" (i.e., offering its securities to the public for the first time). For a number of reasons, insider trading in such cases is unlikely. First, there is no public market for the firm's securities. Without a public market, insider traders cannot easily engage in anonymous insider trading. Although insider trading is still possible in shares of private companies, it is much easier to detect and to trace. Second, the persons canvassed with a view to stating their interest in the issuer's securities are not likely to be the existing shareholders, mitigating the dangers of the unlawful selling of securities described earlier. Third, the price impact of an initial public offering on the issuer's outstanding shares is likely to be different than in the case of a follow-on offering because the creation of a trading market for an issuer's shares should have a positive, rather than a negative, effect.

In short, the law relating to "testing the waters" ought to draw a distinction between firms that are already public and those that are going public. Currently, it does not, despite recommendations that the

---

16 Even internal discussions among management as to whether a primary market offering should be made could be interpreted as an act in furtherance of a trade, and, hence, a trade. It is interesting to note that under U.S. federal securities laws such discussions and negotiations between an issuer and an underwriter that would otherwise trigger a registration requirement are expressly excluded from the definition of "offer to buy." (See U.S. *Securities Act* of 1933, 15 U.S.C. § 77a *et seq.* at s. 2(3).)

law be changed to reflect this distinction,[17] and despite the fact that U.S. law currently allows first-time issuers to test the waters in some circumstances.[18]

Closely related to concerns about "gun jumping" or "testing the water" are concerns about market grooming and the consequent restrictions on pre-offering contact with the media. Regulators are concerned about statements made by issuers around the time of a public offering that could be seen as attempts to "hype" the issuing firm in general or the specific securities to be offered. Most Canadian securities practitioners are familiar with the 1986 *Cambior* matter, in which the OSC Director reprimanded an underwriter and two leading law firms for failing to prevent a corporate issuer for whom they were acting from placing advertisements in three newspapers shortly after filing a preliminary prospectus.[19]

At the same time, not all media communications could, or should, be forbidden because ongoing disclosure of material information is also a requirement of securities law for public companies. Securities regulators have tried to provide some guidance to issuers in drawing the distinction between permissible and impermissible pre-offering (or waiting period) media communications in Uniform Act Policy 2-13[20] as well as in OSC Staff Notices 47-701[21] and 47-703.[22] Briefly, these documents emphasize that the only marketing material that may be distributed during the waiting period is material that complies with the rather bare-bones rules of clause 65(2)(a) of the *OSA*, and that such restrictions also apply prior to the filing of the preliminary prospectus. In the case of media reports, which may, after all, be initiated by journalists and not by the issuer itself, OSC staff has indicated that it is still the responsibility of the issuer "to take appropriate precautions to ensure that media coverage which can reasonably be considered to be in furtherance of a distribution of securities does not occur after a decision has been made to file a preliminary prospectus or during the waiting period."[23] To provide some additional guidance to issuers, OSC staff

---

17   See, e.g., Jeffrey G. MacIntosh, "Regulatory Barriers to Raising Capital for Small Firms," (1994) 6 *Alert* 57–64; *Report of the Task Force on Small Business Financing* (1996), 19 OSCB 5753.

18   See, e.g., in the context of a Regulation A offering, Rule 254, 17 C.F.R. 230.254.

19   *Notice Re Cambior Inc.* (1986), 9 OSCB 3225.

20   (1980), 3 OSCB 234.

21   Originally published (1987), 10 OSCB 2831 (retained and renumbered, 20 April 2001).

22   Originally published (1988) 11 OSCB 1098 (retained and renumbered, 20 April 2001).

23   OSC Staff Notice 47-701, above note 21.

has invited issuers to consider a release of the U.S. Securities and Exchange Commission on the matter.[24] Finally, Canadian securities regulators warned issuers that "posting of new information on a website during a period of distribution may be construed as advertising" and thus could attract regulatory scrutiny.[25]

2) Bought Deal

The bought deal provides the one exception to the general rule against testing the waters. Recall that a bought deal typically begins with an underwriter approaching (or responding to a request from) an issuer that is eligible to use the short-form prospectus rules (a "POP eligible" issuer, to use former terminology). The underwriter proposes purchasing, in a firm-commitment underwriting, a large block of the issuer's securities. In the usual form of firm commitment underwriting, the underwriting agreement is signed at the time the final prospectus is filed. However, in a bought deal, the contract is signed even before the filing of a preliminary prospectus, with a view to filing the preliminary prospectus within two days. The underwriter is allowed to solicit "expressions of interest" from potential purchasers during the two-day window between the signing of the underwriting agreement and the issuance of a receipt for the preliminary prospectus.[26] This rule facilitates bought-deal offerings by allowing the underwriter to reduce the risk of the offering to a more manageable level by canvassing potential purchasers.

F. THE PRELIMINARY PROSPECTUS AND THE WAITING PERIOD

1) What Is a Preliminary Prospectus?

The preliminary prospectus is a draft of the final prospectus that must be delivered in connection with a public offering of securities.[27] It must

---

24   Ibid.

25   National Policy 47-201 (1999), 22 OSCB 8174.

26   National Instrument 44-101 (2000), 23 OSCB (Supp.) 867, s. 14.1. In order to qualify for this privileged treatment, the underwriter and issuer must not only enter into an "enforceable agreement" that requires, among other things, that a preliminary short-form prospectus be filed and a receipt obtained therefor within two business days, but must also immediately issue a press release announcing the transaction.

27   OSA, above note 3, s. 53(1).

"substantially comply" with the rules governing final prospectuses.[28] Once the issuer files the preliminary prospectus with securities regulators, the "waiting period" begins.[29] More technically, the waiting period is the time between the filing of the preliminary prospectus (strictly speaking, the time of issuance by the regulators of a receipt therefor[30]) and the issuance of a receipt for the final prospectus. The underwriter may commence sales of the securities only after the issuance of a receipt for a final prospectus.

Submitting the prospectus in draft form allows the regulators a chance to examine the prospectus to determine whether it complies with the applicable requirements. During the waiting period, OSC staff who have reviewed the preliminary prospectus issue comment letters to the issuer. The issuer is obliged to respond in an effort to resolve any regulatory concerns so that when the issuer files the final prospectus (with any necessary amendments), it can obtain a receipt promptly. As explained in section H below, however, it is no longer the practice of the OSC to review every preliminary prospectus filed.

2) Length of the Waiting Period

The legislation provides that the waiting period shall be at least ten days. The purpose of this requirement appears to be so that the regulators have an adequate opportunity to vet the prospectus. That is not, however, the only justification for the waiting period. The Kimber Committee, upon whose recommendation the mandatory, ten-day minimum waiting period was introduced, suggested that such a period would be useful because it would permit prospective purchasers to "study the merits of the security issue" and "permit underwriters to test the market."[31]

Nonetheless, in the cases of a short-form prospectus (or POP), a shelf prospectus, and an MJDS offering, the rules provide for clearance

---

28   *Ibid.* s. 54.

29   *Ibid.* s. 65.

30   The legislation requires the Director to issue a receipt for the preliminary prospectus upon filing. See *OSA, Ibid.* s. 55. In other words, there is no discretion on the part of the regulators, as there is in the case of the final prospectus, to refuse to issue a receipt for a preliminary prospectus. Despite this requirement, the *OSA* gives the Director the power to cease-trade any of the permitted trading activity in the waiting period if the preliminary prospectus does not comply in a material way with regulatory requirements. (See *OSA, Ibid.* s. 68.)

31   *The Report of the Attorney General's Committee on Securities Legislation in Ontario* (Toronto: Queen's Printer, 1965) [*Kimber Report*] at para. 5.28.

of the prospectus by regulators in fewer than ten days. Issuers that are eligible for these alternative prospectus regimes are large issuers that are well-known to the market and are likely to have sophisticated accounting, legal, and information systems in place. The prospectuses of such issuers generally require minimal review by securities administrators.

As a matter of practice, the waiting period for POP issuers may indeed be as short as a few days. For small companies issuing securities for the first time in public markets, however, the waiting period averages several months and has been known to be upwards of one year. Such issuers frequently have unsophisticated accounting, legal, and information systems, making it difficult to assemble the required information to the standard demanded by securities regulators.

3) Activities Permitted during the Waiting Period

During the waiting period, it is unlawful to sell any of the securities. However, it is permissible for the underwriters to distribute copies of the preliminary prospectus;[32] to solicit "expressions of interest" from prospective purchasers, provided that the underwriter delivers a copy of the preliminary prospectus to the prospective purchasers either before the solicitation or after a prospective purchaser has expressed interest;[33] and to distribute certain limited notices and advertisements, provided any such communication indicates how a copy of the preliminary prospectus may be obtained.[34] As indicated earlier, OSC Staff Notices 47-701 and 47-703[35] attempt to provide some guidance on the sorts of communications permitted during the waiting period.

4) Burden of Disclosure Requirements

The costs of issuing securities in public markets are relatively fixed. The legal, accounting, and other compliance costs of going public do not rise proportionately with the proceeds of the offering. For this reason, the burden of mandatory disclosure requirements tends to fall more heavily on small issuers.[36]

The greatest cost to smaller issuers is likely not the direct cost of regulatory compliance, but rather the opportunity cost associated with compliance. Small issuers often have fewer support staff. In particular,

32   *OSA*, above note 3, s. 65(2)(b).
33   *Ibid.* s. 65(2)(c).
34   *Ibid.* s. 65(2)(a).
35   Above notes 21 and 22.
36   See e.g., MacIntosh, above note 17.

they have fewer dedicated accounting, legal, and information system employees who can participate in assembling the required information. This means that senior managers are often drawn deeper into the process of prospectus assembly than are the managers of large firms. The diversion of managerial focus away from the business can have severe adverse consequences for the business.

5) Preliminary Prospectus Contains Most of What the Final Prospectus Will Contain

The preliminary prospectus contains essentially all of the information that the final prospectus will contain (see below). The preliminary prospectus, however, may omit the auditor's report(s), as well as information concerning (or derived from) the price of the offering.[37] Given that the length of the waiting period can be somewhat unpredictable, the former omission is made because by the time of issuance of the final receipt, the issuer may have to update the financial information contained in the prospectus. The issuer and its underwriter omit the price of the offering because they do not wish to price the issue until just before the receipt for the final prospectus is issued. Market receptivity, whether determined by firm-specific or marketwide factors, may change between the time of filing the preliminary prospectus and the final prospectus.

G. CONTENT OF A PROSPECTUS

Both final and preliminary prospectuses (with the exceptions noted above) must comply with regulatory requirements found in a number of sources.

1) The *OSA*

a)   The Overriding Duty of Full, True, and Plain Disclosure
Most of the content requirements for the prospectus are now prescribed, in Ontario, in the OSC rules. However, the *OSA* contains the overarching requirement that the prospectus supply "full, true and plain disclosure of all material facts relating to the securities issued or

---

37   *OSA*, above note 3, s. 54(1) & (2).

proposed to be distributed."[38] Thus, in deciding what to include in the prospectus, securities lawyers must have regard not merely to those items that are specifically required by the *OSA*, the *OSA Regulation*, and the OSC Rules. Securities lawyers must also make difficult judgments about what *other* information is sufficiently material to be included in the prospectus.

b) No Half-truths

The definition of "misrepresentation" plays a significant role in determining what to include in the prospectus. The *OSA* states that a misrepresentation means not only an untrue statement of a material fact, but also "an omission to state a material fact that ... is necessary to make a statement not misleading in the light of the circumstances in which it was made."[39] This latter part makes half-truths or equivocations (statements that are literally true, but misleading) into misrepresentations.

Suppose, for example, that an issuer with a ten-year life made a profit of $40,000 in its first year and nothing in the subsequent nine years. It would be literally true to say that the issuer's profits averaged $4,000 per year. But, for obvious reasons, this half-truth is highly misleading and amounts to a misrepresentation under Canadian securities law.

c) The Certificate Requirements

The *OSA* further requires that the issuer include a certificate in the prospectus, signed by the "chief executive officer, the chief financial officer, and, on behalf of the board of directors, by any two directors of the issuer, other than the foregoing, duly authorized to sign, and any person or company who is a promoter of the issuer."[40] The certificate must declare that "[t]he foregoing constitutes full, true and plain disclosure of all material facts relating to the securities offered."

Any underwriter in a contractual relationship with the issuer must also supply a certificate for inclusion in the prospectus. The underwriter's certificate must state that "[t]o the best of our knowledge, information and belief, the foregoing constitutes full, true and plain disclosure of all material facts relating to the securities offered."[41]

All of those (both individuals and firms) who sign a certificate and the issuers' directors, whether or not they sign, are potentially civilly liable for any misrepresentation in the prospectus, as described in more detail in section K below. The purpose of these requirements is to

38   *Ibid.* s. 56(1).
39   *Ibid.* s. 1(1) (definition of "misrepresentation").
40   *Ibid.* s. 58(1).
41   *Ibid.* s. 59(1).

induce care in assembling the prospectus on the part of the directors of
the issuer and those who sign the certificates.

Note the difference in form between the issuer's certificate and the
underwriter's certificate. The reason for this difference is that the issuer
has direct access to all pertinent information, while the underwriter
has only secondary access (i.e., the underwriters and their lawyers can
only ascertain the truth of matters by questioning the issuer's officers
and employees).

2) Requirements in the Regulations, Rules, and Forms

The *OSA* states that the prospectus "shall comply with the requirements
of Ontario securities law."[42] which includes the *OSA*, the *OSA Regulation*,
the OSC rules, and decisions of the OSC or the Director. Virtually all of
the additional prospectus requirements for long-form prospectuses are
now found in National Instrument 41-101,[43] Rule 41-501 (plus the
accompanying forms), and Companion Policy 41-501 CP.[44] Rule 41-501
requires that, generally speaking, a prospectus must be prepared in
accordance with Form 41-501 F1.[45] Thus, the content requirements in
the mandated form are made a part of the Rule explicitly, and any breach
of these requirements is a breach of Ontario securities law.

3) Decision of the OSC or the Director

Ontario securities law includes any decision by the OSC or the
Director. Thus, strictly on an *ad hoc* basis and applying to a particular
issuance of securities,[46] the OSC or the Director may require that additional information be disclosed in the prospectus.

4) Policy Statements

In Ontario and other jurisdictions in which regulators have a rule-making authority, policy statements may no longer prescribe the content of
a prospectus (or indeed create any other rule-like proscriptions[47]). In
jurisdictions lacking rule-making authority, policy statements continue

---

42   *Ibid.* s. 56(1).
43   (2000), 23 OSCB 761.
44   (2000), 22 OSCB (Supp.) 767ff.
45   Rule 41-501, *Ibid.* s. 1.1, and *OSA*, above note 3, s. 1.1.
46   A ruling that purports to have general application is outside of the jurisdiction
     of the OSC. See *OSA*, above note 3, s. 143.11, and the discussion in chapter 3.
47   *OSA*, above note 3, s. 143.8(1)(d).

to be a source of prospectus requirements, as they were in the rule-making jurisdictions prior to the reformulation of policy statements into rules. After the *Ainsley*[48] decision, discussed in chapter 3, the legal pedigree of prospectus content requirements found in the policy statements is extremely doubtful.

5) Amending the Prospectus

Once the preliminary prospectus has been filed and a receipt issued by the regulators, if a material *adverse* change occurs before a receipt for the final prospectus is obtained, the issuer must file an amendment to the preliminary prospectus as soon as practicable or within ten days.[49] Once the final prospectus has been filed, the obligation to amend is more onerous. An amendment to the final prospectus must be made in the event of any material change, whether beneficial or adverse, that occurs prior to completion of the distribution, as soon as practicable or within ten days.[50] Recently, the Ontario Superior Court held that a cause of action could be based on financial forecasts contained in a prospectus if, although reasonable at the time they were made, they became misleading between the time the issuer filed the final prospectus and the time of the sale of the securities to investors.[51]

Because the ongoing obligation to amend the prospectus continues as long as the securities are in "distribution," it is important, as a legal matter, to be able to determine when the distribution has been completed. This is not as straightforward a question as it may at first appear. Distribution of the securities does not necessarily end when the transaction is closed (i.e., the time at which the securities are issued, the sale proceeds are paid, and the underwriters receive their fees). The closing of an underwritten offering indicates only that the underwriter has satisfied its contractual obligation to purchase the securities from the issuer. However, sales of the securities by the underwriter to purchasers may continue beyond that date, and the issuer normally has no control over, or even knowledge of, the status of those continuing sales efforts. Accordingly, it is conventional for underwriting agreements to include a covenant on the part of the underwriters to complete the distribution as expeditiously as possible, and to notify the issuer when, in

---

48   *Ainsley Financial Corp. v. Ontario (Securities Commission)* (1993), 14 O.R. (3d) 280 (Gen. Div.), aff'd (1994), 21 O.R. (3d) 104 (C.A.).
49   *OSA*, above note 3, s. 57(1).
50   *Ibid.*
51   *Kerr v. Danier Leather Inc.*, [2001] O.J. No. 950 (Sup. Ct.).

the underwriters' opinion, the distribution has been completed. It should also be noted that, subsection 74(2) of the *OSA* authorizes the OSC to determine whether a distribution of a security has been concluded.[52] Finally, the IDA By-laws provide that "the period of distribution to the public in respect of any securities shall continue until the [IDA] Member shall have notified the applicable securities commission that it has ceased to engage in the distribution to the public of such securities."[53]

H. REVIEW OF THE PROSPECTUS

1) Selective Review of Prospectuses

At one time, the OSC reviewed and commented on every preliminary prospectus filed in respect of a proposed public offering. Receiving and responding to such OSC comment (or deficiency) letters was a routine part of public offerings for issuers, underwriters, and their respective counsel. The OSC and certain other provincial regulators eventually determined, however, that subjecting every prospectus to the same intense review process was not an efficient use of their limited resources. Accordingly, some time ago, these jurisdictions, including Ontario, proposed a system of "selective review."[54] The selective review system has three different standards of review for prospectuses: full review, issue-oriented review (in the case of prospectuses and other filed documents), or no review. (For other periodic disclosure documents, such as AIFs and financial statements, there is yet another standard of review known as "issuer review.") Full review consists of the same sort of detailed review that was formerly undertaken for every prospectus filed. Issue-oriented review, as the name suggests, is a

---

52 There is a second important reason to determine with certainty when the distribution of securities has ended. During the distribution period, the issuer, underwriters, and others are not permitted to purchase or to bid for securities of the same class and series as those being distributed. (See OSC Policy 5.1 (1982), 4 OSCB 418E, as amended, para. 26.) The prohibition prevents market prices from being artificially manipulated. There are limited exceptions to these restrictions that permit dealers to engage in normal market stabilization and "passive market making activities." (*Ibid.* para. 26(x).)

53 Investment Dealers Association of Canada, above note 5, By-law 29.4.

54 See OSC Staff Notice, "Selective Review of Prospectuses and Other Documents" (1994), 17 OSCB 4386. This notice is currently in the process of being reformulated.

review limited to a specific issue or issues. Regulators screen the prospectuses filed and determine the appropriate standard of review to apply. The criteria applied by the OSC to determine the appropriate level of review include subjective and objective components intended to identify the issuers whose prospectuses are most likely to raise matters that would benefit from the review process. For example, prospectuses filed in connection with initial public offerings normally continue to be subject to full review.

2) Mutual Reliance Review System — National Policy 43-201

One of the logistical problems that has long confronted issuers undertaking a public offering in Canada is the requirement to file a prospectus in every province or territory in which securities are to be sold. The use of electronic filing systems in recent years has significantly alleviated the burden of having to complete up to thirteen individual filing packages and to coordinate and respond to multiple regulators. It has also increased the cooperation and coordination of provincial securities regulators. The most recent advance in this respect was the institution of the Mutual Reliance Review System (MRRS) for prospectuses and annual information forms, embodied in National Policy 43-201.[55] Under the MRRS, a prospectus filer designates one securities regulatory authority as its "principal regulator." This principal regulator has the responsibility of reviewing filed documents and has virtually all contact with the filer. Regulators in the other "non-principal" jurisdictions also may review the filed documents and convey any concerns they might have to the principal regulator. In addition, non-principal regulators are permitted to "opt out" of the MRRS system for any particular filing and so deal directly with the filer or the issuer of the securities. Barring such an opt-out, the MRRS allows a prospectus filer to deal with a single regulator. When all comments have been resolved, the prospectus filer receives from that regulator an MRRS decision document, which is functionally equivalent to prospectus receipts issued by every participating securities regulator.[56] Not every provincial or territorial regulator has the resources to act routinely as a principal regulator. Accordingly, the only regulators that have agreed thus far to act as principal regulators are those in British Columbia, Alberta,

---

55   (2002), 25 OSCB 500.
56   The form of legend to appear in the final MRRS decision document for a prospectus is set out in NP 43-201, *Ibid*. s. 7.6(1).

Saskatchewan, Manitoba, Ontario, Quebec, and Nova Scotia.[57] Issuers are not at liberty to select any principal regulator without regard to an appropriate jurisdictional nexus. National Policy 43-201 provides a set of criteria to determine a principal regulator based on geographic links between the issuer's business and the province of the appropriate principal regulator.[58]

Though the MRRS system, operating in conjunction with the SEDAR system, represents a significant improvement over earlier practice, it still falls well short of creating the sort of seamless national filing system that would be possible under a single, national securities law regime.

I. OBLIGATION TO DELIVER PROSPECTUS

Once the final prospectus has been filed with the securities regulators and a receipt has been obtained, the securities may lawfully be sold. However, there would be little point in putting issuers and their advisers to the trouble and expense of producing a detailed disclosure document if prospective purchasers did not have access to it. Accordingly, the *OSA* requires a dealer to deliver a prospectus to anyone who subscribes for or places an order for the offered securities. The prospectus must be delivered either before any sale agreement is entered into or within two days thereafter.[59] Failure to deliver the prospectus constitutes a violation of the Act and could lead to penalties as discussed generally in chapter 11. Moreover, any purchaser who should have received a prospectus has a statutory right of action against the offending dealer for rescission of the purchase contract or damages.[60]

J. PURCHASER'S WITHDRAWAL RIGHTS

The *OSA* provides a special "cooling-off" period for the purchasers of securities in a public offering. Under subsection 71(2), such a purchaser has two business days after receiving the prospectus or any prospectus amendment, to withdraw from any purchase agreement by providing written notice.[61] This withdrawal right is absolute and does

---

57   *Ibid.* s. 3.1.
58   *Ibid.* s. 3.2.
59   *OSA*, above note 3, s. 71(1).
60   *Ibid.* s. 133. (The limitation period for such an action is prescribed by s. 138).
61   *Ibid.* s. 71(2).

not require the purchaser to prove — or even allege — any misrepresentation or deficiency in the prospectus. The rationale behind the withdrawal right is twofold. First, like similar provisions in some other areas of consumer protection law, the withdrawal right is intended to act as an antidote to high-pressure sales techniques. Second, it helps ensure that purchasers have had at least the opportunity to review the detailed information in the prospectus before committing to purchase the securities offered.

K. STATUTORY CIVIL LIABILITY FOR PROSPECTUS MISREPRESENTATIONS

1) Introduction

One of the key aspects of our securities regime is statutory civil liability for prospectus misrepresentations. This statutory provision, found in section 130 of the *OSA*, gives aggrieved investors a weapon in addition to common law actions, such as fraudulent or negligent misrepresentation. Section 130 was introduced chiefly to address the shortcomings in the prior law by providing a remedy, even in cases where prospectus misrepresentations were not made with an intent to defraud, and by relieving investors of the necessity to prove actual reliance upon any such offending statements or omissions. As discussed further immediately below, section 130 prescribes the potential defendants in such a claim, the extent of the defendants' liability, and the available defences.

2) Who May Be Liable?

There are six classes of persons or companies who may be liable under section 130 of the *OSA* to compensate investors who purchased securities pursuant to a prospectus that contained a misrepresentation:

- The issuer (in the case of a primary offering)
- The selling securityholder (in the case of a secondary offering)
- Each underwriter who is required to sign a certificate attached to the prospectus under section 59 of the *OSA*
- Each director of the issuer who was a director at the time the prospectus (or any offending amendment) was filed, even if the director did not sign the issuer's prospectus certificate

- Every person or company who gave consent in connection with reports, opinions, or statements included in the prospectus (e.g., engineers, lawyers, and accountants) but only with respect to the specific reports, opinions, or statements made by them
- Every person or company who signed the prospectus or an amendment, which typically includes the issuer's chief executive officer, chief financial officer, and any promoter,[62] if these people are not already subject to liability under section 130 as directors of the issuer.

3) Extent of Liability

There are three sorts of limitations imposed on the total amount of damages a plaintiff can recover from a defendant in an action under section 130. First, the amount recoverable cannot exceed the offer price of the securities.[63] Second, if a defendant can prove that the damages claimed exceed the "depreciation in value of the [offered] security as a result of the misrepresentation relied upon," the defendant is not liable for any such excess.[64] Third, where an underwriter is a defendant, the underwriter's maximum liability exposure is the portion of the offering price underwritten by that underwriter.[65]

4) Available Defences

a) Defences Available to the Issuer and the Selling Securityholder

The defences available to a claim under section 130 vary depending upon the identity of the defendant. If the defendant is the issuer or the selling holder of the securities sold under the defective prospectus, there is only one available defence: to escape liability, such a defendant must prove that the plaintiff purchased the securities with knowledge of the misrepresentation.[66] No amount of care, good faith, or due diligence on the part of such defendants will otherwise protect them from liability. The rationale behind holding issuers and selling securityhold-

---

62   *Ibid.* s. 58.
63   *Ibid.* s. 130(9).
64   *Ibid.* s. 130(7).
65   *Ibid.* s. 130(6).
66   *Ibid.* s. 130(2).

ers to an almost strict liability standard is clear. Where the prospectus contains a misrepresentation that adversely affects the value of the purchased security, the loss should fall on the seller, not on the buyer.

b) Defences Available to Other Classes of Defendants to Claims under Section 130

i) Non-expertised Portions of the Prospectus

As for other classes of defendants, section 130 draws a distinction between misrepresentations that occur in what might be called the "expertised" portions of the prospectus (i.e., disclosure of statements or opinions of experts) and "non-expertised" portions of the prospectus. Where the misrepresentation occurs in a non-expertised portion of the prospectus, four defences are available: (a) the defendant did not have knowledge of, or did not consent to, the filing of the prospectus;[67] (b) the defendant, upon learning of the misrepresentation, withdrew any consent previously given;[68] (c) any official statement in the prospectus (subsequently found to be false) fairly reflected the official statement, the defendant believed it to be true, and the defendant had no reasonable grounds for believing otherwise;[69] and (d) the defendant did not, in fact, believe there had been a misrepresentation and conducted a "reasonable investigation as to provide reasonable grounds for a belief that there had been no misrepresentation."[70]

The fourth defence is generally referred to as the "due diligence defence" and provides the statutory basis for the extensive due diligence reviews conducted by underwriters and their counsel during the public-offering process. In determining whether grounds for a belief are reasonable, or whether an investigation has been reasonable, the standard to be applied is "that required of a prudent person in the circumstances of the particular case."[71]

---

67 *Ibid.* s. 130(3)(a).
68 *Ibid.* s. 130(3)(b).
69 *Ibid.* s. 130(3)(e).
70 *Ibid.* s. 130(5).
71 *Ibid.* s. 132.

There is some ambiguity surrounding the standard of due diligence and a paucity of helpful Canadian jurisprudence on the issue.[72]

ii) Expertised Portions of the Prospectus

In the case of "expertised" portions of the prospectus, the defences available depend upon whether the defendant is the very expert whose statement is being impugned or is simply a member of one of the other classes of potential defendants under section 130 (other than the issuer or selling securityholder for whom, as explained above, no additional defences are available in any event). The expert has two possible defences. First, the *OSA* provides a kind of *non est factum* defence where the information in the prospectus inaccurately reflected the information that the expert actually furnished. In such a case, the expert is not liable, provided he or she can demonstrate his or her (mistaken) belief, based on reasonable grounds and after a reasonable investigation, that the information in the prospectus fairly represented the original information provided, or that after becoming aware of the mistake, he or she promptly gave notice of the error to the OSC and generally.[73] It seems unlikely that an expert could ever satisfy the first prong of this defence. A "reasonable investigation" would surely include reading the relevant portions of the prospectus. If a material error occurred, it is not clear how the expert could escape liability by claiming not to have discovered that his or her report had been inaccurately presented. Accordingly, it seems that giving notice of the error in such a case constitutes the only practical way for an expert to avoid liability. In other cases, where the expert's information is accurately reproduced, but is, itself, the source of error, section 130 offers the expert a

---

72   In 1997, the Allen Committee asserted that no action had ever proceeded to judgment under s. 130 of the *Securities Act*, citing as authority an article by John J. Chapman, "Class Actions for Prospectus Misrepresentations" (1994) 73 Can. Bar Rev. 492 at 494. See TSE Committee on Corporate Disclosure, *Final Report: Responsible Corporate Disclosure — A Search for Balance* (Toronto: Toronto Stock Exchange, 1997) at 26 [Allen Committee Report].

It might also be noted here that in a recent Canadian case, plaintiffs were permitted to add a law firm and individual partners in that firm as defendants in an action based on negligent misrepresentation in connection with allegedly defective prospectus disclosure. The court indicated that "[e]ffective implementation of [the safeguards in securities legislation] depends to a considerable degree upon the legal counsel who serves in an advisory capacity to the issuers of securities." See *CC&L Dedicated Enterprise Fund (Trustee of) v. Fisherman*, [2001] O.J. No. 4622 at para. 78 (Ont. Sup. Ct.).

73   *OSA*, above note 3, s. 130(3)(d).

due diligence defence that parallels the general due diligence defence described earlier.[74]

Where an expertised portion of a prospectus contains a misrepresentation, it is not only the expert who may be sued. However, non-expert defendants have a defence if they did not believe, and had no reasonable grounds to believe, that there was a misrepresentation.[75] Although the defendants have the burden of proving such belief and reasonable grounds, there is no additional requirement — as there is in the case of non-expertised portions of the prospectus — for the defendants to prove that a reasonable investigation was undertaken to verify the accuracy of the expert's information.

c) Unavailability of Rescission

In a recent Ontario decision,[76] Cumming J. of the Ontario Superior Court held that when securities are purchased from an underwriter in connection with a public offering, the rescission right in section 130 may be exercised only against the underwriter, and not the issuer because, after all, the investor purchases the security from the underwriter, not the issuer.[77] The conclusion would presumably be otherwise in the case of a best efforts or an agency transaction, and the court clearly recognizes the relevance of the agent/underwriter distinction in this context.[78]

L. ALTERNATIVE FORMS OF THE PROSPECTUS

1) Short-form Prospectus

a) Introduction

For certain larger issuers, public offerings of securities can be completed more quickly through the short-form prospectus system. The short-form prospectus system was originally known in Canada as the prompt-offering prospectus (POP) system, and the acronym POP is still

---

74   *Ibid.* s. 130 (4).
75   *Ibid.* s. 130(3)(c).
76   *Kerr v. Danier*, above note 51.
77   *Ibid.* para. 29.
78   *Ibid.* para. 30.

found in many sources, including, at the date of writing, the SEDAR Web site.[79] It is convenient here to refer occasionally to issuers eligible to access this system as POP-eligible issuers, although that term is actually no longer found in the rules that provide for this system.

The requirements for the short-form prospectus system are set out in National Instrument 44-101.[80] The rationale underlying the short-form prospectus system is that for larger issuers about whom a significant body of information is already publicly available and widely disseminated, it makes little sense to require repetition of that information in a prospectus or to submit the prospectus to the same lengthy review process that is needed in the case of issuers about whom less information is widely available. By allowing these large issuers to "piggyback" on previously filed and reviewed public documents, the offering process is expedited, regulatory resources are more efficiently deployed, and the cost of raising capital can be somewhat reduced. The rationale underlying the short-form prospectus accounts for the two fundamental features of the system: (a) the issuer-eligibility criteria, and (b) the AIF and short-form prospectus form requirements.

b)   Issuers Eligible to Use the Short-form Prospectus System

i)   The Rules

Generally speaking, to be eligible to use the short-form prospectus system, an issuer must satisfy the eligibility requirements applicable to one of the following categories of issuer.

1. *Basic issuer:*[81] Eligibility criteria are a minimum twelve-month reporting history, a current AIF, and a market value of outstanding securities of at least $75 million.

2. *Substantial issuer:*[82] Eligibility criteria are that the issuer be a reporting issuer (but with no minimum reporting history required), with a current AIF, and with a market value of outstanding securities of at least $300 million.

3. *Issuer of investment grade non-convertible securities:*[83] Eligibility criteria are a minimum twelve-month reporting history, a current AIF, and non-convertible securities that have received an approved rating

---

79   Available online at <http://www.sedar.com> (site accessed: 20 February 2002).
80   (2000), 23 OSCB (Supp.) 867.
81   *Ibid.* s. 2.2.
82   *Ibid.* s. 2.3.
83   *Ibid.* s. 2.4.

from an approved rating organization (e.g., a rating of at least BBB from Standard & Poor's Corporation for an issue of long-term debt).

4. *Issuer of guaranteed non-convertible debt/preferred share/cash settled derivatives:*[84] Eligibility criteria are that an entity other than the issuer guarantees the issuance; the guarantor (or other credit supporter) satisfies the minimum reporting and/or minimum size requirements similar to those set out in items (2) and (3) above; and if the guarantor or other credit supporter has a market capitalization of less than $75 million, the securities being sold under the short-form prospectus must themselves be investment grade and the guarantor or credit supporter must also have outstanding investment-grade non-convertible securities.

5. *Issuer of guaranteed, convertible, debt/preferred shares:*[85] Eligibility criteria are the issuance is guaranteed by an entity other than the issuer, the securities are convertible into securities of that guarantor or credit supporter (*not* into other securities of the issuer of the convertible securities itself), and the guarantor/credit supporter satisfies eligibility criteria similar to those described in items (2) and (3) above.

6. *Securitization special purpose vehicle:*[86] Eligibility criteria are a current AIF and asset-backed securities that have received an approved rating from an approved rating organization.

The National Instrument also sets out additional eligibility criteria for successor firms formed as a result of reorganizations.

ii) The Rationale Underlying the Eligibility Criteria
It is important that issuers be eligible to use the short-form prospectus system only if key information about them is available to the public and has been widely disseminated. The eligibility requirements include both minimum size thresholds and usually minimum public-reporting periods. For the very largest issuers, the minimum public-reporting periods are relaxed. It is assumed that financial analysts tend to follow larger companies most closely, and the longer an issuer has been a reporting issuer, the more widely information about that company has been disseminated within the investment community.

The minimum-size rules are dispensed with in the case of certain debt issues. Smaller issuers may be eligible to use the short-form

---

84   *Ibid.* s. 2.5.
85   *Ibid.* s. 2.6.
86   *Ibid.* s. 2.7.

prospectus system when they issue investment-grade debt securities. Investment-grade debt refers to debt instruments, such as bonds, debentures, or notes, that have a minimum credit rating from one of the major credit-rating agencies, such as Standard & Poor's. Purchasers of debt instruments are primarily interested in the interest rate payable on the debt and in the issuer's creditworthiness (i.e., the issuer's continuing ability to make payments of interest and principal as they become due). Other company information that might be useful to equity investors seeking to evaluate the future-earning prospects of the firm is less important to debtholders. Moreover, independent rating agencies perform precisely the kind of analysis of creditworthiness that debtholders would undertake themselves if they had the resources, the expertise, and the access to the issuers that is available to rating agencies. For all of these reasons, in the case of an issue of investment-grade debt, regulators have determined that there is no need for a minimum issuer size requirement.

Non-convertible preferred shares are treated in the same way as debt for these purposes. Such shares typically carry a fixed dividend,and do not entitle their holders to any return on their capital above their initial investment. Accordingly, such shares, although they are equity securities for legal purposes, are typically structured, priced, and regarded in the marketplace as analogous to debt. They are, therefore, subject to similar investor concerns.

Where the issuer itself does not satisfy the necessary eligibility criteria, but the issue is fully guaranteed by another entity that does, the rules correctly recognize that the same policy considerations ought to apply and that access to the short-form prospectus procedures ought to be available.

The special eligibility criteria for asset-backed securities deserves closer inspection. It should be noted that, in the case of such an issue, neither a minimum reporting history, nor a minimum issuer size is required. Of course, the issuer size requirement is relaxed for other issuances of investment-grade debt. Relaxing the minimum reporting history, however, is crucial to making the short-form prospectus rules available for securitizations. A securitization (or asset-backed financing) is a type of financing in which one entity (often called the originator) transfers financial assets (such as receivables) to a second entity. This second entity, the purchaser of the transferred assets, issues securities to finance the purchase of the assets from the originator. This second (purchasing) entity is normally a corporation or a trust created specifically for the deal. Indeed, such an issuer is typically referred to as a "special purpose vehicle," which cannot be expected to have been a reporting issuer. The securitization technique has become so common and widely accepted that a policy decision was made to permit these special purpose vehicles to issue investment-grade securities by way of a short-form prospectus. Accordingly, the eligibility criteria for such issuers do not include any minimum public-reporting history.

c) AIF and Short-form Prospectus Forms

The short-form prospectus system depends upon investors having access to information about the issuers in a form, and of a quality, similar to that found in prospectuses. Eligible issuers must, therefore, file each year an Annual Information Form (AIF) with the securities regulators. The AIF contains prospectus-level disclosure about the issuer and its operations. Once the AIF is filed, when the issuer subsequently wishes to sell its securities to the public, it may use a simpler and shorter offering document — a short-form prospectus. The short-form prospectus focuses on the specific securities being sold and omits most general information about the company because that sort of company information is contained in the publicly accessible AIF, which is "incorporated by reference" into the prospectus. Not only can a short-form prospectus be prepared much more quickly than a long-form prospectus, but the securities regulators can also review a short-form prospectus in a matter of days, reducing both costs and risks for the issuer and its underwriter.

The formal requirements of the AIF are set out in Form 44-101 F1, and the requirements for the short-form prospectus are found in Form 44-101 F3.

d) Shorter Review Period

The principal advantage of the short-form prospectus system is that offerings can be completed much more quickly. A significant part of the time savings comes from the shorter length of time required by securities regulators to review short-form prospectuses. National Policy 43-201[87] indicates that, in the case of filings under the MRRS system, the principal regulator will use its "best efforts" to issue a comment letter on a preliminary short-form prospectus within three working days of the issuance of the preliminary MRRS decision document, which func-

---

87   Above note 55, s. 5.3(1).

tions as the preliminary prospectus receipt under the MRRS. By way of comparison, in a long-form prospectus filing, the MRRS indicates that regulators will use their best efforts to issue the first comment letter within ten working days. Moreover, non-principal regulators are to communicate their concerns about a short-form preliminary prospectus by noon (Eastern time) on the working day following the issuance of the principal regulator's comments. In a long-form filing, non-principal regulators use their best efforts to communicate such concerns within five working days of the date of the principal regulator's comment letter (or, where the prospectus has been selected for basic review, within six working days of being notified of such selection). The shorter review periods for preliminary prospectus filings need not, and will not, be observed by regulators when the short-form prospectus relates to a novel or complicated offering.[88] For example, in July 2001, the OSC issued a notice[89] indicating that preliminary short-form prospectuses filed in connection with "equity line financings,"[90] which are still novel in Canada, are subject to the same time lines as long-form prospectuses. Securities regulators also indicate that no specific time frames for regulatory review apply if an issuer elects to file a short-form prospectus outside of the MRRS system.[91]

---

88   *Ibid.* s. 5.4.

89   (2001), 24 OSCB 4515.

90   An equity-line financing refers to an arrangement under which an issuer enters into an agreement with purchasers that, in effect, allows the issuer to put new shares to the purchasers, at the issuer's option, at some agreed discount to the then-market price of those shares. The arrangement is called an "equity line" because it is similar, from the issuer's perspective, to a line of credit, which the issuer may draw down as funds are needed. Unlike a credit line, the draw downs involve the issuance of additional equity rather than additional debt. The U.S. Securities and Exchange Commission offers a useful discussion of equity-line financings in their 31 March 2001 "Current Issues and Rulemaking Projects Quarterly Update," available online at <http://www.sec.gov> (site accessed: 21 February 2002). In June 2001, Oncolytics Biotech Inc. filed a short-form base shelf prospectus in Canada in respect of an equity line financing; available online at <http://www.sedar.com> (site accessed: 12 March 2002).

91   Companion Policy 44-101 CP (2000), 23 OSCB (Supp.) 955, s. 7.6.

2) Shelf Prospectus

a) Overview

The shelf prospectus rules found in National Instrument 44-102[92] offer a second alternative to the long-form prospectus filing process. As the name suggests, a shelf prospectus is a disclosure document that is prepared, filed, and put on the metaphorical shelf (for up to twenty-five months) until the issuer decides that it wishes to take some or all of the qualified securities "off the shelf" and distribute them. At the time of the actual sale, the issuer prepares a relatively brief shelf prospectus supplement, containing specific information about the securities being sold that was not available at the time the base shelf prospectus was prepared and was, therefore, omitted from that earlier document. This information is then incorporated by reference in the base shelf prospectus itself. Any misrepresentation may give rise to statutory civil liability under section 130 of the *OSA*, just as in the case of any misrepresentation in a conventional prospectus.[93] The shelf prospectus procedures are faster than the regular prospectus process because the shelf prospectus supplements are not normally subject to any prior review by the regulators.[94] In fact, in most cases, the prospectus supplements can be filed on the same date that they are first delivered to purchasers or prospective purchasers.[95] In the case of sales of medium-term notes or other continuous distributions, the supplement can be filed up to two business days after it has been sent to purchasers or prospective purchasers.[96] Accordingly, it is possible for issuers to take quick advantage of very narrow windows of market opportunity.

b) Eligibility Criteria

Only issuers eligible to use the short-form prospectus system are eligible to use the shelf system. The short-form prospectus rules in National Instrument 44-101 apply to shelf prospectuses, together with some modifications found in National Instrument 44-102. Thus, as Companion Policy 44-101 CP states,

---

92   (2000), 22 OSCB (Supp.) 985.
93   *Ibid.* s. 6.2.
94   In the case of novel derivatives and asset-backed securities, however, the shelf-prospectus supplement must be precleared with regulators. See *Ibid.* s 4.1.
95   *Ibid.* s. 6.4(2)(a.)
96   *Ibid.* s. 6.4(2)(b).

[i]ssuers qualified to file a prospectus in the form of a short form prospectus and selling security holders of those issuers that wish to distribute securities under the shelf system should have regard to [National Instrument 44-101] and [Companion Policy 44-101 CP] first, and then refer to National Instrument 44-102 and the accompanying policy for any additional requirements.[97]

It should also be noted that the shelf prospectus eligibility rules require an issuer to satisfy the criteria twice: first, at the time the shelf prospectus is filed, and again at the time that the securities are actually sold pursuant to the shelf prospectus.

c) Shelf Prospectus Can Relate to More than One Type of Security

The shelf prospectus system provides great flexibility to issuers. A shelf prospectus can be filed relating to any number and type of securities. The shelf prospectus is not, however, intended to offer issuers a complete blank cheque. Rather, the prospectus must stipulate the total dollar value of securities the issuer proposes to sell under the shelf prospectus, and this value is to be based upon the amount the issuer reasonably expects to sell within twenty-five months following the filing of the prospectus.[98]

3) Post-Receipt Pricing (PREP) Prospectus

The third alternative to the conventional long-form prospectus filing is the Post-Receipt Pricing or PREP prospectus system. The structure of a PREP prospectus offering is similar in many ways to an offering under the shelf prospectus system. For example, the PREP system involves a similar two-step filing process. First, a base document that omits certain deal-specific information is filed and cleared with regulators. Second, at the time of actual sale, a second, shorter supplementing document, which is *not* precleared with regulators, is used. The PREP system, which is provided for in National Instrument 44-103,[99] differs from the shelf system, however, in three main respects:

- The PREP procedures are available to all issuers, not only to those who are eligible to file a short-form prospectus.[100]

---

97 Above note 91, s. 1.5.
98 National Instrument 44-102, above note 92, s. 5.4.
99 (2000), 23 OSCB (Supp.) 1013.
100 See, e.g., Companion Policy 44-103 CP (2000), 23 OSCB (supp.) 1026, s. 1.2.

- The base PREP document has a shorter "shelf life" than a base shelf prospectus: a base PREP prospectus expires ninety days after a receipt is obtained, unless a supplemented PREP prospectus is filed within that time; and, unless a supplemented prospectus has been filed within twenty days after the filing of the base PREP prospectus (or an amended base prospectus), the receipt also expires.[101]
- A PREP prospectus cannot be used to qualify multiple types of securities in the way that a shelf prospectus can. (Note that neither the shelf[102] nor the PREP[103] procedures may be used for a rights offering.)

4) Capital Pool Companies (CPC)

The capital pool company program (CPC) of the CDNX has evidently proved to be a useful alternative to a traditional initial public offering and, so, has prompted Ontario regulators to propose permitting such offerings in Ontario.[104] In some respects, the CPC program resembles an institutionalized system of reverse take-overs. Put simply, the system works as follows. An issuer is permitted to issue and file a CPC prospectus and to obtain a CDNX listing for a company that has no assets and does not yet carry on business. Once the CPC has completed its financing, the CPC has eighteen months within which to use the money raised to complete a "qualifying transaction" and become eligible for regular Tier 1 or Tier 2 listing status on the CDNX. According to data produced by the CDNX, over 1200 CPCs have been formed since the program began in 1987. The obvious advantage of the CPC program is that it helps smaller companies access the capital markets earlier in their development than is normally possible. The OSC's proposed policy to permit CPCs to conduct offerings in Ontario has been adopted by the OSC and delivered to the Minister of Finance in 2002. At the date of writing, it is anticipated that it will come into effect on 15 June 2002.

---

101 Above note 92, s. 3.5.
102 *Ibid.* s. 2.10.
103 *Ibid.* s. 2.1.
104 Proposed OSC Policy 41-601, "Capital Pool Companies" (2001), 24 OSCB 5317.

M. CONCLUSION

In many ways the public-offering process lies at the historical and philosophical heart of modern Canadian securities regulation. Yet, the traditional, transaction-oriented public-offering rules — developed in a different era and under very different market conditions — are gradually yielding to more flexible and more issuer-oriented regimes that offer the dual promise of improving the issuers' access to the capital markets and enhancing the timeliness and quality of information about new offerings available to Canadian investors.

CHAPTER 7

THE EXEMPT MARKET (PRIVATE PLACEMENTS)

A. INTRODUCTION

1) Registration and Prospectus Exemptions

The two fundamental tools of Canadian securities law regulating the sale of securities are the registration requirement and the prospectus requirement. The registration requirement refers to the rules requiring *trades* of securities to be effected through a securities firm that is registered (i.e., licensed) under the *OSA*. The prospectus requirement refers to the rules that require certain kinds of securities trades — *distributions* — to be undertaken only if the seller prepares, files, and delivers to the purchasers a prospectus, as discussed in chapter 6.

The *OSA* does, however, provide exemptions in certain cases from both the registration and the prospectus requirements, and those exemptions are the subject of this chapter.

a) Registration Exemptions
In *almost* every case where a distribution of securities is exempt from the prospectus requirement, that distribution is also exempt from the registration requirement. Therefore, we spend little time discussing registration exemptions separately here. Perhaps the three most fundamental points to be noted about the registration requirement are the following.

175

- *A "Trade" Triggers the Registration Requirement*: The registration requirement is triggered whenever there is a "trade" in securities, even if that trade is not a "distribution." Thus, it may be necessary in a private sale of securities to ensure that a registration exemption is available, even in cases where there is no legal requirement to prepare a prospectus.
- *Securities Sold without a Registrant*: Where securities are sold without the participation of a registrant, care must be taken to ensure that a registration exemption is available. It ought not to be assumed that, if a prospectus exemption is identified, a parallel registration exemption is also available.
- *Sources of Registration Exemptions*: The registration exemptions may be found, primarily, in sections 34 and 35 of the *OSA*[1] and in Rules 45-501,[2] 45-502[3] and 45-503.[4] Application may also be made to the OSC under section 74 of the *OSA* for registration exemptions in individual cases.

For the remainder of this chapter, we focus not on registration exemptions but rather on exemptions from the requirement to file and deliver a prospectus in connection with the distribution of securities.

2) Overview of the Prospectus Exemptions: Primary Offerings

Clearly, assembling a prospectus is not financially feasible for all issuers. For example, putting a prospectus together is out of the question for a small, start-up corporation seeking to raise $50,000 from relatives and friends of the corporation's main shareholders. Any sensible scheme of securities regulation recognizes that a prospectus is not cost effective in such a situation and contains exemptions from the prospectus requirement to recognize the practical realities of financing small ventures.

In other cases, buyers of securities, whether by dint of their bargaining leverage vis-à-vis the issuer or their sophistication in financial matters, do not require the protection afforded by a mandated prospectus. Again, any sensible scheme of securities regulation provides exemptions from the prospectus requirement to accommodate such purchasers. Indeed, many of the most important prospectus exemp-

---

1   *Securities Act* (Ontario), R.S.O. 1990, c. S.5 [*OSA*].
2   (2001), 24 OSCB 7011.
3   (1998), 21 OSCB 3685.
4   (1998), 21 OSCB 7708.

tions in Canadian legislation are based on the notion of the "sophisticated purchaser" who is capable of protecting her own interests without legislative interference.

A third important class of exemptions recognizes that some securities are so inherently safe that it is unnecessary to protect buyers by insisting that the vendor of the securities produce a prospectus. For example, the Government of Canada does not need to prepare a prospectus when issuing securities. For obvious reasons, it is regarded as an extremely creditworthy debtor, more creditworthy than any Canadian corporate issuer.

Virtually all of the prospectus exemptions, whether designed to accommodate small issuers, recognize investor sophistication, acknowledge the inherent safety of the securities offered for sale, or promote other rationales, are implicitly built upon a cost-benefit calculus; that is, in some situations, the cost of requiring the issuer to assemble a prospectus exceeds the likely benefit (e.g., enhanced investor protection) that would be achieved by imposing this requirement.

3) Regulation of Secondary Market Trading

Regulating primary market transactions effectively requires regulating secondary market transactions as well. Suppose, for example, that an "exempt buyer" (again, a person who qualifies to purchase securities under an exemption from the prospectus requirement) buys securities, but immediately resells them to a person who does not qualify as an exempt buyer (i.e., a person who could have purchased the securities only with the benefit of a prospectus). If this sort of "quick flip" were permitted by securities laws, it would provide an easy way to circumvent the requirement that an issuer compile a prospectus when selling to those who do not qualify as exempt buyers.

A transaction that seeks to illicitly circumvent the prospectus requirement is commonly referred to as a "backdoor underwriting." In the closed system, the danger of a backdoor underwriting is addressed by the following means. The default rule (i.e., the rule that applies absent an exemption) requires an exempt purchaser to assemble and distribute a prospectus when reselling the securities that she originally acquired on an exempt basis. Formally, this is done by designating the first trade in securities acquired under an exemption as a "distribution" of those securities.

However, an exempt purchaser may escape the prospectus requirement by either of two means. First, she may sell the securities to a purchaser who is also an exempt purchaser. This simply follows from the fact that exempt purchasers are assumed to be capable of protecting their own interests. They are no less capable of protecting their own interests in secondary market purchases than they are when they purchase directly from the issuer.

Second, provided the issuer is a reporting issuer (and, in certain cases, has been a reporting issuer for a minimum "seasoning period"), an exempt purchaser may escape the prospectus requirement if she has held the securities for a period of time once referred to as the "hold period," but now dubbed the "restricted period." The seasoning and restricted periods under Ontario law range from four to twelve months. The periods vary depending principally upon whether the issuer of the securities is a "qualifying issuer" as defined in Multilateral Instrument 45-102.[5] (The concept of a "qualifying issuer" is explored at greater length below.) The restricted-period requirement ensures that exempt buyers purchase with the intention of holding the securities for investment purposes, rather than with a view to reselling the securities to non-exempt buyers, and so allowing the issuer to circumvent the prospectus requirement.

Sales by "control persons" are also specially regulated in the closed system, whether or not the control person acquired her securities in an exempt transaction. A control person is any person or entity having the power to materially affect the control of an issuer, and is presumed to include any person or entity holding 20 percent or more of an issuer.[6] Sales by control persons are distributions that must be made under a prospectus, just like sales by the issuer.

The rationale for special regulation of sales by control persons is that such persons frequently have access to privileged information concerning the issuer. As in the case of sales by the issuer itself, the requirement that a sale by a control person be accompanied by a prospectus is designed to redress the potential imbalance of information between the seller and the buyer and to ensure that the seller does not take advantage of the buyer.

Sales by control persons and, indeed, all sales that constitute a distribution effected by someone other than the issuer are commonly referred to as "secondary distributions," or, in the case of a control per-

---

5   (2001), 24 OSCB 5522, s. 1.1.

6   The term "control person" is not defined in the OSA. However, clause (c) of the definition of "distribution" in s. 1(1) deems any trade in securities from the holdings of a person with these characteristics to be a "distribution." Moreover, OSC Rule 14-501 (1997), 20 OSCB 2690 defines the term "control person distribution," for the purposes of the rules, to mean "a trade described in clause (c) of the definition of 'distribution' in subsection 1(1) of the Act."

son selling securities using a prospectus, as a "secondary offering." This is because such sales do not occur in the primary market between an issuer and an investor, but rather occur in the secondary market between two investors.

As in the case of sales by the issuer, a control person may escape the prospectus requirement if the person purchasing securities from the control person is an exempt purchaser. A control person may also avoid the prospectus requirement where the issuer is a reporting issuer in at least two different circumstances. First, if the control person is an "eligible institutional investor" as defined in National Instrument 62-101 (i.e., a financial institution, pension, or mutual fund), the control person can sell the issuer's shares without a prospectus, provided the seller does not actually control the issuer or have board representation, the sale is made in the ordinary course of the seller's business, the seller has no knowledge of undisclosed material facts or changes, the securities would not otherwise be subject to a hold period, and no market-grooming efforts are undertaken or extraordinary commissions paid.[7] If the control person is not an eligible institutional investor, the resale rules are somewhat different. Securities may be traded without a prospectus, subject to seasoning and restricted periods that mirror those applicable to exempt buyers, so long as the control person gives the regulators advance notice of the intended sale and formally disclaims knowledge of any undisclosed material information concerning the issuer.[8]

B. DETAILED REVIEW OF THE PROSPECTUS EXEMPTIONS

1) Types of Exemptions

There are a number of types of prospectus exemptions. The most important type is based on the nature of the *trade* or the *identity* of the person acquiring the securities.[9] For example, if the buyer is a bank, the issuer need not compile a prospectus. The rationale that underlies

---

7   National Instrument 62-101 (2000), 23 OSCB 1367.

8   Multilateral Instrument 45-102, (2001), 24 OSCB 5522, s. 2.8. The specific rules applying to sales by control persons or by pledgees of a control person's securities will not be dealt with in any further detail here.

9   *OSA*, above note 1, s. 72, as supplemented by the *OSA Regulation*, R.R.O. 1990, Reg. 1015, and as further supplemented and qualified by Rule 45-501, above note 2.

this type of exemption is that the buyer is able to protect its own interests in purchasing the securities.

The second most important type of exemption is based on the nature of the *security*. For example, bonds issued by a provincial government may be sold free of the prospectus requirement, regardless of the identity of the purchaser.[10] The rationale that underlies this type of exemption is that the type of security is so inherently safe that the protections afforded by securities regulation are unnecessary.

The third most important type of exemption is based on the existence of an alternative regulatory scheme for the protection of the buyers of the securities. For example, on a statutory amalgamation of two companies, the shareholders of each amalgamating company receive new securities in exchange for their old securities. However, as detailed below, corporate law supplies shareholders with sufficient protections (including mandated disclosure), to render the prospectus requirement unnecessary.

A number of other, less important rationales underlie various specific prospectus exemptions. These are discussed below.

a) Exemptions Based on the Ability to Protect One's Own Interests

The prospectus requirement is based on the assumption that the market will not adequately protect buyers from unscrupulous sellers who are willing to exploit their informational advantage for profit. However, it is commonly recognized that there are buyers who have either sufficient bargaining power or sufficient sophistication (or both) to protect their own interests without the intervention of the statutorily mandated prospectus. Where an issuer sells securities to such purchasers, the *OSA* does not require a prospectus. This is formally accomplished by exempting sales to designated purchasers from the prospectus requirement. Such purchasers have long been known in the trade as "exempt purchasers"; however, through recent changes in 2001 to the exempt distribution rules, Ontario law has adopted a modified version of the American securities law concept of "accredited investors," which is discussed further in the next section.

i) *Accredited Investors*

A significant change to Ontario's exempt distribution rules occurred in 2001 with the introduction of a new version of Rule 45-501.[11] The new rule removed several of the prospectus exemptions most frequently

---

10   *OSA*, above note 1, ss. 73(1)(a) & 35(2)1(a).
11   Above note 2, s. 2.3.

relied upon by securities issuers, while introducing a number of important new exemptions. The two most fundamental changes introduced by the new rule are the creation of the "closely-held issuer" exemption, which is discussed later in this chapter, and the "accredited investor" exemption. The "accredited investor" exemption is modelled on a concept found in the U.S. federal securities law limited-offering (i.e., private placement) rules.[12] Generally speaking, accredited investors are purchasers who are sophisticated or are deemed to be sophisticated because of certain characteristics they possess. The term "accredited investors," to whom securities may lawfully be distributed without the requirement to produce a prospectus, includes the following types of buyers.

aa) Designated Institutions[13]
Where the purchaser is a bank, a credit union, a trust or loan corporation, an insurance company, or a registered dealer (in certain registration categories), the issuer need not prepare a prospectus.

bb) Governments[14]
Where the purchaser is the federal government, a provincial government, a municipal corporation, a public board, or a commission, no prospectus is required.

cc) Persons or Companies Who Meet Income or Asset Tests, or
    Who Are Recognized by the OSC as Accredited Investors[15]
Those purchasers who meet certain specified income or asset thresholds fall into this category of accredited investors. Those purchasers who have applied to the OSC for, and have been granted, accredited investor status also fall into this category.

Under the *asset* test, individuals may qualify as accredited investors if they beneficially own, either individually or together with a spouse, net *financial* assets (i.e., cash, securities, certain insurance contracts, and certain certificates of deposit) exceeding $1 million.[16]

---

12 Regulation D, Rule 501, 17 C.F.R. §230.501.
13 Rule 45-501, above note 2, s. 1.1 (definition of "accredited investor"), paras. (a)–(g). Note that the institution must purchase as principal, rather than as agent for someone else (Rule 45-501, s. 2.3). This requirement addresses the danger of a backdoor underwriting (defined in the text, above).
14 *Ibid.* paras. (h)–(j).
15 *Ibid.* paras. (m)–(o), (t), & (u).
16 *Ibid.* para. (m). The $1 million figure is calculated net of "related liabilities," which is also defined in s. 1.1. The concept of related liabilities raised some concerns among commenters to an earlier proposed version of Rule 45-501 because the phrase includes not only liabilities actually incurred to acquire financial assets, but also liabilities "that are secured by financial assets." Some thought that investors with significant real assets (such as home or business assets) that

Under the *income* test, an individual with a net individual income before taxes of more than $200,000 in each of the two most recent years, or with a combined individual and spousal income before taxes of more than $300,000 in the two most recent years, is eligible for accredited investor status but only if the individual "has a reasonable expectation of exceeding the same net income level in the current year."[17]

There is also an asset test for non-individuals. A company, limited partnership, limited liability partnership, trust, or estate, other than a mutual fund or non-redeemable investment fund, with net assets of at least $5 million (as shown on its financial statements) is an accredited investor.[18]

Prior to the new Rule 45-501 regime, the OSC had the authority to recognize certain securities buyers as "exempt purchasers" on a case-by-case basis. Paragraph (u) of the definition of "accredited investor" in section 1.1 of Rule 45-501 indicates that the OSC will continue to have a similar power to recognize buyers as "accredited investors." However, a recent OSC Staff Notice states that they do not expect this provision to be relied upon very often because most applicants for "exempt purchaser" status under the former rule would now satisfy the requirements of one or more of the specifically enumerated categories of "accredited investor" and so would not require any special OSC recognition.[19] Nevertheless, section 8.1 of Rule 45-501 indicates that,

---

were financed with loans that were also secured with interests granted in the owners' financial assets would be unnecessarily, and unfairly, excluded from the class of accredited investors. (See (2001), 24 OSCB 5547.)The OSC did not regard this as a practical problem because, in its view, lenders did not typically take general security interests in loan transactions with individual (as opposed to corporate) borrowers.

17 *Ibid.* para (n). This language has, again, been taken largely from Regulation D, above note 12. But one drafting change has been made that, perhaps, introduces an unintended ambiguity. The comparable language in the final phrase of Regulation D reads, "and has a reasonable expectation of *reaching* the same income level in the current year."[Emphasis added.] By changing the word "reaching" in Regulation D to "exceeding," the drafters evidently intended to conform the language used throughout the paragraph to clarify that the investor's income must *exceed* the $200,000 or $300,000 threshold, as the case may be, in the current year. However, the section could also be misinterpreted to mean that the individual's income in the current year must, in fact, exceed the level of that individual's income in the previous two years, rather than the $200,000 or $300,000 benchmarks.

18 *Ibid.* para. (t).

19 OSC Staff Notice 45-702.

as a transitional matter, anyone previously recognized as an "exempt purchaser" will be considered an "accredited investor" until 30 November 2002. Under the previous "exempt purchaser" exemption, the OSC, for example, recognized funds (such as mutual funds or pension plans) with significant assets (typically at least $5 million) under administration as exempt purchasers. Recognition as an exempt purchaser was granted on a year-by-year basis only. According to an unofficial "registrant listing" prepared by the OSC, as of 15 July 2001, there were approximately 114 exempt purchasers recognized by the OSC.[20] There is an important technical point to be noted here. The *OSA* provided that a person or company could apply for recognition as an exempt purchaser for the purposes of both the prospectus requirement and the registration requirement. However, these two exemption provisions differed slightly. Specifically, following a statutory amendment in 1999, and before a further amendment that came into force in December 2001, an individual (as opposed to a corporation, other legal entity, or other association) could be recognized as an exempt purchaser for the purposes of the registration requirement,[21] but an individual could *not* be so recognized, under clause 72(1)(c) of the *OSA*, for the purposes of the prospectus requirement. Thus, to become exempt from the prospectus requirement, an individual needed to obtain an exemption from the OSC granted not under the exempt purchaser provision in clause 72(1)(c), but under the OSC's general exemption power in section 74.

In 2000, an individual investor did apply to the OSC for just such an order exempting him from the prospectus requirement because as an individual, he was not eligible to seek recognition as an exempt purchaser under clause 72(1)(c).[22] He also sought an order under section 35(1), paragraph 4, recognizing him as an exempt purchaser for the purposes of the registration requirement. The OSC declined to grant the relief sought. The applicant's principal argument was that, under U.S. securities law, he would qualify as an "accredited investor" and would, therefore, be eligible to purchase securities there on an exempt basis. The OSC noted that under the then proposed (and now effective)

---

20   Available online at <http://www.osc.gov.on.ca> (site accessed: 28 July 2001).

21   *OSA*, above note 1, s. 35(1), para. 4. Note that the s. 35(1), para. 4, "exempt purchaser" registration exemption, like the s. 72(1)(c) "exempt purchaser" prospectus exemption, was removed by Rule 45-501, above note 2, s. 3.1. In any event, as of 5 December 2001, s. 72(1)(c) was amended by striking out the phrase "other than an individual" (*Responsible Choices for Growth and Fiscal Responsibility Act* (Budget Measures), S.O. 2001, c. 23, s. 213).

22   *Re McIntyre* (2000), 23 OSCB 7279.

changes to OSC Rule 45-501, a similar "accredited investor" exemption would be recognized in Ontario. However, because the new version of Rule 45-501 had not yet been adopted, the OSC stated that "[w]hat [the applicant] would have us do is agree to apply the proposed revised Rule as though it had been made."[23]

dd) A Promoter[24] of an Issuer or a Spouse, Parent, Grandchild,
    or Child of an Officer, Director, or Promoter[25]

A person or company is considered a "promoter"[26] of an issuer if that person or company founds or organizes an issuer, or receives, in connection with the founding or organizing of an issuer, 10 percent or more of the issuer's securities or 10 percent or more of the proceeds of sale of an issue of securities. Typically, promoters are intimately acquainted with issuers and, generally, are the original, directing mind and will of such issuers. Accordingly, they do not need the protection of securities laws when they purchase the securities of the issuer. Exemptions are, thus, available for sales of securities to promoters, between promoters, and between promoters and control persons of an issuer.

ee) Control Persons, Affiliates of the Issuer,[27] or the Issuer Itself[28]

When an affiliate of the issuer or a control person purchases securities of the issuer, there is little risk of the sort of informational imbalance that underlies the application of the prospectus requirement. Accordingly, such sales are exempt from the prospectus requirements. So, too, are purchases made by issuers of their own outstanding securities, including purchases in the form of redemption of shares. (Of course, purchases by an issuer of its own securities raise questions of a different sort concerning informational imbalance. These are discussed under the heading "Issuer Bids" in chapter 10.)

ii) Trades between Registered Dealers[29]

When a registered dealer sells securities to another registered dealer who is purchasing as a principal (i.e., not as an agent for another party who may not be a sophisticated party), no prospectus is necessary. The purchaser is deemed to be a sophisticated buyer. As discussed in chapter 4, those acting for registered dealers must satisfy certain proficien-

---

23   *Ibid.* at 7280.
24   Rule 45-501, above note 13, para. (p).
25   *Ibid.* para. (q).
26   *OSA*, above note 1, s. 1(1) (definition of "promoter").
27   Rule 45-501, above note 13, para. (r) (definition of "accredited investor").
28   *Ibid.* para. (s).
29   *OSA*, above note 1, s. 72(1)(q).

cy standards before they can carry on business.[30] Registered dealers also typically have market experience in evaluating the worth of securities. (It should be noted that there appears to be some overlap between this exemption and a certain aspect of the "accredited investor" exemption.)[31]

iii) Trades to Underwriters or between Underwriters[32]

Underwriters are market professionals who play key roles in assembling a prospectus, usually for the purpose of selling securities to the public. As key participants in the process, they have access to privileged information concerning the issuer and obviously do not need the protection afforded by the very prospectus that they assist the issuer in preparing.

Trades between underwriters are also exempt from the prospectus requirement because underwriters often subcontract a portion of the sales function to other underwriters. The subcontractors do not participate in the process of assembling the prospectus; however, like those underwriters dealing directly with the issuer, they are required to register with the regulators and must meet proficiency standards in order to carry on business. These underwriters are also savvy investment dealers who are experts in assessing the value of securities. Thus, they do not need the protection afforded by a prospectus.[33]

b) Exemptions Based on the Inherent Safety of the Security Offered

A number of exemptions from the prospectus requirement are based on the intrinsic safety of the securities issued. An example of such a security is a debt instrument issued or guaranteed by a Canadian or foreign government.[34]

Only a few exemptions based on the nature of the securities offered, however, can be supported on this basis alone. For example, debt securities offered by banks, credit unions, trust companies, and insurance companies are all exempted from the prospectus require-

---

30   Why the seller must also be a registered dealer is a little less obvious because the *OSA* seeks to protect the *buyer*, not the *seller*.

31   Rule 45-501, above note 2, para. (g) (definition of "accredited investor").

32   *OSA*, above note 1, s. 72(1)(r).

33   If the prospectus has already gone "final" (i.e., a final receipt has been received from regulators), then underwriters selling to subcontracting underwriters will not need to rely on this exemption.

34   *OSA*, above note 1, ss. 73 (1)(a) & 35(2).

ment.[35] Although at one time these securities were thought to be extremely safe investments, collapses, or near failures, of some Canadian financial institutions within the past twenty years demonstrate that this is no longer invariably the case. Thus, inherent safety, without more, does not seem to be an adequate rationale for these exemptions today, if it ever was.

Indeed, in some of these cases, the existence of an alternative protective mechanism is a better explanation for these exemptions. For example, banks are subject to federal regulation and oversight by the Office of the Superintendent of Financial Institutions, which applies minimum standards of banking conduct and capital adequacy rules to minimize the risk of a bank collapse. Similarly, guaranteed investment certificates issued by trust corporations are regulated under the Ontario *Loan and Trust Corporations Act.*[36] Only those credit unions governed by the *Credit Unions and Caisse Populaires Act, 1994,*[37] are exempt from the prospectus requirement.

Moreover, some of the securities-based exemptions appear to find their footing in the ability of the buyer to protect herself. For example, buyers of securities issued by *private* mutual funds[38] are generally people who are thought to be sufficiently sophisticated to protect their own interests. So, too, are buyers of short-term commercial paper[39] (i.e., negotiable promissory notes with a maturity date of less than one year).

c)   Exemptions Based on the Existence of an Alternative Protective Mechanism

In some situations, a prospectus is not required because those who receive securities in a "distribution" are protected by some alternative mechanism. Examples include amalgamations and other similar corporate combinations or reorganizations, and take-over and issuer bids.

---

35   *OSA, ibid.* ss. 73(1)(a) & 35(2)1(c), (c.1). It should be noted that the exemption for debt instruments issued by banks, trust companies, or insurance companies is not available in the case of sales of debt instruments that are subordinate in right of payment to deposits held by the issuer or guarantor (Rule 45-501, above note 2, s. 3.8).

36   R.S.O. 1990, c. L.25.

37   S.O. 1994, c. 11.

38   *OSA,* above note 1, ss. 73 (1)(a) & 35(2)3. Note, however, that this exemption is not available if the private fund is administered by a trust company, but that trust company is not the promoter or manager of the fund. See Rule 45-510, above note 2, s. 3.3.

39   *OSA, ibid.* ss.73(1)(a) & 35(2)4.

i)   Amalgamations and Other Similar Corporate
Combinations or Reorganizations[40]

When two corporations amalgamate, the *amalgamating* (i.e., predecessor) corporations are subsumed within the body of the *amalgamated* (i.e., continuing) corporation that results from the amalgamation. All the outstanding securities of each of the amalgamating corporations are cancelled. The amalgamation agreement provides for the allocation to the shareholders of the various amalgamating corporations of security interests in the new corporation (or, in the case of a "three-cornered amalgamation," shares in a third-party affiliate). Because the new securities will be exchanged directly by the issuer (i.e., the new amalgamated company) for securities previously held in the "old" amalgamating corporations, there is a trade for valuable consideration. And, because that issuance is a primary market transaction, it constitutes a distribution of securities that would normally require a prospectus.

However, the *OSA* exempts this type of issuance from the prospectus requirement because the shareholders are adequately protected under the applicable corporate law. The shareholders of each amalgamating corporation must consent to the plan of amalgamation by special resolution.[41] Prior to the vote, corporate law requires a "proxy circular" to be sent to the shareholders that contains information similar to that required under a prospectus.[42] Moreover, any individual shareholder who declines to participate in the transaction may insist that the corporation buy his shares from him at a court-appraised "fair value."[43] This exemption extends not only to amalgamations, but also to other statutory procedures with results similar to an amalgamation (e.g., an "arrangement" under applicable corporate law).[44]

40   *Ibid.* s. 72(1)(i); Rule 45-501, above note 2, s. 2.8. Section 2.8 of Rule 45-501 extends the application of the exemption to "three-cornered amalgamations" in which shareholders of one amalgamating company receive shares not in the other amalgamated company itself, but rather in a third-party affiliate. This type of transaction does not appear to fall within the s. 72(1)(i) exemption, which grants an exemption in cases where shares of the issuing company are "exchanged" for other securities and so appears to be limited to cases where shares are issued by the amalgamated entity in exchange for securities of the amalgamating entities. By contrast, s. 2.8 of Rule 45-501 provides an exemption whenever shares are issued "in connection with" an amalgamation or arrangement. See s. 2.6, Companion Policy 45-501 CP (1997), 20 OSCB 5313.
41   See, e.g., *Canada Business Corporations Act*, R.S.C. 1985, c. C-44 [*CBCA*], s. 183.
42   OSC Rule 54-501 (2000), 23 OSCB 8465. See also the general discussion of information circulars in chapter 9.
43   See, e.g., *CBCA*, above note 41, s. 190(1)(c) & (3).
44   For an example of a corporate law statutory plan of arrangement provision, see *CBCA*, above note 41, s. 192.

ii) Take-over Bids[45] and Issuer Bids[46]

In colloquial parlance, a take-over bid occurs when a bidder makes a public offer for the securities of a corporation (the "target").[47] In some cases, the bidder is a corporation that offers its own securities in exchange for those of the target. Such an offer is known as a "securities exchange take-over bid." An issuance of securities in this situation constitutes a distribution because the issuer directly makes the issuance for valuable consideration. There is an exemption, however, from the prospectus requirement because the bidder must prepare a "take-over bid circular" for the benefit of target shareholders. The circular contains the same information provided in a prospectus.[48] A similar exemption applies in the case of a securities exchange issuer bid, provided the issuer is a reporting issuer not in default under securities laws.[49]

d) Exemptions Based on Particular Policy Goals

Some exemptions are based on idiosyncratic policy concerns. Examples include (i) closely-held issuer exemptions; (ii) trades to employees and consultants; (iii) government incentive securities; (iv) securities issued by prospectors or mining companies; and (v) securities issued by non-profit organizations for educational, charitable, religious, or recreational purposes.

i) Closely-held Issuer Exemption[50]

The closely-held issuer exemption is one of the two most important modifications to Ontario's exempt distribution law introduced by new Rule 45-501 in 2001. (The other is the accredited investor exemption discussed above.) Where an issuer meets the requirements to be considered a closely-held issuer, that issuer may distribute securities with a total value of up to $3 million without the need to produce a prospectus. A closely-held issuer is defined in Rule 45-501 as an issuer whose shares (but not necessarily debt securities)[51] may be transferred only with the approval of the directors or the shareholders, and with the outstanding securities beneficially owned by not more than thirty-five

---

45   *OSA*, above note 1, s. 72(1)(j).
46   Rule 45-501, above note 2, s. 2.5.
47   The legal definition of a take-over bid is rather different. See chapter 10.
48   See the discussion in chapter 10.
49   Rule 45-501, above note 2, s. 2.7.
50   *Ibid.* s. 2.1.
51   For discussion of this point, see "Summary of Comments Received by the Commission on Proposed Rule 45-501 — Exempt Distributions" (2001), 24 OSCB 5546 at 5547.

persons or companies. The thirty-five holder limitation, however, excludes shareholders that are accredited investors, current or former directors, officers, or employees of the issuer or its affiliates, and current or past consultants. Based on the current drafting of Rule 45-501, to be excluded from the thirty-five–holder limitation, directors and officers (as well as employees and consultants) must hold only shares issued to them as compensation or under an incentive plan. However, a recent OSC Staff Notice indicates that this was a drafting error and that *all* current and former officers and directors were intended to be excluded from the thirty-five–shareholder threshold, regardless of how they obtained their shares. Although the rule will not be formally amended until at least November 2002, the same Staff Notice indicates that applications should be made for discretionary relief in cases inadvertently caught by this drafting error.[52] The concept of a closely-held issuer replaces (in Ontario) the traditional Canadian securities law concept of a "private company"[53] and the more recent concept of a "private issuer." It is important to emphasize that sales of securities of closely-held issuers (subject to the $3 million limitation) are exempt from the prospectus requirement, regardless of the identity of the purchasers. This exemption clearly represents a trade-off between the need to protect potentially unsophisticated investors and the practical need of smaller enterprises to raise capital in a cost-efficient way. To try to avoid undue exploitation of this new exemption, the rule imposes four qualifications.

---

52   OSC Staff Notice 45-702, above note 19.

53   The term "private company" is defined in s. 1(1) of the *OSA*. Although the definition has not been repealed, the registration and prospectus exemptions formerly accorded to trades in the securities of a private company have been removed by Rule 45-501, above note 2, s. 3.1. The term "private issuer" appeared in an earlier version of Rule 45-501 and provided some flexibility to the fairly restrictive definition of "private company." The "private company" definition required that the three central defining attributes of such a company had to be expressly included in the issuer's constating documents. Even if a company *in fact* possessed the attributes of a private company, it would not technically qualify for the prospectus exemption if the private company clauses were not recited in its articles of incorporation or equivalent document. The "private issuer" definition, on the other hand, could be met by an issuer that satisfied all the indicia of a private issuer, whether or not its articles contained provisions addressing those indicia. It is interesting to note that, in November 2001, the sole officer and director of a private company in Alberta was convicted of illegally selling securities in connection with the sale of shares in a "private company" to at least 170 public shareholders. See Alberta Securities Commission, News Release, "Convicted Securities Offender Gets House Arrest" (14 November 2001), available online at <http://www.albertasecurities.com> (site accessed: 15 November 2001).

- No promoter of the issuer may have acted as a promoter of another issuer that relied upon the closely-held issuer exemption within the previous year.[54] This restriction is evidently intended to prevent an abuse of the thirty-five–securityholder restriction by a promoter seeking to rely upon the exemption for successive sales by closely-held issuers. The OSC indicates, however, that where a promoter is involved in genuinely distinct issuers within a twelve-month period, the promoter can apply for and obtain an appropriate exemption.[55]
- No selling or promotional expenses may be incurred in connection with the exempt trade, other than for the services of a registered dealer.
- The $3 million aggregate limitation is calculated *after* taking into account all trades made in purported reliance on the exemption (i.e., it is not possible to raise more than $3 million in total in reliance upon the exemption).
- The seller must provide the purchasers with an information statement at least four days before the exempt trade. The information statement must be "substantially similar" to Form 45-501 F3. That form comprises a generic statement that, among other things, cautions investors about the risk of investing in small businesses. The issuer is not, however, required to deliver such a statement if, following the exempt trade, the issuer will have five or fewer beneficial owners of its securities.[56]

Where the conditions of the closely-held issuer exemption are satisfied, the exemption is available not only to the issuer itself, but also in respect of any trades by a securityholder of such an issuer.[57] Needless to say, however, the exemption is available in the case of trades by securityholders only while the issuer continues to satisfy all the closely-held issuer criteria. When the issuer no longer satisfies those criteria, a securityholder seeking to resell his or her shares in the closely-held issuer must identify another available prospectus exemption or, as described further below, ensure that the "seasoning-period" requirements of Multilateral Instrument 45-102, section 2.6 are satisfied.[58]

---

54   Rule 45-501, above note 2, s. 2.1(b).
55   See "Notice of Proposed Rule 45-501" (2001), 24 OSCB 4247 at 4252.
56   *Ibid.* s. 2.1(2).
57   Companion Policy 45-501 CP, above note 40, s. 2.3(1).
58   Rule 45-501, above note 2, s. 6.2. Where the securityholder is a promoter of the issuer, the resale is also subject, among other things, to a hold-period requirement. (Rule 45-501, s. 6.1; MI 45-102, ss. 2.8(2) & (3)).

ii) Trades to Employees, Executives, and Consultants[59]

OSC Rule 45-503 effectively enshrines a public policy in favour of employee ownership and, more broadly, in favour of share ownership by a corporation's employees, consultants, and executives. The rule advances this policy goal by exempting from the prospectus requirement distributions of securities to such persons, provided their participation in the trade is voluntary.[60]

iii) Government Incentive Securities[61]

In Ontario, a special exemption exists for "government incentive securities." These are defined as securities that are linked to specific exploration, development, or oil and gas property incentive schemes under the federal *Income Tax Act*.[62] This exemption manifests a compromise of the legislation's overarching policy of investor protection in favour of other policy objectives pursued by the government.

iv) Securities Issued by Prospectors or Mining Companies[63]

Historically, mining has been an important industry in Ontario. To encourage the formation of mining concerns, the legislation contains a variety of exemptions that allow prospectors, prospecting syndicates, and mining companies to issue securities free of the prospectus requirement.

v) Securities Issued by Non-profit Organizations for Educational, Charitable, Religious, or Recreational Purposes[64]

Securities may be issued free of the prospectus requirement by non-profit organizations for educational, charitable, religious, or recreational purposes, provided no commission or other remuneration is paid in connection with the sale.

---

59   Rule 45-503 (1998), 21 OSCB 6571. (This rule effectively supersedes *OSA*, s. 72(1)(n). See Rule 45-503, s. 2.1.)
60   Technically, the voluntariness requirement is not necessary for exempt trades to executives who are not officers (Rule 45-503, *ibid.* s. 3.1(b)).
61   Rule 45-501, above note 2, s. 2.13.
62   *Ibid.* s. 1.1 (definition of "government incentive security").
63   *OSA*, above note 1, ss. 73(1)(a) & 35(2), paras. 11–14.
64   *Ibid.* ss. 73(1)(a) & 35(2), para. 7.

C. OTHER EXEMPTIONS

Although most of the key prospectus exemptions are found in subsections 72(1) and 73(1) of the *OSA* and in Rules 45-501, 45-502, and 45-503, there are a host of additional exemptions scattered throughout other rules. For example, the following rules also contain specific prospectus exemptions:

- *Rule 45-504*: exemption for the distribution of securities to a managed account (i.e., a portfolio account where the manager has full discretion to trade without the client's consent to individual trades);
- *National Instrument 62-101*: exemption for control block distributions by "eligible institutional investors," a term defined in National Instrument 62-103;
- *Multilateral Instrument 45-102*: exemption for control block distributions by sellers other than eligible institutional investors, exemption for sales by pledgees who sell securities pledged by a control person to liquidate a good-faith debt, and ancillary exceptions to what would otherwise be resale restrictions;
- *Rule 32-503*: exemptions for the sale of mutual fund securities by financial intermediaries to corporate-sponsored pension plans and other similar plans, and for the sale of mutual fund securities where the fund itself is a pool of funds that constitutes a commingling of superannuation, pension, or similar plan funds;
- *Rule 35-101*: exemption for the distribution of a foreign security made by a foreign broker-dealer or agent exempt from registration pursuant to Rule 35-101;
- *Rule 72-501*: exemption for the resale of a "restricted security" when the resale occurs on certain markets outside of Ontario;[65]
- *Rule 91-501*: exemption for certain trades in strip bonds;
- *Rule 91-502*: exemption for trades in recognized options by or through a recognized dealer; and
- *Rule 91-503*: exemption for trades of exempt commodity futures or commodity futures option contracts.

---

65   Note that in 2000, a proposed multilateral instrument (MI 72-101 (2000), 23 OSCB 6260) was published for comment. MI 72-101 would provide for certain registration and prospectus exemptions in the case of extraprovincial distributions. MI 72-101 would essentially deal with those situations that, within the U.S. federal securities law regime, are the subject of the SEC's Regulation S. However, in March 2002, the CSA staff indicated it would not be proceeding with this initiative because the subject matter of these proposals would, instead, be considered as part of the recently established uniform securities legislation project referred to in chapter 3. See CSA Staff Notice 72-301, available online at <http://www.osc.gov.on.ca> (site accessed: 22 March 2002).

D. AN OVERARCHING PRINCIPLE: THE RELATIVE COSTS AND BENEFITS OF ISSUING A PROSPECTUS

Securities regulation is often said to be grounded in investor protection; however, what is stated less frequently is that investor protection is not, and could never be, the single, unencumbered goal of securities regulation. If it were, the costliness of the regulation would be irrelevant, and all that would matter would be ensuring that investors' interests were never compromised.

In fact, no scheme of regulation can operate successfully without some implicit notion of cost-effectiveness. This means that investor protection is a moving, not a fixed, target to be pursued to the extent that the cost of the rules necessary to achieve a particular protective end do not exceed the benefit to be achieved. This is now explicitly recognized in the Ontario legislation.[66]

The "closely-held issuer"[67] exemption is an example. Under this exemption, as discussed above, no prospectus is required in connection with the sale of up to $3 million of a closely-held issuer's securities to non-accredited investors. Commenting on a predecessor to the closely-held issuer exemption, the "private company exemption," one commentator suggested that the exemption was based on the view that buyers of securities of private companies are able to protect their own interests.[68] No doubt this is true of some buyers under the exemption; however, it will not be true of many, such as friends and relatives who purchase securities not on the basis of information that they are provided about the investment, but on the basis of their relationship to the promoter. Many such investors are extremely unsophisticated investors.

Rather than being grounded in the sophistication of the buyers, the closely-held issuer exemption is better explained as evidencing an implicit trade-off between the cost and benefit of assembling a prospectus. Assembling a prospectus is extremely expensive. Most small start-up companies cannot possibly afford to comply with the prospectus requirement, even though it would undoubtedly result in better protection for the investors. Thus, although requiring a prospectus would secure a benefit, its cost would greatly exceed the benefit.

The *Final Report of the Ontario Securities Commission Task Force on Small Business Financing* recognized that the exemptions must be

---

66   *OSA*, above note 1, s 2.1(6).
67   Rule 45-501, above note 2, s. 2.1.
68   Victor P. Alboini, *Securities Law and Practice*, vol. 1 (Toronto: Carswell, looseleaf) at para.17.26.1.

grounded in a notion of cost and benefit.[69] The report recommended scrapping a number of exemptions in favour of new exemptions based more explicitly on the trade-off between cost and benefit. In May 1999, the OSC published a concept paper based on the recommendations in the report.[70] This was followed by the new version of Rule 45-501,[71] which came into force 30 November 2001.

E. DISCRETIONARY EXEMPTIONS

Securities statutes in Canada provide legislators with a residual authority to grant discretionary exemptions from the prospectus requirement. In Ontario, for example, the OSC "may, upon the application of an interested person or company, rule ... [that a prospectus is not required] where it is satisfied that to do so would not be prejudicial to the public interest, and may impose such terms and conditions as are necessary.[72] A ruling of this nature may not be appealed to the courts."[73]

It seems clear that this exemptive power is intended to be used in an *ad hoc* fashion in response to applications from particular persons or companies. However, securities administrators take the view that the Director, a senior administrator, has standing as an "interested person" for the purpose of making an application to the OSC. This fiction has been used to justify "blanket rulings" issued by the various securities commissions. These rulings purport to bind *all* persons of a particular character or all parties engaging in specific types of transactions. Moreover, such rulings have been used for objectives other than to exempt classes of persons or transactions from the application of aspects of the securities legislation. By broadly construing the power to "impose ... terms and conditions" when making a discretionary order, the regulators have effectively used blanket rulings to legislate in the securities area. In Ontario, for example, the POP (the prompt-offering prospectus or the "short-form prospectus") system was originally created pursuant to a blanket ruling.[74] The ruling specified that a qualifying issuer was exempted from the prospectus requirement so long as it sold securities under a short form of prospectus whose form and content

---

69   (1996), 19 OSCB 5753.
70   "Revamping the Regulation of the Exempt Market"(1999), 22 OSCB 2835.
71   (2001), 24 OSCB 2187.
72   *OSA*, above note 1, s. 74(1).
73   *Ibid.* s. 74(3).
74   *Re Securities Act and the Prompt Offering Qualification System* (1986), 9 OSCB 6963, replaced by (1993), 16 OSCB 731.

were dictated by an OSC policy statement. The bought deal,[75] the multijurisdictional disclosure system,[76] and the shelf-prospectus system[77] were also originally effected in this manner.[78]

As discussed in chapter 3, in 1994 in Ontario, contemporaneously with the legislative ceding of rule-making powers to securities regulators, the OSC was explicitly deprived of the ability to make blanket orders under the discretionary exemptive power. By contrast, in certain other Canadian jurisdictions, such as British Columbia[79] and Nova Scotia,[80] where the regulators also have been given rule-making powers, the regulators may still, apparently, use blanket orders as well.

F. OFFERING MEMORANDA

When securities are sold by issuers in reliance on a prospectus exemption, it is frequently necessary, as a business matter, to provide investors with pertinent information about the issuer and the securities being sold. The disclosure document used for that purpose is known as an "offering memorandum."[81] Generally speaking, in an exempt offering, an issuer may decide for itself whether it wishes to provide such a document to investors. If the issuer provides an offering memorandum to investors, the *OSA* and the rules, generally, do not mandate the content of such a document or its form. However, in certain cases, the law requires an issuer to provide investors with an offering memorandum. Where an offering memorandum is provided, whether pursuant to one of these requirements or voluntarily, the law provides for civil liability for misrepresentations, similar to the liability that attaches to misrepresentations in a prospectus under section 130 of the *OSA*.

An offering memorandum must be delivered to purchasers and to the OSC where the exempt offering is made in reliance on the "government incentive security exemption."[82] The offering memorandum in

---

75 *Re Securities Act and the Prompt Offering Qualification System and the Solicitation of Expressions of Interest* (1986), 9 OSCB 6993, replaced by (1993), 16 OSCB 2832.

76 (1991), 14 OSCB 2863.

77 (1991), 14 OSCB 1824.

78 Of course, as discussed elsewhere in this book, all of these matters are now governed in Ontario by the OSC Rules implementing National Instruments.

79 *Securities Act*, R.S.B.C. 1996, c. 418, s. 187. This provision actually refers to orders, including blanket orders, pertaining to commission rules.

80 *Securities Act*, R.S.N.S. 1989, c. 418, s. 151A.

81 The term "offering memorandum" is defined in *OSA*, above note 1, s. 1(1).

82 Rule 45-501, above note 2, s. 2.13.

such a case must include the information specified in subsection 2.13(b) of Rule 45-501, which includes a statement concerning the statutory right of action for misrepresentations pursuant to section 130.1 of the *OSA*.

In addition, in some cases, although the seller is not required to deliver an offering memorandum to prospective purchasers, if the seller chooses to deliver one, the purchasers have a statutory right of action, as described in section 130.1 of the *OSA*. A description of this right must be included in the offering memorandum. A copy of the offering memorandum must also be delivered to the OSC, although it does not become a public document. The offering memorandum rules described in this paragraph apply when the exempt offering is made in reliance on any of the following exemptions:[83]

- Rule 45-501, section 2.1 (sales of securities of a closely-held issuer);
- Rule 45-501, section 2.3 (sales to an accredited investor); and
- Rule 45-501, section 2.12 (sales of mutual or non-redeemable investment funds).

G. HISTORICAL/TRANSITIONAL NOTE

1) Certain Prospectus Exemptions Available under Prior Law

A number of other prospectus exemptions were formerly available under Ontario securities law. Some were modified several years ago, and others were removed very recently when the new version of Rule 45-501 came into force. Several of these former exemptions are noted briefly here, including certain exemptions that, perhaps, may have been relied upon by purchasers who still hold such securities. Resales of securities by these purchasers will be subject to transitional resale rules described further below.

a) Persons Purchasing Securities in the Amount of $150,000 or More: The "Private Placement" Exemption

Sales to persons purchasing securities in the amount of $150,000 or more could be effected prior to 30 November 2001, without a prospectus by relying on the exemption set out in clause 72(1)(d) of the

---

83   *Ibid*. ss. 4.1–4.3.

OSA.[84] Such purchasers were assumed (rightly or wrongly) to have sufficient financial sophistication and/or access to expert financial advice to be able to protect their own interests.

This exemption was sometimes referred to as the "private placement" exemption, a phrase that is now used in Companion Policy 45-501 CP[85] to refer to sales made in reliance upon the closely-held issuer and accredited investor exemptions, described above, and, rather more loosely, is occasionally used by practitioners to refer to any sale made under a prospectus exemption. Although a widely used and important provision, the $150,000 aggregate acquisition cost exemption had many shortcomings. The ability of a purchaser to invest $150,000 in a single investment was an arbitrary, and rather dubious, proxy for financial sophistication, especially in recent years. Moreover, the exemption discouraged investors unwilling to risk $150,000 on a single investment from investing lesser amounts in smaller enterprises. For these and other reasons, the accredited investor and closely-held issuer exemptions introduced by the new version of Rule 45-501 appear to address the needs at which the former clause 72(1)(d) exemption were aimed, while eliminating at least some of its deficiencies.

b) Persons Who Were Sophisticated or Well Advised: The Seed Capital Exemption[86]

The *OSA* also provided that a prospectus need not be prepared where, subject to some important qualifications discussed below, all the sales were to persons who "by virtue of net worth and investment experience or by virtue of consultation with or advice from a person or company" were able to evaluate the information provided by the issuer.[87] Issuers would typically assure themselves that purchasers qualified for this exemption by requiring that each purchaser fill out a form declaring that he or she was appropriately qualified. Sales could also be made under this exemption to designated persons, including senior officers and directors of the issuer.

Because this exemption was most often used in the early stages of a company's existence, it was usually referred to as the "seed capital"

---

84   *OSA*, above note 1, s. 72(1)(d); (Old) OSC Rule 45-501 (1998), 21 OSCB 7709, ss. 3.1–3.4 [(Old) Rule 45-501]. See also *OSA*, s. 72(1)(1) and (Old) Rule 45-501, s. 3.5 (exemption for the issue of securities to satisfy the purchase price of assets worth $150,000 or more).
85   (2001), 24 OSCB 5563, s. 1.2.
86   *OSA*, above note 1, s. 72(1)(p) and (Old) Rule 45-501, ss. 3.6–3.7, above note 84.
87   *Ibid*. s. 72(1)(p).

exemption. While the seed capital exemption initially appears to be very wide ranging, it was in fact much more limited. The issuer could solicit no more than fifty prospective purchasers in total, counting solicitations made in any jurisdiction, and could sell to no more than twenty-five, with all the sales essentially completed within a six-month period. Further, if one or more of the purchasers included an entity (such as a corporation) created specifically for the purpose of making the exempt purchase, the number of shareholders (or other partici- pants of a non-incorporated entity) could not exceed the number of permitted purchasers. Moreover, the sale could not be advertised, and the exemption could be used only once in the lifetime of the issuer.

Perhaps the greatest disadvantage of the exemption was that it required each purchaser to have "access to substantially the same infor- mation concerning the issuer that a prospectus ... would provide." Most lawyers interpreted this phrase as requiring an "offering memo- randum" that essentially replicated a prospectus in its informational content. While the expense of assembling an offering memorandum typically falls somewhat short of that associated with assembling a prospectus,[88] the cost was often sufficiently large to transform the seed capital exemption into a simplified prospectus regime, rather than a true exemption from the prospectus requirement.

c)   Exempt Distributions through the Facilities of a Stock Exchange

In Ontario between 1984 and 1994, an issuer with a listing on the Toronto Stock Exchange could choose to make an offering of its com- mon shares through the stock exchange by means of an "exchange- offering prospectus" (or EOP).[89] In such a case, the issuer was exempt from the prospectus requirement, but the offering was required to be made in compliance with the rules of the stock exchange. The stock exchange rules required that the EOP essentially replicate the informa- tion required in a prospectus. The principal benefit of using the EOP

---

88   No "road show" would be necessary, and a translation of the document would not be required unless there were buyers in Quebec. Professional fees and the underwriter's commission would also be lower.

89   Note that the legislation explicitly permits an offering of securities through the facilities of an approved stock exchange upon the filing of a "statement of mate- rial facts." See *OSA*, above note 1, s. 73(1)(b). The EOP system, however, was created pursuant to a series of blanket rulings under s. 74, rather than this statu- tory provision. The last of these rulings may be found at (1994), 17 OSCB 347. While the statutory provision required that the form and content of the prospec- tus be specified in the regulations, the blanket ruling allowed the TSE to formu- late requirements as to the form and content.

rather than a conventional prospectus was that the stock exchange, rather than the OSC, reviewed and ultimately approved the EOP. There is some anecdotal evidence that the exchange performed this review somewhat more quickly and more sympathetically than the OSC.

The EOP system was designed to assist junior resource and industrial enterprises in raising capital. For this reason, it was limited to issuers raising no more than $5 million in any six-month period. This limitation, however, appears to have been its undoing: few offerings in Ontario comply with this size limitation. Thus, the EOP was seldom used and was discontinued at the end of 1994.

2) Contractual Rights of Action

Before the 2001 amendments to Rule 45-501, the statutory right of action in the case of misrepresentations in an offering memorandum prescribed by section 130.1 of the *OSA* was not operative. Although section 130.1 was introduced into the *OSA* in 1999, it initially had no effect because subsection 130.1(8) provided that it would apply only as follows:

(a) to an offering memorandum which has been furnished to a prospective purchaser in connection with a distribution of a security under an exemption from section 53; and

(b) in the circumstances specified in the regulations for the purposes of this section.

At first glance, it might appear that clauses (a) and (b) were intended to describe two different sets of circumstances in which the provisions of section 130.1 would apply. On closer reading, however, it becomes clear that the purpose of clause (b) was not to expand the application of section 130.1 to cases not already covered in clause (a), but was to narrow or limit the application of section 130.1 only to those circumstances where the requirements of *both* clauses were satisfied.[90] Because no regulations of the sort contemplated by clause (b)

---

90   This latter interpretation is based on the definition of "offering memorandum" in s. 1(1) of the *OSA*. An offering memorandum is a document delivered in connection with a sale of securities made in reliance upon an exemption under s. 53 of the *OSA*. Since s. 130.1(8)(a) refers to an offering memorandum furnished in precisely these circumstances, s. 130.1(8)(a) does not limit or extend the definition of offering memorandum; it merely restates that definition. Accordingly, s. 130.1(8)(a) could not, on its own, be seen to prescribe any special circumstances in which s. 130.1 would apply. Therefore, the drafters clearly intended s. 130.1(b) to limit the circumstances in which s. 130.1 would apply.

were passed prior to the promulgation of the new version of Rule 45-501 in late 2001, section 130.1 was not, until that time, an operative provision. However, to make the matter free from doubt, subsection 130.1(8) was amended effective 5 December 2001, to read as follows:

> (8) This section applies only with respect to an offering memoran-dum which has been furnished to a prospective purchaser in con-nection with a distribution of a security under an exemption from section 53 of the Act that is specfied in the regulations for the purposes of this section.[91]

Regulations, it will be recalled, include "rules."[92] Accordingly, the provisions of Rule 45-501 have now brought section 130.1 into effect.

However, even prior to the coming into force of section 130.1, issuers delivering an offering memorandum to prospective private placement purchasers were required, in certain cases, to provide investors with a "contractual right of action" as defined in Rule 14-501.[93] A contractual right of action, as the name suggests, is a right conferred by a contract rather than by a statute, that specifically per-mits an investor to sue for rescission or damages if the offering memo-randum contains a misrepresentation. This right of action was required to "reasonably correspond" to the rights granted under section 130 for prospectus misrepresentations.[94]

---

91 Bill 127, *Responsible Choices for Growth and Fiscal Responsibility Act*, 2d Sess., 37th Leg., Ontario, 2001, cl. 216 (assented to 5 December 2001), S.O. 2001, c. 23.

92 *OSA*, above note 1, s. 1(1) (definition of "regulations").

93 (1997), 20 OSCB 4054, as am. by (1999), 22 OSCB 1173, s. 1.1(2).

94 (Old) Rule 45-501, above note 84, ss. 4.1 & 4.2.

H. REGULATION OF SALES BY EXEMPT PURCHASERS: RESTRICTED AND SEASONING PERIODS

1) Introduction: Restricted and Seasoning Periods

Thus far, we have seen that in order to issue securities in the primary market, an issuer must either compile and distribute a prospectus or find an applicable prospectus exemption. A large number of exemptions from the prospectus requirement are based on the identity of the purchaser. Some persons qualify as exempt purchasers[95] and some do not.

Without more, it would be too easy to evade the prospectus requirement. A person qualifying as an exempt purchaser, for example, might agree, whether for compensation or not, to purchase the securities of a particular issuer and immediately resell them to a non-exempt buyer. This form of circumvention of the prospectus requirement is known as a "backdoor underwriting." An effective scheme for the regulation of primary market offerings must address this danger. The only way to do so is to regulate the first resales (or first trades) of the securities initially sold to exempt buyers.

Prior to the introduction of the closed system, such regulation was done by requiring exempt buyers to fill out a statutory declaration in which the buyer stated that she was purchasing with "investment intent" (i.e., with the intent to hold the securities as an investment and not merely to resell them to non-exempt buyers). This system was difficult to administer, however. Having filled out a statutory declaration and purchased the securities, a buyer might sell them to a non-exempt buyer in a matter of days or weeks, claiming that she had simply changed her intention.

The closed system uses a different means to address the danger of a backdoor underwriting. Securities purchased under some (but not all) of the exemptions become "restricted securities"[96] that cannot freely be resold in the marketplace. Exempt buyers holding restricted

---

95   We use the terms "exempt purchasers" or "exempt buyers" in this section to refer generally to purchasers to whom securities have been sold in reliance upon a prospectus exemption, and not simply to purchasers recognized as "exempt purchasers" by the OSC, pursuant to s. 72(1)(c) of the *OSA*.

96   Readers should be careful not to confuse the term "restricted securities" as we use it here, meaning securities subject to restricted trading rights, with the term "restricted shares," as defined in OSC Rule 56-501 (1999), 22 OSCB 6761, which refers to equity shares subject to a voting or other restriction.

securities are subject to statutory restricted periods (formerly called "hold periods) ranging from four to twelve months (assuming the issuer is a reporting issuer and, in some cases, has been such an issuer for a minimum "seasoning period," as discussed further below). The length of the restricted period varies depending mainly on whether the issuer is a "qualifying issuer" as defined in Multilateral Instrument 45-102. Prior to the elapse of the applicable restricted period, the exempt buyer can resell the securities in either of two ways: (1) after assembling a prospectus for the benefit of prospective buyers, or (2) by reselling to another exempt purchaser. Only after the elapse of the restricted period can the buyer freely resell the securities to whomever she chooses without preparing a prospectus or finding an applicable prospectus exemption. This technique for selling securities free of the prospectus requirement is sometimes referred to below as the "restricted-period resale route."

Restricted periods ensure that those who buy securities under prospectus exemptions do so only with the intention of holding the securities for investment purposes. The underlying theory is that those who know that the securities they purchase will have limited saleability for a period of time ranging from four to twelve months will tend to be locked into their investments. Hence, they will not be tempted to purchase securities in exempt transactions purely with an eye to a quick resale.

In certain cases, the nature of the initial exempt trade is such that the risk of "backdoor underwriting" is very low indeed. In such cases, securities acquired in an exempt distribution may be resold without the need to satisfy any restricted period at all, provided the issuer has been a reporting issuer for a specified minimum period known as the "seasoning period." The seasoning period ensures that information about the issuer has been available to the public for a sufficient length of time to enable that information to be reflected in the market price of the issuer's securities. The restricted-period resale rules and the seasoning-period resale rules are discussed in more detail below.

2) Conditions Applying to Restricted-Period Resales

a)   Multilateral Instrument 45-102, Section 2.5

Although the prospectus exemptions vary from province to province, especially since the introduction of new Rule 45-501 in 2001, the rules applying to the first trade of securities originally acquired in an exempt distribution are increasingly uniform in most of Canada's provinces and territories. This uniformity was achieved with the introduction of Multilateral Instrument 45-102,[97] which has been adopted as a rule, regulation, or policy, as the case may be, in every Canadian securities jurisdiction except Quebec.[98] Reproduced below are the provisions of Multilateral Instrument 45-102 that govern restricted periods:

> 2.5 (1) Unless the conditions in subsection (2) or (3) are satisfied, a trade that is specified by section 2.3 or other securities legislation to be subject to this section is a distribution.
>
> (2) If the issuer of the securities was a qualifying issuer at the distribution date, the conditions are:
>
>> 1. The issuer is and has been a reporting issuer in a jurisdiction listed in Appendix B [i.e., any Canadian province except New Brunswick, Newfoundland, and Prince Edward Island] for the four months immediately preceding the trade.
>>
>> 2. At least four months have elapsed from the distribution date.
>>
>> 3. If the distribution date is on or after the effective date of this Instrument, a certificate representing the securities was issued that carried a legend stating:
>>
>>> "Unless permitted under securities legislation, the holder of the securities shall not trade the securities before [insert the date that is four months and a day after the distribution date]."
>>
>> 4. The trade is not a control distribution.
>>
>> 5. No unusual effort is made to prepare the market or to create a demand for the securities that are the subject of the trade.
>>
>> 6. No extraordinary commission or consideration is paid to a person or company in respect of the trade.
>>
>> 7. If the selling security holder is an insider or officer of the issuer, the selling security holder has no reasonable

---

97   (2001), 24 OSCB 5511 at 5522.

98   However, a number of the key provisions discussed in this chapter, including s. 2.5 (restricted period) and s. 2.6 (seasoning period), do not apply in Manitoba, New Brunswick, Prince Edward Island, or the Yukon Territory (Multilateral Instrument 45-102, *ibid.* s. 2.1).

grounds to believe that the issuer is in default of securities legislation.

(3) If the issuer of the securities was not a qualifying issuer at the distribution date, the conditions are:

1. The issuer is and has been a reporting issuer for the 12 months immediately preceding the trade

    (a) in a jurisdiction listed in Appendix B, if the issuer is an electronic filer under NI 13-101; or

    (b) in the local jurisdiction of the purchaser of the securities that are the subject of the trade, if the issuer is not an electronic filer under NI 13-101.

2. At least 12 months have elapsed from the distribution date.

3. If the distribution date is on or after the effective date of this Instrument, a certificate representing the securities was issued that carried a legend

    (a) if the issuer is a reporting issuer in a jurisdiction listed in Appendix B and is an electronic filer under NI 13-101 on the distribution date, stating:

    "Unless permitted under securities legislation, the holder of the securities shall not trade the securities before [insert the date that is 12 months and a day after the distribution date].";

    or

    (b) if the issuer is not a reporting issuer in a jurisdiction listed in Appendix B at the distribution date, stating:

    "Unless permitted under securities legislation, the holder of the securities shall not trade the securities before the earlier of (i) the date that is 12 months and a day after the date the issuer first became a reporting issuer in any of Alberta, British Columbia, Manitoba, Nova Scotia, Ontario, Quebec and Saskatchewan, if the issuer is a SEDAR filer; and (ii) the date that is 12 months and a day after the later of (A) the distribution date, and (B) the date the issuer became a reporting issuer in the local jurisdiction of the purchaser of the securities that are the subject of the trade."

4. The trade is not a control distribution.

5. No unusual effort is made to prepare the market or to create a demand for the securities that are the subject of the trade.

6. No extraordinary commission or consideration is paid to a person or company in respect of the trade.

7. If the selling security holder is an insider or officer of the issuer, the selling security holder has no reasonable grounds to believe that the issuer is in default of securities legislation.

The various restricted periods referred to in this provision are discussed further below.

b) Prospectus Exemptions That Subject the Resale of Securities to Restricted Periods

Securities acquired pursuant to a prospectus exemption are not always subject to a restricted period. Generally speaking, the greater the risk that an exemption could be used to facilitate "backdoor underwriting," the more likely it is that securities acquired pursuant to that exemption will be subject to a restricted period. More specifically, the first trade of securities obtained in distributions under any of the following exemptions are subject to restricted periods:

1. Securities distributed to accredited investors (Rule 45-501, ss. 2.3 & 6.3)
2. Securities of certain non-reporting mutual fund issuers or non-redeemable investment fund issuers where the initial purchaser's aggregate acquisition cost is at least $150,000 or where the initial purchaser owns $150,000 in securities (Rule 45-501, ss. 2.12 & 6.3)
3. Government incentive securities (Rule 45-501, ss. 2.13, 2.14, & 6.3)
4. Securities distributed to various types of financial institutions (OSA, cl. 72(1)(a))[99]

---

99   Availability of these exemptions after 30 November 2001 has been removed by Rule 45-501, s. 3.1.

5. Securities distributed in an isolated trade (*OSA*, cl. 72(1)(b))
6. Securities distributed to exempt purchasers recognized by the OSC (*OSA*, cl. 72(1(c))[100]
7. Securities distributed with an aggregate acquisition cost of not less than $150,000 (*OSA*, cl. 72(1)(d))[101]
8. Securities distributed in exchange for at least $150,000 worth of assets (*OSA*, cl. 72(1)(l))[102]
9. Securities distributed in exchange for mining claims (*OSA*, cl. 72(1)(m))
10. Securities obtained under the "seed capital exemption" (*OSA*, cl. 72(1)(p))[103]
11. Securities sold by one registered dealer to another (*OSA*, cl. 72(1)(q))
12. Underlying securities acquired from the conversion or exchange of a convertible or exchangeable security where that convertible or exchangeable security was initially acquired by the seller pursuant to a "Type 1 trade" (i.e., an exemption under *OSA* cls. 72(1)(a), (b), (c), (d), (l), (m), (p), or (q); Rule 45-501, ss. 2.3, 2.12, 2.13, or 2.14; or under (Old) Rule 45-501, ss. 2.4, 2.5, or 2.11)) (Rule 45-501, s. 6.5)
13. Certain securities traded to a Registered Retirement Savings Plan or a Registered Retirement Income Fund in certain circumstances (Rule 45-501, s. 6.8)

c) Issuer Must Be a Reporting Issuer: The Seasoning Period

One of the most important things to note about the resale restrictions contained in section 2.5 of Multilateral Instrument 45-102 is that they include two critical elements: a seasoning period and a restricted period. The seasoning period refers to the length of time the issuer of the securities has been a reporting issuer, either in one of the seven provinces that act as principal regulators under the mutual reliance review system[104] or, if the issuer is not a SEDAR filer, in the jurisdiction of the purchaser of the securities that are being traded. In order for a purchaser of exempt securities to freely resell those securities into the

---

100 *Idem.*
101 *Idem.*
102 *Idem.*
103 *Idem.*
104 These seven provinces are Alberta, British Columbia, Manitoba, Nova Scotia, Ontario, Quebec, and Saskatchewan. (See MI 45-102, above note 97, Appendix B.) Note that Quebec is included on this list, even though MI 45-102 has not been adopted in Quebec.

market after the elapse of the restricted (or hold) period, the securities must be those of a *reporting issuer* that has been a reporting issuer for at least four months in some cases, and for at least twelve months in others. "Reporting issuer" is a defined term. In general, only companies that have made an offering of their securities to the public are reporting issuers.[105] (At one time, a take-over bid in which the bidder company offered its securities in exchange for securities of a target company could have resulted in the bidder becoming a reporting issuer. See, e.g., *Re 695274 Ont. Ltd.*[106] This provision, however, came to be regarded as a significant gap in the *OSA*, as discussed further in chapter 10, and was changed in 1999.)

Reporting issuers usually have publicly quoted trading prices.[107] More important, such companies are subject to ongoing (continuous) disclosure requirements, under which they must promptly report all material corporate events.[108] Thus, the informational record concerning reporting issuers tends to be much more complete than the informational record of companies lacking this status.

It is for this reason that the ability to sell securities free of the prospectus requirement after the elapse of a restricted period is limited to reporting issuers and, more particularly, to reporting issuers about whom public information has been available for a minimum period of time. Buyers of securities in such issuers have a market price that serves as a benchmark against which to evaluate the worth of those securities. By contrast, there is no such benchmark for those who buy the securities of a private company, and no well-developed, public-information record to inform them and protect their interests.

If the issuer is *not* a reporting issuer, the exempt purchaser is limited to two options in selling her securities: selling to another exempt buyer[109] or selling via a prospectus.[110]

---

105 It is possible, however, for a company to become a reporting issuer without ever offering its securities to the public. *OSA*, s. 53(2), for example, enables an issuer to become a reporting issuer simply by filing a prospectus, without making a distribution.

106 (1987), 10 OSCB 2685.

107 If the reporting issuer's securities trade on a stock exchange, they will have a quoted price. If the issuer does not have a stock exchange listing and its securities trade in the "over-the-counter" market, one or more dealers in the system may quote prices at which they are willing to buy and sell those securities.

108 See chapter 9. In order to ensure that the public information record is complete, the restricted-period resale route is, in many cases, available only when the reporting issuer is not in default of applicable reporting requirements. See discussion in section (e) below.

109 *OSA*, above note 1, s. 72 (1).

110 *Ibid*. s. 53.

d) No "Hard Sell"

In order to take advantage of the restricted-period resale route, the seller of the securities (or his or her agents) cannot make any "unusual effort ... to prepare the market or to create a demand for the securities," and "no extraordinary commission or consideration" can be paid to effect such a sale. These requirements ensure that the buyers of securities from exempt purchasers are not unduly pressured or enticed by the sellers.

e) Issuer Not in Default

The resale rules include an issuer seasoning-period requirement to provide some protection to subsequent purchasers who may benefit from the public availability of information about the securities issuer. But, those benefits are seriously curtailed if the issuer, although subject to the ongoing securities law reporting rules, does not comply with those rules. Where the seller of an issuer's securities is a stranger to the issuer, with no control over the issuer and no way of knowing whether the issuer complies with its legal obligations, little can be gained by imposing constraints on the sale. But, where the seller is in a position to affect proper compliance by the issuer, making such compliance a condition of resale provides additional discipline on issuers and improves the quality of disclosure available to all investors. Accordingly, where the selling securityholder is an insider or an officer of the issuer, the rules provide that the securities of such a holder will be freely tradeable only if the holder "has no reasonable grounds for believing the issuer is in default of securities legislation."[111]

f) Legended Certificates

The use of "legends" on securities certificates has long been a technique employed to ensure the integrity of share transfer restrictions, not only in Canada, but also in the United States. By expressly noting the transfer restrictions to which a security is subject on the certificate itself, subsequent purchasers of the share are given notice that the security is not freely tradeable. The effectiveness of such legends, however, assumes, among other things, that the certificate will in fact be delivered to the buyer of the security. In Canada, when securities of public companies are transferred, paper certificates rarely change hands. Securities are typically registered in the name of a depository holding the shares on behalf of participants (i.e., brokerage firms). Transfers of securities between individuals, accordingly, represent

---

111 Multilateral Instrument 45-102, above note 97, ss. 2.5(2)7 & (3)7.

transfers of beneficial, rather than legal, ownership and are typically effected by book entries by the depository, their brokerage participants, or both. No paper certificates need ever be delivered because the registered holder — the depository — remains unchanged by such transactions. These limitations, however, while fully recognized by the CSA, were not thought to completely overwhelm the potential value of requiring legends to enforce resale restrictions.[112]

Accordingly, when securities are sold in reliance on a prospectus exemption that subjects the buyer to a restricted or hold period before those securities can become freely tradeable, the securities certificates delivered to the buyer must carry a legend with wording specifically prescribed by Multilateral Instrument 45-102. The wording varies depending upon whether the issuer is a qualifying issuer[113] or a reporting issuer in one of the provincial jurisdictions specified in Appendix B to MI 45-102.[114] The essential message in each case is that the holder of securities is put on notice that the securities represented by the certificates cannot be traded until the applicable restricted period expires.

Of course, legended certificates generally cannot be used to settle trades of exchange-listed securities.[115] However, as the CSA noted in its response to comments received on Multilateral Instrument 45-102, the transfer agent of an issuer is permitted to remove the legends from the certificates after the restricted period expires.

g)   Qualifying Issuers and the Length of the Restricted Period

From the above discussion of provisions of Multilateral Instrument 45-102, it should be noted that the restricted period is shorter for the securities of "qualifying issuers" than it is for the securities of other issuers. Specifically, where an issuer was a qualifying issuer *at the date of the initial exempt trade* and is a reporting issuer with at least a four-month reporting history *by the date of the resale*, the securities obtained in the initial exempt trade are subject to only a four-month restricted period (assuming the other conditions in section 2.5 of MI 45-102 are satisfied). If the issuer was not a qualifying issuer at the date of the initial exempt trade, however, the restricted period is twelve months. Thus, for example, if a qualifying issuer was a reporting issuer for four (or

---

112   See, e.g., (2001), 24 OSCB 5517.
113   Multilateral Instrument 45-102, above note 97, s. 2.5(2)3.
114   *Ibid.* s. 2.5(3)3.
115   See, e.g., s. 625, *Toronto Stock Exchange, Company Manual,* available online at <http://www.tse.ca/en/pdf/CompanyManual0202.pdf> (site accessed: 16 April 2002) and *The Rules of the Toronto Stock Exchange Inc.,* Rule 5-203(f), available online at <http://www.tse.ca/en/pdf/TSERules.pdf>.

more) months on the date of an exempt trade in securities to which section 2.5 of MI 45-102 applies and did not cease to be a reporting issuer throughout the succeeding four months,[116] the person to whom those securities were issued pursuant to the exempt trade could resell the securities freely four months after that initial exempt trade. However, if a purchaser acquires securities of an issuer that is not a qualifying issuer in an exempt distribution to which section 2.5 applies, then the purchaser cannot freely resell the securities until twelve months after the original exempt distribution or until twelve months after the issuer first became a reporting issuer (in the relevant jurisdiction), whichever is later. (Of course, it would be possible during this time period for the securities to be sold in reliance upon a prospectus exemption. The point is that they could not be sold except pursuant to such an exemption.)

The phrase "qualifying issuer" is defined in MI 45-102 to mean an issuer:

(a) that is a reporting issuer in a jurisdiction listed in Appendix B [i.e., Alberta, British Columbia, Manitoba, Nova Scotia, Ontario, Quebec, and Saskatchewan],

(b) that is an electronic filer under NI 13-101,

(c) that has a current AIF filed on SEDAR,

(d) that

    (i) has a class of equity securities listed or quoted on a qualified market [i.e., any of the three Canadian exchanges — except Tier 3 CDNX issuers — the NYSE, the London Stock Exchange, the AMEX, the Nasdaq National Market and the Nasdaq SmallCap Market], has not been notified by the qualified market that it does not meet the requirements to maintain that listing or quotation and is not designated inactive, suspended or the equivalent, or

    (ii) has a class of securities outstanding that has an approved rating [i.e., a BBB rating or above for long-term debt securities and comparable investment-grade ratings for short-term debt and preferred shares].

---

116 Note, however, that although the issuer must continue to be a reporting issuer at the date of the resale, it need not continue to be a qualifying issuer on that date. It is sufficient that it *was* a qualifying issuer on the date of the initial exempt trade. (See Companion Policy 45-102 CP (2001), 24 OSCB 5540, s. 1.7.)

(e) if it is not qualified to file a short form prospectus ... and has a mineral project or oil and gas producing activities, including exploration, that has filed with its current AIF, as if the current AIF were a prospectus, technical reports in accordance with NI 43-101 if the current AIF was filed after the effective date of NI 43-101, or a technical report and certificate prepared in accordance with NP 2-B,

(f) that, if it has received a notice in writing from any regulator that its current AIF, including any technical reports, is unacceptable, has satisfied the regulator that its current AIF is acceptable, and

(g) that, if it is a CPC [i.e., a capital pool company, as discussed in chapter 6], has filed a CPC information circular.

The most common type of "qualifying issuer" is a reporting issuer with a current AIF filed on SEDAR and a class of securities listed on a stock exchange or a class of outstanding debt or preferred shares with an approved rating. Linking shorter restricted (or hold) periods to an AIF filing requirement is derived from the SHAIF system (Shorter Hold Periods for Issuers Filing an AIF) instituted in British Columbia and Alberta in 1998.[117] The CSA has acknowledged that one benefit of the new rules will be to encourage more issuers to become AIF filers, which will, in turn, improve the general level of publicly available information in Canadian capital markets.[118]

Special rules apply when the securities initially sold by the issuer in an exempt trade are convertible into other securities (the "underlying securities") of the issuer at a later date. In such cases, the restricted period for resale of the underlying securities begins to run, not from the date on which the holder first obtained the underlying securities by exercising the conversion right, but from the earlier date on which the convertible securities were first issued.

h) Satisfying the Restricted-Period Rules: Examples

To illustrate the application of the rules governing restricted periods, consider the following examples.

i) Scenario One (Non-convertible Securities)

On 1 January 2002, ABC Ltd. (a "qualifying issuer") issues common shares to Buyer (1) in a transaction exempt from the prospectus

---

117 See "Notice of Proposed Multilateral Instrument 45-102" (2000), 23 OSCB 6234.

118 (2001), 24 OSCB 5518.

requirement by virtue of section 2.3 of Rule 45-501 (the "accredited investor" exemption). Buyer (1) is *not* a control person of ABC Ltd. On 1 February 2002, Buyer (1) wishes to resell her ABC Ltd. common shares to Buyer (2).

Can Buyer (1) lawfully trade the ABC Ltd. common shares to Buyer (2) on February 1 without the need for a prospectus to be prepared?

aa) *Analysis*

Because the original exempt trade to Buyer (1) on 1 January 2002 was exempt from the prospectus requirement under section 2.3 of Rule 45-501, the resale (or "first trade") of those shares is subject to a four-month, pre-trade "seasoning period" and a four-month restricted (or hold) period commencing on the "distribution date" (i.e., the date of the initial exempt distribution — in this example, 1 January 2002). (Rule 45-501, s. 6.3 and MI 45-102, s. 2.5(2)).

Therefore, Buyer (1) cannot freely trade the ABC Ltd. shares on February 1 because the four-month, pre-trade restricted period (January 1 to May 1) has not yet elapsed.

However, Buyer (1) can sell to Buyer (2) if such a sale, itself, is made pursuant to a prospectus exemption. (See Companion Policy MI 45-102 CP, s. 1.2(2).)

ii) *Scenario Two (Non-convertible Securities)*

Assume the same facts as in scenario one and additionally assume that Buyer (2) is also an accredited investor and is not a control person of ABC Ltd.

Therefore, Buyer (1) sells the ABC Ltd. shares to Buyer (2) on February 1, relying on the prospectus exemption in section 2.3 of Rule 45-501.

On 5 May 2002, Buyer (2) wishes to sell to Buyer (3) the ABC Ltd. shares previously acquired from Buyer (1).

Can Buyer (2) lawfully trade the ABC Ltd. shares to Buyer (3) on May 5?

aa) *Analysis*

Because the trade by Buyer (1) to Buyer (2) was made in reliance on the exemption in section 2.3 of Rule 45-501, the first trade of those securities by Buyer (2) is subject to section 2.5 of MI 45-102. (See Rule 45-501, s. 6.3.) The shares can be sold freely if, and only if, the seasoning-period requirement and the restricted-period requirement are satisfied.

Because the date of the proposed sale to Buyer (3) (i.e., May 5) is more than four months after 1 January 2002, and because we know that ABC Ltd. must have been a reporting issuer on 1 January 2002 (because every "qualifying issuer" must be a reporting issuer), it appears that the requirement of the four-month, pre-trade seasoning period is satisfied.

The restricted-period requirement is also satisfied because the four-month restricted period commences *not* on February 1 (the date on which Buyer (2) obtained the shares it now wishes to sell), but rather on January 1 (the date of the initial exempt trade by the issuer of the securities). Section 2.5 of MI 45-102 provides that at least four months must "have elapsed from the *distribution date*" [emphasis added]. "Distribution date" is defined in section 1.1 of MI 45-102 to mean, in this case, "the date the security that is the subject of the trade was distributed in reliance on an exemption from the prospectus requirement *by the issuer*" [emphasis added]. It should be noted that this conclusion is consistent with the expressed policy of the OSC under the prior resale rules to permit "tacking" of hold periods.[119] To make the matter free from doubt the CSA expressly confirms this conclusion — complete with an illustrative example — in Companion Policy 45-102 CP.[120]

iii) Scenario Three (Convertible Securities)
On 1 January 2002, XYZ Ltd., a qualifying issuer, issues convertible preferred shares to Purchaser 1, an accredited investor, in an exempt trade made in reliance on section 2.3 of Rule 45-501. Normally, Purchaser 1 would be able to freely trade the preferred shares by 2 May 2002. (See Rule 45-501, s. 6.3 and MI 45-102, s. 2.5.)

However, on 1 February 2002, Purchaser 1 exercises its conversion right and converts the preferred shares to common shares of XYZ Ltd. The issue of the common shares by XYZ Ltd. to Purchaser 1 on February 1 is exempt from the prospectus requirement pursuant to subclause 72(1)(f)(iii) of the *OSA*.

When will Purchaser 1 be able to freely resell the common shares in XYZ Ltd. that it now holds?

aa) Analysis
The rules governing the resale by Purchaser 1 of the common shares it now holds in XYZ Ltd. depend on which exemption XYZ used when it originally distributed the convertible preferred shares to Purchaser 1

---

119 See, e.g., (old) Companion Policy 45-501 CP (1998), 21 OSCB 6548, s. 2.5.
120 (2001), 24 OSCB 5540, s. 1.9.

without a prospectus.[121] In this case, XYZ issued the preferred shares to Purchaser 1 in reliance on the accredited investor exemption in section 2.3 of Rule 45-501. A trade made in reliance on the accredited investor exemption is a "Type 1 trade," which is defined in Rule 45-501. Therefore, the resale of the underlying securities (in this example, the common shares) is subject to the restricted period prescribed by section 2.5 of MI 45-102. (See Rule 45-501, s. 6.5.) Because XYZ Ltd. is a qualifying issuer, the restricted period is four months from the distribution date assuming all other conditions of section 2.5 are satisfied. (See MI 45-102, s. 2.5(2)2.) The distribution date for underlying securities, such as the XYZ Ltd. common shares, is the "date the convertible security [i.e., in this example, the preferred shares] ... that, directly or indirectly, entitled or required the holder to acquire the underlying security was distributed in reliance on an exemption from the prospectus requirement by the issuer ..." (See Rule 45-501, s. 1.1, definition of "distribution date.") In this example, then, the distribution date is 1 January the date on which the preferred shares were issued to Purchaser 1.

The result of all this is that Purchaser 1 can sell the *common shares* freely after four months have elapsed from the date on which Purchaser 1 first acquired the convertible *preferred shares*. In other words, the underlying common shares become freely tradeable on the same date as the preferred shares would have become freely tradeable had Purchaser 1 chosen not to exercise its conversion right. This is precisely the outcome intended by the regulators and confirmed in Companion Policy 45-102 CP, section 1.10:

> The restricted period or seasoning period applicable to trades in underlying securities is calculated from the distribution date of the convertible security, exchangeable security or multiple convertible security.

---

121 Underlying securities acquired in a distribution exempt from the prospectus requirement by virtue of s. 72(1)(f)(iii) of the *OSA* are subject to (a) the restricted period if the convertible securities (i.e., the securities that were converted into the underlying securities) were originally acquired pursuant to one of the *OSA* prospectus exemptions referred to in Appendix D to MI 45-102, or in a "Type 1" trade as defined in Rule 45-501; or (b) the seasoning period in all other cases except those involving exempt trades to consultants under Rule 45-503, above note 4. (See MI 45-102, above note 97, ss. 2.3, 2.4, Appendix D, and Appendix E, and Rule 45-501, s. 6.5, above note 2.)

3) Exempt Trades for Which There Is No Restricted Period (Seasoning-Period Exemptions)

a) Multilateral Instrument 45-102, Section 2.6

When securities are acquired under some prospectus exemptions, no restricted periods apply. In such cases, securities can be resold freely if the issuer has been a reporting issuer for a specified seasoning period and satisfies the other, usual resale conditions (i.e., that the sale is not a control distribution; no unusual effort is made to prepare the market; no extraordinary commission or consideration is paid; and, if the seller is an insider or officer of the issuer, the seller has no reasonable grounds to believe that the issuer is in default of securities legislation).[122]

The minimum seasoning period varies depending on whether the issuer is a qualifying issuer at the date of the original exempt trade (the "distribution date"), *regardless of whether the issuer is or is not still a qualifying issuer at the date of the resale.* Where the issuer was a qualifying issuer at the distribution date, the seasoning period is four months; that is, the issuer of the securities must have been a reporting issuer for at least four months by the date of the resale. Where the issuer was not a qualifying issuer at the distribution date, the seasoning period is twelve months.

As a practical matter, the effect of the seasoning-period requirements is that if an issuer distributes securities in an exempt distribution before the issuer's initial public offering, the buyers of those securities cannot resell them freely until one year after the issuer goes public. There is one important exception to this one-year seasoning period. If securities are issued to employees of the issuer before the issuer's initial public offering and the issuer subsequently becomes not merely a reporting issuer, but also a qualifying issuer, the seasoning period that must elapse before the employees can resell their shares is four months, rather than twelve.[123] This, of course, is an exception to the general rule that the issuer's status as a qualifying issuer is determined solely as of the distribution date. The exception was included in the final version of MI 45-102 so that employees who receive shares of an issuer before its initial public offering will be on an equal footing with those who receive such shares after the initial public offering. The CSA explains that this exemption was included to encourage issuers to use employee stock options and similar equity incentives.[124]

---

122 Multilateral Instrument 45-102, above note 97, ss. 2.6(3)2–5 & (4)2–5.
123 *Ibid.* s.2.6(5).
124 (2001), 24 OSCB 5513.

b) Types of Issues for Which There Is a Seasoning Period, but No Restricted (or Hold) Period

The following is a list of many of the most frequently encountered prospectus exemptions to which resales (or first trades) are subject to seasoning-period requirements:

1. Securities distributed as stock dividends (*OSA*, subcl. 72(1)(f)(i); MI 45-102, s. 2.4, Appendix E)
2. Securities distributed in the course of a reorganization or winding up (*OSA,* subcl. 72(1)(f)(ii); MI 45-102, s. 2.4, Appendix E)
3. Securities distributed as a result of the exercise of a previously granted right to purchase, convert, or exchange securities (*OSA*, subcl. 72(1)(f)(iii)); or the exercise by the issuer of its right to compel a holder of convertible or exchangeable securities to convert (Rule 45-501, s. 2.6) or exchange (Rule 45-501, s. 2.7), other than in cases where the convertible or exchangeable securities were originally acquired in an exempt trade otherwise subject to the restricted-period rules or where the trade is to an associated or investor consultant as defined in Rule 45-503 (Rule 45-501, s. 6.6; MI 45-102, s. 2.4, Appendix E)
4. Securities distributed in the course of a statutory amalgamation, arrangement, or other similar procedure (*OSA*, cl. 72(1)(i) and Rule 45-501, ss. 2.8 & 6.7)
5. Securities distributed by a bidder in the course of a take-over bid (*OSA*, cl. 72(1)(j); MI 45-102, s. 2.4, Appendix E) (In fact, the first trade of such securities may even be exempt from the section 2.6 rules under certain circumstances. See MI 45-102, s. 2.11)
6. Securities distributed by an issuer in connection with a securities exchange issuer bid (Rule 45-501, ss. 2.5 & 6.7)
7. Securities sold into a take-over bid (*OSA*, cl. 72(1)(k); MI 45-102, s. 2.4, Appendix E)
8. Distributions of rights (*OSA*, cl. 72(1)(h); Rule 45-501, s. 6.4) and distribution of securities upon exercise of rights, unless the rights were originally distributed in a Type 1 trade, as discussed above (*OSA*, cl. 72(1)(h); Rule 45-501, ss. 6.4 & 6.5)
9. Securities distributed to executives and employees of the issuer who purchased the securities voluntarily (*OSA*, cl. 72(1)(n) and Rule 45-503)[125]

---

125   Note that, although MI 45-102, Appendix E, specifically refers to *OSA*, s. 72(1)(n), that prospectus exemption was removed by Rule 45-503, s. 2.1, above note 4. Resales of securities acquired by employees, executives, and consultants are not technically subject to the seasoning-period rules of MI 45-102, above note 97, s. 2.6, but are subject to a seasoning-period regime prescribed in Part 9 of Rule 45-503.

10. Securities distributed pursuant to a dividend reinvestment plan (Rule 45-502, ss. 2.1 & 4.1)[126]
11. Securities distributed pursuant to the closely-held issuer exemption, unless the securities were originally distributed to a promoter of the issuer (Rule 45-501, ss. 6.1 & 6.2)[127]

c)   Mechanics of the Seasoning-Period Requirement

While there is no restricted (or hold) period for securities received under the above exemptions, in order for holders to resell the securities under section 2.6 of Multilateral Instrument 45-102, the issuer must satisfy the seasoning-period requirement. This means that the issuer must have been a reporting issuer for a specified minimum amount of time before its securities can become freely tradeable. If the exempt securities are received *before* the issuer becomes a reporting issuer, the initial exempt purchaser wishing to resell is subject to a *de facto* restricted or hold period equal to at least the length of the seasoning period (or longer, if the issuer does not become a reporting issuer immediately after the exempt distribution). Of course, if the issuer does not immediately become a reporting issuer, the *de facto* restricted period equals the period following the exempt distribution during which the issuer is not a reporting issuer plus the seasoning period, which begins only after the issuer finally becomes a reporting issuer.

Note, however, that if, at the time of the exempt purchase, the issuer already has been a reporting issuer for the required seasoning period, there is no hold- or restricted-period requirement, *de facto* or otherwise.

The length of the required seasoning period varies depending upon whether the issuer of the securities is a qualifying issuer at the time of the initial exempt distribution. Where the issuer was a qualifying issuer on the distribution date, the seasoning period is four months (i.e., the issuer must have been a reporting issuer for at least four months before the resale).[128] Where the issuer was not a qualifying issuer on the date of the initial exempt trade, the seasoning period is twelve months.[129] Of course, even when the seasoning-period requirements are met, the seller

---

126 Such trades are not technically subject to the seasoning-period rules of MI 45-102, above note 97, s. 2.6, but are subject to a seasoning-period regime prescribed in Part 4 of Rule 45-502, above note 3.
127 Where the securities were originally distributed to a promoter, resale by the promoter is subject to MI 45-102, ss. 2.8(2) & (3). (See Rule 45-501, above note 2, s. 6.1.)
128 Multilateral Instrument 45-102, above note 97, s. 2.6(3)1.
129 *Ibid.* s. 2.6(4)1.

must still satisfy the other "usual" resale rules: namely, that the trade is not a control distribution; no unusual effort is made to prepare the market; no extraordinary commission or consideration is paid; and, if the seller is an insider or officer of the issuer, the seller has no reasonable grounds to believe that the issuer is in default of securities legislation.[130]

d) Little Danger of Backdoor Underwriting

Why is there no restricted period for securities purchased under the above exemptions? Resales of securities purchased under these exemptions present comparatively little danger of backdoor underwriting. For example, no restricted period is required to resell securities originally received from a bidder as consideration for tendering shares of a target corporation into a take-over bid.[131] The initial issue of the bidder's shares is exempt from the prospectus requirements because the bidder issuing the securities must assemble an offering circular, which contains the same information as a prospectus.[132] Thus, shareholders of the target company who receive such securities from the bidder are as well protected as the shareholders would have been if the bidder originally issued the securities to the public under a prospectus (although the take-over bid circular, unlike a prospectus, is not subject to prior review by the OSC). The launching of a formal take-over bid, the completion of an offering circular, and the myriad other rules that apply to such a bid ensure that reliance on this prospectus exemption can hardly be viewed as an effective device to circumvent the prospectus requirements. Accordingly, there is no need to make securities issued pursuant to this exemption subject to a restricted period.

Similarly, there is no restricted period for the resale of securities originally received by a take-over bidder from target shareholders who tendered into the bid.[133] Again, there is little danger in such cases of backdoor underwriting. It is improbable that an issuer of securities would engineer a backdoor underwriting by issuing securities to exempt purchasers, and then having the purchasers tender their shares into a take-over bid. The take-over bidder is typically an arm's-length

---

130 *Ibid.* s. 2.6(3)2–5 & (4)2–5.

131 *OSA*, above note 1, s. 72(1)(j).

132 The take-over bid may be exempt from the take-over requirements including the filing of a take-over bid circular (see chapter 10 for further details); however, under MI 45-102, above note 97, s. 2.11, only securities received in a take-over bid in which a securities exchange take-over bid circular was filed are exempt from the seasoning-period provisions of s. 2.6.

133 *OSA*, above note 1, s. 72(1)(k).

third party not acting in concert with the issuer or insiders of the issuer. Moreover, the securities obtained by the bidder are freely trade-able only if the target company has been a reporting issuer for the required seasoning period. Thus, persons subsequently purchasing tar-get securities when they are resold by the bidder have access to public information concerning the issuer of those securities that was in the public market before the bid was made, plus additional disclosure about the target firm contained in the bidder's take-over bid circular.

Similarly, there is no restricted period when securities are received pursuant to a reorganization, a winding-up,[134] a statutory amalgama-tion, or other similar procedure.[135] In each of these cases, once again, the risk of such transactions being used to effect backdoor underwrit-ings and thereby circumvent the prospectus rules is minimal. Imposing a restricted period on holders of securities who very likely received the securities in exchange for securities that were *not* subject to such restrictions is unfair and could needlessly hamper the completion of otherwise sensible corporate reorganizations.

4) Critique of the Restricted-Period Requirements

The primary issues that must be addressed to determine the factors that should influence the length of the restricted period are the likelihood of a backdoor underwriting and the likelihood of purchasers of exempt securities mispricing these securities. How effectively do the resale pro-visions address these issues?

As noted, one factor affecting the restricted period is risk. The securities of qualifying issuers are subject to shorter restricted periods because the securities of qualifying issuers, broadly speaking, are less risky than the securities of non-qualifying issuers. At first blush, the riskiness of a security appears to have little or nothing to do with the risk of a backdoor underwriting or the danger of subsequent buyers mispricing the securities.

It may be tempting to rationalize the relationship between risk and the restricted period on the basis that the riskier the security, the greater the investment risk to subsequent purchasers of that security. But, this amounts to saying little more than "riskier securities are riski-er securities." Modern portfolio theory suggests that the risk of an investor's *portfolio* is important in buying securities, rather than the risk of any individual security in the portfolio. Moreover, the unsys-

---

134 *Ibid.* s.72(1)(f)(ii).
135 *Ibid.* ss.72(1)(i) and Rule 45-501, above note 2, s. 2.8.

tematic component of security risk, on this theory, is unimportant to investors. Only systematic risk is priced.[136] Yet, those proxies for risk explored above seem to address mainly the issue of unsystematic risk. Finally, in order to fully diversify, investors should buy securities at many levels of risk. Thus, it is difficult to argue that risk alone should have any influence on the length of the restricted period.[137]

The relationship between risk and the restricted period might be defended, however, on the basis that securities with high unsystematic risk tend to be those issued by small, speculative companies. Such companies likely find meeting the public-offering requirements onerous. Companies of this nature may have a greater incentive to attempt to illicitly bypass the public-offering requirements by effecting a back-door underwriting. Of course, such issuers must be reporting issuers in order for their shares to become freely tradeable. So, in order to provide investors with freely-tradeable shares, these issuers must prepare a prospectus at some point. However, even if such an issuer was prepared to file a prospectus at one point in its corporate life, it might perhaps seek to raise additional funds without having recourse to the expensive public-offering process again.

Securities issued by small companies are much more likely to be mispriced in the public-trading markets. This is a consequence of a number of factors, including the relative absence of a following among institutional traders, the absence of interest from market analysts and the press, the poorly developed informational record concerning such issuers, and thin trading.

As noted, the depth of the public market for the firm's securities and the depth of the public informational record are the other two factors that affect the length of the hold period. The relationship between these factors and the firm's size is clear: small companies are subject to illiq-

---

136 This conclusion is based on the capital-asset pricing model (CAPM). For a discussion of CAPM and the concepts of systematic (or market) and unsystematic (or unique) risk, see Zvi Bodie and Robert C. Merton, *Finance* (Upper Saddle River: Prentice-Hall, 2000), Chapter 13.

137 In its most restrictive form, the capital-asset pricing model (CAPM) assumes that the risky portion of every investor's portfolio ought to consist of the same optimal portfolio of risky securities. Investors would then tailor their overall portfolio (i.e., the risky plus the risk-free component) by adjusting the proportion they invested in risky securities. Thus, the more risk averse the investor, the more of her or his portfolio would consist of risk-free investments (such as government bonds). While the proportion of each investor's portfolio invested in risky securities would vary, the portion of risky securities of every investor's portfolio would consist of the same securities in the same proportions.

uid trading and have poorly developed public informational records. Such companies are comparatively difficult for purchasers to value.

Risk, liquidity, and quality of the informational record taken together indicate the degree of informational risk that confronts those who purchase securities from exempt purchasers. The greater the informational risk is, the more difficult it is to value the securities, and the greater the danger that subsequent buyers will misprice the securities.

There is typically no informational asymmetry between restricted buyers and those who purchase from them. Thus, the restricted periods perform a second redundant function. In addition to guarding against possible backdoor underwritings, the restricted periods protect against an informational asymmetry that does not exist.

I. PUBLIC/PRIVATE OFFERINGS

One final point merits mention here. The notional distinction between public and private offerings is sometimes blurred in real life. For example, before section 130.1 of the *OSA* took effect, when an issuer sold securities in a private placement to a few institutional investors in Canada and at the same time sold securities of the same class in a public offering in the United States, an issue arose as to whether Canadian purchasers ought to be given a contractual right of action.[138] Moreover, occasionally underwriters approach institutional investors with a view to completing a private placement, then abandon the plan. Instead, the underwriters conduct a public offering of the same securities. In such cases, do the underwriters' pre-prospectus discussions with the institutional investors — which are perfectly legal as part of a planned private placement — nevertheless become illegal acts in furtherance of a distribution in the absence of a prospectus?[139] When an issuer privately

---

138 See Deemed Rule, *Re Certain International Offerings by Private Placement* (1997), 20 OSCB 1219; and OSC Staff Notice, "International Private Placements" (1995), 18 OSCB 1350.

139 See CSA Notice, "Pre-Marketing Activities in the Context of Bought Deals" (1993), 16 OSCB 2822 in which staff indicate that if there were a "bona fide intention to effect an exempt distribution" that was subsequently abandoned, the prior discussions would be considered a "distribution" separate from the eventual distribution in respect of which the prospectus was filed and, therefore, would not be in violation of the *OSA*. Otherwise, however, such discussions would be considered in furtherance of the eventual public offering. Because such an offering would be a distribution, the discussions conducted before a prospectus was filed would constitute, in staff's view, a violation of the *OSA*.

places an issue of special warrants that entitle holders, upon exercise, to purchase common shares, and then files a prospectus to make such common shares freely tradeable, is this a private placement of the warrants, a public offering of the shares,[140] or both? Many issues of this sort have been confronted by U.S. regulators grappling with what is often referred to as a question of "integration of offerings." The problem, in some ways, is less cumbersome in Canada because of the differences between the Canadian and U.S. securities markets and because Canadian prospectus exemptions tend to be more tightly crafted than their U.S. counterparts. However, issues of this sort have, from time to time, challenged Canadian regulators as well.

J. CONCLUSION

The exempt market is a critical source of funds, particularly for small and medium-sized enterprises. The prospectus exemptions and the resale (or "first trade") restrictions are, accordingly, of great importance to the survival and the prosperity of these businesses. While investor protection remains the single most important goal of securities regulation, it must be pursued within a regime that is sufficiently flexible and cost-effective to ensure that the capital markets are not closed to smaller companies, which are often among the most innovative players in our economy. The new exempt distribution regime in Ontario, especially with the flexibility offered by the new "closely-held issuer" exemption, illustrates a regulatory willingness to balance traditional investor protection concerns with the legitimate financial needs of smaller enterprises.

---

140 For a discussion of some of the implications of special warrant financings, see OSC Staff Notice 46-701, "Use of Special Warrants in Connection with Distribution of Securities by Prospectus" (1989), 12 OSCB 2168.

CHAPTER 8

INSIDER TRADING

A. INTRODUCTION

Corporate insiders, such as officers or directors, regularly buy and sell shares issued by their companies and are generally permitted by law to do so, provided they comply with two sorts of rules. First, corporate insiders must report their trades to securities regulators in a form that becomes available as a public record. Second, they must not trade when they have confidential inside information.

There are few subjects in securities law that attract more public attention than insider trading. Many of the villains of the highly publicized securities scandals of the 1980s were (or were thought to be) notorious insider traders who used their informational advantages to scoop up hefty (illegal) profits. Yet, despite the morality-play rhetoric of the so-called "decade of greed," an informed view of insider trading requires a careful analysis of detailed legislative provisions and challenging questions of economics and public policy.

In this chapter, we consider some of the threshold issues surrounding Canadian insider-trading regulation. The questions we address here include:

- What is the precise policy goal of laws restricting insider trading?
- Whom does the law consider to be "insiders"?
- What restrictions should be, and are, placed on the activities of such people?

B. CORPORATE LAW PROHIBITIONS ON INSIDER TRADING

The discussion of insider trading in this chapter relates primarily to the rules contained in provincial securities legislation. It is also important to remember that many Canadian corporate law statutes contain insider-trading provisions. These corporate law rules should not be forgotten. Among other things, they often are not limited, in the way that securities laws typically are, to the trading in securities of reporting issuers (i.e., public companies); the corporate law rules may also extend to the purchase and sale of shares of private companies.[1]

C. WHY REGULATE SECURITIES TRADING BY INSIDERS?

It is useful to begin by reviewing the traditional rationale for imposing legal restrictions on the trading of securities by insiders. Although a myriad of very sophisticated justifications for insider-trading laws have been debated for decades,[2] at the most basic level, there are three principal concerns that insider-trading laws intend to address.

- *Unfairness*: Many commentators object to the perceived unfair advantage that insiders of corporations enjoy because special access to material inside information is not available to other investors, regardless of whether the practice of insider trading has any broader, adverse economic effects.
- *Misappropriation/breach of fiduciary duty*: Underlying this concern is a theory that material undisclosed business information about a firm should be considered to be an asset of the firm itself, so that individuals who profit from the use of such information are essentially stealing from the firm.
- *Economic harm to markets or firms*: Some commentators express concern that widespread insider trading may undermine investors' confidence in the capital markets and/or increase the cost of capital for issuers.

---

1   See, e.g., *Canada Business Corporations Act*, R.S.C. 1985, c. C-44 [*CBCA*], s. 131.
2   For a review of many of the arguments both for and against insider-trading laws, see J.S. Ziegel et al., *Cases and Materials on Partnerships and Canadian Business Corporations*, 3d ed. (Toronto: Carswell, 1994) at 847–61.

1) Unfair Access

An important premise of our securities laws is that all investors and prospective investors ought to be given access to material information relating to the securities they are considering for purchase so that the prospective purchasers may value those securities accurately and make informed investment decisions. Any information about an issuer, therefore, that likely would affect the market value of that issuer's securities should be available on an equal basis to all investors and potential investors. It seems intuitively unfair to many people that corporate insiders with access to important undisclosed information about an issuer might use such information to make large profits in the trading of their own companies' securities.[3] Those who are concerned about the unfairness of insider trading have frequently tried to buttress their case for prohibitions against the practice by arguing that this perceived unfairness damages our capital markets, as discussed in section (3) below.

However, some observers, especially certain law and economics scholars, maintain that allowing insiders to trade on undisclosed information is not unfair in any meaningful sense at all. Briefly put, those who oppose restrictive insider-trading laws argue, among other things, that it is no more unfair for insiders to trade on information that is unavailable to other investors, than it is unfair for corporate officers and directors (who might also be shareholders) to be paid fees or salaries to which ordinary shareholders are not entitled.[4] This conclusion has been critiqued frequently, and the economics of insider trading has been the subject of a considerable, and not entirely consistent, academic literature.[5]

---

3   One leading U.S. academic argues that "the most common argument against insider trading has been that it is unfair." See Stephen Bainbridge, "The Insider Trading Prohibition: A Legal and Economic Enigma" (1986) 38 Univ. Fla. L. Rev. 50 at 55.

4   See, e.g., Frank H. Easterbrook and Daniel R. Fischel, *The Economic Structure of Corporate Law* (Cambridge: Harvard University Press, 1991) at 261–62. The seminal law and economics treatment of insider trading is Henry Manne's 1966 book, *Insider Trading and the Stock Market* (New York: Free Press, 1966).

5   For a recent consideration of the economics of insider-trading prohibitions, including a brief canvass of the prior literature, see Jie Hu and Thomas H. Noe, "Insider Trading and Managerial Incentives"(2001) 25 J. Banking & Finance 681.

2) Information as Corporate Asset

An alternative theory that justifies insider-trading liability is the notion that inside information about an issuer (such as a corporation) is an asset of that issuer. The value of such information belongs to the issuer, not to those people — the insiders — who happen to be in a position to exploit it. Accordingly, allowing insiders to trade with the knowledge of such information is tantamount to allowing them to raid the corporate till. In the United States, this theory appears to have been important in the development of insider-trading law by the courts. In particular, a doctrine known as the "misappropriation theory" underlies the major American insider-trading cases. Under the misappropriation theory, insider trading constitutes a wrong to the *issuer* that is the source of the confidential information, rather than to the uninformed third party with whom the insider completes the impugned securities trade.[6] The suggestion that insider trading is offensive to the issuer was also advocated by the great English corporate law scholar, the late L.C.B. Gower.[7]

To suggest that insiders ought not to profit from the use of corporate information may, at first, seem to invoke traditional standards of fiduciary obligations, such as those articulated in the seminal eighteenth-century case, *Keech v. Sandford*.[8] However, when considered more closely, it is not entirely clear that insider-trading prohibitions fit very neatly within the *Keech v. Sandford* mould after all. The rigid trust rule that a trustee must not benefit from her or his position ensures that such fiduciaries never put themselves into a position where their duty and interest might conflict. Accordingly, the fact that a particular trust beneficiary cannot show any damages suffered as a result of a potential trustee conflict is irrelevant because in other similar situations a beneficiary *might* suffer damages.[9] In the case of insider trading, however, invoking this rigid rule begs the question because it is not

---

6   See *United States v. O'Hagan*, 117 S. Ct. 2199 at 2207 (1997). See also the analysis of this case and the law of insider trading generally, in Joel Seligman, "A Mature Synthesis: O'Hagan Resolves 'Insider' Trading's Most Vexing Problems" (1998) 23 Delaware J. Corporate Law 1.

7   See L.C.B. Gower et al., *Gower's Principles of Modern Company Law*, 5th ed. (London: Sweet & Maxwell, 1992) at 607 where he describes the practice as "objectionable." In an earlier edition of this work, he condemned insider trading as "deplorable" (see L.C.B. Gower, *Gower's Principles of Modern Company Law*, 4th ed. (London: Stevens & Sons, 1979) at 631).

8   (1726), 25 E.R. 223.

9   There is little doubt that this was the principal concern in *Keech v. Sandford*: "[I]f a trustee, on the refusal to renew, might have a lease to himself, few trust estates would be renewed to a *cestui que* use." *Ibid.* at 223.

clear that any similar conflict of duty and interest exists, at least in those cases where an insider *purchases* the securities of an issuer on the basis of undisclosed information. Although such an insider, indeed, might make a profit, the potential to reap such a trading profit does not necessarily compromise the insider's position or distort his or her incentives.[10] To understand why, consider the following. To profit from purchasing shares using inside information, it must reasonably be expected that once the information is made public, it will cause the market price of the issuer's securities to rise. Accordingly, insiders permitted to make these trading profits, arguably would have greater, not lesser, incentives to work diligently to generate such price-improving initiatives. Also, it cannot be said that such a profit otherwise would have flowed to the corporation to which the insider owes a fiduciary duty.[11] In considering this point, it is important to distinguish between the value of possessing an asset and the value of *knowing* that one possesses an asset. Consider a simple example. Suppose a corporation with $1 million of cash and no other assets or liabilities of any kind has ten shares outstanding. Each share is worth about $100,000. The corporation decides to buy a mining property for $1 million (i.e., all of its cash). By good luck, the corporation later discovers rich gold reserves on the property. The property is actually worth $100 million. That value — $100 million — is the value of the property. The corporation possesses all of that value — down to the last penny. Information about the gold reserves neither adds nor detracts from this value *as far as the corporation is concerned*. Information about the property cannot be appropriated from the corporation in any way that will diminish the value of the corporation's asset because the corporation's asset is the land, *not* information about the land.[12]

---

10 See above note 5.

11 At first blush, a proposed take-over bid might appear to offer an exception to this broad statement. If a corporation is planning to make a take-over bid for a target company, an indiscreet insider of the bidding corporation who purchased shares in the target could potentially cause the price of the target's shares to rise, and, therefore, compel the bidder to pay more to complete the take-over. However, what should be immediately apparent from this example is that it does not follow the traditional formulation of insider trading at all because the unscrupulous insider would not be buying or selling shares of his or her own corporation, but rather of another corporation in which he or she had no such special access. (See Easterbrook and Fischel, above note 4 at 255, where they note that "[n]one of the [U.S.] Supreme Court's 'inside trading' cases deals with the manager who trades ahead of public release of corporate news.)

12 We are *not* suggesting here that information about the land would not be material to investors. Clearly, it would be. We are only pointing out that information about the land is not an independent source of value *to the corporation itself*.

Now suppose an insider, knowing about the valuable new gold property, improperly buys up five shares of the corporation before the corporation publicly discloses the new information. The insider wishes to act quickly and, so, offers the sellers of the shares a significant premium over the prevailing market price, paying $1 million for each of the five shares. The sellers are delighted. Indeed, they think the buyer is making a foolish bargain. After all, they were prepared to sell their shares for as little as $100,000 each. So they believe they have garnered a windfall of $900,000 per share. Of course, when the corporation later discloses the news of the gold, the sellers are likely to complain, claiming that they were treated unfairly because they should have received even more than $1 million per share. And yet, if they had sold the same five shares at the same time but to a non-insider for considerably less than $1 million, they would have been far worse off, but would have had no basis upon which to complain. How is it, then, that the insider, by paying ten times the price the sellers were prepared to accept, can be said to have "taken" something — either from the corporation or the selling shareholders? Even if one argues that the insider somehow dealt unfairly with the selling shareholders, there is surely no way that one can say that the insider took value from the company itself. The "information" the insider possessed about the gold reserves was not an independent source of value to the corporation.[13] The corporation's interest was worth $100 million before, during, and after, the insider's purchase of the shares. The corporation has lost nothing.

The situation is different, however, in the case of insiders who *sell* securities on the basis of undisclosed information. Allowing such sales can place insiders in a position where their duty and their interest conflict.[14] An insider permitted to sell shares before the public release of company information likely to trigger a fall in the market price of the shares might not have a strong incentive to increase the firm's value. Moreover, allowing insiders to sell on the basis of undisclosed informa-

---

13   On this point, see also Robert C. Clark, *Corporate Law* (Aspen: Aspen Publishers Inc, 1986) at 266: "[I]t is not clear that in practice the postulated impact of insider trading is either common or important. Consequently, many courts and commentators seem disinclined to believe that rules against insider trading are justified on the theory that the trading harms the corporation."

14   These arguments are discussed in Easterbrook and Fischel, above note 4 at 258. Easterbrook and Fischel (at 260) also raise a somewhat more sophisticated, but related, argument that managers permitted to trade on inside information might have a perverse incentive to increase the volatility of the firm's share price by making suboptimal investment decisions.

tion might encourage the proliferation of the notorious sorts of "pump-and-dump" schemes that seem to have prompted governments to regulate securities markets in the first place. More serious concerns would arise if insiders were permitted not only to sell their securities, but also to engage in "short selling." Short selling is essentially a technique for selling securities that one does not yet own. A short sale is accomplished by borrowing the subject securities from a securities lender, completing the sale, and then, some time later, purchasing securities of the same type in the market so that they may be returned to the lender. Short selling is profitable only if the market price of the securities falls between the date of the original short sale and the date on which the short seller covers his or her short position by purchasing securities in the market. The key concern is that if insiders were permitted to sell securities short, they would actually have an incentive to drive down the value of their own company's shares. (To use a crooked-sporting analogy, it should come as no surprise that corrupt gamblers have been known to bribe athletes to deliberately *lose* games, rather than to try a little harder to win.) It should be emphasized, however, that this potential conflict of duty and interest is created by permitting insiders to engage in short selling under *any* circumstances. It is not a problem that exists only where insiders are permitted to trade on the basis of undisclosed information. Accordingly, it is not surprising to find outright prohibitions against short selling by insiders.[15] The Dickerson Committee curtly declared that "there is nothing to be said in favour" of short selling by insiders.[16] It is by no means clear, however, that this potential abuse adds much to general policy arguments that have been advanced against insider trading.

3) Economic Harm to Markets or Issuers

It has been argued that insider trading is not only morally reprehensible, but also can damage capital markets by undermining investor confidence. According to this argument, prospective investors will refuse to purchase securities if they have reason to fear that insiders will be free to trade on the basis of undisclosed information. Capital markets

---

15   As Easterbrook and Fischel put it, "[a]dvance knowledge allows profitable trading whether the news is good or bad, and bad news is easier to create." Above note 4 at 260. See, e.g., *CBCA*, above note 1, s. 130. Recent amendments to the *CBCA* extend the prohibition in s. 130 against insiders short selling *shares* to include short sales by insiders of *all* securities.

16   Robert W.V. Dickerson et al., *Proposals for a New Business Corporations Law for Canada*, vol. 1 (Ottawa: Information Canada, 1971) at 91.

will then dry up and our economy might collapse. Considerations of this sort influenced the 1965 report of the Kimber Committee, which proposed many of the modifications that now form the basis of Ontario insider-trading law.[17] They also appear to animate the decisions of securities regulators. For example, in 2002, an OSC panel rejected a settlement agreement negotiated by OSC staff and an alleged illegal insider trader in a high-profile manner, stating "illegal insider trading by its very nature is a cancer that erodes public confidence in the capital markets. It is one of the most serious diseases that our capital markets face."[18] Although this argument is logically coherent, it is difficult to find strong empirical evidence to support it. Moreover, opponents of restrictive insider-trading rules argue that to the extent that this is a genuine risk, companies are in a better position than regulators to gauge that risk and, therefore, should be left to respond with their own internal restrictions on insider trading, when and if necessary.

Even if insider trading does not threaten to destroy capital markets, it has been argued that it might, nevertheless, increase the cost of capital for issuers. If investors believe that insider trading was rampant in Canadian capital markets, investors might continue to buy securities from Canadian issuers, but demand *ex ante* compensation for their expected insider-trading losses in the form of lower prices (or, equivalently, in the form of higher interest rates or higher rates of return) for issued securities.[19] Such investor demands would result in an increased cost of capital for Canadian issuers. Thus, a legal regime that constrains insider trading — and is perceived to constrain insider trading — benefits issuers. A link between actual or perceived levels of insider trading and the issuers' costs of capital is difficult to establish, empirically. As Ziegel et al. note, however, it can be demonstrated that securities dealers who trade with known insiders adjust their prices accordingly by increasing the price of securities they sell (the "ask price") and by decreasing the price at which they are prepared to buy

---

17   *The Report of the Attorney General's Committee on Securities Legislation in Ontario* (Toronto: Queen's Printer, 1965) [*Kimber Report*] at 10: "The ideal securities market should be a free and open market with the prices thereon based upon the fullest possible knowledge of all relevant facts among traders. Any factor which tends to destroy or put in question this concept lessens the confidence of the investing public in the market place and is, therefore, a matter of public concern."

18   *In the Matter of M.C.J.C. Holdings Inc. and Michael Cowpland* (2002), 25 OSCB 1133. See also *Larry Woods* (1995), 18 OSCB 4625 at 4627, quoted with approval in *M.C.J.C. Holdings Inc.*

19   This argument is based upon the economics of asymmetric information for which George Akerlof, Michael Spence, and Joseph Stiglitz were recently honoured with the 2001 Nobel Prize in Economics.

(the "bid price").[20] This observation falls well short of establishing a general link between insider-trading laws and the cost of capital, but indicates, at the least, that the concern for the implications of the cost of capital is credible.

D. LAWFUL TRADING BY INSIDERS

Although illegal insider trading preoccupies the financial press and the popular media, it is important to understand the requirements insiders must meet to permit them to trade *lawfully* in securities of issuers to which they have special access.

1) Who Is an "Insider"?

The term "insider" is used in at least two different senses: one is narrow and technical, and the other broad and somewhat imprecise. Canadian securities statutes use the narrow, technical meaning to identify persons who must comply with special reporting requirements. The broader definition often appears in the financial press and elsewhere in reports describing certain illegal transactions. However, as will be seen, Canadian securities rules forbidding what is popularly described as "insider trading" actually restrict trading by a much wider class of persons than are included within the statutory definition of "insider." Accordingly, it is important that the two following statutorily defined terms are clearly distinguished and understood:

- "*insider*": a term defined in the *OSA* mainly for the purposes of specific public reporting requirements
- "*person or company in a special relationship with a reporting issuer*": a broader term that includes, but is by no means limited to, "insiders," is the term that is pivotal to the *OSA*'s rules against unlawful trading using material undisclosed information

a) Insiders

i) Definition of "Insider"
Subsection 1(1) of the *OSA*[21] defines "insider of a reporting issuer" as follows:

> (a) every director or senior officer of a reporting issuer,

---

20 Ziegel et al., above note 2 at 859.
21 *Securities Act* (Ontario), R.S.O. 1990, c. S.5 [*OSA*], s. 1(1).

(b) every director or senior officer of a company that is itself an insider or subsidiary of a reporting issuer,

(c) any person or company who beneficially owns, directly or indirectly, voting securities of a reporting issuer or who exercises control or direction over voting securities of a reporting issuer or a combination of both carrying more than 10 percent of the voting rights attached to all voting securities of the reporting issuer for the time being outstanding other than voting securities held by the person or company as underwriter in the course of a distribution, and

(d) a reporting issuer where it has purchased, redeemed or otherwise acquired any of its securities, for so long as it holds any of its securities.

The *OSA* contains additional, extended definitions that ensure that certain persons and companies are considered insiders. Mutual fund management and distribution companies are considered insiders of the mutual funds with which they are associated.[22] When one company acquires another, if one of the companies is a reporting issuer, the senior officers and directors of the other company are deemed to have been insiders of the reporting issuer for up to six months prior to the acquisition.[23] This deeming provision deters insiders from profiting unfairly from their prior knowledge of the impending takeover or other acquisition. As discussed further below, deeming insiders of one company that participates in such a transaction to be insiders of the other company for a period of six months prior to the closing obliges such insiders to file reports listing all the securities that the insiders have purchased or sold in either company during those six months.

The purpose of these definitional provisions is twofold. First, these provisions establish the class of persons to whom the insider-reporting obligations in Part XXI of the *OSA* apply. Second, they define one important class of persons to whom the insider-trading prohibitions in section 76 of the *OSA* extend.

ii) Insider-Reporting Obligations

Insiders of a reporting issuer are generally permitted to buy and sell shares of that issuer, provided the insiders do not have access to material undisclosed information at the time of the trade. When an insider

---

22   *Ibid.* s. 1(7).
23   *Ibid.* s. 1(8) & (9). These provisions are not specifically linked to acquisition transactions, but it is apparent that this is the main focus of the legislation.

trades, however, she or he is subject to specific public reporting requirements.

aa) Initial Insider Report

The first such filing requirement is found in subsection 107(1) of the *OSA*, which requires a person or company who becomes an insider of a reporting issuer to file a report within ten days from the date the person or company became an insider. The obligation to disclose cannot be avoided merely by setting up a holding company to own the relevant securities because the statute requires the insider to disclose "any direct or indirect beneficial ownership of or control or direction over securities of the reporting issuer." Subsection 1(1), paragraph 5 of the *OSA* ensures that any shares beneficially owned by a company are deemed to be beneficially owned by the controlling person of that company. Similar rules deem companies to own beneficially any securities beneficially owned by their affiliates.[24] Where a person or company is deemed to have been an insider of a reporting issuer for the previous six months, by virtue of subsection 1(8) or 1(9) of the *OSA*, that person or company must file insider-trading reports in respect of the prior period during which the person or company was deemed to be an insider.[25] As discussed above, this reporting requirement attempts to deter insiders of companies that participate in merger transactions (including take-over bids) from trading shares in those companies before the transaction has been formally announced. Moreover, the date on which an insider is considered to have acquired beneficial ownership of securities can be earlier than the date on which a sale transaction for such securities is finally closed. Clause 106(1)(c) of the *OSA* provides that, for the purposes of the reporting rules in section 107, "[o]wnership shall be deemed to pass at such time as an offer to sell is accepted by the purchaser or the purchaser's agent or an offer to buy is accepted by the vendor or the vendor's agent."[26]

bb) Subsequent Insider-Trading Reports

After filing the initial insider report, whenever the insider's holdings in the reporting issuer change, the insider must file an additional report within ten days of that change.[27]

Because many public companies are reporting issuers in more than one Canadian province, insiders are frequently subject to similar insider-reporting requirements in several jurisdictions. To facilitate compliance

---

24 *Ibid.* s. 1(5) & (6).
25 *Ibid.* s. 107(3).
26 *Ibid.* s. 106(1)(c).
27 *Ibid.* s. 107(2).

with multiple reporting requirements, Canadian securities regulators and the federal Director under the *CBCA* have agreed on a common form for insider-reporting purposes. That form in Ontario is found in OSC Rule 55-501.[28] Although the filing of insider reports by facsimile has been permitted since 1998,[29] the system remains paper-based and, therefore, somewhat cumbersome. Regulators have recently launched a new System for Electronic Disclosure by Insiders (SEDI).[30] The principal advantages of the new SEDI system are twofold. First, it is a truly national system, simplifying the filing process by eliminating multiple filings in different provinces. Second, because SEDI is an Internet-based system, it allows for filings to become public more quickly than is possible in the current paper-based system, and facilitates access to, and searching of, filed reports. (In early 2002, technological problems resulted in SEDI going offline for an indefinite period.)

In May 1999, the OSC released *A Guide to Insider Reporting in Ontario*.[31] This useful document summarizes the *OSA*'s insider-reporting rules, and includes detailed examples to assist the reader in determining when insider-reporting obligations arise. It should be noted, however, that, at the date of writing, the *Guide* was not updated to reflect amendments to the *OSA* made in 1999[32] that affected the time for filing insider-trading reports. Under the law that was in force when the *Guide* was drafted, insider-trading reports had to be filed within ten days following the end of the month in which the trade occurred.[33]

iii) Exemptions from Insider-Reporting Requirements
The insider-reporting requirements are extremely broad and, if read literally, prove particularly problematic in three situations:

1. Where directors and senior officers of one company that is deemed to be an insider of a second company are, in turn, deemed to be insiders of that second company. (This is especially problematic where the first company is deemed to be an insider only by the operation of subsection 1(5) of the *OSA*.)

---

28 (1996), 19 OSCB 821.
29 OSC Rule 55-502 (1998), 21 OSCB 2327.
30 National Instrument 55-102 (2001), 24 OSCB 4414.
31 Available online at <http://www.osc.gov.on.ca> (site accessed: 25 February 2002) [*Guide to Insider Reporting*].
32 S.O. 1999, c. 9, s. 214.
33 This timing was based on an earlier U.S. requirement found in s. 16(a) of the *Securities Exchange Act of 1934*, 15 U.S.C. § 78a *et seq*. See *Kimber Report*, above note 17 at 13.

2. Where directors and senior officers acquire securities from a reporting issuer automatically, such as pursuant to dividend or interest reinvestment plans or when the reporting issuer issues a stock dividend or effects a stock split or other corporate transaction that affects all the shareholders in the same way
3. Where reporting issuers repurchase their own securities through normal-course issuer bids

To deal with the burdensome and unnecessarily onerous insider-reporting requirements that would otherwise apply in these three situations, the OSC adopted National Instrument 55-101 as an OSC Rule and Companion Policy 55-101 CP as a policy.[34] These regulatory instruments provide relief from the strict reporting rules of the Act and are discussed in the following sections.

aa) Directors and Officers of Insider Company Affiliates

Because the definition of "insider" of a reporting issuer includes officers and directors of companies that are themselves insiders of that reporting issuer, the reporting obligations in Part XXI of the *OSA*, on their face, apply to many individuals who, in fact, have no special access to information about a reporting issuer. Where, for example, Company ABC owns 10.1 percent of the voting shares of Company XYZ (and XYZ is a reporting issuer), ABC is an insider of XYZ. What's more, if ABC has an affiliate, DEF Ltd., DEF is also deemed to be an insider of XYZ, even if DEF owns no shares of XYZ whatsoever. The combined effect of clause (c) of the definition of "insider" and subsection 1(6) of the *OSA* leads to this outcome. Subsection 1(6) provides that "[a] company [e.g., DEF] shall be deemed to own beneficially securities beneficially owned by its affiliates [e.g., ABC]."

Thus, every director and senior officer of ABC and every director and senior officer of DEF would be considered an insider of XYZ. Yet, it is very likely that the directors and officers of ABC have no special access to XYZ. And, it is almost certain that the directors of DEF have no such access. National Instrument 55-101 provides exemptions in two such situations. First, a director or officer of a subsidiary of a reporting issuer is not required to file insider-trading reports, unless the subsidiary is a "major subsidiary" as defined in the instrument[35] or unless the director or officer "receives or has access to" inside informa-

---

34   (2001), 24 OSCB 1293.
35   A major subsidiary is, essentially, a subsidiary with assets or revenues that are at least 10 percent of the consolidated assets or consolidated revenues, respectively, of the reporting issuer, including all the subsidiaries whose financial information is included in the reporting issuer's consolidated financial statements.

tion before it is generally disclosed.[36] Second, officers and directors of affiliates of insider companies (such as DEF, in the above example) are exempt from the insider-reporting requirements, unless the officers or directors receive or have access to inside information or unless the affiliate is a material supplier or otherwise has a material contractual relationship with the reporting issuer.[37] In the earlier example, the directors and senior officers of DEF are exempt from the insider-reporting requirements, unless DEF is a major subsidiary of XYZ or a major supplier/contractor of XYZ. It should be noted, however, that the National Instrument does not automatically exempt directors and senior officers of insider companies (i.e., of ABC, in the example) from the insider-reporting requirements. This omission is intentional. The OSC considers applications for exemptions from such individuals on a case-by-case basis, but generally applies the principles reflected in National Instrument 55-101.[38]

bb) Dividend and Reinvestment Plans and "Issuer Events"
There are a host of circumstances in which a director or senior officer of a reporting issuer may acquire securities of that reporting issuer without ever exercising any independent investment decision. For example, an officer might participate in a dividend reinvestment plan under which quarterly dividend payments are automatically used to purchase additional shares in the issuer for the officer. Or, the reporting issuer might decide to effect a stock split, which would result in all shareholders receiving additional shares proportionate to their current shareholdings. In such cases, the director or officer who receives additional shares makes no investment decision at the time of the issuance and, therefore, cannot time the trades to take advantage of inside information. Accordingly, it is unnecessary for such share acquisitions to trigger any insider-reporting obligations. National Instrument 55-101, therefore, exempts such transactions from the insider-reporting requirements.[39] Some stock purchase plans, however, allow participants to make voluntary payments and thereupon acquire additional securities in exchange for such additional investment. Purchases of shares in these circumstances raise the same insider-trading concerns as regular market purchases and are not covered by the exemption.[40]

---

36   *Guide to Insider Reporting*, above note 31, ss. 2.1 & 2.2.
37   *Ibid.* s. 3.2 & 3.3.
38   (2001), 24 OSCB 1284.
39   National Instrument 55-101, Part V (automatic securities purchase plan) and Part VII (issuer events), above note 34.
40   *Ibid.* s. 5.1.

cc) Normal-Course Issuer Bids

An issuer bid refers to any offer by an issuer to acquire securities of its own issue other than non-convertible debt securities.[41] Popular terms for an issuer bid include a "share repurchase" and a "share buyback." If a corporation's articles authorize the corporation to issue an unlimited number of shares, Canadian corporate law statutes generally require that when such corporations buy back their own shares they must immediately cancel them.[42] However, even in cases where a corporation promptly cancels shares after a repurchase, the corporation nevertheless would own shares of its own issue from the time of the purchase until the time of the cancellation. Because the OSA states that every reporting issuer that purchases its own shares is deemed to be an insider of itself,[43] such transactions trigger insider-reporting requirements. Securities regulators determined, however, that the ten-day reporting regime was unnecessarily burdensome in the case of "normal-course" issuer bids (i.e., purchases by an issuer of its own securities that do not exceed 5 percent of the class over a twelve-month period).[44] Accordingly, where an issuer repurchases its own securities pursuant to a normal-course issuer bid, the reporting deadline is relaxed, and insider-trading reports must be filed on the tenth day following the end of the month in which the purchases were completed.[45]

E. PROHIBITED INSIDER TRADING

1) Introduction

Insider-trading liability occurs when a person in a special relationship with a reporting issuer trades with knowledge of an undisclosed material change or material fact, or discloses such information (i.e., "tips") to others who then profit by trading with knowledge of such information. The OSA restrictions apply only to trades of securities issued by reporting issuers, although, as noted earlier, Canadian corporate legislation often imposes similar restrictions on private companies.

---

41 OSA, above note 21, s. 89(1).
42 See, e.g., CBCA, above note 1, s. 39(6).
43 OSA, above note 21, s. 1(1)(d) (definition of "insider").
44 Issuer bids, including normal-course issuer bids, are discussed in more detail in chapter 10.
45 National Instrument 55-101, ss. 6.1 and 6.2, above note 34.

The insider-trading prohibition is found in section 76 of the *OSA*, and the specific provisions for penalties and statutory civil liability for those who engage in such practices are prescribed in sections 122 and 134.[46] The fundamental features of the regime created by these restrictions are as follows:

- Restrictions apply to any "person or company in a special relationship with a reporting issuer" (not just to an "insider" as defined in subsection 1(1))
- Liability attaches when securities are sold or purchased with knowledge of a "material fact" or a "material change" (It is not necessary to establish that the trader made use of that knowledge.)[47]
- The *OSA* restricts both trading and informing others (tipping) who trade
- Trading restrictions apply to a broad range of securities and derivative instruments
- Breach of the rules can lead to administrative sanctions, special fines and other quasi-criminal penalties, and statutory civil liability

2) Person or Company in a Special Relationship with a Reporting Issuer

Although it is common to refer to the provisions of section 76 of the *OSA* as the "insider-trading restrictions," in fact, the rules in that section apply to a much wider class of persons and companies than are included within the term "insider" as defined in section 1.

---

46   Perhaps the most celebrated example of an insider-trading proceeding in recent Canadian history is the Bennett/Doman matter. See *Doman* v. *British Columbia (Superintendent of Brokers)*, [1998] B.C.J. No. 2378 (C.A.), leave to appeal to S.C.C. denied.

47   Before 1988, there was a defence available under the insider-trading provisions where the trader proved that she or he did not make use of this knowledge. For a discussion of the implications of the removal of this defence, see *R.* v. *Woods* (1994), 17 OSCB 1189. It is noteworthy that, in the United States, there had long been debate over the same question as to whether prosecution for unlawful insider trading required proof that the defendant actually made use of the inside information, or whether it was sufficient to establish that the defendant knowingly possessed such information at the time of the impugned trade. In 2000, the SEC attempted to eliminate the confusion by promulgating Rule 10b5-1 (17 C.F.R. 240.10b5-1). This rule, similar to the current Ontario rule, provides that "a purchase or a sale of a security of an issuer is 'on the basis' of material non public information about that security or issuer if the person making the purchase or sale was aware of the material non public information when the person made the purchase or sale." (*Ibid.* 240.10b5-1(b)).

Indeed, the key definition in section 76 is not insider at all, but rather a "person or company in a special relationship with a reporting issuer." That phrase is defined in subsection 76(5). Although the phrase certainly includes all insiders of a reporting issuer, it is not limited to insiders.

Specifically, the phrase is defined as follows:

(a) a person or company that is an insider, affiliate ["affiliate" is defined in subsection 1.1(2)] or associate ["associate" is defined in subsection 1(1)] of,

    (i)   the reporting issuer,

    (ii) a person or company that is proposing to make a take-over bid, as defined in Part XX, for the securities of the reporting issuer, or

    (iii) a person or company that is proposing to become a party to a reorganization, amalgamation, merger or arrangement or similar business combination with the reporting issuer or to acquire a substantial portion of its property;

(b) a person or company that is engaging in or proposes to engage in any business or professional activity with or on behalf of the reporting issuer or with or on behalf of a person or company described in subclause (a)(ii) or (iii);

(c) a person who is a director, officer or employee of the reporting issuer or of a person or company described in subclause (a)(ii) or (iii) or clause (b);

(d) a person or company that learned of the material fact or material change with respect to the reporting issuer while the person or company was a person or company described in clause (a), (b) or (c);

(e) a person or company that learns of a material fact or material change with respect to the issuer from any other person or company described in this subsection, including a person or company described in this clause, and knows or ought reasonably to have known that the other person or company is a person or company in such a relationship.[48]

_____

48   *OSA*, above note 21, s. 76(5).

This definition casts an extremely broad net. This section applies not only to directors and senior officers of the reporting issuer, but also to all other officers and even employees. This coverage is broader than anticipated by the Kimber Committee, which recommended against introducing statutory sanctions for trading based on undisclosed confidential information by junior officers and employees, arguing that any such abuses were best controlled by corporate management.[49] It should also be noted that the restrictions extend not only to those who work within the reporting issuer, but also to those who work within other firms proposing to launch a take-over bid for the reporting issuer's shares or proposing to enter into some other major business combination with the reporting issuer. Moreover, advisers to any such firms (such as lawyers or investment bankers) are also subject to section 76, pursuant to clause 76(5)(b). Thus, the situation that gave rise to the recent leading U.S. Supreme Court case on insider-trading, *United States* v. *O'Hagan*,[50] is explicitly dealt with under the Ontario statute.

Section 76 also extends to the critical issue of "tipping." Tipping refers to the act of providing confidential information about a reporting issuer to another person who then uses that information to profit by trading in securities of the reporting issuer (or who further "tips" someone else). Section 76 makes it clear that it is an offence not only for any person in a special relationship with a reporting issuer to "tip" (subsections 76(2) and (3)), but also for any person who obtains knowledge of a material fact or material change from such a source (a "tippee"[51]) to trade with knowledge of that information before it is generally disclosed, unless the tippee did not know, or ought not reasonably to have known, that the tipper was a person or company in a special relationship with the reporting issuer.[52] The provision also catches tippees who, themselves, convey information they have received to others.

3) Material Fact and Material Change

Insider-trading liability turns on the two critical concepts of "material fact" and "material change." These expressions are both defined in sub-

---

49   *Kimber Report*, above note 17 at 11.
50   Above note 6. *O'Hagan* involved trades by a lawyer in securities of a firm that was the target of a take-over bid about to be launched by a client of the lawyer's firm.
51   The term "tippee" is said to have been coined by U.S. securities law scholar, the late Louis Loss. See, e.g., Seligman, above note 6 at 3.
52   *OSA*, above note 21, s. 76(5)(e).

section 1(1) of the *OSA*. Members of the practising bar and others have expressed concern about these two statutory definitions, especially in the context of current proposals to impose statutory civil liability for misrepresentations in continuous disclosure documents. One particular technical issue relates to the potentially retrospective aspect of the "material fact" definition. Recently, these issues were canvassed in CSA Notice 53-302,[53] which is discussed further in chapter 9.

In proposed National Policy 51-201, discussed in section F below, the CSA summarizes the effect of certain policy statements of the TSE, the CDNX, and the Bourse de Montreal (formerly the Montreal Exchange), relating to the determination of materiality.[54] The proposed policy specifically recommends that reporting issuers adopt internal insider-trading monitoring policies, including policies that specifically prohibit any trading by employees during certain times, such as the period prior to the release of regular earnings information.

4) Section 76 Defences and Exemptions

a) Defences
Section 76 of the *OSA* does not create an absolute liability offence. Accordingly, a defence is available to an alleged inside trader who proves that he, she, or it reasonably believed that the undisclosed material fact or material change had in fact been "generally disclosed" before the impugned trade.[55]

There are two important aspects to this defence provision First, the onus is on the accused to prove that he, she, or it had such a reasonable belief. Second, there is a technical question as to the meaning of the phrase "generally disclosed." The *OSA* does not define the phrase "generally disclosed," but it seems clear that the mere issuing of a press release, without more, is not sufficient.[56] In *Re Harold P. Connor*,[57] the OSC suggests that determining whether information is generally disclosed involves a two-pronged test: (a) the information must first be "disseminated to the trading public"[58] and (b) the public must then be given a sufficient amount of time to "digest such information given its

---

53   (2000), 23 OSCB 1.
54   (2001), 24 OSCB 3308, s. 4.2.
55   *OSA*, above note 21, s. 76(4).
56   See *Green v. Charterhouse Group Can. Ltd.* (1976), 12 O.R. (2d) 280 at 302–3 (C.A.).
57   [1976] OSCB 149 at 174.
58   *Ibid.*

nature and complexity."[59] While the OSC concedes that the amount of time necessary for such "digestion" varies from case to case, it indicates that "[a] safe working rule would be that an insider should wait a minimum of one full trading day after the release of the information before trading."[60]

In addition to the defence specifically provided for in subsection 76(4), the courts have recognized a "reasonable mistake of fact" defence to charges based on a violation of section 76. In *Lewis v. Fingold*,[61] the accused was a director of a reporting issuer who became aware of certain confidential information about the issuer at a directors' meeting. The accused sold shares in the issuer with knowledge of that information and before it had been generally disclosed. The court found that the information constituted a "material fact" that would reasonably be expected to have a significant effect on the market price of the issuer's shares. Yet, the trial judge also found that the accused did not believe that the information would have a substantial effect on the company's share price and that there was at least some basis for that belief. Thus, the accused had established a defence of reasonable mistake of fact; that is, a reasonable belief "in a mistaken set of facts which, if true, would render the prohibited act an innocent one."[62] Accordingly, because the offence created by sections 76 and 122 was characterized by the court as a strict liability offence, to which such a "reasonable mistake of fact" defence must be available, the accused was acquitted at trial, and this decision was upheld on appeal.

b) Exemptions

i) Introduction

Because the prohibitions in section 76 of the *OSA* are so broad, they potentially could prove untenable for certain professional firms, such as, in particular, investment banking firms. Major investment banking firms, or integrated securities firms, regularly engage in brokerage or proprietary trading activities and provide advisory services that may result in their being privy to information that could constitute undisclosed material facts. Such a firm, as a single corporate entity, theoretically, has access to undisclosed material information in one area of the firm, while it simultaneously engages in trading activities in another

---

59   *Ibid.*
60   *Ibid.*
61   (1999), 22 OSCB 2811.
62   *Ibid.* at 2822.

area of the firm. However, the policy considerations underlying section 76 are not offended by such trading, provided that the individuals making the trading decisions do not, in fact, have knowledge of the undisclosed information. Accordingly, in an attempt to recognize these practical realities, and to deal with them sensibly, section 175 of the *OSA Regulation*[63] provides for exemptions and OSC Rule 33-601 contains guidelines.[64] Each of these is discussed in turn below.

ii) OSA Regulation, Section 175

Section 175 of the *OSA Regulation* provides exemptions from subsection 76(1) and section 134 of the *OSA* for trades by persons or companies in a special relationship with a reporting issuer with knowledge of an undisclosed material fact or material change in the following circumstances:

* Where the individuals who participated in or advised on the trading decision did not have actual knowledge of the undisclosed material information
* Where the purchase or sale of the securities occured pursuant to a pre-existing agreement, plan, or commitment
* Where the person or company was acting as an agent for a third party pursuant to "a specific unsolicited order"

In each case, the burden of proof lies with the person or company that would otherwise be guilty of acting in violation of section 76. The *OSA Regulation* provides that, in determining whether the burden of proof is discharged, the internal policies and procedures that the person or company has put into place to prevent contravention of the *OSA*'s insider-trading prohibitions are relevant considerations.[65] Although the OSC has not specifically prescribed a code to be followed by securities firms in developing such internal policies, it has offered "general guidelines" in OSC Policy 33-601.[66]

iii) OSC Policy 33-601

When OSC Policy 33-601 first came into effect, the OSC made it clear that failure to comply with the policy did not mean that a person or company could not seek the exemption in section 175 of the *OSA Regulation*. Similarly, however, the OSC indicated that compliance with

---

63   *OSA Regulation*, R.R.O. 1990, Reg. 1015 [*OSA Regulation*], s. 175.
64   (1998), 21 OSCB 619.
65   *OSA Regulation*, above note 63. s. 175(3).
66   OSC Policy 33-601, above note 64, s. 1.2.

the policy did not guarantee that the person's or company's policies and procedures would be considered adequate.[67] These concepts are also expressed in Policy 33-601 itself.[68]

Policy 33-601's guidelines are organized around four areas:

- Employee education
- Containment of inside information
- Compliance
- Restriction of Transactions[69]

aa) Employee Education

The guidelines in OSC Policy 33-601 recommend implementing programs to ensure that employees are informed of both their legal and ethical responsibilities.[70]

bb) Containment of Inside Information

The guidelines in OSC Policy 33-601 relating to information containment are premised on the well-known concept of notional information "firewalls" between different departments of the same firm.[71] Such "firewalls" (also called "Chinese walls" or "ethical walls") are well understood in the financial industry. Essentially, employees in different departments of a firm are expected to act as though their departments were separate firms. Confidential information possessed by one department is not disclosed to anyone outside of that department. In *Transpacific Sales Ltd. (Trustee for)* v. *Sprott Securities Ltd.*,[72] Stinson J. commented on the common use (and propriety) of such intrafirm institutional "walls":

> Regardless of whether they are technically bound to do so, the evidence before me establishes that brokers employ the "Chinese wall" approach in relation to these transactions. In all the circumstances, I am loathe [sic] to tinker with existing practices. If a change is necessary, I agree that the legislature and the regulators are best suited to make it.[73]

---

67   *Ibid.*
68   *Ibid.*
69   *Ibid.* s. 2.1.
70   *Ibid.* s. 2.2.
71   *Ibid.* s. 2.3.
72   [2001] O.J. No. 597 (Sup. Ct.).
73   *Ibid.* at para. 97.

cc) Restrictions of Transactions

The guidelines in OSC Policy 33-601 relating to the restriction of transactions employ the concept of classified lists ("grey lists" and "restricted lists") of issuers about which the firm has, or may have, inside
information.[74] To illustrate the use of such lists, consider the following
example. Red Suspenders Securities Inc. is an integrated securities firm
that provides corporate finance and merger and acquisitions advice to
its investment-banking clients, and brokerage services to its institutional and retail clients. Red Suspenders also engages in proprietary
trading for its own account. Whale Corp., a reporting issuer, retains
Red Suspenders. Whale Corp. proposes to make an unsolicited take-
over bid for Jonah Ltd. When Whale Corp. first consults Red
Suspenders, Red Suspenders places both Whale Corp. and Jonah Ltd.
on the "grey list," which is a "highly confidential" list of issuers about
which Red Suspenders has "inside information." The grey list is not
generally circulated to other members of the firm, but is made available, as necessary, to compliance officers. Once Whale Corp. publicly
announces its intention to make a bid, Red Suspenders moves Whale
Corp. and Jonah Ltd. from the highly confidential "grey list" to a
"restricted list." The restricted list is a list of issuers about which the
firm *may* have inside information, obtained from providing continuing
advisory services in the course of the take-over bid. The restricted list
is disseminated throughout Red Suspenders, and trading in securities
of issuers on the list normally stops, except in the case of "normal
market-making or other permitted activities." Once the take-over bid
is completed, Red Suspenders removes Whale Corp. and Jonah Ltd.
from the restricted list.

dd) Compliance

OSC Policy 33-601 provides a number of specific suggestions for ongoing trade monitoring, reviewing, and compliance policies and procedures.[75] Among other things, the policy suggests that a senior officer of
the firm be made responsible for these measures, and that the firm's
policies and procedures be subject to regular review to ensure that they
are adequate and effective.

---

74   Above note 64, ss. 2.4–2.6.
75   *Ibid.* s. 2.7.

5) Trading in Options and Other Derivative Instruments

Subsection 76(6) of the *OSA* deems certain financial instruments to be securities of a reporting issuer for the purposes of the insider-trading restrictions. Such financial instruments include options to purchase shares of the issuer (calls), options to sell shares of the issuer (puts), and other securities that derive their value, in a material respect, from the market price of the securities of the issuer. This section was added to the *OSA* in 1987.[76] To ensure the integrity of the insider-trading prohibitions, it is essential that those who possess undisclosed material information are restricted from profiting from such information regardless of the form of financial instrument they trade to realize the profit. Consider an insider who has information that, when publicly revealed, could be expected to cause the market price of a reporting issuer's shares to rise. It makes little sense to forbid the insider from purchasing shares in the issuer, yet still permit him or her to purchase call options that enable the insider to purchase those same shares after the information is publicly disclosed but at the lower pre-announcement price. Where the reporting issuer itself issues such options, the options clearly constitute securities of the reporting issuer within the definition of security in subsection 1(1) of the *OSA*.[77] However, such instruments are frequently issued not by the reporting issuer itself, but by financial intermediaries such as investment banks. The reporting issuer is a complete stranger to such contracts, but the purchase and sale of such contracts still trigger the public policy considerations underlying section 76 of the *OSA*. It is for this reason that the deeming provision in subsection 76(6) is needed. Further, Victor Alboini suggests that the reference in clause 76(6)(b) to securities that vary in price with the market price of the reporting issuer's securities could include securities issued by one company that are exchangeable into securities issued by another.[78] For certain tax reasons, the issuance of exchangeable securities is a technique frequently used when a foreign corporation acquires a Canadian corporation.[79] Whether the rules in section 76 are broad

---

76   S.O. 1987, c. 7, s. 7.

77   *OSA*, above note 21, s. 1(1)(d) (definition of "security").

78   Victor P. Alboini, *The 1997 Ontario Securities Act Annotated* (Toronto: Carswell:1996) at 475.

79   For a discussion of this point, see Peter H. Blessing and Elinore J. Richardson, "Cross Border Acquisitions and Mergers: Canadian and U.S. Structures and Tax Issues" in *Mergers and Acquisitions: Strategies for Creating Value and Growth* (Toronto: Insight Press, 1999) at 299–304.

enough to catch the most sophisticated uses of derivatives, however, remains a matter of debate and regulatory concern.[80]

6) Penalties for Violation of Section 76 of the *OSA*

a) Introduction

There are at least five sorts of sanctions or liability to which a person or company who violates section 76 may be exposed:

- Penal sanctions
- Statutory civil liability
- Administrative sanctions
- Civil court proceedings
- Stock exchange or self-regulatory organization (SRO) sanctions

The subject of enforcement is dealt with in detail in chapter 11, and, accordingly, only a brief discussion of each of these five enforcement avenues is provided here.

b) Penal Sanctions

A violation of section 76 constitutes a breach of Ontario securities law. An offender may be prosecuted under the "quasi-criminal" provisions in section 122 of the *OSA*. Anyone convicted of an offence under section 122 faces a possible fine of up to $1 million, a two-year term of imprisonment, or both.[81] However, special additional penalties apply to insider-trading violations. A person or company convicted of such a violation is liable to pay a fine equal to the amount of the profit made or the loss avoided by the transaction, and indeed is potentially liable to pay as much as three times the amount of the profit made or the loss avoided.[82] These sanctions can include, and on occasion have resulted in, terms of imprisonment. In the recent case of *R. v. Harper*,[83] for example, the accused was convicted under clause 122(1)(c) of the *OSA* on two counts of insider trading contrary to section 76. He was originally sentenced to one year's imprisonment in respect of each count to be served concurrently. These custodial sentences were imposed in

---

80 See Ontario Securities Review Advisory Committee, *Issues List* (2000), 23 OSCB 3035 at 3044; Christopher C. Nicholls, *Corporate Finance and Canadian Law* (Toronto: Carswell, 2000) at 212.

81 *OSA*, above note 21, s. 122(1).

82 *Ibid.* s. 122(4).

83 [2000] O.J. No. 3664.

addition to fines totalling almost $4 million. (On appeal, the sentence was reduced.)

c)   Statutory Civil Liability

Section 134 of the *OSA* provides, in the case of unlawful insider trading, a statutory civil remedy to four classes of plaintiffs:

- Those who are the innocent counterparties to unlawful insider trades[84]
- Those who are the innocent counterparties to trades with tippees[85]
- Mutual funds or the clients of portfolio managers or registered dealers in cases where someone with access to information concerning the investment program of the funds, managers, or dealers benefits by trading on the basis of such information[86]
- Reporting issuers whose insiders, affiliates, or associates have gained by trading with the knowledge of undisclosed material information or have communicated such information to others[87]

In several respects, the statutory civil liability under section 134 of the *OSA* mirrors the insider-trading liability under section 76. So, for example, defences are available to claims brought under section 134 in those cases where (a) the person who traded on the basis of the undisclosed information reasonably believed the information was publicly disclosed, or (b) the information was known, or ought reasonably to have been known, to the plaintiff.[88] These defences are similar to the defences to the quasi-criminal charge of unlawful insider trading found in subsection 76(4) of the *OSA* and in subsection 175(5) of the *OSA Regulation*.

It also should be noted that the basis for liability under section 134 of the *OSA* differs depending upon whether the plaintiff is an innocent party to the unlawful trade or is the issuer to which the undisclosed information relates (or is, in some cases, the client of a portfolio manager when information about the manager's investment program was used improperly). Innocent counterparties to unlawful trades are entitled to recover any damages they may have suffered as the result of such trades.[89] However, in the case of actions brought by issuers (or by the clients of portfolio managers), the basis for liability is different. The

---

84   *OSA*, above note 21, s. 134(1).
85   *Ibid.* s. 134(2).
86   *Ibid.* s. 134(3).
87   *Ibid.* s. 134(4).
88   *Ibid.* s. 134(1).
89   *Ibid.* s. 134(1).

liability of insiders, affiliates, and associates of a reporting issuer is measured not by the amount of loss or damage suffered by the reporting issuer, but by the extent of any gain realized by the insider, affiliate, or associate that traded on the basis of the undisclosed material information. (Note that this special rule applies *only* in the case of unlawful trades by insiders, affiliates, and associates, and *not* in other cases involving persons or companies in a special relationship with the reporting issuer.) Such liability is evidently premised on the theory, discussed above, that corporate information is an asset of the corporation itself. Any person or company who trades on the basis of information concerning the investment program of a mutual fund or a portfolio manager faces a similar liability to account for benefits or gains.[90]

To facilitate the bringing of such actions to account for benefit or gain pursuant to subsections 134(3) and (4), the *OSA* provides a procedure in section 135 not unlike the derivative action found in typical Canadian corporate law statutes.[91] Section 135, essentially, provides a method by which the OSC, the securityholders of a reporting issuer, or the securityholders of a mutual fund may institute or continue an action under subsections 134(3) or (4), in the name of the issuer or the mutual fund against defendants who have traded unlawfully. The procedure prescribed by section 135 may be used when the reporting issuer or mutual fund to whom the section 134 remedy is provided has chosen not to pursue such an action itself. It is clear why such a derivative-type procedure is necessary. A senior officer or director of a reporting issuer might profit from illegal insider trading. Yet, that same individual may well be in a position to decide whether the issuer will pursue a remedy under section 134. It is fair to surmise that such an individual would have little interest in causing the issuer to bring an action against himself or herself. The section 135 procedure, therefore, offers a possible solution.

d) Administrative Sanctions

The OSC is empowered to make orders in the public interest where, among other things, the *OSA* has been breached. In the case of an insider-trading violation committed by a securities professional, such as a broker, the OSC's most potent weapon is to suspend, restrict, or terminate the registration of the offender. In cases of violations by others, the OSC can, among other things, exclude the offender from trading in Ontario's markets, remove the offender, or prohibit the offender from

---

90 *Ibid.* s. 134(3).
91 See, e.g., *CBCA*, above note 1, s. 239.

acting, as a director or officer of an issuer, or reprimand the offender. As discussed in chapter 11, the OSC does not have the power to order an offender to pay monetary penalties, although, on occasion, the OSC has negotiated substantial payments in the settlement of proceedings.

e)   Civil Court Proceedings

The OSC may apply to the Superior Court of Ontario "for a declaration that a person or company has not complied with or is not complying with Ontario securities law."[92] Where the court makes such a declaration, it has broad powers to issue an appropriate remedial order.[93]

f)   Securities Exchange or IDA Sanctions

Where the securities of a company are listed on a stock exchange, or where an insider trader is subject to the jurisdiction of an exchange, or is a member of a self-regulatory organization, such as the Investment Dealers Association of Canada, additional polices and sanctions may apply to insider trading.[94]

7) The U.S. "Short-Swing" Rules

U.S. federal securities laws do not, for the most part, include the same tightly drafted insider-trading prohibitions as Canadian provincial securities statutes; however, there is an additional feature of U.S. law that is frequently encountered by Canadian lawyers and business people that deserves brief mention here. Under the *Securities Exchange Act of 1934*,[95] directors, officers, and beneficial owners of more than 10 percent of any class of equity security of a reporting issuer are liable to account for any profit realized on a round-trip transaction (i.e, a purchase followed by a sale, or a sale followed by a purchase) in a security of that reporting issuer that occurs within a six-month period.[96] This restriction against "short-swing profits" is expressly aimed at "preventing the use of information which may have been obtained" by such persons.[97] However, liability under the 1934 Act does not require any actual use or misuse of

---

92   *OSA*, above note 21, s. 128(1).

93   *Ibid.* s. 128(3).

94   See, e.g., *Toronto Stock Exchange, Company Manual*, s. 423.4, available online at <http://www.tse.ca/en/pdf/CompanyManual0202.pdf> (site accessed: 16 April 2002) and *Rules of the Toronto Stock Exchange*, s. 7-106, available online at <http://www.tse.ca/en/pdf/TSERules.pdf> (site accessed: 16 April 2002).

95   15 U.S.C. § 78c, s. 16.

96   *Ibid.* s. 16(b).

97   *Ibid.*

such informational advantage. Thomas Hazen has noted that "the legislative history [of this section] reveals congressional recognition of such a great potential for abuse of inside information so as to warrant the imposition of strict liability."[98] The Kimber Committee, in its proposals for the reform of Ontario's securities laws, considered, but explicitly rejected, the American "short-swing profit" rules.[99]

F. SELECTIVE DISCLOSURE

Closely related to the topic of insider trading is the question of "selective disclosure." Selective disclosure in general, and the recent OSC settlement relating to the 2000 Air Canada selective disclosure matter in particular, are discussed in greater detail in chapter 9. In Canada and in the United States there is concern about the common corporate practice of meeting with financial analysts in connection with pending earnings guidance (i.e., providing information upon which financial analysts can issue forecasts of a company's future earnings) and in connection with other information that is not necessarily provided to retail investors. Regulators fear that there is a significant grey area between appropriate information gathering by financial industry professionals and the use of information in a way that resembles insider trading. These concerns prompted the SEC to introduce Regulation FD[100] in the United States, which took effect in October 2000. In Canada, similar concerns have led to a proposed, new national policy, National Policy 51-201,[101] but not to any new legislative initiatives. At the date of writing, this proposed policy was still at the comment stage. The details and implications of these initiatives are explored in Chapter 9. However, it is relevant for the purposes of this chapter to mention the aspects of proposed National Policy 51-201 that touch upon issues of insider trading and tipping.

The proposed policy seeks to provide guidance in the interpretation of the phrase "in the necessary course of business" as it appears in subsection 76(2) of the *OSA*. Material non-public information may be

---

98 Thomas Lee Hazen, *The Law of Securities Regulation*, 3d ed. (St Paul: West Publishing Co., 1996) at 716.

99 *Kimber Report*, above note 17 at 17. The Kimber Committee seemed, in particular, to be concerned that such a rule had led to a proliferation of lawsuits instigated by lawyers seeking fees — an outcome they criticized as "an unseemly procedure."

100 Securities Exchange Act Release No. 34-43154, (15 August 2000).

101 National Policy 51-201, above note 54.

lawfully disclosed only where it is in the necessary course of business to do so, which makes the regulators' views on the meaning of this phrase especially useful. The proposed policy provides an illustrative list of permitted communications, which includes, among other things, communications with vendors, suppliers, employees, professional advisors, regulators, and credit-rating agencies.[102] Expressly excluded, however, is selective disclosure to members of the media, financial analysts, institutional investors, and other market participants.

G. CONCLUSION

A precise, empirically verifiable economic rationale for insider-trading liability remains somewhat elusive. However, there is some evidence that the practice may harm capital markets. And, in any event, Canadian securities law, Canadian securities regulators, the financial press, and the popular media universally condemn the practice of insider trading. Accordingly, it is clear that prohibitions against the practice will continue. It appears to be increasingly important for reporting issuers and their advisers to take proactive steps to deter, detect, and prevent improper insider trading, as well as to ensure compliance with all insider-reporting requirements. Thoughtful approaches to these preventive programs require a careful consideration of both the letter and the spirit of insider-trading prohibitions.

---

102 *Ibid.* s. 3.3(2).

CHAPTER 9

CONTINUOUS DISCLOSURE

A. INTRODUCTION AND OVERVIEW

As discussed in chapter 6, when a company (an issuer) first sells its securities to the public, it is required to produce a detailed information disclosure document called a prospectus. The prospectus provides "full, true and plain disclosure of all material facts relating to the securities"[1] being sold to the public. However, most Canadians who own securities did not purchase them directly from the issuer at the time of a public offering. Rather, they acquired them in the secondary market, usually through the facilities of a stock exchange. People who purchase securities in the secondary market do not receive a copy of the prospectus that was produced by the company when those securities were first distributed to the public. But, even if such a prospectus were delivered to these secondary market purchasers, it would be of little, or no, use to them. The prospectus would have been prepared by the issuer months or even years in the past. Such a stale-dated document cannot be relied upon by an investor trying to assess the current value of a company's securities.

Accordingly, it is important that public companies provide regular, up-to-date information to current and potential investors. The requirement to produce such information is generally referred to as a continuous disclosure obligation. The importance in Canadian securities law

---

1 *Securities Act* (Ontario), R.S.O. 1990, c. S.5, [*OSA*] s. 56(1).

of ongoing or continuous disclosure by public companies is growing as we move increasingly from a system of transaction-based disclosure to a system of integrated or issuer-based disclosure.

The *OSA* requires reporting issuers, as defined, to comply with rules relating to two basic types of continuous disclosure obligations:

1. Regular or periodic disclosure of, among other things, annual and quarterly financial statements, annual reports, and information circulars in connection with soliciting proxies for shareholders' meetings
2. Timely disclosure of material business developments when they occur

The increased regulatory emphasis on continuous disclosure has led, in recent years, to important developments and proposals in several related areas, including the following:

- Civil liability for misrepresentations in continuous disclosure documents, including common law remedies and statutory civil liability
- Selective disclosure. Communication with beneficial owners of securities where those securities are registered in the name of a nominee
- An issuer-based "integrated disclosure system"

Each of these issues is canvassed later in this Chapter.

Of course, the rapid increase in the use of the Internet also has important implications for the ongoing disclosure of information by securities issuers. Some of those implications and the regulatory initiatives relating to Internet use are also discussed briefly here.

B. REPORTING ISSUER

Only "reporting issuers" are subject to the *OSA*'s continuous disclosure rules. "Reporting issuer" is defined in section 1 of the *OSA*. Although the definition contains seven clauses, the most common way in which an issuer of securities becomes a reporting issuer is by filing a prospectus and obtaining a receipt for it.[2]

Once an issuer becomes a reporting issuer, it is subject to all of the periodic and timely disclosure obligations (discussed in more detail below) until such time, if any, that the issuer applies to the OSC and is granted an order deeming that it has "ceased to be a reporting

---

2   *OSA, ibid.* s. 1(1)(b) (definition of "reporting issuer").

issuer."[3] Prior to 1999, only reporting issuers with fewer than fifteen securityholders were permitted to apply for such an order, but the OSC now has greater latitude to grant such an order, provided it is not prejudicial to the public interest.

The concept of "reporting issuer" was introduced into Ontario law in 1978;[4] but, the idea came from an important OSC committee report, commonly referred to as the *Merger Report*.[5] The *Merger Report*, in turn, borrowed the concept from U.S. federal securities legislation.[6] The concept is fundamental to the so-called closed system. Those issuers that choose to access Ontario's public markets obligate themselves to ensure that current information about their businesses is readily available to the investing public. Investors buying or selling securities of such issuers in the secondary markets are, therefore, better able to make informed trading decisions. Moreover, the fact that a body of information about such issuers exists, and is regularly updated, facilitates the development of more streamlined procedures for additional public financings, such as the short-form, shelf, and PREP procedures discussed in chapter 6.

In 1999, the *OSA* was amended to add section 83.1. This new section provides the OSC with the authority to deem an issuer to be a reporting issuer where it would not be prejudicial to the public interest to do so.[7] The section is primarily aimed at ensuring that companies with publicly traded shares — especially companies that have completed public offerings in other Canadian jurisdictions — may, in appropriate circumstances, acquire the benefits, and simultaneously be subject to the obligations, of reporting issuers in Ontario. In 2001, the OSC promulgated a policy statement outlining the procedures and information relating to the granting of orders under section 83.1, principally with respect to reporting issuers with securities listed for trading on the CDNX and other issuers from various Canadian provinces that were reporting issuers in their home jurisdictions for at least one year.[8]

---

3   *Ibid.* s. 83.
4   *Securities Act, 1978*, S.O. 1978, c. 47.
5   Ontario Securities Commission, *Report of the OSC on the Problems of Disclosure Raised for Investors by Business Combinations and Private Placements*. (Toronto: Department of Financial and Commercial Affairs, 1970) [*Merger Report*].
6   *Securities Exchange Act of 1934*, 15 U.S.C. 78a *et seq.*
7   *OSA*, above note 1, s. 83.1.
8   See "Notice of Proposed Ontario Securities Commission Policy 12-602" (2001), 24 OSCB 1531.

C. PERIODIC DISCLOSURE REQUIREMENTS

The most fundamental regular or periodic disclosure requirements to which reporting issuers are subject under Ontario securities law are the following:

- The filing and delivery of quarterly and annual financial statements, and outstanding share data
- The filing of an annual information form
- The filing and delivery of an information or proxy circular

1) Financial Statements

a) Annual and Quarterly Statements

Reporting issuers are required to prepare, file, and deliver certain financial statements in respect of each completed financial year and each completed financial quarter.

Annually, each reporting issuer must, within 140 days[9] following the end of its financial year, file with the OSC[10] and deliver to the holders of its voting, and certain other, securities, other than debt securities,[11] comparative financial statements relating to both the most recently completed financial year and the immediately preceding financial year. The financial statements for each of these years that must be so filed and delivered are as follows:

- Balance sheet
- Income statement
- Statement of retained earnings
- Cash flow statement[12]

In most cases, these financial statements must be reviewed by the issuer's audit committee,[13] approved by the board of directors, and signed by two directors indicating such approval.[14] The statements must be prepared in accordance with Canadian generally accepted

---

9   There have been recent suggestions that this reporting requirement should be reduced from 140 days to 90 days.

10   *OSA*, above note 1, s. 78.

11   *Ibid.* s. 79: OSC Rule 56-501 (1999), 22 OSCB 6804, s. 2.1(7); *Re Certain Reporting Issuers* (1997), 20 OSCB 1219, at para. (10). This deemed rule is currently being reformulated as Rule 51-502.

12   OSC Rule 52-501 (2000), 23 OSCB 7303, s. 2.1.

13   *Ibid.* s. 2.1(4)

14   *OSA Regulation*, R.R.O. 1990, Reg. 1015, s. 11 [*OSA Regulation*].

accounting principles[15] and must be accompanied by a report of the issuer's auditor.[16] The term "generally accepted accounting principles," when used in the *OSA*, refers to those principles in the *CICA Handbook*.[17]

Most reporting issuers include their annual financial statements in the annual report they send to their shareholders. However, it must be emphasized that, in Ontario, there is no legal requirement for issuers to prepare or distribute an annual report. In other words, although the financial statement disclosure is mandatory, the rest of the typical annual report is optional. There are, however, requirements relating to the filing of another annual document — the annual information form (AIF), which is discussed further below. It is important to understand that the AIF is very different from the traditional corporate annual report. The annual report is typically a glossy, promotional document intended to persuade shareholders (and potential investors) that the company has had "another successful year." The financial statements, the auditor's report, and the management's discussion and analysis (which is explained further in section 1(b) below) are generally included at the back of the annual report and often provide the "hardest" information found in the document. The AIF is a much more detailed and regulated, prospectus-like disclosure document and is discussed further below.

Reporting issuers also are required to file with the OSC[18] and deliver to voting and certain other securityholders, other than debtholders,[19] interim financial statements within sixty days following the end of each financial quarter.[20] This interim financial information consists of the same four financial statements that must be filed annually, as discussed above. The quarterly statements must provide "year-to-date" information in all statements and specific information for the particular quarter in the income and cash flow statements. To help readers of the financial statements evaluate the performance of the issuer, issuers are required to include comparative information. Specifically, interim statements also must include a balance sheet for the most recently completed financial year; and an income statement, a statement of retained earnings, and a cash flow statement, covering the corresponding period in the previous financial year.[21]

---

15   *OSA*, above note 1, s. 78(1).
16   *Ibid.* s. 78(2).
17   See National Policy 27 (1992), 15 OSCB 6089 at 3.2 and *CICA Handbook* (Toronto: Canadian Institute of Chartered Accountants, 1968 looseleaf).
18   *OSA*, above note 1, s. 77.
19   *Re Certain Reporting Issuers*, above note 11.
20   *OSA*, above note 1, ss. 77 & 78.
21   OSC Rule 52-501, above note 12, s. 2.2.

Interim statements need not be audited;[22] however, the issuer's board of directors or the audit committee must review the statements before they are filed and delivered.[23] In a recent policy statement the OSC indicated that the board of directors ought to consider engaging an auditor to review the interim statements.[24] OSC staff recently undertook a review of the interim finacial statements filed by some 150 reporting issuers for the three-month period ended 31 March 2001.[25] That review revealed, among other things, that a significant number of reporting issuers failed to include an interim balance sheet in their interim statements and, in particular, failed to include a comparative balance sheet as at the end of the most recently completed financial year, as specifically required by Rule 52-501, s. 2.2(a).

b) Management Discussion and Analysis (MD&A)

In addition to filing and delivering financial statements, certain larger reporting issuers are required to prepare a special narrative document, known formally as "management's discussion and analysis of financial condition and results,"[26] but referred to almost universally by the initialism "MD&A." The essential philosophy underlying MD&A is that financial statements, alone, do not provide an investor or prospective investor with the subjective insights about an issuer's business that managers possess. Financial statements are static and really speak to only an issuer's financial history. What matters most to investors, of course, is how the issuer is likely to perform going forward. To make such a forward assessment requires, among other things, subjective inferences to be drawn from the financial statements. MD&A attempts to fill that informational gap. In the words of Canadian regulators,

> MD&A is supplemental analysis and explanation that accompanies, but does not form part of, an issuer's financial statements. MD&A provides management with the opportunity to discuss an issuer's current financial results, position and future prospects. MD&A is intended to give a reader the ability to look at the issuer through the eyes of management by providing both a historical and prospective analysis of the business of the issuer.[27]

---

22   *Ibid.* s.2.1(10)

23   *Ibid.* s. 2.2(6) and (7).

24   Companion Policy 52-501 CP (2000), 23 OSCB 7306 at s. 2.1.

25   See OSC Staff Notice 52-713 (February 2002). Available online at <http://www.osc.gov.on.ca> (site accessed: 12 March 2002).

26   See OSC Rule 14-501 (1997), 20 OSCB 2436 (definition of "MD&A").

27   National Instrument 44-101 (2000), 23 OSCB 926, Form 44-101F2, Instructions.

MD&A had its genesis in U.S. federal securities law, specifically Item 303 of Regulation S-K.[28] Loss and Seligman indicate that the current U.S. approach to MD&A began in 1980,[29] following a recommendation of an SEC advisory committee on corporate disclosure. Loss and Seligman note that the current SEC rules on MD&A (from which the Canadian rules have been developed) are a "key part of the evolution of the Commission's approach to accounting from an emphasis on 'hard facts' to its present emphasis on 'soft,' or predictive, information."[30] In Ontario, MD&A rules were first introduced in 1989.[31]

Not all reporting issuers are required to provide MD&A with their financial statements. OSC Rule 51-501 states that MD&A is required only in the case of reporting issuers that meet one of two minimum size requirements: (1) shareholders' equity or revenues in excess of $10 million, or (2) market capitalization of at least $75 million.[32]

Every issuer that exceeds one of these thresholds is required to file MD&A with its annual financial statements and deliver the annual MD&A to its securityholders with the financial statements. Issuers typically satisfy the delivery obligation by including MD&A in their annual reports — a practice that has been specifically acknowledged by the OSC.[33] Thereafter, issuers are required to file and deliver updated MD&A with their interim financial statements.

The form of an issuer's annual MD&A is prescribed by Form 44-101F2. The disclosure outlined in this form is actually mandated for inclusion in an issuer's AIF (discussed in the next section), through the combined effect of OSC Rule 51-501 and Form 44-101F1 under National Instrument 44-101.[34] The annual MD&A forms the foundation for the subsequent interim MD&A. The interim MD&A updates the information in the annual report and provides additional analysis on the issuer's interim financial condition and performance.[35]

---

28 17 C.F.R. § 229.303.

29 Louis Loss and Joel Seligman, *Securities Regulation*, 3d ed., vol. II rev. (Aspen: Aspen Law & Business, 1999) at 690.

30 *Ibid.* at 689.

31 OSC Policy Statement 5.10 (1989), 12 OSCB 4275.

32 (2000), 23 OSCB 8311 at s. 1.2(1).

33 OSC Companion Policy 51-501CP (2000), 23 OSCB 8311, s. 2.1.

34 OSC Rule 51-501, above note 32, s. 2.1(1), requires issuers subject to the rule to file an AIF in accordance with Form 44-101F1. Form 44-101F1, in turn, requires filers to include MD&A in accordance with Form 44-101F2. See National Instrument 44-101, above note 27 at Form 44-101F1, Item 6.1(1). It should be noted that for issuers eligible to use the short-form prospectus system, it is National Instrument 44-101, *ibid.* s. 3.1(1), that requires the AIF to be in the form of Form 44-101F1.

35 OSC Rule 51-501, above note 31, s. 4.2.

In the United States, the SEC has taken enforcement action against a number of issuers for deficiencies in their MD&A. Two of the most notable are the 1992 proceeding against Caterpillar, and the 1998 proceeding against Sony Corporation.[36]

c) Outstanding Share Data

Since 15 March 2000, reporting issuers have been required, under National Instrument 62-102,[37] to provide disclosure about their outstanding voting or equity securities (and securities convertible or exchangeable into voting or equity securities) in, or as a supplement to, their annual and interim financial statements. In its recent review of reporting issuers' filings,[38] OSC staff described National Instrument 62-102 as a "little known NI"[39] and pointed out that the disclosure required by 62-102 is share information prepared "as of the latest practicable date." In other words, the share information should be brought down to a date as close as possible to the date of actual filing of the financial statements. Merely filing share information current as of the last date in the accounting period to which the financial statements relate is not sufficient.

2) Annual Information Form (AIF)

a) Introduction

An increasingly important disclosure document for larger reporting issuers is the Annual Information Form (AIF). The AIF is a lengthy and detailed, prospectus-like document that "is intended to provide background information that is essential to a proper understanding of the nature of an issuer and its operations and prospects."[40] The AIF was introduced in Ontario in 1982.[41] It was originally designed to be completed voluntarily by qualifying issuers wishing to take advantage of the short-form prospectus system, or the prompt-offering prospectus (POP) system as it was then known.[42] The value of the information dis-

---

36   For a discussion of these and other SEC MD&A enforcement actions, see Linda C. Quinn and Ottillie L. Jarmel, "MD&A: An Overview" in *33rd Annual Securities Institute on Securities Regulation*, Vol. 1, (New York: Practising Law Institute, 2001) 387 at 406ff.
37   (2000), 23 OSCB 1370.
38   OSC Staff Notice 52-713, above note 25.
39   *Ibid.* s. 7.1.
40   National Instrument 44-101, above note 27, at Form 44-101F1 AIF.
41   See former OSC Policy 5.6 (1982), 4 OSCB 461E. The short-form prospectus system and its predecessor, the "POP" system, are discussed in chapter 6.
42   *Ibid.*

closed in an AIF to all investors was well recognized, and, since November 1989, the filing of an AIF has been mandatory for certain larger issuers, regardless of whether or not they wish to access the short-form prospectus system.[43] Because reporting issuers file AIFs with the OSC, the AIFs are publicly available and easily accessible through the SEDAR system to anyone with Internet access. Issuers are not required, however, to deliver copies of their AIFs to their securityholders, and, indeed, it would be quite unusual for a Canadian issuer to do so.

b) Requirement to File an AIF

The issuer-size thresholds that trigger the requirement to file an AIF are the same as those that trigger the MD&A requirement;[44] namely shareholders' equity or revenues in excess of $10 million or market capitalization of at least $75 million. Reporting issuers subject to the AIF requirement must file their AIFs with respect to each financial year within 140 days following the end of that financial year. The prescribed form for AIF disclosure is Form 44-101F1.[45]

The similarities between an AIF and a prospectus become obvious when one compares the items of Form 44-101F1 with those disclosure items that relate to the *issuer* (as opposed to those prospectus items that deal with the securities being distributed) prescribed by the general prospectus form, Form 41-501F1.[46] AIF items 2, 3 and 4, for example, are substantially similar to items 4, 5 and 6 in the general prospectus form. AIF items 5 and 6 correspond to item 8 in the general prospectus form. AIF Item 8 corresponds to Item 16 in the general prospectus form and so on. These disclosure provisions in both the AIF and the general prospectus form require summary financial information as well as general background information about the issuer and its business. This type of disclosure is often referred to by practitioners as the "story" of the company, and it contains information that would be of interest to owners or potential purchasers of any of the issuer's securities, but especially those of its equity securities. By providing a base document, such as the AIF, the issuer can maintain a complete and current body of company-level information available to the market simply by updating the AIF. This not only helps investors in the secondary markets make informed trading decisions, but also provides a foundational document for the short-form prospectus system, expediting the process of issuing new securities, as discussed in chapter 6.

---

43   The current requirements are found in OSC Rule 51-501, above note 31, s. 1.2.
44   *Ibid.* s. 1.2.
45   *Ibid.* s. 2.1(1).
46   (2000), 23 OSCB (Supp.).

3) Proxy Circular

a) Proxy Solicitation

Corporate law requires every public company to convene a meeting of its shareholders approximately once a year.[47] At this annual meeting, the shareholders receive the company's financial statements, elect directors for the coming year, and appoint an auditor. If the meeting deals with only these three matters, the meeting is said to be a "general" meeting. Annual general meetings are frequently referred to by the initials "AGM." Where the company convenes the meeting to consider any business other than (or in addition to) the three general matters referred to above, the meeting is deemed a "special" meeting.[48] The right of voting shareholders to attend and vote at annual general or special meetings is considered one of the most fundamental attributes of share ownership. Yet, in the case of large companies, many shareholders live in different parts of the country or even in different countries, making it impractical for many, or most, of them to attend the annual meeting. Accordingly, in order to ensure that shareholders have a voice in the affairs of the companies in which they have invested, the law permits those who cannot attend a shareholders' meeting in person to appoint others to act as their representatives or proxies. Of course, the right of a shareholder of a public company to appoint a proxy is only valuable if the shareholder is aware of this right. So, the law imposes an obligation on public companies to solicit proxies from their shareholders in connection with each meeting of the shareholders.

Proxy solicitation is an important example of an area where corporate law and securities law overlap. The conduct of shareholder meetings is an internal corporate matter, historically governed by corporate, not securities, legislation. If the shareholders' voting rights and right to be notified of upcoming meetings are not respected by corporations, however, the value of the shares and the integrity of the capital markets themselves could be compromised. Accordingly, securities regulators take the view that they, too, have the authority, and even the obligation, to regulate the proxy solicitation procedures of public companies that have shareholders residing in the regulators' jurisdictions. Thus, proxy solicitation requirements may be found both in corporate law statutes[49]

---

47   See, e.g., *Canada Business Corporations Act*, R.S.C. 1985, c. C-44 [*CBCA*], s. 133. Technically, under the *CBCA*, a corporation's "annual meetings" can be as much as fifteen months apart (*CBCA*, s. 133(1)(b)).

48   See, e.g., *CBCA*, *ibid.* s. 135(5).

49   See, e.g., *CBCA*, *ibid.* Part XIII.

and in securities legislation. In Ontario, to prevent duplication and potential conflicts, section 88 of the *OSA* relieves an issuer from complying with the *OSA* proxy rules if the corporate law rules to which the issuer is subject (and with which it is properly complying) are substantially similar to those in the *OSA*. Although the balance of this section focuses only on the proxy requirements of the *OSA*, readers should note that many reporting issuers in Ontario, in fact, are subject to only the proxy rules prescribed by their governing corporate statute.

b) Fundamental Components of the Proxy Solicitation Rules

Ontario's proxy rules have three fundamental components:

- Proxy solicitation by management is mandatory.
- Proxy solicitation requires the use of an "information circular."
- The content of information circulars and instruments or forms of proxy are subject to specific regulation.

i) *Management Proxy Solicitation Is Mandatory*

One of the most important recommendations of the Kimber Committee in 1965 was that the management of all public companies should be obligated to solicit proxies from their shareholders in connection with every shareholders' meeting.[50] This requirement is now found in section 85 of the *OSA*. The mandatory solicitation provision requires a form of proxy to be provided to all the shareholders. A shareholder signs the form of proxy to authorize someone else to vote on the his or her behalf at the shareholders' meeting. The proxy form must comply with section 177 of the *OSA Regulation*. That provision requires, among other things, that the proxy state in bold type whether or not management solicited it.[51] The proxy must also provide the means for a shareholder to indicate that her or his shares be voted for or against the matters identified in the notice of meeting, other than the matters customarily dealt with at the annual general meeting — namely, the election of directors and the appointment of auditors.[52] The requirement that the proxy specifically permit shareholders to vote for or against a matter may seem rather obvious; however, it was common practice at the time of the *Kimber Report* for companies to furnish forms of proxy that permitted shareholders either to vote in favour of a management-sponsored resolution or to refrain from voting. The

---

50   *The Report of the Attorney General's Committee on Securities Legislation in Ontario* (Toronto: Queen's Printer, 1965) [*Kimber Report*], s. 6.24.
51   *OSA Regulation*, above note 14, s. 177(1).
52   *Ibid.* s. 177(4).

Kimber Report quoted from a brief submitted by the Toronto Stock Exchange, which condemned this practice because "[t]he vote, in these circumstances, is either a vote for management or the vote is lost!"[53]

It should be reiterated, however, that the regulations do *not* require the form of proxy to provide a means for shareholders to vote against every matter that may come before the meeting. In fact, in the case of votes in respect of the appointment of auditors and the election of directors, the regulations require that the proxy must permit the securityholders' securities to be voted or to be withheld from voting.[54]

ii) Information Circulars

The requirement of management to solicit proxies ensures that shareholders are aware of their right to vote by proxy, but it is the obligation to produce a disclosure document known as an information circular that ensures shareholders receive the information necessary to use their proxies effectively. With limited exceptions, discussed below, the *OSA* requires anyone soliciting proxies from securityholders to send an information circular to those securityholders.[55] The statutory definition of solicitation of proxies is very broad and includes the following:

(a) any request for a proxy whether or not accompanied by or included in a form of proxy,

(b) any request to execute or not to execute a form of proxy or to revoke a proxy,

(c) the sending or delivery of a form of proxy or other communication to a securityholder under circumstances reasonably calculated to result in the procurement, withholding or revocation of a proxy,

(d) the sending or delivery of a form of proxy to a securityholder under section 85 [i.e., the provision of the *OSA* that makes management solicitation of proxies mandatory][56]

Thus, for example, a letter to shareholders from a dissident shareholder group urging the shareholders not to execute a form of proxy previously delivered by the company's managers was held to be a solicitation under a similar provision of the *CBCA*, even though the letter expressly stated that no rival proxies were (yet) being solicit-

---

53 *Kimber Report*, above note 50, at para. 6.12.
54 *OSA Regulation*, above note 14, s. 177(6).
55 *OSA*, above note 1, s. 86(1).
56 *Ibid.* s. 84.

ed.[57] In a recent British Columbia Supreme Court decision, it was suggested that the proxy rules could have broad application in the merger context. It is common practice, in the context of negotiated merger transactions, for corporations to enter into agreements with major shareholders. Those agreements typically include provisions pursuant to which the shareholders agree to support the planned transaction by, among other things, committing to deliver proxies in favour of approval of the transaction at shareholders' meetings called for the purpose of seeking such approval. The British Columbia Supreme Court held that such agreements constitute proxy solicitations, and because no information circular was provided in that particular case prior to or at the time that such proxies were solicited, the agreements were, thus, "illegal."[58] This characterization was based on the court's interpretation of subsection 150(1) of the *CBCA*, which states that a person must not solicit proxies unless a circular "is sent ... to each shareholder." The court held that this language mandates the sending of a circular before, or at the same time as, the proxy solicitation. Merely ensuring, for example, that a circular is sent after the proxy solicitation — even if it is still well in advance of the meeting — is not sufficient in the court's view. The British Columbia Court of Appeal appeared to disagree with this reading of section 150 (although without definitively deciding the point). However, it suggested that an agreement to deliver proxies can never be enforceable in any event because "proxies are always revocable."[59] This statement is curious because it suggests that the Court of Appeal drew no distinction between a contractual commitment to perform a certain action and the subsequent actual performance of that action. However, one notes that both statements appear to have been *obiter dicta* because the court ultimately approved the arrangement under which the proxies had been solicited.

Because the solicitation definition is so broad, shareholders of public companies often find it difficult to communicate with one another, fearing that any communication might be considered a "solicitation," which would trigger the obligation to undergo the time and expense involved in producing an information circular. In response to such concerns, recent amendments to the *CBCA* were passed to loosen the solicitation rules.[60]

---

57 *Brown v. Duby* (1980), 28 O.R. (2d) 745 (H.C.J.). It should be noted that recent amendments to the *CBCA* have relaxed the rules relating to dissident proxy circulars. See text accompanying note 60 below.

58 *Re Pacifica Papers Inc.*, [2001] B.C.J. No. 1484 (S.C.).

59 *Re Pacifica Papers Inc.*, [2001] B.C. J. No. 1714 at para. 15. (C.A.).

60 See recent amendments in Bill S-11, below note 70, to definitions of "solicit" and "solicitation" in s. 147 of the *CBCA*, and to s. 150 of the *CBCA*, regarding exceptions to the requirement to prepare and send a dissident's proxy circular.

The delivery of a satisfactory information circular is crucial to the integrity of the voting process. Where shareholders are not provided with adequate information, any resolutions passed at a meeting at which shareholders voted by proxy may be declared void.[61] The *OSA*, however, provides three limited exceptions to the requirement that an information circular be produced whenever proxies are solicited, including a *de minimis* exception that applies when the number of securityholders whose proxies are being solicited is fifteen or fewer. This *de minimis* exception applies only when the proxies are solicited by someone other than management of the issuer.[62] In the case of proxies solicited by management, a copy of the circular must accompany the notice of the meeting in which the proxy is to be used.[63] Thus, public companies must prepare a management information (or proxy) circular each year for the annual general meeting of its shareholders. It is for this reason that the information circular may be viewed as yet another component of a company's periodic reporting obligations.

The information that must be contained in an information circular is generally prescribed by Form 30.[64] The information must be current as of a date no more than thirty days before it is sent to securityholders.[65]

Special rules apply to information circulars in at least two cases: (1) where proxies are being solicited for a meeting to approve a business transaction that involves the issuance or transfer of securities, and (2) where proxies are being solicited from the non-registered beneficial owners of securities.

---

61   See, e.g., *Garvie v. Axmith*, [1962] O.R. 65 (H.C.).

62   *OSA*, above note 1, s. 86(2)(a). Proxies might be solicited by persons other than management of an issuer in cases where the securityholders who are opposed to management proposals (often referred to as "dissidents" — see, e.g., *Canada Business Corporations Act Regulations*, SOR/2002-512 s. 60) seek to gain support for positions opposed by managers. When opposing factions actively solicit proxies on opposite sides of an issue, they are said to be engaged in a "proxy contest" or, to use a somewhat more provocative term, a "proxy war." As discussed in chapter 10, a proxy contest can be used as an alternative to a take-over bid because it could enable a rival management group, if successful, to replace a company's board of directors at a shareholders' meeting. For a recent example of just such a proxy contest, see the proxy circulars distributed to shareholders of FPI Limited by Clearwater Fine Foods Limited and by Management of FPI Limited in connection with the FPI Limited shareholders meeting of 1 May 2001, available online at <http://www.sedar.com> (site accessed: 30 April 2002).

63   *OSA*, above note 1, s. 86(1)(a).

64   *OSA Regulation*, above note 14, s. 176(1).

65   *Ibid.* s. 176(2).

In the first case, OSC Rule 54-501[66] requires that the information circular include prospectus-type disclosure in connection with the securities being issued or transferred.[67] Such disclosure permits shareholders to make informed decisions about the value of the securities involved in the transaction, and to exercise informed votes on whether to approve the transaction.

The second case, involving the non-registered beneficial owners of the shares, requires a more detailed explanation. In Canada, most individual investors who own shares do not, in fact, have those shares registered in their own names. Of course, many Canadians choose to invest through pooled investment vehicles, such as mutual funds, and do not expect to become registered shareholders of the corporations whose shares are held by the mutual fund. However, even those Canadians who buy shares in specific issuers directly, rather than through a mutual fund, are unlikely to hold those shares in their own names. Instead, individual investors typically hold their securities through accounts that they maintain with their brokers. The brokers, in turn, hold their securities through participation arrangements with a depository, such as the Canadian Depository for Securities Limited (CDS). The depository is typically the registered holder of the securities. This system of securities holding makes it much easier and faster to clear and settle trades (i.e., to match orders to buy with orders to sell, and to ensure that buyers receive their securities and sellers receive their sale proceeds). Traditionally, however, Canadian corporate law has emphasized the importance of registered ownership. Accordingly, Canadian corporations are generally entitled, as a matter of corporate law, to treat the registered owners of shares as the true owners for all purposes.[68] The implications of this emphasis on registration are many. In 1996, for example, the Supreme Court of Canada held that a beneficial owner of shares registered in the name of a trustee was not permitted to submit a shareholder proposal to the corporation.[69] (It should be noted, however, that recent amendments to the *CBCA* specifically permit beneficial owners of shares, as well as registered holders, to submit a shareholder proposal.)[70]

---

66   (2000), 23 OSCB 8465.
67   *Ibid.* at para. 2.1(1).
68   See, e.g., *CBCA*, above note 47, s. 51(1).
69   *Verdun v. Toronto-Dominion Bank*, [1996] 3 S.C.R. 550.
70   See *CBCA* above note 47, s. 137(1) and (1.1).

In certain contexts, securities regulators also indicate a preference for relying on the register as determinative of security ownership.[71] Yet, securities regulators do not wish to discourage the use and development of the book-based depository system because that system contributes significantly to the efficiency and safety of Canadian capital markets.[72] They do, however, wish to ensure that shareholders holding their interests through a depository are not, effectively, disenfranchised. Consequently, in 1987, the CSA introduced National Policy No. 41,[73] which outlines a detailed set of procedures to ensure that the beneficial owners of shares obtain proxy material essentially through a kind of depository-broker-shareholder relay system. When all goes well, this system is invisible to the individual shareholder who may never be fully aware of the complex series of steps taken to enable him or her to attend an annual meeting or appoint a proxyholder to attend on his or her behalf.

When the OSC obtained rule-making power in 1995, National Policy No. 41 was made a "deemed rule" under section 143.1 as a transitional matter. At the date of writing, National Policy No. 41 is in the process of being reformulated as National Instrument 54-101.[74] In addition to a number of technical changes, NI 54-101 deals with the important, and somewhat controversial, concept of "non-objecting beneficial owners" (NOBOs). Briefly put, NOBOs are beneficial owners of an issuer's securities who do not object to having their names and addresses disclosed to the issuer. It often comes as a surprise to Canadian securityholders that public companies have no way of determining the identities of most of their shareholders. At the same time, some shareholders prefer that their identities not be revealed to the companies in which they have invested. And many financial intermediaries, for administrative reasons, commercial confidentiality, and per-

---

71   See, e.g., *Re Med-Tech Environmental Limited* (1998), 21 OSCB 7607 at p. 7614:
"We are inclined to view that 'holders' when used in clause [93(1)] (d), means registered holders. This approach results in a simpler and easier determination of whether the exemption is available, and a test which does not require what might be a difficult inquiry into beneficial ownership. In addition, it seems to us that, absent specific language to the contrary, 'holder' normally means the person shown as the shareholder on the register of shareholders at the relevant time." For further discussion of s. 93(1)(d) of the *OSA*, see Chapter 10.

72   For a recent discussion of the increasing importance of book-based systems, see Canadian Capital Markets Association, Dematerialization Working Group, *Dematerialization White Paper* (31 October 2001), available online at <http://www.ccma-acmc.ca> (site accessed: 26 February 2002).

73   (1987), 10 OSCB 6307.

74   (2000), 23 OSCB 5875. See also chapter 12.

haps other business reasons would also prefer that issuers not be in a position to communicate directly with investors.

4) Annual Filing

In those cases where management of a reporting issuer is not required to file an annual information circular, the *OSA* and the *OSA Regulation* require such a reporting issuer to make an annual filing on *OSA Regulation* Form 28.[75]

D. TIMELY DISCLOSURE REQUIREMENTS

1) Introduction

In addition to the ongoing periodic disclosure requirements described above, reporting issuers are subject to "timely disclosure" obligations.

Timely disclosure alerts the market to news affecting a reporting issuer promptly after the reporting issuer becomes aware of it. Without timely disclosure obligations, those investors lucky enough to have special access to such corporate information would have an unfair advantage over others.

The obligation of reporting issuers to publicly disclose certain relevant information on a timely basis raises three subsidiary issues:

1. How soon must new information be publicly disclosed?
2. How should new information be publicly disclosed?
3. What information triggers an obligation to make public disclosure?

2) Timing of Disclosure

The *OSA* requires that when a "material change occurs in the affairs of a reporting issuer," the issuer must disclose the change "forthwith."[76] The meaning of "material change," and the various regulatory extensions and glosses that have been introduced, are discussed below. At

---

75   *OSA*, above note 1, s. 81(2); *OSA Regulation*, above note 14, s. 5; Form 28. This obligation does not extend, however, to issuers that are exempt from the requirement to file a proxy circular by virtue of *OSA*, s. 88. Rather, it would apply, for example, in cases where an issuer's voting securities were held by a single shareholder, but where it had public debt outstanding. See OSC Policy 7.1 (1983), 4 OSCB 514E (as amended), E1.
76   *OSA*, above note 1, s. 75(1).

this point, it is only noted that, where a reporting issuer has an obligation to disclose new information, that information must be disclosed
immediately. Although the *OSA* requires reports of material changes to
be filed with the OSC within ten days, this filing requirement does not
qualify the primary obligation to make public disclosure at once.

3) Material Information

A reporting issuer's obligation to disclose information generally turns
upon the materiality of that information. A number of technical legal
issues surround the concept of materiality and, in particular, the concepts of "material change," "material fact," and "material information."

a) Material Change

The *OSA* states that the obligation to make timely disclosure is triggered when "a material change occurs in the affairs of a reporting
issuer."[77] The phrase "material change" is defined in subsection 1(1) of
the *OSA*. The definition raises a number of challenging questions, some
of which are canvassed below. However, quite apart from these matters,
the interpretation of the disclosure obligation in section 75 of the *OSA*
is further complicated by National Policy No. 40,[78] which purports to
"supplement" the requirement to publicly disclose material changes.

National Policy No. 40 is discussed in more detail in the next section. At this point, however, it is important to understand why
Canadian securities regulators consider National Policy No. 40's broader approach necessary. It is useful, therefore, to consider certain interpretive difficulties raised by the *OSA*'s definition of "material change."
First, the *OSA* defines a material change as an internal corporate development that is "a change in the business, operations or capital of the
issuer."[79] Yet, it is possible for a development that does not constitute
such an internal change to have an impact on the market price of an
issuer's securities. In this context, one notes that the *OSA*'s definition of
the related term "material fact" is not similarly confined to facts concerning the business, operations, or capital of an issuer.

The fact that the *OSA* requires disclosure only in the case of "material changes" has led to some confusion. The disclosure obligation is
evidently limited to "material *changes*" because of the assumption that

---

77   *Ibid.*
78   National Policy No. 40 is to be rescinded when proposed National Policy 51-201
      is adopted.
79   *OSA*, above note 1, s. 1(1).

all material facts that do not constitute material changes have already been disclosed by the issuer.[80] However, the limited meaning of material change has led to at least one unfortunate judicial decision. In *Pezim v. British Columbia (Superintendent of Brokers)*,[81] the British Columbia Court of Appeal determined that favourable assay results on a mining property owned by an issuer could not constitute a material change, notwithstanding that, when publicly disclosed, such results would have a dramatic effect on the price of the issuer's shares. The majority in the Court of Appeal reasoned that such results "[m]ay constitute a basis for a perception that there has been a change in the value of an asset. But that is a far different thing than a change in an asset."[82] A number of commentators criticized the Court of Appeal's decision in *Pezim*.[83] On appeal, the Supreme Court of Canada expressly rejected the narrow view of material change articulated by the British Columbia Court of Appeal.[84] Nevertheless, the case illustrates the potential problems posed by the use in section 75 of the narrowly defined term "material change."

The second troublesome feature of the definition of "material change" is that it includes "a decision to implement such a change made by the board of directors of the issuer or by senior management of the issuer who believe that confirmation of the decision by the board

---

80 Former OSC Chairman Peter Dey, speaking in 1983, framed the issue this way: "This theory for the distinction is supported by the requirement that timely disclosure be made only of material changes and not of material facts because the material facts should all be in the public realm. If all material facts should be in the public realm, I ask myself: Why is there a prohibition against tipping material facts? The answer must be that material information about an issuer can arise without there being a change in the business operations or capital of the issuer. And then I ask myself, why shouldn't this information have to be disclosed under s. 75?" Peter Dey, "Consolidation of Remarks of Peter J. Dey Concerning Disclosure Under the Securities Act made to Securities Lawyers in Calgary and Toronto on June 7 and 9 [1983]" (1983), 6 OSCB 2361.

81 (1992), 66 B.C.L.R. (2d) 257 (C.A.), rev'd in part [1994] 2 S.C.R. 557 [*Pezim*].

82 *Ibid.* at 268 (cited to B.C.L.R.).

83 See, e.g., George C. Stevens and Stephen D. Worley, "Murray Pezim in the Court of Appeal: Draining the Lifeblood from Securities Regulation" (1992) 26 U.B.C. L. Rev. 331.

84 *Pezim*, above note 81 at 600 (cited to S.C.R.): "In the mining industry, mineral properties are constantly being assessed to determine whether there is a change in the characterization of the property. Thus, from the point of view of investors, new information relating to a mining property (which is an asset) bears significantly on the question of that property's value. Accordingly, I agree with the approach taken by the Commission, namely that a change in assay and drilling results can amount to a material change depending on the circumstances."

of directors is probable."[85] As commentators have noted, this phrase limits material changes to those matters that require approval by the board of directors. Yet, many important business decisions, which could certainly have a material effect on the price of an issuer's shares, can be made by senior managers without any need to seek board approval. Surely, a company must be obliged to disclose those matters as well.

A third issue concerning the definition of "material change" relates to the test of materiality itself. The definition states that a change is material if it "would reasonably be expected to have a significant effect on the market price *or value* of any of the securities of the issuer."[86] It is not entirely clear, however, when the value of securities would be affected with no corresponding effect on their price. Nor is it clear why regulators ought to be concerned with changes that would not affect the price of securities. Alboini suggests that the definition needs to refer to both price and value "because of the susceptibility of the market price of an issuer's securities to factors other than material changes."[87] An example he offers is a material change that would improve the value of an issuer's securities at a time of a general market downturn. Such a change, he says, ought to be disclosed, even though, upon disclosure, the market price of the issuer may still fall rather than rise. With respect, however, Alboini's argument is unpersuasive. Such important positive information would, indeed, be expected to have a significant effect on the market price of the issuer's securities: the effect would be to prevent the price from declining as steeply as it might otherwise have done. The reference to value adds nothing useful in this example. More generally, some suggest that the reference to value prevents attempts by managers to invoke technical arguments to avoid compliance with the *OSA*. Because the obligation to disclose is triggered by changes that "would reasonably be expected" to have an effect on an issuer's securities, and not merely by changes that are *subsequently observed* actually to have such an effect, the possibility of any such technical defence being invoked inappropriately is, to say the least, remote.[88] Accordingly, the reference to value adds nothing useful to the

---

85 *OSA*, above note 1, s. 1(1) (definition of "material change").

86 *Ibid.* [Emphasis added.]

87 Victor P. Alboini, *The 1997 Ontario Securities Act Annotated* (Toronto: Carswell, 1996) at 447.

88 In this context, it is illumibating to consider the court's analysis of "material fact" and the defence of reasonable mistake of fact in the insider trading context in *Lewis v. Fingold* (1999), 22 OSCB 2811, discussed in chapter 8 [*Fingold*].

concept of market price, is potentially susceptible to misuse in the hands of overzealous regulators, and could safely, and usefully, be deleted from the definition.

A final critical issue concerning the definition of "material change" relates to the timing of the disclosure, particularly in the case of transactions that are still subject to negotiation. In an important 1988 decision, *Basic Inc. v. Levinson*,[89] the United States Supreme Court discussed this issue in the context of merger negotiations. The case involved a company, Basic, that had been approached by another firm concerning a possible merger. Basic made three public statements denying that it was involved in merger discussions. When a merger deal was finally announced, and Basic's share price increased dramatically, many investors who had sold their shares in Basic prior to that announcement sued, alleging that they had suffered losses as a result of their reliance on Basic's untrue denials of the merger talks. The United States Supreme Court held that the general test to apply in determining whether information is material is the test previously adopted by the court in the context of proxy solicitations in *TSC Industries Inc. v. Northway, Inc.*[90] The test of materiality articulated in *TSC Industries* was that "[a]n omitted fact is material if there is a substantial likelihood that a reasonable shareholder would consider it important in deciding how to vote,"[91] and that "there must be a substantial likelihood that the disclosure of the omitted fact would have been viewed by the reasonable investor as having significantly altered the 'total mix' of information made available."[92] In the specific context of preliminary merger discussions, the court acknowledged that it was inappropriate to attempt to formulate a bright-line test as to the moment at which such discussions become material.[93] Rather, materiality in such cases is fact specific and depends "on the probability that the transaction will be consummated, and its significance to the issuer."[94] (In Canada, the question of disclosure of ongoing negotiations is dealt with specifically in National Policy No. 40, discussed in the next section.)

---

89   485 U.S. 224 (1988) [*Basic Inc.*].
90   426 U.S. 438 (1976) [*TSC Industries*].
91   *Ibid.* at 449.
92   *Ibid.*
93   Certain lower courts previously took the view that such discussions did not become material until an agreement in principle had been reached between the parties.
94   *Basic Inc.*, above note 89, at 250.

b) National Policy No. 40

Many of the technical problems posed by the restrictive definition of "material change" in section 75 of the *OSA* prompted Canadian securities regulators in 1987 to adopt the TSE's approach to continuous disclosure[95] through the promulgation of National Policy No. 40.[96] National Policy No. 40 purports to "supplement" the continuous disclosure provisions of provincial securities legislation, including the *OSA*. The technicalities of the "material change" definition are overcome in the policy statement by imposing a "requirement" upon issuers to disclose "material information" as soon as it becomes known to management.[97] Material information is not limited to material changes, but rather is defined as "any information relating to the business and affairs of an issuer that results in or would reasonably be expected to result in a significant change in the market price or value of any of the issuer's securities."[98] National Policy No. 40 also expressly states that material information includes *both* material facts and material changes.[99] National Policy No. 40 was originally issued many years before the OSC and other Canadian securities regulators were granted rule- or regulation-making authority. The regulators attempted to soften what would otherwise appear to be indirect legislative amendment by advising the following in the introduction to the policy statement:

> Where the requirements of the Policy go beyond the technical requirements of existing legislation, the securities administrators and stock exchanges *request* that issuers, their counsel, and market professionals regard such requirements as *guidelines* to follow in order to assist in the operation in Canada of an open and fair marketplace which merits the trust and confidence of the investing public.[100]

National Policy No. 40 was in place at the time of the *Pezim* case, referred to above. The British Columbia Court of Appeal in *Pezim* made reference to the policy, specifically stating that the regulators had no authority to impose "more exacting standards than those specifically adopted and imposed by the legislature."[101] As one of the authors of this

---

95 See *Toronto Stock Exchange, Company Manual*, available online at <http:www.tse.ca/en/pdf/CompanyManual0202.pdf> (site accessed 2 May 2002), s. 406 [*TSE Company Manual*].

96 (1987), 10 OSCB 6295.

97 *Ibid.* at para. D.

98 *Ibid.* at para. D.

99 *Ibid.*

100 *Ibid.* at para. A. [Emphasis added.]

101 Above note 81 at 270 (cited to B.C.L.R.).

book noted in an earlier paper, although the Supreme Court of Canada reversed the British Columbia Court of Appeal's decision, it made no adverse comments on this aspect of the Court of Appeal's reasons.[102] It is also worth noting that National Policy No. 40 was "restated" by regulators with some minor changes to update statutory references after the British Columbia Court of Appeal rendered its judgment in *Pezim*.[103]

Admittedly, however, National Policy No. 40 does not only purport to widen the *OSA's* disclosure rules, but also attempts to balance legitimate issuer concerns about maintaining confidentiality — especially in the context of sensitive ongoing negotiations — against the value of complete public disclosure. Accordingly, the policy expressly acknowledges the following:

> In certain circumstances disclosure of material information concerning an issuer's business and affairs may be delayed and kept confidential temporarily where immediate release of the information would be unduly detrimental to the issuer's interests.[104]

Confidential disclosure is discussed in section 4(c) below.

In 2001, the CSA proposed rescinding National Policy No. 40, and introducing in its place National Policy 51-201.[105] National Policy 51-201 is referred to further below. At the date of writing, the comment period for the proposed policy had not yet expired.

c) Stock Exchange Requirements

As noted above, National Policy No. 40 is based on the TSE's timely disclosure policies, which may be found at Part IV B of the *TSE Company Manual*. Although the TSE's policies are consistent with those of National Policy No. 40, in the case of companies with shares listed on the TSE, the TSE enforces its own disclosure rules.[106]

d) Material Fact

Even if a reporting issuer's timely disclosure obligations were triggered, unambiguously, not only in the case of material changes, but also in any case where management had knowledge of previously undisclosed material facts, a number of perplexing problems would remain. For example, the definition of "material fact" in the *OSA* appears to have

---

102 Jeffrey G. MacIntosh, "Securities Regulation and the Public Interest: Of Politics, Procedures and Policy Statements — Part I" (1995) 24 Can. Bus. L.J. 77 at 81.

103 (1993), 16 OSCB 2722.

104 National Policy No. 40, above note 96 at para. G..

105 Proposed National Policy 51-201 (2001), 24 OSCB 3301.

106 *TSE Company Manual*, above note 95, s. 406.

an inappropriate retroactive element. The definition, it will be recalled, refers not only to facts that would reasonably be *expected* to have an impact on the price or value of securities, but also to facts that do, *in fact*, have such an effect. Thus, it is theoretically possible for managers of a reporting issuer to be liable for failure to disclose information that, in fact, affected security prices unexpectedly, even if such information could not reasonably have been expected to have such an effect at the time the managers first became aware of it.[107]

4) Method of Disclosure

a) News Release

A reporting issuer making timely disclosure of material information must disclose that information in two ways: by issuing a news release and by filing that release and a material change report with the OSC. A senior officer of the issuer must authorize the news release. The *OSA* does not specify how or to whom a reporting issuer must issue the news release to satisfy the requirements of section 75. A commonly cited test for general disclosure is found in the Ontario Court of Appeal's decision in *Green v. Charterhouse Group Can. Ltd.*[108] However, National Policy No. 40 provides that issuers must use media that will facilitate quick and wide dissemination of the information. The policy statement provides as follows:

> Media releases should be made to news services that disseminate financial news nationally, to the financial press and to daily newspapers that provide regular coverage of financial news.[109]

Alboini suggests that issuers commonly issue news releases to the following media outlets:

1.   the wire services, such as Canada News-Wire Limited;

2.   the stock exchange where the reporting issuer's securities are listed;

---

107 This potentially retroactive aspect of the "material fact" definition was specifically referred to by the Allen Committee. See TSE Committee on Corporate Disclosure, *Final Report: Responsible Corporate Disclosure — A Search for Balance* (Toronto: Toronto Stock Exchange, 1997) at 80 [*Allen Committee Report*]. See also, however, *Fingold*, above note 88.

108 (1976), 12 O.R. (2d) 280 (C.A.). The CSA specifically refers to the *Green v. Charterhouse* decision in its recently proposed National Policy 51-201. See text accompanying note 163 below.

109 National Policy No. 40, above note 96 at para. F.

3. the Globe and Mail, the Toronto Star and other daily newspapers in other provinces or jurisdictions where security holders are resident or where there may be investor interest in the securities of the reporting issuer; and

4. securities administrators in the other provinces, in order to comply with their timely disclosure requirements or the SEC.[110]

Where a reporting issuer has a class of securities listed on a stock exchange, such as the TSE, the reporting issuer must also comply with the exchange's rules. The *TSE Company Manual* mandates the use of "a wire service (or combination of services) ... which provides national and simultaneous coverage."[111] The *Company Manual* sets out the criteria that acceptable news services must satisfy and mandates the use of services that carry the full text of news releases, rather than edited versions.[112] Unfortunately, issuing a news release to the media does not guarantee that the media will publish it. Issues have occasionally arisen as to whether news that has been released to the media has been adequately disseminated in cases where the media chooses not to publish the release.[113]

b) Material-Change Report

In addition to issuing a news release when there has been a material change, the reporting issuer must make a public filing with the OSC. The required filing consists of a copy of the news release filed "forthwith"[114] and a material-change report.[115] As indicated above, the filing of the material change report must be made "as soon as practicable and in any event within ten days" of the change.[116] Although the *OSA Regulation* states that a material-change report must be prepared in accordance with Form 27,[117] the form[118] indicates that it is intended only as a guideline, and that the material-change report requirements may be satisfied by way of "a letter or other document."[119]

---

110 Alboini, above note 87 at 453.
111 *TSE Company Manual*, above note 95, s. 417.
112 *Ibid*.
113 For a discussion of this issue, see Alboini, above note 87 at 453–54.
114 *OSA*, above note 1, s. 75(1).
115 *Ibid*. s. 75(2).
116 *Ibid*.
117 *OSA Regulation*, s. 3(1)(a).
118 *OSA Regulation*, Form 27, Note.
119 *Ibid*.

c) Confidential Disclosure

Reporting issuers confront a particularly thorny problem when they have knowledge of sensitive confidential information that is material, and that certainly must be disclosed eventually, but is not quite "ripe" for disclosure. Premature disclosure of such information could, in certain cases, cause an issuer to lose valuable opportunities to the detriment of the issuer and its investors. Suppose, for example, an oil company is involved in negotiations to acquire a property that the company has good reason to believe has substantial reserves. Until a binding agreement is signed, it is imprudent for the oil company to disclose the negotiations publicly because the news might attract rival bidders, drive up the cost of the land, and, so, harm the oil company. Yet, the fact that a lucrative deal is imminent is surely material information. In view of the policy considerations underlying section 75 of the *OSA*, there are compelling reasons not to allow the company to remain "silent" and make no disclosure whatsoever. In cases such as this, the *OSA* and National Policy No. 40, as discussed above, permit reporting issuers to disclose the information on a confidential basis to the OSC only. The *OSA* provides for two instances in which such confidential disclosure may be made:

> Where,
>
> (a) in the opinion of the reporting issuer, the disclosure required by subsections [75(1) and (2)] would be unduly detrimental to the interests of the reporting issuer; or
>
> (b) the material change consists of a decision to implement a change made by senior management of the issuer who believe that confirmation of the decision by the board of directors is probable and senior management of the issuer has no reason to believe that persons with knowledge of the material change have made use of such knowledge in purchasing or selling securities of the issuer.[120]

A material-change report filed on a confidential basis is normally expected to be made public within ten days. If the issuer seeks to retain confidentiality for longer than ten days, the issuer must specifically advise the OSC.[121] While such material information remains confidential, the issuer is required to take steps to ensure that the information is not leaked, and to monitor trading in its securities for signs of any improper leaks. If the information is disclosed inadvertently or other-

---

120 *OSA*, above note 1, s. 75(3).
121 *Ibid.* s. 75(4).

wise, the issuer must immediately announce the information publicly.[122] Thus, confidential disclosure gives the OSC the means to deter the exploitation of confidential information by insiders, but does not force issuers to disclose sensitive information publicly before such disclosure is prudent.

d) No Individual Remedy

The Ontario Superior Court[123] has indicated that, where an issuer is alleged to have failed to comply with its timely disclosure obligations under section 75 of the *OSA* "a shareholder is not empowered to seek an order for disclosure from the court."[124] It is for the OSC, and the OSC alone, to take action to compel compliance.

E. CIVIL LIABILITY FOR CONTINUOUS DISCLOSURE MISREPRESENTATIONS

1) Common Law Remedies

The increasing importance of secondary market trading and of the rigorous ongoing disclosure standards for reporting issuers leads to a consideration of the remedies available to investors when those standards are breached. Where a reporting issuer engages in outright fraud, traditional common law causes of action in fraudulent misrepresentation can be pursued by disgruntled investors. But, outright fraud is comparatively rare and often notoriously difficult to prove. Accordingly, investors who purchase shares in the secondary market after a reporting issuer makes public statements that are inaccurate, incomplete, or misleading — but which have not been made fraudulently — often face almost insurmountable barriers. In 1997, the TSE Committee on Corporate Disclosure (the Allen Committee) stated that "the remedies available to investors in secondary trading markets who are injured by misleading disclosure are so difficult to pursue and to establish, that they are as a practical matter largely academic."[125] The well-recognized shortcomings of our existing legal regime have spurred two sorts of ini-

---

122 National Policy No. 40, above note 96 at para. G. Where the issuer's securities are listed on the TSE, the applicable requirements are found in the *TSE Company Manual*, above note 95, s. 423.3.
123 *Stern v. Imasco*, [1999] O.J. No. 4235 (Sup. Ct.).
124 *Ibid*. para. 44.
125 *Allen Committee Report*, above note 107 at p. vii.

tiatives: (1) attempts by creative lawyers to find innovative ways to lower the hurdles facing plaintiffs in such cases, including attempts to import the U.S. notion of "fraud-on-the-market theory" into Canada; and (2) proposals to amend securities legislation to provide for statutory civil liability for misrepresentations in continuous disclosure.

a)   Fraud-on-the-Market Theory

"Fraud-on-the-market theory" is an American judicial creation designed to facilitate class actions in certain securities law cases. The U.S. Federal Rules of Civil Procedure provide that class actions may be pursued only where common questions of fact and law predominate over such questions affecting only individual plaintiffs.[126] In cases where investors allege that they suffered damages as a result of false statements made by a public company, it is necessary for each plaintiff to demonstrate that he or she relied on those false statements. Such proof of individual reliance makes it impossible to conclude that common questions predominate over individual questions, and, so, the availability of class actions in such cases is all but eliminated. The fraud-on-the-market theory solves this problem by obviating the need for individual plaintiffs to prove actual reliance on the impugned statements. In *Basic Inc.* v. *Levinson*[127] the U.S. Supreme Court endorsed the following explanation of the fraud-on-the-market theory, citing from *Peil* v. *Speiser*:[128]

> The fraud on the market theory is based on the hypothesis that, in an open and developed securities market, the price of a company's stock is determined by the available material information regarding the company and its business ... Misleading statements will therefore defraud purchasers of stock even if the purchasers do not directly rely on the misstatements. ... The causal connection between the defendants' fraud and the plaintiffs' purchase of stock in such a case is no less significant than in a case of direct reliance on misrepresentations.[129]

---

126 See U.S. Federal Rules of Civil Procedure, 28 U.S.C.A. Rule 23(b)(3):

> An action may be maintained as a class action if ...

> (3) the court finds that the questions of law or fact common to the members of the class predominate over any questions affecting only individual members ...

127 *Basic Inc.*, above note 89.
128 806 F.2d 1154 at 1160–61 (3d Cir. 1986).
129 Quoted in *Basic Inc.*, above note 89 at 241-42. For a more detailed discussion of "fraud-on-the-market theory," including its link to efficient market theory, see Christopher C. Nicholls, *Corporate Finance and Canadian Law* (Toronto: Carswell, 2000) at 96–99.

At one time, Canadian commentators speculated that the fraud-on-the-market theory might usefully be attempted by Canadian class action plaintiffs as well.[130] The most recent Canadian judicial pronouncement on the doctrine is not, however, very promising. In a decision relating to the 1997 collapse of Bre-X Minerals Ltd., the Ontario Court (General Division), now the Ontario Superior Court, specifically held that the fraud-on-the-market theory could not be used by plaintiffs in a Canadian class action to circumvent the clear requirement in Canadian law that, in an action based on negligent misrepresentation, plaintiffs must prove actual reliance on the alleged misrepresentation.[131] However, although fraud-on-the-market theory appears to have been formally rejected, an innovative attempt to introduce a similar approach under a different name has recently survived a motion to strike in Ontario. In *CC&L Dedicated Enterprise Fund (Trustee of)* v. *Fisherman*,[132] the plaintiffs advanced the theory that "the market price of ... shares ... reflected the 'Representation' made in the [defendant auditors'] audit opinion. Thus, [they argued] a court could conclude that by purchasing ... shares each class member relied upon the 'Representation'."[133] The plaintiffs had not pleaded "fraud-on-the-market theory," and the court expressly stated that if they had done so, their claim could not succeed (because "fraud on the market" is not recognized in Ontario law). Nevertheless, the court accepted that this very similar argument could be allowed to stand, distinguishing it from fraud-on-the-market theory on the basis that "the case law recognizes that a person's reliance upon a representation may be inferred from all the circumstances."[134] Because this matter came before the court in the context of a motion to strike pleadings (where the threshold for plaintiffs to succeed is very low), the court allowed the claim to proceed.

---

130 See, e.g., Mark R. Gillen, *Securities Regulation in Canada*, 2d ed. (Toronto: Carswell, 1998) at 212.

131 See *Carom v. Bre-X Minerals Ltd.* (1998), 41 O.R. (3d) 780 (Gen. Div.). For a more complete explication of the reasoning of the court on this issue, see Christopher C. Nicholls, "Lessons from the Bre-X Scandal: When Systems Fail" (1999) 45 *Rocky Mt. Min. L. Instit.* 3-1 at 3-17 to 3-19.

132 (2001), 18 B.L.R. (3d) 260 (Ont. Sup. Ct.)

133 *Ibid.* at 274

134 *Ibid.* at 277.

2) Statutory Civil Liability for Continuous Disclosure

a) Introduction
The practical difficulties encountered by investors pursuing common law negligent or fraudulent misrepresentation claims against issuers for lapses in continuous disclosure have led to calls in recent years for possible amendments to the *OSA*. Reformers argue that legislative change is needed to provide for *statutory* civil liability in the case of continuous disclosure misrepresentation.

b) The Allen Committee Report
In 1997, the Toronto Stock Exchange's Committee on Corporate Disclosure, under the chairmanship of Thomas I.A. Allen, released its final report, *Responsible Corporate Disclosure — A Search for Balance*.[135] The Allen Committee Report was issued less than a year after the release of the influential SEC advisory committee report, the Wallman Report, in 1996.[136] The Wallman Report, in turn, followed a series of initiatives aimed at integrating the provisions of the *Securities Act of 1933* (which regulates the disclosure requirements of issuers when they distribute their securities to the public) with the ongoing issuer-reporting requirements of the *Securities Exchange Act of 1934*. The goal of integrating the disclosure provisions of these two statutes was to create an "integrated disclosure system."[137] Canadian securities law has followed a different path. But, it has been recognized in Canada, as in the United States, that as more information about reporting issuers is

---

135 Allen Committee Report, above note 107.

136 *Report of the Advisory Committee on the Capital Formation and Regulatory Processes* (Washington: SEC, 1996), available online at <http://www.sec.gov/news/studies/capform.htm> (site accessed 31 March 2002) [*Wallman Report*].

137 The term "integrated disclosure system" was used by the SEC to describe the 1982 initiative to reduce duplication in disclosure, and streamline the offering process. (See Sec. Act. Release No. 33-6383 (3 March 1982).) Hazen says that the concept of integrated disclosure may be traced to the American Law Institute's Proposed Federal Securities Code. (See Thomas Lee Hazen, *The Law of Securities Regulation*, 3d ed. (St. Paul: West Publishing Co., 1996), 119 n.) In its 1996 release, following receipt of the Wallman Report, the SEC suggested that the roots of the integrated disclosure system may be found in a 1966 paper by Milton Cohen, "Truth in Securities' Revisited" (1966), 79 Harv. L. Rev. 1340. See SEC, "Effects on 1933 Act Concepts on Capital Formation," Concept Release, CCH Federal Securities Law Reporter ¶85,823.

available to, and accessible by, the public, it becomes less necessary, and potentially wasteful, to require such issuers to repeat that information each time they wish to raise capital by distributing securities. The notion that Canadian securities regulation ought to shift more from transaction-based disclosure to issuer-based disclosure was advocated in the 1970 *Merger Report*,[138] as discussed in section G below.

The Allen Committee Report advanced the discussion on this issue in at least two critical respects. First, the report recommended upgrading current disclosure rules, including making the filing of an AIF mandatory for every reporting issuer and requiring material-change reports to meet prospectus-level disclosure standards.[139] Secondly, the report discussed at length a proposal for improving the quality of continuous disclosure by providing a statutory civil remedy for aggrieved investors in the case of misrepresentations in such disclosure. This latter proposal is discussed in the following section.

c) The 1998 Proposal for Statutory Civil Liability

Reporting issuers are required to provide up-to-date material information to the market. As discussed above, where such information is deficient or misleading, Canadian investors traditionally have had available to them largely ineffective common law remedies.[140] There is no statutory civil remedy in Ontario to address the shortcomings of the common law in this area as there is, for example, for misrepresentations in prospectuses,[141] certain private placement offering memoranda,[142] take-over bid circulars, issuer bid circulars, and directors' circulars.[143] There is international precedent for a statutory remedy for continuous disclosure misrepresentations. Such a remedy exists, for

---

138 Above note 5. For a discussion of this point, see Mary G. Condon, *Making Disclosure: Ideas and Interests in Ontario Securities Regulation* (Toronto: University of Toronto Press, 1998) at 177–78.
139 Allen Committee Report, above note 107 at viii.
140 See discussion in section D(1) above.
141 See *OSA*, above note 1, s. 130. The Allen Committee Report, above note 107 at 26, citing a 1994 article, noted: "No actions have proceeded to judgment under the existing sections 130 and 131 of the Ontario *Securities Act*, or similar provisions in other provinces' legislation." However, despite the lack of reported judgments, there is little doubt that the existence of s. 130 and 131 has an important effect on the diligence of issuers and other market participants.
142 *OSA*, above note 1, s. 130.1. (As discussed in chapter 7, the liability provisions of s. 130.1 apply only in certain prescribed circumstances.)
143 *Ibid.* s. 131.

example, under the federal securities laws of the United States.[144] The Allen Committee Report regarded the lack of a similar remedy in Canada as a significant weakness in our law and recommended statutory amendments to introduce civil liability for misrepresentations in continuous disclosure that would be expressly aimed at deterring wayward issuers rather than at compensating aggrieved investors.[145]

In 1998, the CSA issued a proposal for comment for a new statutory civil remedy for continuous disclosure representations that reflected, in the main, the Allen Committee Report proposal.[146] The CSA received twenty-eight comments on its 1998 proposal.[147] After considering these responses, the CSA issued a revised proposal, as Notice 53-302, in November 2000.[148]

d) CSA Notice 53-302

In its November 2000 notice, the CSA indicated that its current version of the proposed legislative amendments to create a statutory civil remedy for continuous disclosure misrepresentations was to be recommended to governments in at least some of the CSA members' jurisdictions.

The 2000 draft legislation, if passed, would introduce a continuous disclosure liability regime including the following features.

i) Leave of the Court

In an effort to prevent coercive "strike" suits of no real merit, that have been launched to pressure managers to settle rather than incur litigation costs, plaintiffs would be required to obtain leave of the court before initiating an action under the new section. Such a leave requirement already exists in Canadian corporate law derivative action provisions.[149]

---

144 In the United States, aggrieved investors who purchased securities in the secondary markets may pursue a civil remedy pursuant to § 10(b) of the *Securities Act of 1934* and Rule 10b-5 promulgated thereunder. Paradoxically, this U.S. *statutory* civil remedy is, in effect, a judicial creation. Nothing in § 10(b) or Rule 10b-5 specifically refers to civil actions. However, as the U.S. Supreme Court explained in *Basic Inc.*, above note 89 at 231, "[j]udicial interpretation and application, legislative acquiescence, and the passage of time have removed any doubt that a private cause of action exists for a violation of § 10(b) and Rule 10b-5, and constitutes an essential tool for enforcement of the 1934 Act's requirements."

145 Allen Committee Report, above note 107 at 41.

146 (1998), 21 OSCB 3367.

147 Canadian Securities Administrators Notice 53-302 (2000), 23 OSCB 7383.

148 *Ibid.*

149 See, e.g., *CBCA*, above note 47, s. 239. The leave requirement for *CBCA* derivative actions was included for precisely the same reason, to prevent U.S.-style "strike suites." See Robert W.V. Dickerson et al., *Commentary, Proposals for a New Business Corporations Law for Canada*, vol. 1 (Ottawa: Information Canada, 1971) at para. 488.

ii) Damage Limits

Because the express purpose of the proposed civil remedy is deterrence rather than full compensation, the new proposal would limit the maximum total amount recoverable from a defaulting issuer (in actions commenced in all jurisdictions) to the greater of $1 million and 5 percent of the offending corporation's market capitalization. For individuals, such as directors and officers, the limit would be the greater of $25,000 and 50 percent of the individual's annual compensation.

iii) Court Approval of Settlements

Closely related to the leave requirement is the proposal that any settlement agreement must be approved by the court. This proposal is also intended to deter "strike suits."[150]

iv) Proportionate Liability

Many prospective defendants might be found liable in the case of a misrepresentation, including the issuer, officers, directors, controlling shareholders, and experts. The proposed liability regime would not make such defendants jointly and severally liable, but would rather apportion liability according to individual responsibility, except in the case of defendants who knowingly participated in the making of a misrepresentation.[151]

v) "Material Fact" and "Material Change" Definitions

The original 1998 proposal of the CSA suggested changes to the statutory definitions of material change and material fact. The most dramat-

---

150 A recent Ontario decision provides a clear illustration of how a requirement of court approval of settlements can, indeed, be an effective way to discourage strike suits. In *Epstein v. First Marathon Inc.*, [2000] O.J. No. 452, Cumming J. of the Ontario Superior Court drew an inference "from the record that [a class action plaintiff's] class proceeding constituted a so-called 'strike action' that, in reality, was initiated by counsel simply for the benefit of counsel"(at para. 40). Indicating that the case before him raised the question of "whether one minor shareholder, with only a few shares, apparently motivated by an entrepreneurial lawyer, may attempt to interfere with corporate restructuring that is not objected to by any of the corporation's other shareholders," Cumming J. concluded that the plaintiff did not satisfy the court that a class action settlement agreement ought to be approved. He declined to approve it, expressing the view that "the plaintiff's class proceeding constitutes an example of litigation of the kind the [*Class Proceedings Act*] was never designed to reward" (at para. 69).

151 One notes in this regard recent amendments to the *CBCA* that would also provide for proportionate liability in the case of a suit for financial loss arising from errors or omissions in corporate financial information. See new section 237.3 of the *CBCA*, above note 47.

ic change envisioned by the 1998 proposal in this regard was the proposed adoption of the *TSC Industries Inc. v. Northway*[152] standard of materiality, discussed above. The test for materiality would be based not on the likely effects on the price or value of an issuer's securities, but rather on whether the information would be considered "important to a reasonable investor in making an investment decision."[153] The adoption of this American approach did not survive the 2000 revisions; however, a more modest amendment to the definition of material fact was proposed to eliminate the potential retroactive effect of the current definition identified by the Allen Committee Report, which is discussed under the heading "material fact" above in section D. 3(d).

F. SELECTIVE DISCLOSURE

1) Introduction

It has long been common practice for reporting issuers to meet formally, and informally, with financial analysts who "cover" the company. Such meetings are considered important to analysts who seek to develop an "informational mosaic"[154] about the companies they follow. Financial analysts attempt to acquire as much information about reporting issuers as possible; however, regulators have been concerned for some time that in the course of analyst meetings, reporting issuers may disclose information selectively that is not generally available to the trading public. The problem of selective disclosure was specifically addressed in the 1997 Allen Committee Report.[155] The Allen Committee raised concerns about the practice in its earlier interim report and, evidently, received many negative comments from analysts and others who were concerned that tighter rules on selective disclosure could result in an unhealthy "disclosure chill."[156] The Allen Committee Report, however, concluded

---

152 *TSC Industries*, above note 90.
153 CSA Proposal, above note 146 at 3367.
154 References to the "informational mosaic" or "mosaic theory" are frequently encountered in discussions of the role of financial analysts. Indeed, reference to the concept appears in the SEC's Regulation FP Release, below note 158: "[A]n issuer is not prohibited from disclosing a non-material piece of information to an analyst, even if, unbeknownst to the issuer, that piece helps the analyst complete a 'mosaic' of information that, taken together, is material."
155 Allen Committee Report, above note 107 at 75–77.
156 *Ibid.* at 76.

that the risk of a disclosure chill was "preferable to selective disclosure that disadvantages large sectors of the market."[157] Since that time, there has been a major, and rather controversial, U.S. SEC selective disclosure initiative as well as recent Canadian regulatory developments.

2) SEC's Regulation FD

One of the most provocative SEC initiatives in recent memory is the introduction of Regulation FD (i.e., fair disclosure) in 2000.[158] The purpose of the regulation is to end selective disclosure essentially by mandating that when material non-public information is disclosed intentionally to analysts, it must be made public *simultaneously*. When such information is disclosed to analysts unintentionally, it must be made public as soon as practicable and, in any event, within twenty-four hours or before the commencement of the next day's trading on the New York Stock Exchange. The SEC indicated, at the time Regulation FD was promulgated, that the regulation is necessary because of certain deficiencies in U.S. insider-trading law. In particular, the U.S. Supreme Court's decision in *Dirks v. SEC*,[159] held that a tippee could not be liable for insider-trading unless she or he received inside information from an insider who received some personal benefit from tipping. Regulation FD, then, was largely aimed at closing this gap.

Breach of Regulation FD can result in SEC administrative action, but cannot be grounds for a private lawsuit because of the express provisions in the new regulation. Yet, even before the regulation came into full effect in October 2000, many market participants predicted dire consequences from the implementation of the new regime. Analysts feared that Regulation FD would make their jobs impossible. They claimed that issuers would either refuse to meet with analysts individually, or even if they did meet, that issuers would be so overly cautious that the meeting would be a waste of time for the issuers and the analysts alike. Issuers were equally concerned. The possibility for liability for inadvertent disclosures seemed immense. There was even suspicion that the SEC had promulgated Regulation FD for the purpose of having a powerful new enforcement tool. At the date of writing, it appears uncertain just what the overall impact of Regulation FD has been or will be; however, the passage of Regulation FD appears to be a catalyst for renewed attention to the issue of selective disclosure in Canada.

---

157 *Ibid.*
158 Selective Disclosure and Insider Trading: Securities Exchange Act Release No. 34-43154 (15 August 2000).
159 463 U.S. 646 (1983).

In October 2000 — the very month in which Regulation FD came into effect in the United States — an example of selective disclosure by a public company occurred in Canada. On the evening of 5 October 2000, an investor relations representative of Air Canada, acting on the instructions of Air Canada's chief financial officer, left detailed voice mail messages for thirteen financial analysts, indicating that Air Canada's not-yet-released third- and fourth-quarter earnings would be lower than expected. Air Canada's share price fell materially on the next trading day. Although Air Canada did issue a press release that day, the release did not contain all of the information provided to the analysts the previous evening. In a subsequent settlement agreement with the Ontario and Quebec securities commissions, Air Canada agreed to pay each commission $500,000, plus an amount in respect of costs. Air Canada also agreed to a review by its auditors for the following four quarters to ensure compliance with the disclosure rules.[160]

3) Proposed National Policy 51-201

As noted above, Canadian regulators have recognized the problem of selective disclosure for some time. Indeed, the Allen Committee Report's proposed approach to selective disclosure shares many of the features of the SEC's Regulation FD. Following a survey of the industry's selective disclosure practices published by the OSC in July 2000,[161] and the release of Regulation FD in the United States, and a similar initiative in Australia, the CSA, in May 2001, issued Proposed National Policy 51-201.[162]

The OSA provisions dealing with insider-trading are considerably tighter than the U.S. law on this point. The perceived deficiencies in U.S. insider-trading law that led to the promulgation of Regulation FD do not exist in Ontario.[163] The CSA essentially reached this conclusion when it determined that it was not necessary to promulgate a rule

---

160 The facts of the Air Canada case, and the details of the settlement are set out in *Re Air Canada Settlement Agreement* (2001), 24 OSCB 4697.

161 (2000), 23 OSCB 5098. This survey was initially conducted in 1999.

162 (2001), 24 OSCB 3301.

163 In particular, there is no U.S. federal securities law equivalent to the anti-tipping provisions in s. 76(2) of the *OSA*, discussed in chapter 8, which make it unlawful for reporting issuers and persons or companies in a special relationship with a reporting issuer to "inform, other than in the necessary course of business, another person or company of a material fact or material change with respect to the reporting issuer before the material fact or material change has been generally disclosed."

comparable to the SEC's Regulation FD.[164] Nevertheless, Proposed National Policy 51-201 provides interpretive guidance relating to disclosure issues, including selective disclosure. It is proposed that, if National Policy No. 51-201 is approved, National Policy No. 40 will be rescinded.

It is worth noting that, unlike National Policy No. 40, Proposed National Policy 51-201 does not attempt to extend the continuous disclosure obligation to cover matters other than material changes. Indeed, proposed NP 51-201 explicitly affirms that the timely disclosure obligation applies "generally" to only material changes.[165] In addition to reiterating statutory rules, NP 51-201 provides guidance on the interpretation of a number of *OSA* concepts, including the following:

- The meaning of "necessary course of business" to determine whether a person in a special relationship with a reporting issuer has illegally "tipped" someone else pursuant to subsections 76(2) or (3) of the *OSA*
- The meaning of "generally disclosed" for the purposes of section 76. The CSA essentially adopts the two-pronged test of (i) public dissemination and (ii) reasonable time for the public to analyze, articulated in *Re Harold P. Connor*,[166] as previously discussed in chapter 8.

The policy also provides guidance on a number of other practices and proposed practices, including earnings guidance, written corporate disclosure policies, and quiet periods and employee-trading blackout periods. Each is discussed in turn below.

a) Earnings Guidance

It was common practice, particularly before the promulgation of Regulation FD, for financial analysts to have "cat-and-mouse" discussions with corporate officers aimed at assisting the analysts in forecasting the corporation's earnings for a future accounting period. Indeed, some companies would be fairly explicit in discussing expected earnings ranges. The proposed policy warns issuers of the risks to issuers of engaging in such private discussions. The proposed policy also provides commentary on matters such as the publication by issuers of earnings or revenue projections.

---

164 Above note 162 at IV.
165 *Ibid.* s. 3.1(3). It is not clear, however, what the intended significance of the word "generally" is in this provision.
166 (1976), OSCB 149 at 174.

b) Written Corporate Disclosure Policies

The proposal urges issuers to adopt written disclosure policies and provides specific suggestions as to the subjects such policies should include.

c) Quiet Periods and Employee-Trading Blackout Periods

The proposal recommends that companies observe quiet periods around the time of the release of quarterly financial results to avoid the risk of selective disclosure. It also recommends that companies adopt "blackout" periods forbidding employees from trading in the issuer's securities around such times.

4) Crawford Committee Recommendations

In October 2001 the final report of the Securities Industry Committee on Analyst Standards[167] was released. This report, discussed in chapter 4, includes a specific recommendation concerning selective disclosure. Recommendation 32 reads as follows:

> We recommend that public companies include the media and investors in analyst meetings and conference calls, thereby avoiding the risk of selective disclosure.[168]

This recommendation generally reflects the practice that has developed in the United States under the Regulation FD regime.

G. INTEGRATED DISCLOSURE SYSTEM PROPOSAL

The most recent initiative in the continuing evolution of Canadian securities regulation from a transaction-based to an issuer-based regime is the CSA's concept proposal for an integrated disclosure system (IDS), published for comment in January 2000.[169]

The basic philosophy behind the proposed integrated disclosure system is already found in the short-form prospectus system described in chapter 6. Under the proposed system, issuers would file an exten-

---

167 Securities Industry Committee on Analyst Standards, *Setting Analyst Standards: Recommendations for the Supervision and Practice of Canadian Securities Industry Analysts* (October 2001).

168 *Ibid.* at p. 14.

169 (2000), 23 OSCB 633.

sive issuer-based disclosure document annually and update the information with periodic and timely disclosure filings. When the issuer
wished to access the capital markets, it could do so on a fairly expedi-
tious basis by producing a disclosure document that focuses principally on the terms of the securities being issued, and by relying on the
previously filed issuer-based documents, which would be "incorporated by reference" in the offering document, to provide investors with
information about the issuer.[170]

The proposed integrated disclosure system is not a wholly new
approach, but rather is an extension of an existing approach.
Specifically, the IDS proposes that the cornerstone issuer-disclosure
document, the AIF, include additional items not required under the
current system. The IDS would be available to more issuers than is the
current short-form prospectus system. Quarterly periodic disclosure
would be in the form of a quarterly information form (QIF), and timely disclosure would be made by way of supplementary information
forms (SIF) rather than material change reports. A major change to the
current continuous disclosure regime, however, is that the QIFs and SIFs
would need to be accompanied by certificates of senior officers and
directors, certifying that the documents constitute full, true, and plain
disclosure. This more extensive base of annual and continuous disclosure documents would streamline the offering process. IDS prospectuses
would be even more succinct than the short-form prospectuses used
under the current system, and review of the IDS prospectus by regulators
would be more limited and, therefore, faster. Finally, the more comprehensive base of prospectus-level disclosure available to the public on an
ongoing basis would alleviate many of the concerns that have led to
restrictions on securities-marketing activities, permitting many of the
existing rules on such activities to be relaxed.

---

170 It is interesting to note that a system very much along these lines was proposed
in Ontario as early as 1970 in the *Merger Report* above note 5 at 25–26:

> 2.18 We have concluded that the disclosure system initiated in *The Securities
> Act, 1966* provides the basis for a completely integrated continuing dis-
> closure system ...

> 2.21 An investor disclosure system would commence with a cornerstone
> prospectus. The facts then available concerning the issuer would con-
> stitute 'full, true and plain disclosure' of all material facts relating to
> the affairs of the issuer. This initial material would be subject to review
> by the Commission staff in the same fashion a prospectus is reviewed
> today. After the initial prospectus disclosure the prospectus as we
> know it should disappear for further public issues and be replaced
> with some simpler and more basic document which for the purpose of
> this report we call the 'offering circular.'

At the date of writing, the IDS proposal has not been implemented. Many features of the proposal will doubtless be subject to further consideration and refinement; however, in view of the recent direction in which securities law appears to be developing in both Canada and the United States, it seems likely that this proposal, or one similar to it, will eventually be adopted.

H. ELECTRONIC INFORMATION

The improvement in electronic communication technology, particularly the increased use and accessibility of the Internet, has prompted regulators to reconsider traditional ongoing disclosure document delivery rules. One important regulatory initiative in this area is National Policy 11-201.[171] NP 11-201 establishes guidelines concerning the electronic delivery of documents in cases where securities law does not mandate a specific method of delivery. The policy indicates that proper electronic delivery of documents depends on the issuer addressing four basic "components":[172]

- Notice to the recipient
- Easy access by the recipient
- Evidence of delivery
- No variation from the original delivered document

To satisfy the notice, evidence, and access components, the policy recommends — though does not, strictly speaking, require — that an issuer receive an informed consent to electronic delivery from any intended recipient of an electronic document. The policy even includes a sample consent form as an appendix. The emphasis on the prior consent of a recipient to electronic delivery of documents indicates that electronic delivery is still regarded as the exception rather than the rule. Needless to say, this is likely to change over time. In their April 2000 "issues list," the Securities Review Advisory Committee, struck to review Ontario securities law, invited comment on the question of whether regulators should move beyond NP 11-201, and "shift the onus on to shareholders" to request specifically that information otherwise available on a firm's Web site or through the SEDAR system be sent to them, rather than retain the onus on issuers to deliver documents *unless* recipients otherwise consent.[173]

---

171 (1999), 22 OSCB 8163.
172 *Ibid.* s. 2.1(2).
173 Securities Review Advisory Committee, "Issues List" (2000), 23 OSCB 3034 at 3039.

I. FOREIGN ISSUERS

The continuous disclosure rules discussed in this chapter raise special challenges for foreign issuers that are incorporated and subject to securities regulation abroad, yet are also reporting issuers for Canadian purposes. Although Canadian regulators could insist that all issuers seeking access to Canada's capital markets must adhere in every respect to Canadian reporting rules, such insistence would be impractical. Canada's capital markets constitute no more than 2 percent of the world's total market capitalization. Rigid insistence by Canadian regulators upon Canadian rules would likely drive foreign issuers away from our comparatively small market, to the detriment of Canadian investors. This result would be especially counterproductive in the case of those foreign issuers subject to rules in their home jurisdictions that, while not identical to Canada's, are functionally similar. Accordingly, Canadian securities regulators have been prepared, in certain circumstances, to exempt foreign issuers from certain aspects of Canada's continuous disclosure requirements, through formal rules[174] and policies[175] in some cases and on a case-by-case basis in others.[176]

The most recent development in this area is proposed OSC Rule 72-502,[177] "Continuous Disclosure and Other Exemptions Relating to Foreign Issuers," which, at the date of writing, has not yet been adopted, but which is proposed to come into force in July 2002. This proposed rule would replace OSC Policy 7.1 (subject to certain transitional provisions) and certain related deemed rules. The new rule would introduce a kind of "unilateral reliance" scheme, pursuant to which issuers from specified foreign jurisdictions would be permitted to satisfy Ontario's continuous disclosure requirements by complying with comparable requirements in the foreign jurisdiction. (Eligible U.S. issuers will, in certain cases, be permitted to choose between exemptions available to them under the new rule and exemptions available under the mulitijurisdictional disclosure system.)[178]

---

174 See, e.g., NI 71-101 (1998), 21 OSCB 6919, Parts 14-17.
175 See, e.g., OSC Policy 7.1 (1982), 4 OSCB 514E, as amended.
176 See CSA Notice 5, "Proposed Foreign Issuer Prospectus (FIPs) and Continuous Disclosure System" (1995), 18 OSCB 1893.
177 Available online at <http://www.osc.gov.on.ca> (site accessed: 12 March 2002).
178 See Companion Policy 72-502 CP, s. 1.2(2), available online at <http://www.osc.gov.on.ca> (site accessed: 12 March 2002.)

I. CONCLUSION

Although the *OSA* creates, in theory, a modified "blue sky" (or merit-based) jurisdiction, in practice, Ontario regulators and market participants have increasingly come to view Ontario law as if it were primarily a disclosure-based regime, like its federal U.S. counterpart. Historically, the disclosure that mattered most of all was the information found in an issuer's prospectus at the time of a public offering. But, we have seen, and should expect to see, continuous disclosure becoming ever more the linchpin of modern securities regulation. As secondary market trading has come to constitute 94 percent of Canadian capital market activity,[179] a regulatory model focused principally on primary market activity must yield to initiatives designed to protect the mass of investors who do not purchase securities at the time of a public offering. Thief Willie Sutton is famously credited (apparently erroneously) with explaining that he robbed banks because that's where the money is.[180] Similarly, if securities regulators are to protect investors, they must focus on the secondary markets because that's where the investors are.

---

179 CSA Notice 53-302, "Proposal for a Statutory Civil Remedy for Investors in the Secondary Markets," (2000), 23 OSCB 7383.
180 Willie Sutton (with Edward Linn), *Where the Money Was: The Memoirs of a Bank Robber* (New York: Viking Press, 1976) at 120. Referring to the quotation famously attributed to him, Sutton writes: "I never said it. The credit belongs to some enterprising reporter who apparently felt a need to fill out his copy. I can't even remember when I first read it. It just seemed to appear one day, and then it was everywhere."

TAKE-OVER AND ISSUER BIDS

A. INTRODUCTION

Canadian securities laws protect investors and foster fair and efficient capital markets. Historically, these objectives have been pursued primarily by regulating the activities of those who seek to sell securities to investors; however, in the past several decades it has become clear that sometimes it is the purchasers of securities, rather than the sellers, whose actions must be regulated to achieve the twin goals of our securities laws. Such is often the case when (a) one company seeks to acquire control of another by purchasing a significant block of shares, or (b) a company wishes to repurchase some of its own outstanding shares from its existing shareholders.

The securities law implications of both of these types of transactions — take-over bids and issuer bids, respectively — are the principal subjects of this chapter. Closely related to take-over and issuer bids are transactions undertaken to transform a publicly traded corporation to a private or closely-held corporation. The law relating to such "going-private transactions" is also canvassed here.

B. TAKE-OVER BIDS

Take-over bid rules were introduced into Ontario securities laws following a recommendation by the Kimber Committee in 1965.[1] The Kimber Committee's recommendation came in the wake of public criticism concerning various significant acquisition transactions in Ontario in the early 1960s. The concerns raised by such transactions are apparent from the nature of the Kimber Committee's response, which advocated take-over rules based on the following fundamental principles:

- The primary objective of take-over legislation is to protect the interests of the shareholders of the offeree (or the "target" company).[2]
- The take-over rules should ensure that such shareholders receive adequate time,[3] adequate information,[4] and equal treatment[5] from any bidder.

As discussed below, although the mechanics of Ontario take-over law have changed since 1966, these principles continue to lie at the heart of the modern take-over regime.

1) The Statutory Framework

a) Introduction
There are many ways in which one company may effectively acquire control of the business of another.[6] Informally, all of these methods might be described by members of the media or other non-lawyers as "take-overs." Canadian take-over bid law, however, deals with only one

---

1   *The Report of the Attorney General's Committee on Securities Legislation in Ontario* (Toronto: Queen's Printer, 1965) [*Kimber Report*].

2   *Ibid.* at para. 3.10.

3   *Ibid.* at para. 3.15

4   *Ibid.*

5   The *Kimber Report* did not expressly articulate equal treatment as a goal of take-over law, but it is implicit in its recommendations of *pro rata* acceptance of bids (which would end "first-come–first-served" bids) and of payments of increased bid prices to all offeree shareholders (*ibid.* at paras. 3.15–3.17 and 3.22).

6   For a discussion of some of these alternative methods, see Christopher C. Nicholls, *Corporate Finance and Canadian Law* (Toronto: Carswell, 2000) at 308 ff; J-P. Bisnaire and T.A. Smee, "Planning a Public Merger" in *Critical Issues in Mergers and Acquisitions: Domestic and International Views. Papers Presented at the 6th Queen's Annual Business Law Symposium* (Kingston: Queen's University, 1999) at 1.

specific type of control transaction: the purchase of outstanding shares of one company (the "offeree issuer" or, colloquially, the "target") by another person (the "offeror" or, colloquially, the "bidder"). This narrow legislative focus reflects a deliberate policy decision. The Kimber Committee, in proposing Ontario's first modern take-over rules, found that the other principal change of control transactions "do not seem to require any particular legislative reform."[7]

b) Overview of the *OSA's* Take-over Bid Provisions

In the most general sense, the *OSA* take-over provisions operate as follows. The legislation adopts a broad definition of "take-over bid" that, as discussed below, includes not only purchases of sufficient shares to give the bidder legal control of the target, but also purchases of much smaller numbers of shares intended to catch virtually all transactions in which *de facto* control might change hands. Any bidder making a "take-over bid" (as defined) is required to either (a) follow a detailed set of bidding rules that provide shareholders of the target company with reasonable time, adequate information about the bid, and fair and equal treatment, or (b) find an available exemption in the *OSA* from these rules or persuade the OSC that it ought to grant the bidder a special exemption from the rules for sound policy reasons. A detailed series of specific rules, exemptions, exceptions, and exclusions implements this basic statutory scheme. These detailed provisions maintain the integrity of the basic rules and principles, and prevent the use of avoidance tactics by bidders. They also allow for exemptions where rigid application of the take-over rules would impose unnecessary costs with little or no benefit to the investors. The sections that follow attempt to navigate through this ocean of legislative complexity.

c) Meaning of "Take-over Bid"

i) The Statutory Definition

The statutory framework regulating significant share acquisitions relies extensively on a series of carefully crafted definitions. The most fundamental of these is the definition of "take-over bid" itself. The *OSA* defines "take-over bid" as follows:

> an *offer to acquire* outstanding *voting* or *equity securities* of a class made to any *person or company* who is in Ontario or to any security holder of the *offeree issuer* whose last address as shown on the books

---

7   *Kimber Report*, above note 1, at para. 3.2.

of the *offeree issuer* is in Ontario, where the securities subject to the *offer to acquire*, together with the *offeror's securities*, constitute in the aggregate 20 percent or more of the outstanding securities of that class of securities at the date of the *offer to acquire*.[8]

The first general observation to be made about this definition is that it is extraordinarily broad in at least two specific senses. First, it deems a share purchase to be a take-over bid when the number of shares involved constitutes only 20 percent of the outstanding shares of a class, which is considerably less than the 50 percent plus one normally required to obtain legal control of a company. Second, this 20 percent threshold is based not on the number of shares to be acquired, but rather on the total number of shares being acquired *plus* the number of shares already owned by the bidder. Thus, in cases where a bidder already owns 20 percent of the shares of a target, an offer by such a bidder to purchase even a single share constitutes a "take-over bid" within the meaning of the *OSA*.

Indeed, the coverage is broader still because of the definition of the "offeror's securities." That definition ensures that, in calculating whether the 20 percent threshold is reached, one includes not only those securities held by the offeror itself, but also any securities owned by any person or company "acting jointly or in concert with the offeror."[9] Moreover, when calculating how many securities of a class an offeror or a joint actor beneficially owns, the *OSA* includes more than just securities currently held. The statute also requires other securities of the class to be included if the offeror or joint actor has a *right* (or is under an *obligation*) to acquire them through the conversion of securities of another class or type or through the exercise of options or similar rights.[10] In fact, securities subject to such conversion or option rights have to be included in the calculation, even if the offeror's or the joint actor's rights to acquire them are subject to conditions that have not yet been satisfied.[11]

Finally, when a bidder acts jointly or in concert with another person or company in making a bid (or bids) for a target, subsection 90(2) of the *OSA* requires both the bidder and the joint actor to count all the shares subject to all such bids as though each of the bidder and the joint actor had bid, by itself, for all such shares. In other words, it is

---

8   *Securities Act* (Ontario), R.S.O. 1990, c. S.5 [*OSA*], s. 89(1). [Emphasis added to indicate that these words and phrases are also specifically defined in the *OSA*.]

9   The concept of acting "jointly or in concert" is discussed in s. 91 of the *OSA*, *ibid*.

10   See *OSA*, *ibid*. ss. 89(3) & 90(1).

11   *Ibid*.

not possible for people who are working together to avoid making a "take-over bid" by breaking up the total bid into smaller pieces.

Moreover, section 92 of the *OSA* provides that offers to acquire include both direct and indirect acquisitions. This rule was introduced into the *OSA* following a recommendation of the 1983 *"Practitioner's Report."*[12] The *Practitioner's Report* refers to the draft rule from which section 92 emerged as "a general anti-avoidance provision"[13] aimed at protecting the securityholders of "true target issuers."[14] The framers of the report were concerned that an offeror might seek to avoid application of the take-over bid rules in the following way. Suppose the take-over target was a public company with one major shareholder holding a block of shares large enough to constitute control. If that major shareholder was not an individual, but was a *private* corporation, the bidder might attempt to buy all of the outstanding shares of that private corporation (rather than the shares it held in the public company target), and thereby acquire indirectly a controlling interest in the public company target. The provision recommended by the *Practitioner's Report* dealt more specifically with this sort of "true target issuer" question than does section 92, but section 92 is intended, at the very least, to include just this type of indirect acquisition.

ii)   Illustrative Examples
To understand why the *OSA*'s take-over provisions were drafted in this way, it is useful to consider a few hypothetical examples based on the following basic scenario.

Scenario: Bidco Inc. wishes to acquire *de facto* control of Target Limited (Target). Target is a widely held company with 100 million common shares outstanding. The ownership of Target's shares is so dispersed that Bidco believes it can, effectively, control Target by owning just twenty million (i.e., 20 percent) of Target's outstanding common shares. Of course, if Bidco makes an outright offer to purchase twenty million of Target's shares, that offer will constitute a take-over bid and will require Bidco to prepare an expensive disclosure document and observe specific time limits and other rules that Bidco may find inconvenient.

---

12   Gordon Coleman, Garfield Emerson, and David Jackson, *Report of the Committee to Review the Provisions of the Securities Act (Ontario) Relating to Take-over Bids and Issuer Bids* (Toronto: Ontario Securities Commission, 1983) [*Practitioner's Report*].

13   *Ibid.* at 12.

14   *Ibid.*

aa) Example A

Bidco tries to gain control without making an outright purchase of 20 percent of Target's shares by first purchasing $100 million face amount of outstanding convertible debentures originally issued by Target. These debentures include a conversion feature permitting the holder, at any time, to convert the debentures into common shares at a price of $5 per share. This debenture purchase would not constitute a take-over bid. First of all, debentures are not, typically, "voting or equity securities." In any event, however, for reasons explained later, even if all twenty million shares into which the debenture can ultimately be converted were treated as outstanding shares, they do not constitute 20 percent of the total shares of the class. Of course, if the debentures had been purchased directly from Target, rather than from another holder of the outstanding debentures, the purchase would not even constitute a purchase of "outstanding" securities and so, again, would fall outside the definition of "take-over bid." Bidco, after buying these debentures, makes an offer to purchase only five million of Target's outstanding common shares, which is significantly less than 20 percent of the class.

Analysis: Bidco's offer to purchase the five million shares is a take-over bid. Bidco is the "offeror," and Target is the "offeree issuer." An offer to acquire is a take-over bid if the number of shares subject to the offer (five million in this example) plus the number of the offeror's securities is at least 20 percent of the class. Subsection 90(1) of the OSA deems the offeror's securities to include securities of the class that the offeror can acquire within sixty days pursuant to the exercise of a conversion privilege. Therefore, Bidco is deemed to have beneficial ownership of twenty million Target shares on the date of the offer. These twenty million shares, when added to the five million that are the subject of the offer, produce a total of twenty-five million shares. What is the total size of the class? Recall that the total number of outstanding Target common shares is 100 million. However, under subsection 90(3), if unissued shares — such as the twenty million shares into which Bidco's debenture may be (but has not yet been) converted — are included in calculating the offeror's securities (as they are required to be in this case, under subsection 90(1)), then that same number of shares must also be deemed to be outstanding when determining whether a take-over bid has been made. Therefore, for the purposes of the take-over bid calculation, Target is deemed to have 120 million shares outstanding. Twenty percent of 120 million is twenty-four million. Thus, the number of shares subject to Bidco's offer (five million) plus the number of the offeror's securities, including the twenty million shares deemed to be beneficially owned by Bidco under subsection 90(1), equals twenty-five million shares. This is more than twenty-four million and, therefore, is more than 20 percent of the class; so, Bidco has made a take-over bid.

bb) Example B

On Day 1, Bidco acquires nine million outstanding shares of Target. On that same day, Joint Actor Corp., an affiliate of Bidco, acquires an additional nine million outstanding Target shares. Neither of these purchases, separately or in the aggregate, constitutes a take-over bid because they involve in total only 18 percent of Target's shares, which is less than 20 percent of the total number of shares outstanding. On Day 20, Bidco makes an offer to acquire ten million additional outstanding Target shares.

Analysis: Bidco's offer to acquire an additional ten million shares constitutes a take-over bid. A take-over bid occurs when the number of shares subject to the offer to acquire (in this case ten million shares) plus the offeror's securities totals at least 20 percent of the class. In calculating the "offeror's securities," one must include not only the shares held by the offeror itself (i.e., the nine million shares held by Bidco), but also the shares held by anyone acting jointly or in concert with the offeror (in this case, Joint Actor Corp.). Therefore, the offeror's securities, at the time of Bidco's Day 20 offer to acquire, total eighteen million shares. When that eighteen million is added to the ten million shares that are subject to the offer, the total exceeds 20 percent of Target's total outstanding common shares. Therefore, Bidco's Day 20 offer constitutes a take-over bid.

cc) Example C

On Day 1, Bidco acquires four million Target shares. Joint Actor Corp. likewise acquires four million shares. On Day 25, Bidco makes an offer to acquire nine million additional outstanding shares of Target. Joint Actor Corp. makes a similar, but separate, offer to purchase nine million shares from Target shareholders at about the same time.

Analysis: The offers by both Bidco and Joint Actor Corp. to acquire nine million shares of Target constitute take-over bids. Subsection 90(2) of the *OSA* deems the number of shares subject to the offer to acquire made by the offeror (Bidco) to be counted as though they were subject to an offer to acquire by a person acting jointly or in concert with the offeror (Joint Actor Corp.). The section similarly deems the number of shares subject to Joint Actor Corp.'s offer to acquire to be treated as though they were also subject to Bidco's offer to acquire. Thus, Bidco is deemed to have made an offer to acquire eighteen million shares. When added to Bidco's four million shares, the total exceeds 20 percent of Target's outstanding common shares. The same analysis applies to Joint Actor Corp. Note that, for the reasons explained in Example B, even if Bidco and Joint Actor Corp. originally purchased as few as one million shares each, followed by separate offers to acquire nine million shares each, they both still would be deemed to have made take-over bids.

dd) Example D (*Note: The Basic Scenario will be modified for this example*)
Target Limited is a public company whose shares trade on the TSE, but 51 percent of Target's shares are held by Holdco Inc., a private holding company owned by a wealthy individual, Hy Networth. Holdco has no assets other than the Target shares and has no liabilities. Bidco wishes to acquire control of Target. However, instead of buying shares of Target directly, Bidco offers to buy from Hy Networth all of the issued and outstanding shares he owns in Holdco. Bidco offers to pay Mr. Networth a price for his Holdco shares that values the Target shares held by Holdco at 30 percent above the current trading price of Target shares on the TSE. Bidco argues that, because Holdco is a private company, this purchase is exempt from the *OSA*'s formal take-over bid rules.

Analysis: Bidco's offer to buy the shares of Holdco constitutes an indirect offer for the shares of Target, pursuant to section 92 of the *OSA*, and is, therefore, a take-over bid for the shares of Target. Accordingly, Bidco is subject to the formal take-over bid rules. The private agreement exemption, discussed below, is not available to Bidco because Bidco is offering to pay Mr. Networth a price greater than 15 percent above the market price.

iii) Acting "Jointly or in Concert"
The question of when parties will be found to be acting jointly or in concert is one of great potential significance. Section 91 of the *OSA* makes it clear that the question is always a matter of fact and provides specific examples of relationships that give rise to a presumption that the parties are joint actors. There is also something of a gloss on the term offered in OSC Companion Policy 61-501 CP.[15] It is well beyond the scope of this chapter to attempt to delineate precisely when parties will be found to be acting jointly or in concert. One particular point,

---

15 (2000), 23 OSCB 2679.

however, merits mention here. It is common for bidders to negotiate with major shareholders of a potential take-over target before launching a formal take-over bid. These advance negotiations are intended to improve the likelihood of the bid's eventual success.

The bidder, typically, does not wish to purchase outright the shares held by the major shareholders before launching the formal take-over bid for at least two reasons. First, if the bid fails, the bidder is left holding a minority share position that might be difficult to sell without adversely affecting the market price of the shares. Second, if the bid succeeds, and the bidder obtains a clear majority of the target's outstanding securities, although it is less than 100 percent, the bidder's ability to complete a second-stage going-private transaction to eliminate the remaining minority interests can be more difficult because of the minority approval requirements in Rule 61-501.[16] (For a more detailed explanation of this issue, see the discussion of going-private transactions later in this chapter.) Accordingly, bidders frequently negotiate "lock-up agreements" with the major shareholders. Under the terms of a typical lock-up agreement, the bidder agrees to launch a take-over bid within a particular period of time and at a certain minimum share price, and one or more of the major shareholders agree to tender the shares if, and when, such a bid is made.

Signing a lock-up agreement potentially has two implications. First, because the agreement gives the bidder the right to acquire the shares of the target company — even though it is subject to conditions — the bidder might be deemed to be the beneficial owner of the shares subject to the agreement pursuant to subsection 90(1) of the OSA. If the shares constitute more than 10 percent of the outstanding voting shares of the target, the bidder would then be deemed an "issuer insider" of the target, pursuant to Rule 61-501.[17] Any subsequent bid made by the bidder would thus be considered an "insider bid,"[18] which is, normally, subject to additional requirements discussed later in this chapter. Second, it might be argued that the lock-up agreement constitutes an agreement of the sort referred to in paragraph 91(1)2 of the OSA. This means that the bidder and the selling shareholder might be considered to be acting jointly or in concert for the purposes of Part XX of the OSA.

---

16   (2000), 23 OSCB 2679.

17   Ibid. s. 1.1(1). It is not clear, however, that the deemed beneficial ownership provisions of s. 90 actually apply to the definition of issuer insider. Subsection 1.2(2) of Rule 61-501 states that the s. 90 rules apply with respect to the definition of "related party" and s. 1.1(2) of s. 61-501; however, the definition of issuer insider appears in s. 1.1(1).

18   Ibid. s. 1.1(3).

Neither of these consequences would be consistent with the policy of the *OSA*, however. A typical lock-up agreement, after all, does not entitle the selling shareholder to receive a share price higher than that of the other target shareholders. Moreover, the selling shareholder merely disposes of her or his own shares and does not act together with the bidder to acquire a greater equity interest. Accordingly, specific exemptions and exceptions are available. Subsection 2.1(2) of Rule 61-501 provides an exemption from the insider bid provisions in the case of such lock-up agreements. Companion Policy 61-501CP states that it is the OSC's view that "an ordinary lock-up agreement with an identically treated shareholder should not in and of itself generally result in arm's length parties being seen to be acting jointly or in concert."[19]

iv) Outstanding Securities

It should also be noted that the definition of take-over bid refers to only an acquisition of "outstanding" securities. In other words, a purchase of previously unissued shares from treasury (i.e., new shares purchased directly from the issuing corporation, rather than from another shareholder) would not constitute a take-over bid even if the number of shares so purchased constituted more than 20 percent of a class. The OSC confirmed this interpretation in *Trizec Equities*.[20]

v) Voting or Equity Securities

The take-over bid rules apply only to offers to acquire "voting or equity securities." Both of these terms are defined in the *OSA*. An equity security is defined in subsection 89(1) to mean "any security of an issuer that carries a residual right to participate in the earnings of the issuer and, on the liquidation or winding up of the issuer, in its assets." It should be noted that, to constitute an equity security, the holder must have a residual right to participate *both* with respect to the issuer's earnings and with respect to its assets. For example, a preferred share that entitles the holder to receive a fixed preferential dividend but confers no further right to participate in earnings is not an equity security, even if it carries a right to participate with the issuer's common shareholders in any distribution of the issuer's assets on a liquidation or a winding-up.

---

19   Companion Policy 61-501CP, above note 15, s. 2.3(2).
20   *Re Trizec Equities Limited and Bramalea Limited* (1984), 7 OSCB 2033 [*Trizec Equities*]: "The Act clearly contemplates that a take-over bid results from an offer made to security holders and not to the issuer whose securities may be the subject of the take-over bid."

The rationale for limiting the take-over regime to purchases of voting or participating equity securities is twofold. First, the purchase of debt and debt-like securities (such as conventional preferred shares) does not involve the shift in control of the corporation that is the fundamental concern of the take-over legislation. Second, the value of fixed-income securities (i.e., debt and preferred shares) is not subject to the same wide potential variances resulting from informational advantages. The value of fixed-income securities is affected chiefly by changes in market interest rates and the creditworthiness of the issuer.

The term "voting security" is not defined in Part XX of the *OSA*, where the take-over bid rules and most of the specialized definitions are found. Rather, it is defined in subsection 1(1) as "any security other than a debt security of an issuer carrying a voting right either under all circumstances or under some circumstances that have occurred and are continuing."[21] The final clause in this definition is the most problematic. It is a common feature of many fixed-dividend preferred shares that, if the issuer fails to pay such a dividend for a period of time (often two years), the preferred shareholders become entitled to elect a specified number of directors to the issuer's board. It might not always be obvious whether non-equity shares with such contingent voting rights constitute "voting shares" for the purposes of the *OSA*. Therefore, whenever a significant acquisition of shares is planned — even if those shares appear at first blush to be non-voting, non-equity shares — it is critical to make proper inquiries to avoid an inadvertent violation of the *OSA*'s take-over bid rules.

d) Exempted Take-over Bids

i)   Introduction

When a transaction constitutes a take-over bid as defined in the *OSA*, it is subject to a complex series of rules (discussed in more detail below). Complying with these rules significantly increases the cost to a bidder of completing the transaction and may also result in significant delays. These added costs and potential delays are considered to be justified for change-of-control transactions involving public companies whose shareholders might otherwise be exploited by aggressive bidders. But, the expansive definition of "take-over bid" that was crafted to prevent easy avoidance also sweeps in many transactions for which the costs of complying with the *OSA*'s complex take-over regime far outweigh any possible benefit to investors. Accordingly, the *OSA*

---

21   *OSA*, above note 8, s. 1(1).

offers a number of exemptions from the take-over bid requirements that are found in section 93.

ii)   Stock Exchange Bid Exemption

Bids undertaken through the facilities of a recognized stock exchange are exempt from the *OSA*'s formal take-over bid rules[22] if the bid is made in compliance with all the applicable "by-laws, regulations and policies" of that exchange.[23] The exchanges recognized for this purpose are the Toronto Stock Exchange (TSE), the Montreal Exchange (now the Bourse de Montreal), and the Canadian Venture Exchange.[24]

The exemption recognizes that the stock exchanges provide their own rules to regulate bids and to protect investors. Accordingly, provided an offeror complies with those alternative rules, the underlying policy objectives of the *OSA* are still achieved. The TSE's take-over bid rules are found in Part 6 of the *Rules of the Toronto Stock Exchange*, Appendix F to the *Toronto Stock Exchange Company Manual*, and in the TSE's "Policy Statement on Stock Exchange Take-over Bids and Issuer Bids." It should be noted that clause 93(1)(a) extends the stock exchange bid exemption to only sections 95 to 100 of the *OSA*, and not to every provision contained in Part XX.[25] Accordingly, a number of important *OSA* rules continue to apply to stock exchange take-over bids. These include the pre-bid integration and ongoing and post-bid acquisition rules, as well as the early warning rules. All of these rules are discussed in greater detail below in section (e).

---

22   *Ibid.* s. 93(1)(a).
23   *Ibid.* s. 93(4).
24   OSC Order 21-901 (1997), 20 OSCB 1034. See also, (2000), 23 OSCB 6055.
25   Technically, all of the exemptions in s. 93(1), not simply the s. 93(1)(a) stock exchange exemption, purport to exempt bids from only the requirements of ss. 95 to 100. However, s. 94 of the *OSA*, which includes, among other things, the pre-bid integration and post-bid acquisition rules, does not apply to every take-over bid in the first place. Section 94 applies only to offerors making a "formal bid," other than a bid that is exempt under the *de minimis* exception in s. 93(1)(e). The definition of "formal bid" in s. 89(1) would not extend to most exempt bids. However, a formal bid includes, among other things, a bid that is exempt from the requirements of ss. 95 to 100 by virtue of s. 93(1)(a), where the offeror is required to deliver to Ontario shareholders a "deemed take-over bid circular" (pursuant to s. 131(10)). The result of this rather complex set of rules is that a stock exchange take-over bid may be exempt from the rules in ss. 95 to 100, but, unlike some other exempt bids, remains subject to the other rules in *OSA* Part XX, including the rules in s. 94.

iii) Normal-Course Purchase Exemption

The take-over bid definition focuses on the total number of shares to be held by an offeror *after* the completion of an offer to acquire, rather than on the number of shares subject to such an offer to acquire. Consequently, very small share purchases by large shareholders may be considered take-over bids under the OSA. Indeed, for a shareholder who already owns 20 percent of the outstanding equity shares of an issuer, any additional purchase, even of a single share, is a take-over bid. Needless to say, it would be cumbersome, inefficient, and unnecessary to subject such minor purchases to the OSA's formal take-over bid requirements. Accordingly, the OSA provides an exemption in the case of modest, normal-course share purchases, provided that an offeror does not purchase more than 5 percent of the outstanding securities of a class in any twelve-month period, and does not pay a premium above the market price for such securities (where there is a published market for them).[26] The "market price" for securities acquired on a published market,[27] typically a stock exchange, means the price of the last board lot of securities of that class purchased prior to the acquisition.[28] (A board lot, or round lot, refers to a standard number of traded shares on an exchange that can typically be traded without requiring the payment of special "odd lot" commissions. On the TSE, the size of a board lot varies depending on the market price per share. But, for most TSE issuers, a board lot is 100 shares.)[29] In the case of any other purchase, the term "market price" essentially means the average closing price for the securities over the previous twenty business days.[30] Where the market in which the securities trade does not provide a closing price, the price is the average of the average highest and lowest trading prices over the previous twenty business days.[31]

iv) Private Agreement Exemption

Perhaps the most important exemption to the formal take-over bid requirements is the so-called private agreement exemption found in clause 93(1)(c) of the OSA. This exemption permits an offeror to make a take-over bid without complying with the formal bid requirements, provided that the bid consists of purchases made from not more than five per-

---

26 OSA, above note 8, s. 93(1)(b).
27 The term "published market" is defined in OSA, *ibid*. s. 89(1).
28 OSA Regulation, R.R.O. 1990, Reg. 1015, s. 183(5) [OSA Regulation].
29 See *Toronto Stock Exchange Company Manual*, Part I, para. 825-104. Available online at <http://tse.ca/en/pdf/Company Manual0202.pdf> (accessed 2 May 2002).
30 OSA Regulation, above note 28, s. 183.
31 *Ibid*.

sons or companies, the price paid for the securities does not exceed 115 percent of the market price (i.e., 15 percent more than the market price), and the bid is not made generally to all securityholders of the class.

A number of general policy issues and specific technical questions arise in connection with clause 93(1)(c). At the most general level, the rationale for the exemption was explained by James C. Baillie, former OSC chairman, when the legislative predecessor to clause 93(1)(c) was first debated. He said that it was a "compromise between two opposing views about how far we should go in this area."[32] The opposing views referred to were, on the one hand, the views of those who considered it improper to place limitations on the rights of securityholders to deal with their property as they saw fit and, on the other, the views of those who believed that any premium paid to securityholders in exchange for gaining control of a corporation should be shared among all securityholders.[33]

The issues relating to various attempts made to exploit the private agreement exemption are more technical. Perhaps the most difficult aspect of clause 93(1)(c), from an enforcement perspective, is the requirement that eligible purchases be made from not more than five persons or companies. Attempts have been made from time to time to break up large purchases into smaller chunks in order to squeeze the transactions within the literal wording of clause 93(1)(c). Additional rules were included to prevent such avoidance. Consider the following simplified examples.

aa) Example A

Bidco Limited wishes to acquire a controlling position in Target Corp., a publicly traded corporation. Bidco already holds a 40 percent interest in Target Corp. and neither wants, nor is prepared to pay for, more than an additional 11 percent stake. Certainly, Bidco does not wish to undertake an expensive formal take-over bid for Target Corp. shares. Twenty-five Target Corp. shareholders, holding an aggregate 11 percent of Target Corp.'s shares, would like to sell their shares to Bidco at a 15 percent premium to market. In order to fit within the words of the exemption in clause 93(1)(c), these shareholders incorporate a new holding company (Holdco.). The twenty-five shareholders transfer all

---

32   Quoted by Mary G. Condon, *Making Disclosure: Ideas and Interests in Ontario Securities Regulation* (Toronto: University of Toronto Press, 1998) at 212.

33   There is fairly extensive academic literature on this topic. For further discussion of this issue see, e.g., Robert C. Clark, *Corporate Law* (Aspen: Aspen Publishers, Inc. 1986) at 491–98; and Frank H. Easterbrook and Daniel R. Fischel, *The Economic Structure of Corporate Law* (Cambridge: Harvard University Press, 1991) at 126 ff.

of their Target Corp. shares to Holdco. Holdco, then, sells all of these Target Corp. shares to Bidco. The purchase by Bidco is a take-over bid because the shares purchased, plus the shares already held by Bidco, exceed 20 percent of Target's outstanding equity securities. However, because Bidco is now purchasing the shares from only one seller, Holdco, instead of from twenty-five individuals, Bidco hopes to rely on the clause 93(1)(c) exemption from the formal take-over bid rules.

Analysis: Bidco will not be permitted to rely on the clause 93(1)(c) exemption. Clause 93(2)(b) specifically anticipates this sort of avoidance transaction. It provides that where a company (like Holdco) acquires securities "in order that the offeror [i.e., Bidco] might make use of" the private agreement exemption, then each person or company from whom the securities were acquired (the twenty-five individual shareholders, in this example) must be included in determining the number of sellers. Clause 93(2)(a) contains a similar rule for securities held in trust. In such a case, the beneficial owners must be counted in determining whether the requirements of clause 93(1)(c) are met. There are two exceptions to the trust rule: (1) where the trust is an *inter vivos* trust established by a single settlor, and (2) where the trust was created by a will, and the interest of the beneficiaries has not yet vested. These two exceptions do not represent attempts to circumvent the policy underlying clause 93(1)(c). After all, the settlor of an *inter vivos* trust, acting in his or her personal capacity, could lawfully have sold the same shares pursuant to clause 93(1)(c), and a testator, before her or his death, likewise could have chosen to sell such securities to a purchaser in reliance on the exemption.

bb) Example B

Offerco Inc. wishes to acquire a controlling position in Target Limited without making a formal take-over bid. Offerco, at the moment, holds no Target Limited securities. Offerco purchases common shares totalling 19 percent of Target Limited's shares from forty separate Target Limited shareholders at a price greater than 25 percent above the market price. Moments after completing the transaction, Offerco purchases an additional 42 percent of Target Limited's shares from five other shareholders, paying exactly 15 percent above the market price. Offerco argues that the first purchase from the forty shareholders does not trigger the formal take-over bid requirements because it involves less than 20 percent of Target Limited's common shares and is, therefore, simply not a take-over bid. Offerco admits that the subsequent acquisition from the five additional shareholders is a take-over bid but argues it falls clearly within the clause 93(1)(c) exemption.

Analysis: Example B is loosely modelled on the facts considered by the OSC in *Re Med-Tech Environmental Limited*.[34] The OSC ruled that the offeror could not take advantage of clause 93(1)(c) because the offeror, while making all of the purchase transactions, in fact, was engaged in a single, continuing take-over bid, rather than merely making discreet purchases. Accordingly, in the words of the OSC, "[t]o fabricate an artificial series of closings as was, in our view, done here, seems to us to violate not only the spirit, but also the letter, of the take-over bid provisions of the Act."[35]

cc) Allowable Premium

The final aspect of the clause 93(1)(c) exemption that must be considered is the question of the allowable premium. A bidder seeking to rely on the exemption is permitted to pay no more than 15 percent above the market price for purchased shares. "Market price" is determined in accordance with the *OSA Regulation*. The regulation defines "market price" as the average of the closing price for the previous twenty business days or, where the relevant market does not provide a closing price, the average of the highest and lowest trading price averages over the previous twenty business days.[36] However, the regulation deals with only the market price of securities that trade in a published market.[37] Accordingly, because the clause 93(1)(c) exemption can be relied upon only where such a market price can be determined, the exemption is unavailable to companies whose securities do not trade on such a market. Yet, where the shares of a target company do not trade in a published market, there is actually less need of formal take-over bid protections. In recognition of this, section 184 of the *OSA Regulation* provides a further take-over bid exemption, analogous to the clause 93(1)(c) exemption. Section 184 exempts from the formal bid rules any purchase of securities of a company for which there is no published market when the purchase is made from not more than five holders and when the bid is not made generally to other holders of the class.[38]

One technical issue with which the OSC has had to grapple in the context of this exemption is determining the date on which the "market price" is to be calculated when the purchase of securities is made pursuant to the exercise of an option. The OSC makes it clear that there

---

34   (1998), 21 OSCB 7607 [*Med-Tech*].
35   *Ibid.* at 7615.
36   *OSA Regulation*, above note 28, s. 183.
37   *Ibid.* s. 183(1).
38   *Ibid.* s. 184.

is no hard and fast rule — no "bright-line grail."[39] There are, however, sound reasons for considering the following analysis (which is based on the *Enfield* and *Trizec Equities* cases) as a first approximation. Where a bidder acquires securities pursuant to the exercise by an offeree shareholder of a previously granted put option, the market price ought to be determined as of the date on which the option was originally granted.[40] By contrast, when the bidder acquires securities pursuant to the exercise *by the bidder* of a previously granted call option, market price ought to be determined as of the date on which the option is exercised.[41] The logic of this distinction is that, in the case of a put option, the investment decision (i.e., the definitive offer by the bidder to acquire the shares at a stated price) is made on the date the put option is sold by the bidder to the offeree shareholder(s). However, in the case of a call option, the bidder makes no definitive offer to buy until (and, indeed, unless) the bidder actually chooses to exercise the call option.

v) Private (Target) Company Exemption

Just as the *OSA* and related rules provide exemptions from the registration and prospectus requirements[42] for trades and distributions of the securities of "closely-held issuers," so too do they provide an exemption from the formal take-over bid rules when the target is a private issuer. The take-over bid exemption, found in clause 93(1)(d) of the *OSA*, is commonly referred to as the private company exemption, although the defined term "private company" does not appear in the clause. The clause 93(1)(d) exemption is available in the following circumstances:

> [The offeree issuer] is not a reporting issuer, there is not a published market in respect of the securities that are the subject of the bid, and the number of holders of securities of that class is not more than fifty, exclusive of holders who are in the employment of the offeree issuer or an affiliate of the offeree issuer, and exclusive of holders who were formerly in the employment of the offeree issuer or an affiliate of the offeree issuer and who while in that employment were, and have continued after that employment to be, security holders of the offeree issuer.[43]

---

39 *Re Enfield Corporation Limited* (1990), 13 OSCB 3364 [*Enfield*].

40 *Ibid.*

41 *Trizec Equities*, above note 20.

42 OSC Rule 45-501 (2001), 24 OSCB 7011, s. 2.1. As discussed in Chapter 7, the closely-held issuer exemption replaced the former "private company" and "private issuer" exemptions that exempted trades in securities of companies with attributes similar to those described in the s. 93(1)(d) take-over bid exemption.

43 *OSA*, above note 8, s. 93(1)(d).

This description differs from the definition of "private company" in section 1 of the *OSA* in the following respects:

* Clause 93(1)(d) refers to company attributes that must in fact be true rather than to attributes that must formally be provided for in the company's constating document.
* The limitation in the number of securityholders is less restrictive in clause 93(1)(d) than in the definition of "private company" in section 1 because clause 93(1)(d) permits employees or former employees of affiliates (and not simply of the company itself) to be excluded in determining whether the total number of shareholders exceeds fifty.
* The clause 93(1)(d) exemption does not specifically require that the issuer's constating document include a restriction on the right to transfer shares or a prohibition against public invitations to subscribe for securities.
* The clause 93(1)(d) exemption expressly requires that the issuer not be a reporting issuer, and that there be no published market for the issuer's shares. (These attributes are, of course, implicit in the private company definition.)

In *Re Med-Tech Environmental Limited*,[44] the issue arose as to whether, in determining the number of a company's shareholders for purposes of clause 93(1)(d), regulators should consider the number of registered shareholders or the number of beneficial shareholders. It will be recalled that, traditionally, for corporate law purposes, corporations are entitled to treat their registered shareholders as shareholders for all purposes.[45] The OSC favoured using the same approach when interpreting clause 93(1)(d).[46]

vi) De Minimis *Exemption*
The *OSA* also provides for an exemption from the formal take-over bid rules when the number of Ontario shareholders is not significant. Specifically, clause 93(1)(e) provides that a bid is exempt where the target company has fewer than fifty securityholders with an Ontario address holding, in total, no more than 2 percent of the outstanding securities of the class. To take advantage of this exemption, however,

---

44 Above note 34.
45 See, e.g., *Canadian Business Corporations Act*, R.S.C. 1985, c. C-44 [*CBCA*], s. 51(1). However, see also recent amendments to *CBCA* s. 137 that extend proposal rights to beneficial owners of shares.
46 *Med-Tech*, above note 34 at 7614.

the bid must be made in accordance with the take-over rules of another recognized jurisdiction, and all of the bid material sent to securityholders in that other jurisdiction must also be sent to the Ontario securityholders. The jurisdictions recognized for the purposes of clause 93(1)(e) include all other Canadian provinces except New Brunswick and Prince Edward Island (which do not have take-over bid legislation comparable to Part XX of the *OSA*), the United States (where the *Securities Exchange Act of 1934* is complied with), and the United Kingdom (where *The City Code on Take-overs and Mergers* is complied with).[47]

vii) Exemption Regulations and OSC Exemption Orders

In addition to the specifically enumerated take-over bid exemptions, the *OSA* provides that further exemptions may be provided by regulation.[48] Moreover, the OSC may, on application, grant special exemptions from the requirements of Part XX of the *OSA* if doing so is not contrary to the public interest.[49]

e)   Basic Rules Governing a Formal "Circular" Take-over Bid

i)   Introduction

Thus far we have considered the circumstances under which an offeror making a take-over bid, as defined by the *OSA*, nevertheless, may avoid the cumbersome and expensive procedures that are required when such a bid is a non-exempt formal take-over bid. In this section, we consider the formal take-over bid rules in some detail.

It will be recalled that the three guiding principles of Ontario take-over bid law are that shareholders of a company that is the target of a take-over bid should be provided with (1) reasonable time to consider an offer for their shares, (2) adequate information to make an informed decision as to whether to tender their shares to a bid, and (3) equal treatment. How those principles undergird all of the take-over rules should become apparent.

ii)   Commencement of the Bid

There are two ways in which a formal take-over bid may be launched: by delivering a formal bid document to all of the target securityhold-

---

47   OSC Order 62-904 (1997), 20 OSCB 1035.
48   *OSA*, above note 8, s. 93(1)(f).
49   *Ibid.* s. 104(2)(c).

ers,[50] or by publishing a detailed announcement of the bid in a major daily newspaper and filing and delivering a copy of the bid to the office of the target company.[51] This copy of the bid must be accompanied by a take-over bid circular.[52] The advantage to a bidder in commencing a bid by way of public advertisement is that it speeds up the process of completing the transaction. As will be seen below, every formal take-over bid must remain open for at least thirty-five days. This thirty-five-day minimum period begins to run from the date the bid is commenced. A public advertisement announcing a bid can generally be placed as much as ten days earlier than a bid document can be mailed to shareholders because, in order to mail a bid document, the offeror first must have a list of all the target company's shareholders. Typical Canadian corporate statutes permit an offeror to obtain such a list, but also permit the target corporation up to ten days to produce such a list.[53] Thus, in the case of a hostile take-over bid (i.e., a bid that is opposed by the managers of the target corporation), the efforts of an offeror to commence its bid could be stalled for almost two weeks were it not for the OSA provision permitting a bid to be initiated by a newspaper ad.[54]

The rules permitting a bid to be commenced by advertisement also respond, at least in part, to a peculiar shortcoming in the prior law. Offerors planning to launch a hostile bid would generally issue, in advance of their bid, a public statement indicating their intent. Indeed, under the continuous disclosure rules, as discussed in chapter 9, they typically would be under an obligation to do so. Yet, nothing in the OSA imposed any obligation on the offeror, after making such a public announcement, to formally commence its bid within a specified mini-

---

50   *Ibid.* s. 100(2).

51   *Ibid.* s. 100(7). In order for the thirty-five-day bid period to begin to run from the date of the advertisement, the bidder must also have requested a list of the target securityholders to whom the bid must be delivered. The bid must be delivered to the relevant target securityholders within two business days following the receipt by the bidder of this list.

52   *Ibid.* s. 98(1).

53   See, e.g., *CBCA*, above note 45, s. 21(3).

54   Prior to 31 March 2001, formal take-over bids in Ontario could be commenced only by delivering a bid document. The amendments to Ontario take-over bid law that took effect in 2001 were originally passed by the Ontario legislature in the *More Tax Cuts for Jobs, Growth and Prosperity Act* (S.O. 1999, c. 9). They followed a series of recommendations by a 1996 Committee of the Investment Dealers Association under the chairmanship of Adam Zimmerman (the "Zimmerman Committee"). It should be noted that not every Canadian jurisdiction has uniform take-over bid rules.

mum time period. Although under the new formal bid rules, a bidder may still choose to commence a bid by delivering the bid documentation to the securityholders rather than by public advertisement, the new regime provides incentives to the offeror to commence the bid by public advertisement. Once the bid is so commenced, the *OSA* imposes specific obligations to ensure prompt delivery of the bid documents thereafter.

iii) Minimum Bid Period/Withdrawal Rights

All formal bids must be made to all securityholders of the class in Ontario, and the bid documents must be sent to those securityholders as well as to any holders of securities that are convertible into securities of that class before the bid expires.[55] The reason for this extended delivery obligation is obvious. Holders of convertible securities may wish to exercise their conversion rights to be eligible to tender to the bid. Bids must remain open for at least thirty-five days[56] to permit the target shareholders sufficient time to consider the offer, and to provide the directors of the target corporation, in the case of hostile bids, sufficient time to explore other alternatives to the bid, including possibly attracting a rival bidder who is willing to pay a higher price. During that thirty-five-day period, the bidder cannot "take up" any shares deposited by selling shareholders.[57] The term "taking up" refers to the acceptance to purchase by the offeror. Until her or his shares are taken up, a shareholder who has tendered shares to the bid is permitted to withdraw them.[58] Such a withdrawal right is important not only because it allows a shareholder to change her or his mind, but also because if a second bid is made at a higher price per share, a shareholder who has tendered shares to the first bid may take them back and tender them to the higher bid instead. By providing target shareholders with such a right, the *OSA* makes it difficult for bidders to put undue pressure on the shareholders, and also makes it feasible for directors of the target corporation to seek out alternative offers.

iv) Pro Rata Take-up of Tendered Securities

Often a bidder does not seek to purchase all the outstanding shares of a target corporation. Instead, it may find it more economical to attempt to acquire control with some lesser interest, such as 66-⅔ percent of all outstanding shares — the percentage needed to pass special resolutions

---

55   *OSA*, above note 8, s. 95(1).
56   *Ibid.* s. 95(2).
57   *Ibid.* s. 95(3).
58   *Ibid.* s. 95(4).

under most Canadian corporate law statutes.[59] In such a case, the bidder chooses to make a partial bid, offering to purchase a specified maximum number of shares. If more shares are tendered to the bid than the bidder is prepared to purchase, the OSA requires the bidder to purchase some of the shares from all tendering shareholders, proportionately, according to the number of shares they each tendered. A brief example may help to illustrate this rule and to indicate why it is important. Suppose Target Limited has a total of one million issued and outstanding common shares. Bidco Corp. (Bidco) wishes to acquire exactly 666,667 of those shares at a price of $100 each, which represents a very generous premium above the market price of Target Limited's shares. Shareholder A tenders 500,000 shares to the bid, Shareholder B, 300,000, and Shareholder C, 100,000. The total number of shares tendered (900,000) is more than Bidco wishes to buy. If the OSA did not prohibit it from doing so, Bidco might choose to buy all of the shares tendered by Shareholder A, all of the shares tendered by Shareholder C, and just 66,667 of the shares tendered by Shareholder B. This would be unfair to Shareholder B, who, after all, would like the same opportunity to share in the premium. Accordingly, the proportionate take-up rules require Bidco to purchase 370,371 shares from Shareholder A,[60] 222,222 shares from Shareholder B,[61] and 74,074 shares from Shareholder C.[62]

v) Taking Up and Paying for Tendered Securities

Bidders have a specific incentive to take up shares as soon as they are permitted to do so: namely, to end the withdrawal rights that tendering shareholders enjoy until their shares are taken up.[63] Therefore, to prevent bidders from being quick to take up, but slow to pay for, tendered securities, the OSA includes a prompt payment provision. Any shares taken up must be paid for as soon as possible, but, in any event, payment must be within three business days.[64] If the bidder waits until the bid expires before taking up any shares, the statute requires all shares tendered to the bid to be taken up within ten days after expiry of the bid.[65]

While a bid is open, individual securityholders might tender their securities at different times. To try to ensure the success of its bid, the

59   See, e.g., CBCA, above note 45, s. 2(1) (definition of "special resolution").
60   (500,000/900,000) × 666,667.
61   (300,000/900,000) × 666,667.
62   (100,000/900,000) × 666,667.
63   OSA, above note 8, s. 95(4)(i).
64   Ibid. s. 95(10).
65   Ibid. s. 95(9).

bidder might wish to take up deposited securities as soon as the mini-mum statutory withdrawal period expires. Yet, if the bid is still open when the bidder first takes up the deposited shares, more securities might be tendered after that date. If bidders were permitted to delay paying any shareholders who tendered late, target shareholders might feel pressured to tender early to an offer to avoid having their payments delayed. It was precisely this sort of pressure that the take-over rules were intended to prevent. Accordingly, the *OSA* provides that once the bidder has taken up *any* tendered securities, the bidder must then take up, and pay for, *all* additional securities that are subsequently tendered to the bid within ten days of their deposit.[66]

vi) Extending Bid

Like any offer to purchase, take-over bids do not remain open forever. Bidders specify in their bid document the time at which the offer to purchase will expire. However, as the expiry date draws near, bidders frequently wish to extend their bids to give securityholders more time to tender their securities. There are many reasons such a bid extension might make sense. If it becomes clear that a bid for all outstanding shares will be largely successful, the bidder may wish to provide addi-tional time to sweep in the few remaining stragglers. Or, perhaps a bid might have been delayed by court or OSC proceedings; if the bidder remains interested in the target, the bidder may, again, wish to extend the bid. Whatever the reason, in cases where all the terms or conditions of the bid are met (other than the conditions that the bidder chose to waive), it is unfair to permit an extension of the bid if such an exten-sion would result in a delay of payment to the securityholders who ten-dered their shares by the original expiry date. Accordingly, the *OSA* provides that a bid can be extended only in such cases if the securities previously deposited are first taken up.[67] (And, once the securities are taken up, the bidder must pay for them in no less than three business days.) Of course, if the bid is extended while tendering shareholders continue to enjoy a withdrawal right, it is not necessary, or possible, to require a bidder to take up the shares before extending its bid. Thus, in such circumstances, no mandatory take-up of shares is required before the bid is extended.[68]

In addition to these instances in which the bidder chooses to extend its bid, the *OSA* requires that the time period of a take-over bid

---

66   *Ibid.* s. 95(11).
67   *Ibid.* s. 95(12).
68   *Ibid.* s. 95(12.1).

must be extended in certain circumstances. Specifically, when the terms of a bid are changed, securityholders must be given at least ten days from the date of the variation to deposit their securities,[69] and must be given withdrawal rights during those ten days.[70] It is customary for the contractual obligations of a bidder to be subject to a host of conditions specified in the bid document. For example, the bid might be conditional on the satisfaction of competition law requirements or on the absence of any material adverse change having occurred in the target's business. Most of such conditions are included in the bid document for the same reason that they are included in negotiated agreements of purchase and sale at the request of purchasers — to protect the offeror. Indeed, such conditions are solely for the benefit of the offeror. Accordingly, if the offeror chooses to waive such conditions in an all-cash bid, this change does not alter the position of the target shareholders to their detriment. It simply makes completion of the bid more probable. Thus, if the only change to the bid is to increase the price or to waive a condition provided for in an all-cash bid, there is no need to provide the tendering shareholders with an extended time to withdraw their securities; thus, no extension is required in these circumstances.[71]

vii) Identical Consideration

aa) Subsection 97(2) of the OSA

Equal treatment of target shareholders is one of the most fundamental animating principles of Ontario take-over law for two reasons. First, the *OSA* seeks to prevent a small number of controlling shareholders from capturing a disproportionate share of the premium a buyer may be willing to pay for control of the corporation, as discussed in connection with the clause 93(1)(c) exemption above. Second, by requiring equality of treatment, the *OSA* seeks to curb variations of the two-tier bid tactic that has long been regarded as coercive because it can pressure shareholders into tendering to a bid even when they may consider the bid price inadequate. The *OSA* thus contains a number of rules to ensure that all shareholders of a company that is the target of a take-over bid receive equal consideration for their shares. These rules regulate actions occurring before, during, and after a take-over bid. The basic rule is found in section 97 of the *OSA*, which requires all holders of the target's securities to be offered identical consideration in the take-over bid.[72] If the bid-

---

69   *Ibid.* s. 98(5).
70   *Ibid.* s. 95(4)(ii).
71   *Ibid.* ss. 98(6), s. 95(5)(ii) & (iii).
72   *Ibid.* s. 97(1).

der increases the bid price after some securityholders have already tendered their shares, the higher price must be paid to every tendering
securityholder, even to those whose securities had already been taken up
by the bidder before the price increase was announced.[73] To prevent the
indirect payment of additional consideration to certain securityholders
(i.e., special "sweetheart" deals), section 97 provides a "no collateral
benefit" rule.[74] This rule forbids a bidder from entering into a separate
agreement with a securityholder — even an agreement ostensibly unre-
lated to the purchase of that securityholder's securities — which has the
effect of providing to that securityholder a higher price for his or her
securities than the price offered to the other securityholders.

bb) OSC Exemption

Occasionally, an offeror has good reasons to enter into a separate agreement with a target securityholder — reasons other than to attempt to
coax that securityholder into tendering her or his shares to a bid. For
example, the offeror may want to ensure that a key senior employee of
the target company remains with the company following the offeror's
acquisition. Yet, if that senior employee also owns securities of the class
subject to the bid, an attempt to enter into a separate agreement with
that employee could be construed as an impermissible collateral benefit. Accordingly, the *OSA* provides specifically for a procedure by which
"an interested person" may apply to the OSC for a decision that any
such agreement is made "for reasons other than to increase the value
of the consideration paid to the selling security holder" for the purposes of subsection 97(2).[75]

cc) Collateral Benefit Exemption and Majority of Minority Approval

There is one quite technical matter surrounding the collateral benefit
rules that deserves mention here. In 2000, the OSC's then Director of
Take-over/Issuer Bids, Stan Magidson, commented on the important
relationship between an OSC exemption from subsection 97(2) and a
technical provision in the going-private rules.[76] The going-private rules
are discussed in more detail below in section D. Briefly put, however,
the going-private rules govern the procedures by which the majority
shareholder of a company may complete a transaction that has the
effect of eliminating (or "squeezing" or "cashing" out) the interests of

---

73   *Ibid.* s. 97(3).
74   *Ibid.* s. 97(2).
75   *Ibid.* s. 104(2)(a).
76   Stan Magidson, "More Recent Developments in the Regulation of Take-
     over/Issuer Bids, Going Private and Related Party Transactions" (2000), 23
     OSCB 3952.

the minority shareholders. The rules generally require such a transaction first to be approved by a "majority of the minority" shareholders (i.e., a vote by those shareholders other than the majority shareholder that has initiated the transaction). But, there is a special exception to these voting rules when a going-private transaction for a company follows the completion of a successful take-over bid for that company. The rules, after all, were intended to protect minority shareholders from abuse, not to permit the holders of very small share interests to hold up any transaction they please, no matter how beneficial that transaction is perceived to be by the overwhelming majority of shareholders.[77] Therefore, as long as the consideration received by the minority shareholders in the going-private transaction is at least as much as the consideration received by those other shareholders who tendered their shares to a recently completed take-over bid,[78] the rules permit the votes attached to the shares acquired by the majority holder in the bid to be counted in determining whether the transaction has received the necessary majority of the minority approval. In effect, the shareholders who tendered to the bid indicate, by tendering, their approval of the price at which the remaining shareholders will be "cashed out." There is one important qualification to this rule, though. If shares were acquired in the bid from a person who received a collateral benefit, such shares may not be counted as minority shares, unless the OSC Director grants a specific exemption otherwise. Of course, any such collateral benefit is illegal unless the OSC granted an order under clause 104(2)(a) permitting it.[79] Therefore, the question arises as to whether the OSC, in permitting the collateral benefit in the first place, has also tacitly agreed that the shares acquired from the person receiving that benefit can be counted in any subsequent going-private transaction minority vote. Magidson's view was that the two issues, though similar, are distinct, and must be so treated:

> In essence, you need to apply to the Commission for a s. 104(2)(a) order, [to permit the collateral contract] then you're going to need an exemption from the Director under Rule 61-501, too, if you want to count the shares tendered by any party to the collateral agreement. The fact that you obtained a s. 104(2)(a) order doesn't negate the fact that the tendering securityholder was treated differently than the

---

77   The fact that requiring majority of minority approval could lead to abuse by intransigent or unreasonable minority shareholders is referred to in the companion policy to OSC Rule 61-501. See Companion Policy 61-501 CP (2000), 23 OSCB 2679 at s. 3.1.

78   Specifically, a bid completed no more than 120 days before the going-private transaction. See Rule 61-501, above note 16 at s. 8.2(b).

79   See the discussion in section (b) above.

other securityholders in the bid. ... [S]ometimes staff will recommend that both exemptions will be granted. In some circumstances, however, staff anticipates that it may recommend that the Commission grant relief under clause 104(2)(a) but recommend against the relief requested under Rule 61-501.[80]

Magidson suggests that regulators would be concerned with any collateral benefit that reasonably might be assumed to have influenced the securityholder's decision to tender to the bid in the first place.

viii)   Pre-bid Integration/Post-bid Acquisitions

To ensure the effectiveness of the identical consideration rule, the OSA also restricts attempts by bidders to enter into preferential deals with individual shareholders immediately prior to and immediately following the making of a take-over bid. Thus, if an offeror purchases securities from a target shareholder within ninety days before making a take-over bid, the eventual take-over bid price must be at least equal to the price paid in the pre-bid transaction. If the bidder makes more than one purchase in that time period, the bid price must be at least equal to the highest price paid. Also, the total percentage of outstanding securities that are subject to the bid must be at least as great as the highest percentage of the shares acquired from any seller in a pre-bid transaction.[81] Thus, for example, if the bidder purchased 90 percent of the shares held by a shareholder for $10 per share in a pre-bid transaction, the subsequent bid must be a bid for at least 90 percent of all outstanding shares of the target company and the bid price must be at least $10 per share. Further, to prevent favourable side deals after the completion of the bid, the OSA forbids any purchases of securities of the same class as those subject to a take-over bid that is not generally available to securityholders of the class for a twenty-business-day period following the expiry of the bid.[82] There is an exception to the pre-bid integration and the post-bid acquisition restriction rules in the case of normal-course purchases on a published market.[83]

ix) Permitted Purchases during a Bid

During a formal bid, the bidder is permitted to purchase a limited number of securities other than pursuant to the bid itself provided (a) the intention to make such purchases is stated in the take-over bid circular, (b) the purchases are made through the facilities of a recognized

---

80   Above note 76 at 3960.
81   *OSA*, above note 8, s. 94(5).
82   *Ibid.* s. 94(6).
83   *Ibid.* s. 94(7).

stock exchange, (c) the total number of securities so purchased does not exceed 5 percent of the total outstanding securities, and (d) the bidder issues and files a news release each day such purchases are made.[84] Note that this exemption does *not* stipulate that the price paid in any such exchange transaction must be the same price offered in the take-over bid. The OSC recently confirmed, in the *Chapters/Trilogy* decision,[85] that identical consideration is not a condition of the subsection 94(3) exemption and, accordingly, is not qualified in this respect by the general policy objective expressed in subsection 97(1) on this point. Otherwise, no other purchases during the bid are permitted.[86]

The *Chapters/Trilogy* matter also provided an occasion for the OSC to consider the meaning of the phrase "through the facilities of a stock exchange" for the purposes of this exemption. When large blocks of shares (block purchases) of an exchange-listed company are traded, the sales are not concluded in the same speedy, electronic way as small orders. Instead, the sales are negotiated and arranged in the so-called "upstairs market" (i.e., they are arranged privately, through the direct matching of buy and sell orders by securities dealers). The trade is subsequently "brought to the floor" of the exchange (i.e., the trade is processed through the facilities of the exchange). Block purchases, though processed through the exchange, are not normal-course exchange purchases. When such purchases were made by the bidder in the course of a hostile take-over bid for Chapters Inc. in 2001, the target argued that the purchases ought not to be permitted under subsection 94(3) of the *OSA*. The OSC disagreed, noting that subsection 94(3) does not stipulate that purchases must be normal-course purchases to enjoy the benefit of the exemption. Accordingly, because trades initiated in the upstairs market and then processed through the exchange are considered by the TSE's own rules to be trades made through the facilities of the exchange, the OSC held that such trades fell within the subsection 94(3) exemption.[87]

However, subsequent to the *Chapters/Trilogy* case, notice of proposed OSC Rule 62-501 was published. Rule 62-501, if passed, would effectively overrule that aspect of the *Chapters/Trilogy* decision that permits transactions completed in the upstairs market to qualify for the exception in subsection 94(3). In its notice of the proposed rule, the OSC indicated the following:

---

84   *Ibid.* s. 94(3).
85   See *Re Chapters Inc. and Trilogy Retail Enterprises L.P.* (2001), 24 OSCB 1663 [*Chapters/Trilogy*].
86   *OSA*, above note 8, s. 94(2).
87   *Chapters/Trilogy*, above note 85.

The purpose of the Proposed Rule is to ensure that the equal treatment principle is not violated in the context of purchases made pursuant to the exemption in subsection 94(3). The Proposed Rule would vary the application of subsection 94(3) so that it would apply only to normal course stock exchange trades and would not apply to trades that are arranged privately and subsequently completed or "crossed" on the stock exchange.[88]

x)   Offeror's Circular

aa)   General

The most important distinguishing feature of a formal take-over bid is the requirement for the bidder to produce and deliver a disclosure document known as a take-over bid circular. The requirement to produce and deliver such a document is found in section 98 of the OSA. The content of such a circular is prescribed by regulation to be the information required by Form 32.[89] Failure to deliver a take-over bid circular as required by the OSA is an offence punishable in accordance with the provisions of section 122 and could also lead to administrative action by the OSC under section 127 or to court proceedings under section 128 of the OSA. In addition, any securityholder of a target corporation to whom a take-over circular was required to be delivered may have a statutory right of action against the offeror, if, in fact, no circular was delivered.[90]

A take-over bid circular is a disclosure document intended to provide selling securityholders with the information necessary to make informed decisions as to whether to tender their shares to a bid. The offeror is responsible for the accuracy of statements in the circular, and the OSA provides a statutory civil remedy in the event that there is a misrepresentation in the circular against the offeror, the directors of the offeror, the experts whose opinions appear in the circular, and others who sign a certificate in the circular.[91] This remedy is similar to the statutory civil liability remedy provided in section 130 for misrepresentations in a prospectus. Like the section 130 remedy, the section 131 remedy provides various defences, including a due diligence defence, to defendants other than the offeror itself. Subsection 131(4) provides the offeror's only defence, which is to prove that the securityholder had knowledge of the misrepresentation. The take-over bid circular must

---

88   Notice of Proposed Rule 62-501, December 14, 2001. Available online at <http://www.osc.gov.on.ca> (site accessed: 27 February 2002).
89   OSA, above note 8, s. 98(7); OSA Regulation, above note 28, s. 189 (a); Form 32.
90   OSA, above note 8, s. 133.
91   Ibid. s. 131.

include a statement of these section 131 rights.[92] The OSC recently stated that the test to determine the adequacy of disclosure in a take-over bid circular is the same standard articulated by the U.S. Supreme Court in *TSC Industries Inc. v. Northway Inc.*[93] in the proxy circular context:

> An omitted fact is material if there is a substantial likelihood that a reasonable shareholder would consider it important in deciding how to vote ... [or in deciding whether to tender his shares in the case of a take-over bid.][94]

bb) Securities Exchange Take-over Bid Circular

It is not uncommon for bidders to offer to acquire securities of a target corporation in exchange for securities of the bidder itself rather than for cash. In the case of such a securities exchange offer, in order for securityholders of the target company to make informed decisions as to the value of the offer, they must necessarily judge the value of the bidder company's securities. Such a decision is essentially an investment decision that is no different, in any material respect, from the investment decision a prospective purchaser of securities must make when an issuer undertakes a public offering. It is for this reason that the bidder's circular for a securities exchange offer must include prospectus-level disclosure.[95] However, the issuing of shares by the bidder in such a case, though clearly a distribution as defined in section 1 of the *OSA*, nonetheless is exempt from the normal prospectus requirements.[96] Accordingly, there is no review of the take-over bid circular by securities regulators, notwithstanding its prospectus-like features. The decision to exempt take-over bid circulars from regulatory review, even in the case of securities exchange offers, was a deliberate policy choice recommended by the Kimber Committee in 1965:

> The Committee recognizes that the issuance by a company of its own securities as part of a share exchange take-over bid does not differ in any essential constituent from the issuance of its securities in the course of primary distribution to the public. However, because of the importance of speed and secrecy to the success of a take-over bid or a counter bid and because the procedural and substantive recommendations which comprise the suggested code for take-over bids should,

---

92   *OSA Regulation*, above note 28, s. 200.
93   426 U.S. 438 (1976).
94   *Re MacDonald Oil Exploration Ltd.* (1999), 22 OSCB 6453 at 6456, quoting *Re Standard Broadcasting Corporation Limited* (1985), 8 OSCB 3671 at 3676.
95   *OSA Regulation*, above note 28, Form 32, Item 15.
96   *OSA*, above note 8, s. 72(1)(j).

on a logical basis, be applicable to both cash bids and share exchange bids, we recommend ... that there be no requirement that the take-over bid circular be reviewed by or filed with the Ontario Securities Commission or other governmental agency.[97]

Of course, take-over bid circulars must be filed with the OSC[98] together with a separate report on Form 42.[99] This filing, however, is not made before the take-over bid begins. The point is that regulators do not subject the circular to a pre-transaction vetting in the way they do a prospectus. It is worth noting here that, prior to 1999, it was possible for a company to become a reporting issuer by filing a securities exchange take-over bid circular even though the circular was not subject to the prospectus vetting process and even in cases where the take-over bid was not completed. Needless to say, this easy way out of the closed system was thought to be a serious loophole and was, apparently, subject to some abuse.[100] Amendments to the *OSA* in 1999 changed the definition of "reporting issuer," however, to eliminate this method of automatically becoming a reporting issuer for securities exchange take-over bid circulars filed after the amendment came into force.

xi) Target Company Directors' Circular

Once the offeror has delivered its take-over bid circular, the directors of the target company must respond with a circular of their own.[101] The purpose of this directors' circular is to further help target shareholders to make informed decisions by providing them with, what is hoped to be, the educated views of those in the best position to assess the value of the target company. The shareholders, therefore, are better able to determine whether the offeror's bid is adequate. The circular must be delivered to securityholders within fifteen days of the bid and must generally contain a recommendation to accept or reject the bid supported by reasons. It is possible for the circular to state that the directors make no recommendation, but, again, the directors must provide reasons for this position. Frequently, directors need additional time to assess the offeror's bid. The directors may indicate in their circular that

---

97 *Kimber Report*, above note 1 at 26, para. 3.24.

98 *OSA Regulation*, above note 28, s. 203.

99 *Ibid.* s. 203.1.

100 The OSC's concerns in this regard can be found in s. 2.2 of the companion policy to the previous (pre-30 November 2001) version of Rule 45-501, which was promulgated before the amendment to the *OSA* that eliminated this "loophole." See (Old) Companion Policy 45-501 CP (1998), 21 OSCB 6548 at s. 2.2.

101 *OSA*, above note 8, s. 99.

they are still considering their position, and may advise securityholders not to tender their shares until they receive a final recommendation from the directors.[102] Such a recommendation must be made at least seven days before the bid expires.[103] It is also possible for individual officers or directors to issue their own circulars containing their own independent recommendations.[104]

xii) Defensive Tactics

When one considers the role of the directors of a target company in the context of a take-over bid, it is difficult to ignore the thorny question of defensive tactics. When a take-over bid is commenced on an unsolicited or hostile basis (i.e., against the wishes of the board of the target company), it has long been recognized that the target company's directors and officers are in a position of potential conflict. If the bid succeeds, it is highly likely that the directors and senior officers will be replaced. Faced with such potentially dire personal consequences, how can the directors and officers reasonably be expected to assess the value of such a bid for their shareholders in a fair and disinterested fashion? Directors' attempts to stall or defeat hostile bids using various defensive tactics, including "poison pills," (or, more formally, shareholder rights plans), are canvassed at length elsewhere. Although securities regulators have taken an active and highly visible role in policing such measures, ultimately the issues raised by take-over defence tactics are essentially matters of corporate, rather than securities, law. These issues involve the consideration of the discharge by directors and officers of their fiduciary duties, a subject on which securities regulators are reticent to express definitive views. Accordingly, as important as these matters are, a discussion of take-over bid defences is beyond the scope of this book, and we invite interested readers to pursue this topic in a number of other sources.[105] Only the following two points will be mentioned here.

---

102 *Ibid.* s. 98(4).

103 *Ibid.* s. 98(5).

104 *Ibid.* s. 99(3).

105 For a discussion of defensive tactics from a corporate law perspective, see J. Anthony Van Duzer, *The Law of Partnerships and Corporations* (Toronto: Irwin Law, 1997) at 335–38. See also, Christopher C. Nicholls, *Corporate Finance and Canadian Law* (Toronto: Carswell, 2000) at 340–367; Stephen H. Halperin and Robert Vaux, "The Role of Target's Directors in Unsolicited Control Transaction" in *Critical Issues in Mergers and Acquisitions: Domestic and International Views, Papers Presented at the 6th Queen's Annual Business Law Symposium 1999* (Kingston: Queen's University, 2000) at 109; Jeffrey G. MacIntosh, "The Poison

First, the CSA issued a policy statement on take-over bid defensive tactics, National Policy 62-202.[106] The policy explicitly affirms the Kimber Committee's original notion that the primary purpose of take-over laws is to protect the *bona fide* interests of the shareholders of target companies. The policy also states that a secondary purpose is to provide an even-handed regulatory framework for take-overs. It indicates that, although regulators are "reluctant" to interfere in bids, nevertheless, they will oppose defensive measures that prevent shareholders of target companies from making their own informed decisions as to whether to tender to a hostile bid. In that context, the policy mentions three particular types of defensive tactics that might attract regulatory scrutiny: (1) issuing a significant number of securities or options to purchase securities of the issuer; (2) selling or granting an option to purchase significant assets of the issuer; and (3) taking steps or entering into contracts out of the normal course of business.

Second, securities regulators have made a number of important rulings with respect to defensive tactics employed by companies that are the target of hostile bids, particularly with respect to "poison pills" or shareholder rights plans. A recent joint decision of the Alberta, British Columbia, and Ontario Securities Commissions that reviewed many of the principles and much of the previous regulatory "jurisprudence" on this issue is *Re Royal Host Real Estate Investment Trust and Canadian Income Properties Real Estate Investment Trust.*[107] The issue was also revisited by the OSC in 2001.[108]

f) The "Early Warning" System

Although the key take-over bid threshold is 20 percent of the voting or equity securities of a target company, the *OSA* provides for an early warning system when an offeror comes to hold at least 10 percent of a reporting issuer's voting or equity securities. This early warning system is modelled on subsection 13(d) of the U.S. *Securities Exchange Act of 1934*, which was introduced to prevent creeping take-over bids[109] by providing the market (including the target company itself) with

---

Pill; A Noxious Nostrum for Canadian Shareholders" 15 Can. Bus. L.J. 276 (1989); P. Anisman, "Poison Pills: The Canadian Experience" in *Corporations, Capital Markets and Business in the Law* (London: Kluwer, 2000) at 1.

106 (1997), 20 OSCB 3526.

107 (1999), 22 OSCB 7819.

108 See *Chapters/Trilogy*, above note 85.

109 See Thomas Lee Hazen, *The Law of Securities Regulation*, 3d ed. (St Paul: West Publishing Co., 1996) at 603.

advance notice that a particular person or company is accumulating a significant block of shares in a public company.

The Ontario early warning rules require that any offeror whose ownership interest in a class of a reporting issuer's voting or equity securities increases to at least 10 percent of the total must issue and file a news release,[110] file a report with the OSC,[111] and refrain from making additional purchases for one business day from the date the report is filed.[112] In other words, the offeror must refrain from purchasing more securities during the period beginning with the purchase that first triggers the obligation to file a report, and ending after the expiry of one business day after the filing of the report. Once the initial early warning report is filed, subsequent reports are required only where the offeror acquires additional securities of the class totalling at least 2 percent of the total. Because the purpose of the section is to detect potential changes of control, no filing is necessary for offerors who already own or control 20 percent or more of the target company's securities.[113]

There is an alternative monthly-reporting regime for eligible institutional investors. These investors, such as banks, pension funds, mutual funds, and investment managers, must acquire the shares for investment, not for control purposes, and generally speaking, they may satisfy the requirements of section 101 of the OSA by filing reports within ten days after the end of the month in which they made purchases that would have otherwise triggered a reporting obligation under section 101.[114]

g) Mini-tenders

The issue of mini-tenders has attracted some recent regulatory attention and deserves mention here. A mini-tender, as explained in CSA Staff Notice 61-301,[115] is a widespread offer to purchase the shares of a public company at a *below-market* price. Typically, such offers are made for less than 20 percent of the shares of a target company and, so, do not constitute take-over bids. As the CSA notes, the only rational reason for a shareholder to tender his or her shares to such a below-market mini-tender is if that shareholder holds less than a board lot of shares.[116] Such a shareholder cannot otherwise easily liquidate his or

---

110 *OSA*, above note 8, s. 101(1)(a). The news release must contain the information prescribed in Appendix E to National Instrument 62-103 (2000), 23 OSCB 1372.
111 *OSA*, above note 8, s. 101(1)(b).
112 *Ibid.* s. 101(3).
113 *Ibid.* s. 101(4).
114 National Instrument 62-103 at Part 4, above note 110.
115 (1999), 22 OSCB 7797.
116 Board lots are explained in section (d)(iii) above.

her holdings without paying brokerage commissions that may, in extreme cases, actually exceed any sale proceeds that the shareholder would realize on the disposition of those shares. Shares typically can be sold to mini-tender offerors without any brokerage commissions. CSA Staff have raised concerns, however, that some shareholders who receive such offers may not follow the market price of their shares, and may assume incorrectly that the mini-tender, like a typical take-over bid offer, is made at an above-market price. Reasonable people may differ on the utility of mini-tenders. A shareholder who has happily liquidated an otherwise locked-in, odd lot position may be grateful for the making of a certain mini-tender and may be disappointed if overzealous regulation were to stamp them out altogether. Nevertheless, there is no legitimate reason to oppose disclosure rules that ensure that shareholders who receive mini-tender offers are made fully aware that an offered price is below the market price. The CSA Staff Notice suggests disclosure guidelines to ensure that selling shareholders are able to make informed decisions.

2) Insider Bids

Much of Canadian take-over law is premised on the notion that shareholders of target companies have less information about those companies than bidders. Regulation, accordingly, is aimed at addressing any potential unfairness that might arise from such informational asymmetry. Concerns over informational imbalance are dramatically increased, however, when the offeror is not an outsider, but has access to inside information about the target company. Such bids, called "insider bids," are, therefore, subject to rules in addition to the take-over bid rules previously discussed.

Most of these additional rules may be found in OSC Rule 61-501. Rule 61-501 defines an insider bid as a take-over bid for the securities of an issuer made by an "issuer insider" of that issuer or by associates, affiliates, or those acting jointly or in concert with the issuer.[117] The special phrase "issuer insider," which is defined elsewhere in the rule, is used instead of the more general term "insider" because it is intended to differ slightly in meaning from the definition of "insider" in the OSA.

The additional rules applicable when a take-over bid is an insider bid relate mainly to additional disclosure and valuation requirements. Specifically, a take-over bid circular used in an insider bid must disclose every valuation of the target company completed within the pre-

---

117 Rule 61-501, above note 16 at s. 1.1(3).

vious two years, provide background information about the bid, disclose any *bona fide* offer for the securities received by the issuer within the previous two years and, perhaps most important, include a copy or a summary of a formal valuation obtained at the expense of the offeror.[118] The valuation must be prepared by an independent valuator chosen by an independent committee of the target company's board of directors, and the offeror must enable that committee to supervise the preparation of the valuation.[119]

Exemptions from the formal valuation requirement are available in certain cases. The exemptions essentially involve instances where (1) the offeror, though technically an insider, in fact, has no special access to information about the target, or (2) the price offered for the securities has been determined demonstrably by market forces, as evidenced by such things as a significant, recently completed, arm's-length transaction at the same or a lesser price.[120]

C. ISSUER BIDS

Corporations frequently find it advantageous to repurchase some of their own outstanding shares. The publicly disclosed reasons for such repurchases often include the following three suggestions: (1) the market is undervaluing the issuer's shares, and they are, therefore, a good bargain; (2) the company can find no worthwhile investment projects and, so, is returning capital to its shareholders in a more tax-efficient manner than through the declaration of a dividend; and (3) the company seeks to increase its earnings per share, which, if firm earnings remain constant, is the certain arithmetic result of reducing the number of outstanding shares by a share repurchase.

For a host of reasons beyond the scope of this chapter, financial economists occasionally question the completeness of the reasons publicly offered by companies announcing stock repurchases and advance various academic theories to explain them.[121] A thoughtful discussion of these theories is, unfortunately, beyond the scope of this book. We

---

118 *Ibid.* ss. 2.2(1) & 2.3(1).
119 *Ibid.* ss. 2.3(2) & s. 6.1(1).
120 *Ibid.* s. 2.4.
121 See, e.g., S. Stewart, "Should a Corporation Repurchase Its Own Stock?" (1976) 31(3) J. Fin. 911; T. Vermaelen, "Common Stock Repurchases and Market Signaling" (1981) 9 J. Fin. Econ. 138.

focus instead on the central securities law issues raised when a corporation seeks to buy back its own outstanding shares.

In most material respects, the *OSA* treats issuer bids very much like take-over bids, although an issuer bid is defined in terms of any offer by an issuer to acquire or redeem its own securities (other than non-convertible debt securities), regardless of the number of securities subject to such offer.[122] There is, in other words, no 20 percent threshold (or any other threshold for that matter) for issuer bids. The formal bid rules set out in sections 95 to 98 and 100 of the *OSA*, as described above, apply equally to issuer bids, except those bids that qualify for an exemption from these requirements. The disclosure document that must be delivered by an issuer making a non-exempt issuer bid is an issuer bid circular.[123] The potential liability where such a circular contains a misrepresentation is, again, essentially the same as in the case of a take-over bid circular.[124]

The regulation of issuer bids is also based on similar policy grounds as the regulation of take-over bids. When an issuer undertakes the purchase of its own shares, regulators must be concerned about the possible exploitation of informational advantage. Who, after all, has better information about the underlying value of an issuer's shares than the issuer itself? This policy concern also helps to account for a number of the exemptions from the issuer bid rules provided by the *OSA*. The exemptions, which are in many cases similar to the formal take-over bid exemptions, include the following:

- Purchases made pursuant to redemption, retraction, or other similar pre-existing rights of the company or the holder attaching to the securities[125]
- Purchases from current or former employees of the issuer, provided the price paid does not exceed the market price and the total number of securities so purchased does not exceed 5 percent of the total number or amount of such securities[126]
- Bids made through the facilities of a recognized stock exchange[127]
- Normal-course issuer bids for which the issuer publishes a notice of intention and engages in open-market purchases of not more than 5

---

122 See definition of "issuer bid," *OSA*, above note 8, s. 89(1).
123 *OSA*, above note 8, s. 98(1).
124 See, e.g., *ibid.* s. 131(3).
125 *Ibid.* s. 93(3)(a), (b) & (c).
126 *Ibid.* s. 93(3)(d).
127 *Ibid.* s. 93(3)(e).

percent of the total outstanding number or amount of such securities within a twelve-month period[128]

- Purchases made by an issuer that is, in effect, a private company[129]
- Purchases made by an issuer with fewer than fifty Ontario security-holders holding less than 2 percent of the outstanding securities of the class being acquired, provided the bid is made in compliance with the rules of a recognized jurisdiction and all materials distributed in that jurisdiction are also sent to the Ontario holders[130]
- Bids exempted by regulation

Because issuer bids, like insider bids, raise particular asymmetric informational concerns, OSC Rule 61-501 imposes additional requirements on them. As in the case of insider bid take-over bid circulars, an issuer bid circular must contain additional disclosure, including a description of the background to the issuer bid,[131] every prior valuation of the issuer within the previous two years,[132] every *bona fide* offer received by the issuer relating to the securities subject to the issuer bid within the previous two years,[133] discussion of the process followed by the issuer in connection with the bid,[134] information relating to parties expected to accept the bid, and the probable effect of the bid on the voting interests of interested parties (a term defined in Rule 61-501).[135] Finally, except in certain cases, the issuer must obtain and disclose the results of a formal valuation by an independent valuator of the securities subject to the bid.[136]

---

128 *Ibid.* s. 93(3)(f). The necessary "notice of intention" must contain information prescribed in Form 31. See *OSA Regulation*, above note 28, s. 187.

129 *Ibid.* s. 93(3)(g). The term "private company" is not used, but the description of companies eligible for this exemption is substantially identical to that of companies for which the take-over bid private company exemption in s. 93(1)(d) is available.

130 *Ibid.* s. 93(3)(h).

131 Rule 61-501, above note 116 at s. 3.2(1)(b).

132 *Ibid.* s. 3.2(1)(c).

133 *Ibid.* s. 3.2(1)(d).

134 *Ibid.* s. 3.2(1)(e).

135 *Ibid.* s. 3.2(1)(f).

136 *Ibid.* s. 3.3(1). Exemptions from the formal valuation requirement are found in s. 3.4.

D. GOING-PRIVATE TRANSACTIONS

1) Introduction

When a private company first decides to sell its securities to outside investors, we say that such a company is "going public." The securities law implications of such public offerings were discussed in chapter 6. The process can also work in reverse: a public company can be converted into a private company by arranging for most of the outstanding public shares to be purchased, leaving a small number of shareholders, or perhaps just a single shareholder, holding all of the company's shares. A transaction that has the effect of transforming a public company into a private company in this way is often referred to, informally, as a "going-private transaction." As will be seen, however, the issues raised by such transactions prompted regulators to introduce a complex set of rules surrounding them. The principal concern of regulators is to ensure that securityholders whose shares are purchased in such transactions receive a fair price and are otherwise treated fairly. The heightened concern for fairness arises from the fact that large shareholders who wish to obtain 100 percent control of the subject company typically initiate going-private transactions. These same large shareholders, for a variety of reasons, typically have access to better information about the company than the small public shareholders whose interests they seek to eliminate. Thus, the rules relating to going-private transactions are aimed mainly at addressing this information imbalance.

When a complex regulatory framework is introduced to deal with a particular sort of transaction, it becomes important to define that sort of transaction with precision. Accordingly, Ontario securities rules offer a specific definition of the phrase "going-private transaction." That definition is examined more closely below.

Although going-private transactions can be initiated at any time in a company's life, often a going-private transaction is undertaken immediately following a take-over bid in which the bidder managed to acquire most, but not all, of the remaining outstanding shares of the target company. That bidder often seeks to acquire 100 percent ownership through such a separate, post-bid transaction. It is for that reason that we consider going-private transactions in this chapter.

2) 90 Percent Compulsory Acquisition

To understand the delicate policy issues surrounding going-private transactions, it is useful first to consider a provision found in many Canadian corporate law statutes that is intended to facilitate the post-bid acquisition of small minority securityholder interests. Such provisions, of which section 188 of the Ontario *Business Corporations Act* is an example, typically permit a bidder whose bid was recently accepted by holders of at least 90 percent of the securities subject to the bid to subsequently force any of the remaining shareholders to sell their securities to the bidder within a specified time following the bid.[137] In some cases, where a bidder chooses not to initiate such a purchase transaction, corporate law provides a parallel right to minority shareholders to compel the bidder to acquire their shares.[138] Minority shareholders might choose to exercise such a right if they perceived that their minority interests would otherwise become illiquid (i.e., there would be little or no trading market for their shares, given the large controlling interest now owned by the successful take-over bidder). The price that the bidder must pay for the remaining securities is the same price previously paid to those holders who accepted the bid or, at the option of any securityholder, the "fair value" of those securities as determined by a court in accordance with the statute.

The *OBCA* provides this compulsory acquisition right to offerors because, without it, a company with just a handful of public shareholders might have to remain a reporting issuer subject to all of the reporting and continuous disclosure obligations imposed on such issuers. Among other things, such a company must continue to prepare proxy material and to convene formal annual shareholder meetings, notwithstanding that the remaining public shareholders do not have any significant economic interest in the company and do not, in any event, have sufficient votes to oppose any initiative of the majority shareholder. In certain cases, this situation could arise merely because a small number of shareholders failed to tender to the bid owing to a simple lack of interest or a lack of attention. Worse still, some minority share-

---

137 Under s. 188 of the *Business Corporations Act* (Ontario), R.S.O. 1990, c. B.16 [*OBCA*], the bid must have been accepted by holders of at least 90 percent of the securities subject to the bid within 120 days after the bid commenced. The offeror then has up to 60 days following the expiry of the bid (or 180 days after the bid commenced, whichever is earlier) to exercise its rights under s. 188.

138 See *OBCA, ibid.* s. 189. Recent amendments to the *Canada Business Corporations Act* would grant a similar right to securityholders of *CBCA* corporations. See *CBCA*, above note 45, s. 206.1.

holders might attempt to use their positions to pressure the company into buying their securities at an inflated price reflecting their "nuisance value" rather than their genuine economic value. If the law did not provide a means of eliminating these small interests after the completion of a *bona fide* and essentially successful take-over bid, many shareholders might choose not to tender to a bid, even where the price was fair, in the hope of engaging in such post-bid pressure tactics. As a result, many otherwise beneficial bids might be forestalled.

The utility of allowing bidders to compel the remaining shareholders to sell is, therefore, clear. But, what about the price at which bidders may force minority shareholders to sell? Shareholders of target companies are protected from receiving an unfairly low acquisition price for their shares because the compulsory acquisition provisions are available only in cases where 90 percent of the shares *not already owned by the offeror* at the commencement of the bid have been tendered to the bid. Such overwhelming acceptance of the bid offers objective evidence that the bid price is a fair one. But to remove any doubt, shareholders also may seek to have the court fix a "fair value" for their shares. Thus, the reasonable goals of the successful bidder are carefully balanced against the interests of the minority shareholders.

Where the original bid was not an all-cash bid, however, interpretation of the compulsory acquisition provisions becomes somewhat more complex. In *Shoom v. Great-West Lifeco Inc.*[139] an offeror completed a take-over bid for London Insurance Group under which London Insurance shareholders were given the option of selling their shares for cash or exchanging them for shares in Great-West Life Assurance Company. The number of shares available for the share exchange option, however, was subject to a specific limit. Therefore, if a substantial number of London Insurance Group shareholders chose the share exchange option, such that the maximum number of available Great-West Life shares was reached, all tendering shareholders electing the share exchange option would be allocated Great-West Life shares on a *pro rata* basis, with the remaining amount of the purchase price paid to them in cash. Indeed, the maximum number of available shares was reached, and these shares were allocated *pro rata* to the relevant tendering London Insurance Group shareholders. Then, following the bid, the offeror sought to acquire the remaining outstanding shares of London Insurance Group pursuant to the 90 percent compulsory acquisition provisions. The offeror argued that it was not required to

---

139 (1998), 42 O.R. (3d) 732 (C.A.) [*Shoom*].

offer a share exchange option to the remaining minority shareholders because all of the Great-West Life shares available for such an option had already been exhausted. The Ontario Court of Appeal disagreed and held that the offeror was required to offer the same share option subject to the same *pro rata* distribution made to shareholders who had tendered to the bid. The court based this conclusion on the language of the statute, which requires that dissenting shareholders may elect either to receive fair value for their shares or to transfer their shares to the offeror "on the terms on which the offeror acquired the shares of the offerees who accepted the take-over bid."[140] Because the offeror had acquired shares from tendering shareholders who had elected the share exchange option on terms that included a *pro rata* distribution of Great-West Life shares, the offeror had to offer those same terms to the dissenting shareholders. The court further noted that this conclusion not only was required by the clear wording of the statute, but also was consistent with the policy underlying the 90 percent compulsory acquisition provision, which is to ensure that shareholders are not pressured to tender to a take-over bid in the first place.[141]

Many of the same competing policy goals that underlie the compulsory acquisition provisions also underlie the "going-private transaction" rules.

3) The Definition of "Going-Private Transaction"

The regulation of going-private transactions is an area in which corporate law and securities law intersect. Thus, the *OBCA* contains a definition of "going-private transaction" that applies to corporations incorporated under that Act. Ontario securities law, as explained below, offers a somewhat different definition of the term, which applies to transactions affecting Ontario securityholders, regardless of the jurisdiction of incorporation of the entity that issued the securities. Although the *OBCA's* going-private transaction rules have not been repealed, they are, for practical purposes, superseded by the securities law rules.[142]

---

140 *CBCA*, above note 45, s. 206(3)(c)(i).

141 *Shoom*, above note 139 at 736.

142 Technically, s. 190(6) of the *OBCA*, above note 137, provides that an interested person may apply to the OSC for an exemption from the *OBCA's* going-private rules, including (a) the circular requirement, (b) the minority approval requirement, and (c) the valuation requirement. OSC Rule 61-501 then provides, essentially, that a transaction that meets the *OBCA's* definition of a going-private transaction will be automatically exempt from the *OBCA* circular, minority

OSC Rule 61-501[143] defines a going-private transaction, not only for the purposes of the rule itself, but also for the purposes of the *OSA*, the *OSA Regulation*, and all other rules, as follows:

> an amalgamation, arrangement, consolidation, amendment to the terms of a class of participating securities of the issuer or any other transaction with or involving a person or company that is a *related party* of the issuer at the time the transaction is agreed to, as a consequence of which the interest of a beneficial owner of a participating security of the issuer in that security may be terminated without the beneficial owner's consent other than [five specific types of transactions, including 90 percent compulsory acquisitions described above, where the potential abuses that the going-private rules are intended to address are of limited or no concern.][144]

We have highlighted the phrase "related party" within the definition because it is the participation of a related party of an issuer in a going-private transaction involving that issuer that gives rise to regulatory concerns. Rule 61-501[145] defines the term "related party" to include various persons and companies who might reasonably be expected to have access to superior information about an issuer. Thus, a person or company is a related party of an issuer if he, she, or it is, among other things, a director or a senior officer of the issuer who, either alone or with others, owns more than 10 percent of the voting securities of the issuer, owns sufficient securities to affect the control of the issuer materially, or manages or directs the issuer.

4) A Going-Private Transaction Illustration

Put simply, a going-private transaction is a transaction that has the effect of eliminating the interest of a holder of an equity security without the holder's consent. For example, consider the case where one company, Bidco Ltd., launches a take-over bid for all of the outstanding shares of Target Inc., a public company. Bidco, it will be assumed, held no shares of Target Inc. before launching its bid. Most, but not all, of the Target Inc. shareholders decide to tender their shares to Bidco's

---

approval and valuation requirements without the need for any exemption application to be made, if the transaction is exempt from the application of the Rule 61-501 requirements, or is conducted in accordance with those requirements. (See OSC Rule 61-501, above note 116 at ss.4.3, 4.6 & 4.9.)

143 OSC Rule 61-501, above note 116.
144 *Ibid.* s. 1.1(3) [Emphasis added].
145 *Ibid.* s. 1.1(1).

bid. Thus, when the bid is completed, Bidco finds that it owns a total of 85 percent of Target Inc.'s outstanding shares. Bidco does not wish for Target Inc. to continue to be a reporting issuer, and, therefore, wishes to acquire the remaining 15 percent share interest. However, Bidco cannot take advantage of the 90 percent compulsory acquisition provisions under corporate law because only 85 percent, not 90 percent, of the outstanding shares were tendered to the bid. So, Bidco, instead, decides to undertake an "amalgamation squeeze."

An amalgamation squeeze refers to an amalgamation between two or more corporations that has the effect of eliminating the equity interest of the minority shareholders of one of those corporations. In this hypothetical case, Bidco amalgamates with Target Inc. to form an amalgamated corporation, Amalco Corp. The amalgamation agreement provides that, on amalgamation, the shareholders of Bidco will receive common shares of Amalco and the minority shareholders of Target Inc. will receive redeemable preferred shares of Amalco. Immediately after the amalgamation, Amalco redeems the preferred shares for cash, leaving the former Bidco shareholders as the only shareholders of Amalco. Because the equity interest of the minority Target Inc. shareholders is extinguished without their consent, this amalgamation squeeze constitutes a going-private transaction. Such a transaction may be completed if certain securities law requirements designed to ensure that the minority shareholders are treated fairly are met. These requirements are discussed in the following sections.

5) Going-Private Transaction Requirements

a) Introduction

When a going-private transaction, as defined in Rule 61-501, is undertaken, the transaction is normally subject to three basic requirements intended to protect the minority shareholders. These three requirements are set out below:

- The transaction must be approved by the minority shareholders. (This requirement is referred to frequently by practitioners as the "majority of the minority" approval.)
- An information circular with prescribed information must be delivered.
- A formal valuation of the affected securities must be obtained.

Exemptions from each of these requirements are available in appropriate circumstances, as discussed further below.

b) Majority of the Minority Approval

The central protection for minority shareholders when a related party of the issuer initiates a going-private transaction is the requirement in Rule 61-501 that such a transaction be approved by a majority of those securityholders whose interests would be eliminated as a result of the transaction. An important qualification to these rules applies to a going-private transaction that is undertaken immediately following a take-over bid. Simply put, Rule 61-501 permits securities that were tendered to the take-over bid to be voted by their new owner (namely, the bidder) just as if they were held by minority shareholders for the purpose of obtaining the required minority approval. In other words, to return to the Bidco/Target example above, the "amalgamation squeeze" proposed by Bidco would require minority approval. But, at the shareholders' meeting convened to seek that approval, Bidco would be permitted to vote all of the shares that it had recently acquired pursuant to its take-over bid. Because in this example, Bidco acquired shares representing 85 percent of all outstanding shares, it could easily outvote the remaining 15 percent interest held by the other shareholders and, so, could proceed with the transaction.

The policy justification for permitting shares tendered to a bid to be counted in this way is much the same as that underlying the 90 percent compulsory acquisition provision described earlier. Regulators are reluctant to provide minority shareholders with an effective veto over transactions where such a veto could be misused to pressure issuers into buying out their interests at premiums not available to other selling shareholders. If most other shareholders willingly tendered their shares to a recently completed take-over bid, that fact provides objective evidence that the bid price was perceived to be a fair one. Therefore, if the remaining minority shareholders receive the same price for their shares as the price paid to those who tendered to the bid — and so long as there is no other reason to doubt the fairness of that price — it seems unreasonable to allow shareholders with very small interests to hold up commercially reasonable transactions. Accordingly, the conditions that must be satisfied before a bidder may vote previously tendered shares at a meeting convened to approve a post-bid going-private transaction all relate to two crucial issues: *information* and *value*.[146] These conditions include the following:

- The tendering securityholders, whose shares the bidder has acquired and now wishes to vote, must have received consideration identical to that received by other beneficial shareholders and must not con-

---

146 *Ibid.* s. 8.2.

tinue to hold participating securities of the issuer. (The explanation for this rule is the following. A tendering shareholder who continues to hold participating securities in the issuer might have agreed to sell his or her other shares at a below-market bid price in the hope of receiving future benefits as a continuing securityholder. No such future benefits would be available to those shareholders who tendered all of their shares (non-continuing shareholders). Thus, there is no reason to doubt that those non-continuing shareholders genuinely regarded the bid price as a fair one, and, thus, there is no reason to prevent the bidder from voting the shares acquired from non-continuing shareholders.)

- The going-private transaction must be completed within 120 days after the expiry of the formal bid.
- The going-private transaction must be proposed by the person who made the formal bid and must relate to those securities that were the subject of the bid.
- The consideration offered to securityholders in the going-private transaction must be no less than the amount offered under the bid and, where applicable, must be in the same form.
- The take-over bid circular must have disclosed (a) the bidder's intention to complete a post-bid going-private transaction; (b) formal valuation information concerning the subject securities; (c) the requirement of minority approval of the subsequent going-private transaction, identifying any securities entitled to a separate class vote and stating which securities must be excluded in determining whether such minority approval had been obtained; (d) relevant tax consequences of the bid and the subsequent going-private transaction, if known, or at least the fact that the tax consequences of tendering to the bid might be different depending on whether one tendered one's shares to the bid or, instead, had one's interest acquired pursuant to the subsequent going-private transaction. (Again, it should be clear that this disclosure is all designed to ensure that shareholders who tendered to the bid made their decisions on an informed basis.)

c) Meeting and Information Circular

Where minority approval of a going-private transaction is necessary, Rule 61-501 requires that a meeting be convened to seek such approval, and that an information circular be sent to holders of affected securities to enable them to make informed decisions when they vote at the meeting. The information circular must comply with specific disclosure requirements, which are aimed at providing minority shareholders, to the greatest extent possible, with access to all of the information that might affect the assessment of the adequacy of the consideration that the minority shareholders would receive for their securities if the going-private transaction were approved. For example, the circular must disclose any known valuations of the issuer completed within the previous two years, any *bona fide* offer relevant to the transaction received by the issuer within the previous two years,[147] and details of the review and approval process adopted by the board and any independent committee of the board of the issuer.

d) Formal Valuation

The principal concern of securities regulators in the case of going-private transactions is that the related party that initiates the transaction and seeks to eliminate the interests of the minority securityholders is likely to have better information about the issuer and about the value of the outstanding securities of the issuer than the minority securityholders. Accordingly, to help minority securityholders arrive at informed decisions as to the value of their securities, Rule 61-501 requires that when a going-private transaction is undertaken, a formal valuation must be prepared by an independent valuator, unless an exemption from that requirement is available.

The exemptions to the valuation requirement set out in Rule 61-501 describe circumstances in which some other reliable, objective evidence is available as to the value of the affected securities, thus making a formal valuation unnecessary.

For example, if a going-private transaction is announced while one or more other going-private transactions, or one or more formal take-over bids, are outstanding, there is no need for a formal valuation, provided the issuer has not given better access to one of the bidders or deal promoters than it has to any of the others.[148]

Similarly, if there were previous arm's-length negotiations that resulted in sales of securities of the same class as those subject to the going-private transaction, such recent comparable sales would generally be a far better indication of market value than a formal valuation and, so, would make a valuation unnecessary. The Rule thus provides an exemption from the valuation requirement when such previous arm's-length negotiations have been completed;[149] however, the exemp-

---

147 This requirement deals squarely with circumstances of the sort addressed by the court in *Percival v. Wright*, [1902] 2 Ch. 421.

148 OSC Rule 61-501, above note 116 at s. 4.5(1)3.

149 *Ibid.* s. 4.5(1)2.

tion is complicated because regulators wish to ensure that a previous arm's-length sale offers *reliable* evidence of value. A recent purchase and sale of a single share, for example, even if conducted at arm's length, would reveal very little about the value of a company's shares. Thus, the rule requires that, to satisfy the exemption, the previous sale must have been substantial, involving a total of 20 percent of the issuer's securities in the aggregate and a purchase of at least 10 percent (or in some cases 5 percent) of the issuer's securities from a single holder.[150] Moreover, care must be taken to ensure that those holders who sold their securities in the prior transaction had complete information and were not influenced by extrinsic factors that might have affected the price that they were prepared to accept for their securities. Care must also be taken to ensure that there was no undisclosed material information that might have affected the price of the securities either at the time of the prior sales or at the time of the proposed going-private transaction.[151]

Valuation exemptions are also available in the case of non-redeemable investment funds that provide public information about their net asset values regularly.[152] As well, exemptions may be granted on a discretionary basis by the Director.[153]

There is yet another valuation exemption upon which we would especially like to focus in this section because it relates to the one type of going-private transaction of most concern in the take-over bid context: a "second-step" going-private transaction. A "second-step" going-private transaction is undertaken by a take-over bidder after the completion of a successful take-over bid to which most, but not all, of the target shares were tendered. The goal of such a second-step transaction is to acquire the few shares still remaining in the hands of minority shareholders. In such a case, it is the successful take-over bid itself that offers the kind of objective evidence of value that makes a formal valuation superfluous. Rule 61-501 provides an exemption from the valuation requirement for a second-step going-private transaction if certain conditions, described below, are satisfied. These conditions parallel the requirements, discussed earlier, that must be satisfied in

---

150 *Ibid.* s. 4.5(1)2(b) & (c).
151 *Ibid.* s. 4.5(1)2(d), (e), (f) & (g).
152 *Ibid.* s. 4.5(1)5.
153 *Ibid.* s. 4.5(1)1 & s. 9.1.

order for a bidder to be permitted to vote shares tendered to the bid at the meeting seeking minority approval:

- The going-private transaction must be effected by the offeror who made the formal bid (or an affiliate) and must be in respect of securities of the same class as those that were the subject of the bid.
- The going-private transaction must be completed within 120 days following the expiry of the take-over bid. (The bid price, in other words, must have been a relatively recent, not a stale, price.)
- The take-over bid circular must have disclosed the bidder's intention to complete a second-step going-private transaction. (Security-holders tendering to the bid must be seen to have made an informed choice. If no going-private transaction was contemplated at the time of the bid, some shareholders might have tendered their shares fearing that, if they failed to do so, they might end up holding a small minority interest in a company with a controlling shareholder. Such an interest could have a fairly thin trading market, making such a minority interest illiquid. If shareholders tendered their shares fearing this outcome, they might have been prepared to accept a less than fair price for their shares. Thus, the bid price would not necessarily be a reliable indicator of value.)
- The amount offered to minority securityholders in the going-private transaction must be at least as much as the bid price, and, where the bid price was paid in a form other than cash, the same form of consideration must also be offered to the minority securityholders in the going-private transaction.
- The take-over bid circular must have disclosed the relevant tax consequences of the bid and the subsequent going-private transaction, if known, or at least the fact that the tax consequences of tendering to the bid might be different depending on whether one tendered one's shares to the bid or, instead, had one's interest acquired pursuant to a subsequent going-private transaction. (This requirement, once again, is intended to ensure that shareholders who tendered to the formal bid made their decisions on an informed basis, so that the price they accepted may be considered a reliable indicator of value.)

e) Filing Requirement
Subsection 203.2(1) of the *OSA Regulation* requires that an issuer file a Form 44 report within ten days of delivering an information circular in respect of a going-private transaction.

E. CONCLUSION

Securities regulation began with a concern that purchasers of securities were at risk of being exploited by the sellers of those securities who possessed superior information and, perhaps, superior resources. The same essential policy concern — to protect the informationally weak from the informationally strong — underlies modern take-over and issuer bid regulation. Take-over and issuer bids can be useful, economically beneficial, and efficient; but, they must be conducted in a manner that ensures, to the greatest extent possible, that smaller securityholders are treated fairly and equitably. These rather simple goals have led to the sophisticated structure of Canadian take-over bid and issuer bid regulation. These simple goals also provide the key to unwinding and to understanding the complexities of that regulation.

CHAPTER 11

SECURITIES LAW ENFORCEMENT

A. INTRODUCTION

The regulatory framework created by Canadian securities laws is formidable. But, without effective enforcement, the protections that should be afforded by such laws would be only so many words on a page.

Securities regulators, such as the Ontario Securities Commission (OSC), play a pivotal role in enforcing securities laws. Enforcement is a central part of the OSC's mandate and commands a material share of the OSC's time and resources. In fact, when the OSC first became an autonomous, self-funded agency in 1997, one of the top priorities identified by the chairman was the expansion of staff "with the focus on increasing resources in the compliance and enforcement areas."[1]

B. FORMS OF ENFORCEMENT ACTION

When securities laws are alleged to have been breached, enforcement actions typically take one or more of four forms:

- *Criminal Code* prosecution for certain specific violations
- Quasi-criminal prosecution

---

1   Ontario Securities Commission, *1998 Annual Report* at 9. Available online at <http://www.osc.gov.on.ca/en/About/Publications/annual_report_1998.html> (site accessed: 28 March 2001).

- Administrative enforcement action
- Civil court proceeding

Although only one of these avenues of enforcement involves a hearing before the OSC, the OSC plays a critical "gatekeeping" and quasi-"prosecutorial" role with respect to the other enforcement channels.

Closely related to the enforcement mechanisms referred to above are securities law provisions authorizing investigations and examinations into possible infractions, including measures for interprovincial reciprocal enforcement and assistance.

Of course, many securities industry participants are subject to the jurisdiction of stock exchanges or other recognized self-regulatory organizations, such as the Investment Dealers Association of Canada. These bodies also play a role in policing the markets.

Finally, it should be remembered that the OSA[2] provides certain civil remedies that are in addition to any remedies that might otherwise be available at common law. These statutory civil remedies may be pursued by private plaintiffs who have been harmed by particular securities law infractions. The most important of these statutory civil remedies are found in section 130 (civil liability for misrepresentations in a prospectus), section 130.1 (liability for misrepresentations in an offering memorandum),[3] section 131 (liability for misrepresentations in a take-over bid circular, an issuer bid circular, or a director's circular), section 133 (liability for nondelivery of a required prospectus or bid document), and section 134 (liability for certain insider-trading violations). These civil remedies are discussed in the chapters dealing with the obligations that these remedies are designed to enforce and, accordingly, are not dealt with further here.

1) *Criminal Code*

There are at least six sections of the *Criminal Code* that describe offences that relate to trading in securities. Perhaps the most important of these is section 400, which provides that it is an indictable offence to engage in the following activities:

> [make, circulate, or publish] a prospectus, a statement or an account, whether written or oral, [known to be] false in a material particular with intent

---

2   *Securities Act* (Ontario), R.S.O. 1990, c. S.5 [*OSA*].
3   For a discussion of s. 130.1, see Chapter 7.

(a) to induce persons, whether ascertained or not, to become share-holders or partners in a company,

(b) to deceive or defraud the members, shareholders or creditors, whether ascertained or not, of a company, or

(c) to induce any person to

(i) entrust or advance anything to a company, or

(ii) enter into any security for the benefit of a company[4]

A person convicted of an offence under section 400 is liable to a maximum penalty of ten years' imprisonment.

The other relevant offences in the *Criminal Code* are found in sections 380 to 384. Among other things, these sections make it a criminal offence to engage in any of the following acts:

- "[Affecting] the public market price of stocks, [or] shares" "by deceit, falsehood or other fraudulent means ... with intent to defraud"[5]
- Using the mails "for the purpose of transmitting...circulars concerning schemes devised or intended to deceive or defraud the public, or for the purpose of obtaining money under false pretences"[6]
- Manipulating the price of traded securities through devices known colloquially as matched orders and wash sales[7]
- Committing certain acts "with intent to make gain or profit by the rise or fall in price of the stock of an incorporated or unincorporated company" but without the intention of actually acquiring or selling, as the case may be, such shares[8]
- Selling shares (in the case of a broker who holds shares purchased on margin for a customer) in the same issuer from his or her (that is the broker's) own account where that sale intentionally reduces the amount of such shares that the broker ought to be carrying for all of his or her customers[9]

These *Criminal Code* provisions were in place well before the dawn of the modern era of complex securities laws and the evolution of well-funded provincial securities regulatory authorities. The existence of both federal and provincial legislation in this area prompts the peren-

---

4   *Criminal Code*, R.S.C. 1985, c. C-46.
5   *Ibid.* s. 380(2).
6   *Ibid.* s. 381.
7   *Ibid.* s. 382.
8   *Ibid.* s. 383(1).
9   *Ibid.* s. 384; *OSA Regulation*, R.R.O. 1990, Reg. 1015 [*OSA Regulation*], s. 47.

nial Canadian constitutional law question. Because many of the actions prohibited by the *Criminal Code*, as described above, also constitute offences under provincial securities statutes, are the relevant provincial or federal legislative provisions *ultra vires* the respective legislature that purports to enact them?

This issue was confronted squarely by the Supreme Court of Canada in *R. v. Smith*.[10] In Smith, the court determined that there was "no repugnancy"[11] between what is now section 400 of the *Criminal Code* and the legislative predecessor to what is now section 122 of the *OSA*. The court concluded that the *OSA* and *Criminal Code* provisions could continue to co-exist because the provincial provision was not one "the pith and substance of which is to prohibit an act with penal consequences."[12] The main purpose of the provincial enactment was, instead, "to ensure the registration of persons and companies before they are permitted to trade in securities, coupled with what is essentially the registration of the securities themselves."[13] The prohibition and penal consequences of the *OSA* section were "merely incidental."[14] Accordingly, the *OSA* section did not constitute criminal law and so did not encroach on a matter of exclusive federal legislative authority.

2) Quasi-criminal Prosecution

a) Offences

Subsection 122(1) of the *OSA* creates a number of specific securities law offences. Two of these offences relate to including false, misleading, or incomplete information in various disclosure documents or in submissions to securities regulators.[15] The third is a catch-all offence committed whenever a person or company "contravenes Ontario securities law."[16]

In each case, on conviction, the guilty party is normally liable to a maximum fine of $1 million, or a term of imprisonment of two years, or both. The maximum fine can actually exceed $1 million, though, in respect of one particular *OSA* breach: namely, a violation of section 76,

---

10   [1960] S.C.R. 776 [*Smith*].
11   *Ibid.* at 780.
12   *Ibid.*
13   *Ibid.* at 781.
14   *Ibid.* at 780.
15   *OSA*, above note 2, s. 122(1)(a) & (b).
16   *Ibid.* s. 122(1)(c).

which prohibits unlawful insider trading.[17] The special rules that apply in such a case are discussed further below.

Although these quasi-criminal offences are tried before a judge, the role of the OSC is still fundamental. A prosecution under section 122 cannot be commenced unless the OSC consents.[18] Once the OSC consents, OSC staff assist in the prosecution function.

Because a person convicted of an offence under section 122 may be subject to a fine, imprisonment, or both, persons charged with such offences are afforded the procedural protections available to those charged with criminal offences. This means, among other things, that prosecutors bear the burden of proving their case "beyond a reasonable doubt." This is not an insignificant fact particularly because the OSC has discretion to decide how to proceed against an alleged securities law violater. Some of the implications of this discretion were canvassed in the recent Ontario Court of Appeal decision, *Wilder* v. *Ontario (Securities Commission)*[19] which is discussed further below.

b)   Unlawful Insider Trading

Special fines may be imposed when a person or company is convicted of engaging in unlawful insider trading. Insider trading is dealt with in greater detail in chapter 8. For the purposes of this chapter, one needs to recall only that unlawful insider trading can generate significant ill-gotten gains. Regulators may find sophisticated unlawful insider-trading activities difficult both to detect and to prosecute successfully. This combination of high potential gains for violators and low probability of detection represents a serious challenge for regulators. The need to address this challenge in order to deter insider-trading accounts for the *OSA*'s additional insider-trading penalties. A person or company convicted of insider trading, contrary to section 76 of the *OSA*, is liable to a fine that is not limited to $1 million, but that can be as great as "an amount equal to triple the profit made or loss avoided ... by reason of the contravention."[20]

The terms "profit made" and "loss avoided" are specifically defined for the purposes of section 122.[21] It should be emphasized that this provision refers to a *fine* and not — as occasionally encountered in U.S. regulatory statutes — "treble *damages*." However, a separate section of

---

17   *Ibid.* s. 122(4).
18   *Ibid.* s. 122(7).
19   (2001), 53 O.R. (3d) 519 (C.A.), aff'g (2000), 47 O.R. (3d) 361 (Div. Ct.) [*Wilder*].
20   *OSA*, above note 2, s. 122(4)(b).
21   *Ibid.* s. 122(6).

the *OSA* provides for statutory civil liability for unlawful insider trading.[22] The civil damages to which a guilty party is exposed are not a multiple of the profit made or losses avoided by that person, but rather are based on the actual losses incurred by the innocent party to the offending trade. Where an "insider, affiliate or associate" of a reporting issuer carries out a wrongful trading in the securities of that issuer, the errant trader is also liable to account to the issuer itself.[23]

3) Administrative Enforcement Action

a) Introduction

The OSC has the authority under section 127 of the *OSA* to make various orders in the public interest. Orders under section 127 may provide, among other things, for the following:

- Suspension or termination of registration or recognition under securities law or imposition of conditions in respect of such a registration or recognition
- Cessation of all trading in a specific security (a "cease trade order")
- Removal of exemptions otherwise provided for by securities law
- A review of a market participant's practices
- Relief from provision or amendment of certain disclosure documents by a market participant
- Reprimand of a person or company
- Forced resignation of a person as an officer or director of an issuer, or prohibition against a person becoming an officer or director of an issuer

The OSC may make an order under section 127 of the *OSA* only after a hearing.[24]

A number of important observations relating to section 127 merit brief mention here, including the following:

- *No Power to Fine*: The OSC, unlike regulators in several other Canadian jurisdictions, has no power to impose fines (or "administrative penalties") under section 127.[25]

---

22   *Ibid.* s. 134.
23   *Ibid.* s. 134(4)
24   *Ibid.* s. 127(4)
25   Legislation in Alberta (*Securities Act*, S.A. c. S-6.1, s. 165.1), British Columbia (*Securities Act*, R.S.B.C. 1996, c. 418, s. 162), Nova Scotia (*Securities Act*, R.S.N.S. 1989 c. 418, s. 135), and Saskatchewan (*The Securities Act*, S.S. 1988-89, c. S-42.2, s. 135.1(2)(a)) provide for the levying of monetary penalties by

- *Power to Reprimand Any Person or Company*: The OSC's enforcement power is not limited to registrants under the *OSA* or even to market participants,[26] but rather extends to any "person or company."
- *Preventive vs. Remedial*: The OSC's public interest jurisdiction allows it to act only to prevent future abuses, not to punish past conduct.
- *Actions Triggering the Commission's Public Interest Discretion*: The OSC has, from time to time, purported to exercise its public interest jurisdiction to prevent actions it perceives to be abusive, even where the letter of the law has not been violated.
- *The Bluntness of the Cease Trade Order*: Not infrequently, a cease trade order can actually harm the very people (public investors) that the OSC is seeking to protect.
- *Appropriate Standard of Judicial Review*: Courts have shown the OSC considerable deference by adopting an intermediate standard of judicial review when a decision of the OSC has been appealed.
- *Enforcement of Commission Decisions*: OSC decisions can become enforceable as orders.

Each of these matters is discussed briefly below.

b) No Power to Fine

Although the OSC has no authority to impose fines pursuant to section 127, it does have the power to make an award of costs in respect of any hearing or investigation. It has also adopted the practice, in certain cases, of negotiating substantial settlement payments in some high-profile section 127 cases.

The statutory authority for the OSC to make costs awards is found in section 127.1 of the *OSA*. The power in section 127.1 is broad, and permits the OSC to make an order for costs following a hearing, even if a person or company was not found to be in breach of securities law, provided that the OSC considers that such person or company "has not acted in the public interest."[27]

One of the most recent examples of a negotiated settlement payment occurred in connection with the 2000 RT Capital "high-closing" matter.[28] Pursuant to its settlement with the OSC, RT Capital agreed to pay $3 million, "to be allocated to such third parties as the Commission

---

the securities commission in these provinces. In most cases, the maximum administrative penalty is $100,000, but in Alberta, in the case of offences committed by persons or companies other than individuals, the maximum penalty is $500,000.

26 *OSA*, above note 2, s. 1(1) (definition of "market participant").

27 *Ibid.* s. 127.1(2)(b).

28 (2000), 23 OSCB 5177.

may determine for purposes that will benefit investors in Ontario."[29] Other recent examples are referred to elsewhere in this book.[30]

In Canadian jurisdictions where securities regulators have the power to impose administrative penalties, it has occasionally been argued that such penalties ought to be regarded as penal, rather than administrative, in nature. The significance of such a characterization is, among other things, that individuals subject to such sanctions ought to enjoy the protections afforded by section 11 of the *Canadian Charter of Rights and Freedoms*.[31] The British Columbia Supreme Court recently rejected this argument when it concluded that "fines imposed by the Commission are properly classified as administrative."[32]

c) Power to Reprimand Any Person or Company

In most Ontario statutes, the word "person" includes a corporation.[33] Under the *OSA*, however, the word "person" does not include incorporated entities.[34] Instead, the *OSA* uses the term "company" when the drafters wish to refer to incorporated bodies.[35] Accordingly, the phrase "person or company" occurs throughout the *OSA* whenever a provision is intended to apply not only to individuals, but also to associations of all sorts — incorporated or otherwise. It is this broad phrase that appears in paragraph 127(1)6. Based on the plain meaning of these words, it might seem uncontentious to conclude that the OSC has the authority to reprimand anyone when it appears to be in the public interest to do so. However, such an interpretation was recently challenged on behalf of an Ontario lawyer in a case before the Ontario Court of Appeal, *Wilder v. Ontario (Securities Commission)*.[36]

In *Wilder*, the OSC sought to hold a hearing pursuant to section 127 to determine whether certain statements made to the OSC by a

---

29   Settlement Agreement, para. 48(f). Available online at <http://www.osc.gov.on.ca> (site accessed: 27 February 2002).

30   See, e.g., chapter 9 of this book for a discussion of a settlement payment made by Air Canada in 2001 in connection with selective disclosure, and chapter 4 for discussion of settlement payments made by three U.S.-based online brokerage firms in connection with trading activities conducted in the absence of Canadian registration.

31   Part I of the *Constitution Act, 1982*, being Schedule B to the *Canada Act 1982*, (U.K.), 1982, c. 11 [*Charter*].

32   *Johnson v. British Columbia (Securities Commission)* [1999] B.C.J. No. 552 at para. 112 (S.C.) aff'd but with cross appeal allowed, [2001] B.C.J. No. 2103 (C.A.).

33   *Interpretation Act* (Ontario), R.S.O. 1990, c. I.11, s. 29(1).

34   *OSA*, above note 2, s. 1(1).

35   *Ibid.*

36   *Wilder*, above note 19.

lawyer in the course of representing a client were misleading, untrue, or incomplete, and if appropriate based on such determination, to determine whether or not to reprimand the lawyer. The lawyer challenged the OSC's jurisdiction to conduct such a hearing, making the following three arguments:

1. The allegations against him fell squarely within the wording of section 122, but by choosing to proceed under section 127, rather than pursuing the matter in the courts under section 122, the OSC denied the applicant certain procedural advantages (including the benefit of the criminal burden of proof).
2. A reprimand is punitive in nature and therefore beyond the powers of the OSC, which has only a remedial jurisdiction (as discussed in section (d) below).
3. Only the Law Society of Upper Canada, the governing body of the Ontario legal profession, ought to have the authority to discipline Ontario lawyers acting in the course of their professional practices.

The applicant's arguments were rejected, first by the Ontario Divisional Court, and then by the Ontario Court of Appeal. Some observers were surprised by this outcome in light of the history of section 127. Prior to 1994, the OSC had no authority to issue reprimands. In February 1990, the OSC published a discussion paper that contained a proposed set of amendments to the enforcement provisions of the *OSA*.[37] Included in that discussion paper was a proposal that the OSC be given the power "[t]o order a private or public reprimand of a person (including a lawyer ...) for misconduct in the marketplace, either with or without further sanctions attached."[38]

Subsequently, in May 1991, new draft proposed amendments were published.[39] These proposed amendments included provisions that would have empowered the OSC to discipline "a professional person or company acting in a professional capacity" where such person or company "has counseled a breach of the securities law, assisted in conduct which constitutes a breach of the securities law, or provided an opinion, advice or information to the Commission or its staff which is deceptive or misleading."[40]

Many members of the practising bar objected to the proposal to grant the OSC such disciplinary powers. When the enforcement provi-

---

37   (1990), 13 OSCB 405.
38   *Ibid.* at 421.
39   (1991), 14 OSCB 1907.
40   *Ibid.* at 1945.

sions of the *OSA* were finally amended in 1994, the amendments made no specific reference to the OSC's power to reprimand "professional persons." Accordingly, many lawyers critical of the original proposals assumed that the OSC had relented in its pursuit for the power to discipline professionals. These critics appear to have been mistaken. Swinton J. of the Ontario Divisional Court reviewed much of this history in the *Wilder* decision and rejected the argument that the legislature's failure to include specific reference to professionals meant that the words "person or company" were to be read as though they excluded professionals.[41]

d) Preventive or Remedial Power?

The OSC interprets its power under section 127 as wholly remedial, rather than punitive. For example, in *Re Mithras Management Ltd.*,[42] the OSC explained its role as follows:

> We are not here to punish past conduct; that is the role of the courts ... We are here to restrain, as best we can, future conduct that is likely to be prejudicial to the public interest in having capital markets that are both fair and efficient.[43]

The Supreme Court of Canada, in its 2001 decision in *Committee for Equal Treatment of Asbestos Minority Shareholders v. Ontario (Securities Commission)*[44] agreed with this limitation on the OSC's powers:

> [P]ursuant to s. 127(1), the OSC has the jurisdiction and a broad discretion to intervene in Ontario capital markets if it is in the public interest to do so. However, the discretion to act in the public interest is not unlimited. In exercising its discretion, the OSC should consider the protection of investors and the efficiency of, and public confidence in, capital markets generally. In addition, s. 127(1) is a regulatory provision. The sanctions under this section are preventive in nature and prospective in orientation. Therefore, s. 127 cannot be used merely to remedy *Securities Act* misconduct alleged to have caused harm or damages to private parties or individuals.[45]

The distinction between remedial and punitive jurisdiction is far from a mere technical issue. If the OSC has no remedial power under section 127 of the *OSA*, then it would be improper for the OSC to make an

---

41   *Wilder*, above note 19.
42   (1990), 13 OSCB 1600.
43   *Ibid.* at 1610–11.
44   2001 SCC 37 [*Asbestos Shareholders*].
45   *Ibid.* at para.45.

order against a person or company, no matter how abusive such person or company's actions were, unless making such an order would prevent future abuses. Indeed, in the *Asbestos Shareholders* case, the OSC concluded that certain actions of the Quebec Government and the Société nationale de l'amiante were "abusive of minority shareholders and were manifestly unfair."[46] Yet, the OSC declined to make an order under subsection 127(1) because of its concerns as to whether the impugned actions had a sufficient connection to Ontario. As indicated by both the Ontario Court of Appeal[47] and the Supreme Court of Canada,[48] such a consideration was perfectly appropriate. After all, the OSC's public interest jurisdiction under section 127 cannot be exercised to punish wrongdoers for past abuses. It can be invoked only if it is necessary to prevent future harm to Ontario's capital markets.

e) Actions Triggering the OSC's Jurisdiction

One of the more controversial aspects of the OSC's public interest jurisdiction has now become well-settled law. The OSC clearly has the authority to make an order under section 127 where there has been no breach of securities law. This proposition was advanced by the OSC in its 1978 decision in *Re Cablecasting Ltd.*[49] There the OSC expressly held that it has the authority to issue a cease trade order to stop a proposed transaction that violated no law, but that nevertheless contravened the "intent" of securities regulation.[50] Nine years later, the OSC reiterated the proposition in *Re Canadian Tire Corp.*,[51] a decision that was upheld by the Ontario Divisional Court. The legal basis for this position is twofold. First, there is nothing in section 127 that specifically makes the OSC's granting of an order under that section conditional on a finding of a breach of the law. Second, as a matter of policy, the OSC could be severely constrained from fulfilling its mandate to prevent market abuses if it were not permitted to act until the letter of the law was contravened. Accordingly, it is clear that the OSC may, and will, act when securities laws or policies have been breached, as well as when the "animating principles"[52] of securities regulation are violated. The OSC,

---

46   (1994), 17 OSCB 3537 at 3560.
47   (1999), 43 O.R.(3d) 257 (C.A.).
48   *Asbestos Shareholders*, above note 44.
49   [1978] OSCB 37 [*Cablecasting*].
50   *Ibid.* p. 41. Although the OSC found that it had the authority to issue a cease trade order even in the absence of an express violation of securities law, it ultimately decided not to issue such an order in the *Cablecasting* matter.
51   (1987), 35 B.L.R. 56, aff'd (1987), 59 O.R. (2d) 79 (Div. Ct.).
52   *Ibid.* at 100 (cited to B.L.R.).

however, recognizes that, in the absence of an actual contravention of securities law or policy, it must "proceed with caution."[53]

Although the OSC's power to act in the absence of an express violation of the law has been upheld by the courts, it remains a source of some concern to securities practitioners and others. For practising lawyers, the difficulty of a regime in which action may be taken for violations of the "spirit" of a law are obvious. One leading Canadian securities practitioner, James Turner, explains that "lawyers shouldn't be giving advice based on what they *think* a regulator *thinks* the law should be."[54] Of course, it should be emphasized that, as the Supreme Court of Canada has recently confirmed, the OSC's discretion, although broad, is by no means unlimited.[55]

f) The Bluntness of the Cease-Trade Order

One enforcement tool that has long been available to Canadian securities regulators is the "cease-trade order," which is an order forbidding the trading in securities of an issuer.[56] One well-recognized shortcoming of the cease-trade order is that it can be a very imprecise enforcement weapon. For example, where an issuer is in default of its obligations under securities laws, regulators may impose a cease-trade order in an effort to compel the issuer to bring itself into compliance. However, the immediate effects of such a cease-trade order are felt, not by the issuer, but by the holders of the securities that have been cease-traded who become unable to deal with their interests. This is a particularly unfortunate and paradoxical outcome because the goal of the regulators is to help investors, not hurt them.

The OSC has recognized this problem, and has sought to address the matter recently by introducing the concept of a "Management and Insider Cease Trade Order" in OSC Policy 57-603.[57] Briefly, Policy 57-603 indicates that, where an issuer has failed to file certain financial statements as required by the *OSA*, a cease-trade order can be issued to affect only the securities of the defaulting issuer held by specified managers and insiders. The OSC has indicated that this would be the only

---

53   *Ibid.* at 99.
54   James E.A. Turner, "Comments on 'Gatekeepers and the Commission: The Role of Professionals in the Regulatory System'," in *Securities Regulation: Issues and Perspectives — Papers Presented at the Queen's Annual Business Law Symposium 1994* (Toronto: Carswell, 1995) at 270.
55   *Asbestos Shareholders*, above note 44.
56   See, e.g., *OSA*, above note 2, s. 127(1)2.
57   (2001), 24 OSCB 2700.

cease-trade order issued, provided the issuer remedies the default within two months and publishes information in compliance with the "Alternative Information Guidelines" referred to in Policy 57-603 during the period of default.

g) Appropriate Standard of Judicial Review

As discussed in Chapter 3, final decisions of the OSC may generally be appealed to the Ontario Divisional Court.[58] The OSC is an administrative tribunal and, accordingly, appeals of OSC decisions must be considered in light of the applicable principles of administrative law. One important administrative law principle relates to the proper standard of review a court must apply when reviewing a tribunal decision.

Traditionally, courts have shown considerable deference to such OSC decisions on appeal. More technically, courts have held consistently that the appropriate standard of judicial review for OSC decisions on issues relating to its specialized expertise is that of "reasonableness." Unless the court finds the OSC's decision on such a matter unreasonable, it will not be overturned. The court need not agree with the correctness of the OSC's decision. Iacobucci J. explained this standard in a recent Supreme Court of Canada decision:

> [I]t cannot be contested that the OSC is a specialized tribunal with a wide discretion to intervene in the public interest and that the protection of the public interest is a matter falling within the core of the OSC's expertise. Therefore, although there is no privative clause shielding decisions of the OSC from review by the courts, that body's relative expertise in the regulation of the capital markets, the purpose of the Act as a whole and s. 127(1) in particular, and the nature of the problem before the OSC, all militate in favour of a high degree of curial deference. However, as there is a statutory right of appeal from the decision of the OSC to the courts, when this factor is considered with all the other factors, an intermediate standard of review is indicated. Accordingly, the standard of review in this case is one of reasonableness.[59]

It should be emphasized that this intermediate standard of review is not necessarily applicable when the OSC renders decisions outside of its area of expertise. In certain instances, where the OSC is called on to render decisions on general matters of law outside of its specialized

---

58   *OSA*, above note 2, s. 9(1).
59   *Asbestos Shareholders*, above note 44 at para. 49.

area of expertise, the standard of review is the more demanding "correctness" standard.[60]

h) Enforcement of Commission Decisions

Although the OSC is not a court, decisions of the OSC may be filed with, and thereby become enforceable as orders of, the Superior Court of Justice.[61]

4) Civil Court Proceedings

a) Introduction

In addition to the OSC's own fairly limited administrative sanctions and the quasi-criminal enforcement mechanism for which it essentially acts as a gatekeeper, the OSC has the power under the *OSA* to apply to the Ontario Superior Court for a declaration and a consequent remedial order in cases of securities law violations. The power to bring such an application is set out in section 128 of the *OSA*. The court has broad remedial powers under section 128 and is free to exercise those powers to make any order, notwithstanding any penalties or administrative sanctions already imposed under sections 122 and 127 for the same violations.

Section 128 lists sixteen specific orders that a court is authorized to make, but makes it clear that this list is not intended to be exhaustive.[62] Among other things, the court is specifically authorized under section 128 to order a person or company to pay compensation, make restitution,[63] and pay general or punitive damages.[64]

However, it is for the OSC alone to determine whether or not to seek an order that an issuer is not in compliance with the *OSA*. An individual investor does not have the authority to do so. Breach of the *OSA*, unless specifically provided, does not entitle individuals to a private right of action.[65]

b) Actions on Behalf of an Issuer

As discussed in Chapter 8, when a person in a special relationship with a reporting issuer violates the *OSA*'s insider-trading prohibitions, that

---

60 See, e.g., *Coughlan v. WMC International Ltd.*, [2000] O.J. No. 5109 at para. 34 [*Coughlan*].

61 *OSA*, above note 2, s. 151.

62 *Ibid.* s. 128(3).

63 *Ibid.* s. 128(3)13.

64 *Ibid.* s. 128(3)14.

65 See, e.g., *Stern v. Imasco Ltd.*, [1999] O.J. No. 4235 (Sup. Ct.).

person, among other things, is accountable to the reporting issuer.[66] There are similar remedies available when persons or companies improperly make use of special information concerning the investment program of a mutual fund or portfolio manager.[67] The obvious problem with such statutory civil remedies is that the onus is on the issuer to bring the action. Yet, the insider (or insiders) who breached the prohibitions may be the same corporate officers or directors who normally decide whether to authorize the issuer to commence legal proceedings. Concerns of precisely this sort led to the regime for pursuing derivative actions found in modern Canadian corporate statutes.[68] The *OSA* provides for a similar derivative-type action to assist in the enforcement of claims under subsections 134(3) and 134(4). Section 135 provides for this action. Where a reporting issuer or mutual fund has a cause of action under section 134, but does not pursue it, the OSC, or any securityholder of the reporting issuer or mutual fund, may apply to the court for an order permitting the OSC or the securityholder to commence or continue the action.

5) Limitation Period

Section 129.1 of the *OSA* imposes a general six-year limitation period from the date of the occurrence of the last event on which the proceeding is based for the commencement of enforcement proceedings. Before a 1994 amendment to this provision, the limitation period began to run from the date on which "the facts upon which the proceedings are based first came to the knowledge of the Commission." Needless to say, this language gave rise to difficult interpretation questions.[69] It must be noted that section 129.1 is a default provision that applies only in the absence of specific limitation periods provided for elsewhere in the statute. Various other limitation periods are so provided elsewhere, including section 138, which provides shorter limitation periods for the *OSA*'s statutory civil remedies, and section 136, which provides shorter limitation periods for actions that seek the rescission of certain contracts.

---

66 *OSA*, above note 2, s. 134(4).
67 *Ibid.* s. 134(3).
68 See, e.g., *Canada Business Corporations Act*, R.S.C. 1985, c. C-44 [*CBCA*], s. 239. For an excellent discussion of the policy concerns surrounding derivative actions, see Robert W.V. Dickerson et al., *Commentary*, vol. 1 of *Proposals for a New Canadian Business Corporations Law for Canada* (Ottawa: Information Canada, 1971) at 160–165.
69 See, e.g., *Lewis v. Fingold* (1999), 22 OSCB 2811.

b) Investigations, Examinations, and Interim Property Preservation Orders

a) Power to Order

The *OSA* gives the OSC broad powers to order investigations[70] as well as rather narrower powers to order financial examinations of market participants[71] to further the OSC's mandate to regulate capital markets and enforce compliance with securities laws. The power to order both an investigation and an examination may be exercised, not only to enforce Ontario securities law, but also "to assist in the due administration of the securities laws or the regulation of the capital markets in another jurisdiction."[72]

The constitutional validity of this extraterritorial aspect of the comparable investigation power in the British Columbia *Securities Act*[73] was recently upheld by the Supreme Court of Canada in *Global Securities Corp. v. British Columbia (Securities Commission).*[74]

As well, the OSC has the power, in certain instances, to issue a direction to any person or company requiring that person or company to retain and hold "funds, securities or property of any person or company."[75]

b) *Charter* Implications

The *OSA* gives broad powers to persons carrying out such an investigation or examination including the power to summon witnesses and to compel them to testify under oath.[76] This statutory power has proved controversial and has been the subject of litigation. In *British Columbia Securities Commission v. Branch,*[77] for example, the Supreme Court of Canada considered a provision in the British Columbia *Securities Act* similar to section 13 of the *OSA*, and rejected the argument that the provision offended sections 7 and 8 of the *Canadian Charter of Rights and Freedoms.*[78] Writing for the majority, Sopinka and Iacobucci JJ. quoted from the court's earlier decision in *Pezim v. British*

---

70   *OSA*, above note 2, s. 11.
71   *Ibid.* s. 12.
72   *Ibid.* ss. 11(1)(b), & 12(1)(b).
73   R.S.B.C. 1996, c. 418.
74   [2000] 1 S.C.R. 494.
75   *OSA*, above note 2, s. 126.
76   *Ibid.* s. 13.
77   [1995] 2 S.C.R. 3 [*Branch*].
78   Above note 31.

Columbia (Superintendent of Brokers),[79] and stated that the "protective role" of securities commissions "gives a special character to such bodies which must be recognized when assessing the way in which their functions are carried out under their Acts."[80] The court found that the purpose of the British Columbia *Securities Act* "justifies inquiries of limited scope" that serve "an obvious social utility"[81] and necessarily involve compelling testimony. Because the testimony is not elicited for the purposes of incriminating the deponents and the individuals would be entitled to claim evidentiary immunity (i.e., to ensure that any evidence taken is not subsequently used against them), the court concluded that the provision did not violate section 7 of the *Charter*. As for section 8 of the *Charter*, the court noted that what is an "unreasonable" search or seizure depends on the context. It cited with approval the observation of La Forest J. in *Thomson Newspapers Ltd. v. Canada (Director of Investigation and Research, Restrictive Trade Practices Commission)*,[82] that "the degree of privacy the citizen can reasonably expect may vary significantly depending on the activity that brings him or her into contact with the state."[83] Applying this principle to the securities arena, the majority of the court asserted that "in our opinion, persons involved in the business of trading securities do not have a high expectation of privacy with respect to regulatory needs that have been generally expressed in securities legislation."[84] This low expectation of privacy, coupled with the relatively unobtrusive method of demand for production contemplated by the British Columbia *Securities Act* and the nature of the documents to be produced (i.e., business, rather than personal documents) satisfied the majority of the court that the provisions do not contravene section 8 of the *Charter*.

c) Confidentiality of Information

The fact that the OSC can compel the creation of such an evidentiary record, however, gives rise to an additional issue. To whom, and under what circumstances, should such information become available?

Sections 16 and 17 of the *OSA* provide a (partial) statutory answer to some of these questions. Section 16 states that orders made under section 11 or section 12 are confidential and can be disclosed only as permitted under section 17. Similarly, all information acquired pursuant

---

79   [1994] 2 S.C.R. 557 [*Pezim*].
80   *Ibid.* at 595.
81   *Branch*, above note 77 at 27–28..
82   [1990] 1 S.C.R. 425.
83   *Ibid.* at 506.
84   *Branch*, above note 77 at 39.

to section 13, including the name of anyone examined, is not to be disclosed. The restrictions delineated in section 16 apply to everyone with knowledge of an order made under section 11 or section 12, or of an examination conducted under section 13, including the OSC itself.

Section 17 outlines a series of exceptions to these prohibitions against disclosure. These exceptions, for example, permit a court, in the context of a prosecution initiated by the OSC, to compel production to enable a defendant to make a full answer and defence.[85] Moreover, a person conducting an investigation or examination under the *OSA* is permitted to disclose or produce information for the purpose of conducting the examination, or for the purpose of a proceeding initiated by the OSC.[86] Much of section 17 is concerned with the circumstances under which the OSC can authorize the disclosure of information when the OSC considers "that it would be in the public interest" to do so.[87]

In *Biscotti v. Ontario Securities Commission*,[88] the Ontario Court of Appeal considered the principles that ought to guide the OSC in determining whether to disclose information acquired pursuant to an OSC-ordered investigation. *Biscotti* was decided prior to the statutory amendments that added sections 16 and 17 to the *OSA*, but the Ontario Divisional Court has recently suggested that the current statutory scheme is essentially a codification of the prior law, including *Biscotti*.[89]

In *Coughlan v. WMC International Ltd.*,[90] the Ontario Divisional Court overturned the OSC's decision to permit certain transcripts and other documents produced in connection with a section 13 investigation to be disclosed to a third party (Westminer). Westminer was a defendant to a civil action commenced in another jurisdiction (Nova Scotia) and argued that the information was relevant to its defence of that action.

The investigation in the *Coughlan* case had its genesis in a failed Nova Scotia gold mining company. Westminer had acquired control of the company by way of a hostile take-over bid in 1988. Westminer subsequently discovered that the company did not, in fact, possess valuable gold reserves and so alleged that the former CEO (Coughlan) had made misrepresentations about the firm. The OSC conducted an investigation that included examining Coughlan under oath.

---

85   *OSA*, above note 2, s. 17(5).
86   *Ibid.* s. 17(6).
87   *Ibid.* s. 17(1).
88   (1991), 1 O.R. (3d) 409 (C.A.) [*Biscotti*].
89   *Coughlan*, above note 60 at para. 15.
90   *Ibid.*

Westminer sued Coughlan (and others) in Ontario. Coughlan, in turn, sued Westminer in Nova Scotia, alleging conspiracy to injure. Coughlan's Nova Scotia action succeeded. The court there held, among other things, that Coughlan had acted honestly and in good faith, and had not breached the *OSA*. However, in the meantime, Coughlan attempted to form and finance a new company. When the underwriter engaged to help finance the new company learned of the pending Ontario action against Coughlan, it withdrew. The new company then collapsed, and certain guarantors of the company's debts were required to honour their guarantees. Those guarantors brought the Nova Scotia action against Westminer that then prompted Westminer to seek disclosure of the evidence previously furnished by Coughlan to the OSC.

In ruling that the OSC's decision to permit such disclosure was unreasonable, the Ontario Divisional Court noted, in addition to a number of circumstances unique to the case, that, as a general matter, the public interest in maintaining the confidentiality of such information did not end when the OSC's investigation ended or when the limitation period under the *OSA* for commencing proceedings had elapsed. Although these matters certainly should be relevant factors in considering the issue of whether disclosure is in the public interest, they cannot, in the Ontario Divisional Court's view, be determinative. Moreover, the OSC gave Coughlan express assurances of confidentiality. The court held that, although the OSC is not bound in law to honour such assurances, they ought not to be "simply dismissed out of hand as 'not binding.'"[91] Closely related to this general notion of respect for prior assurances of confidentiality is the legal doctrine of legitimate expectations. In this case, Coughlan argued that he had a legitimate expectation that confidentiality would be respected. The court reiterated that, although the OSC "was not bound by the doctrine of legitimate expectations to exercise its discretion in a particular way,"[92] it certainly ought to have taken the doctrine into account. Finally, the court was critical of the OSC's procedure for disclosure. Specifically, the court said that the OSC ought to have inspected the material to be disclosed to determine whether only part of the material obtained would need to be disclosed, given the specific policy reason being invoked to justify the disclosure.

---

91   *Ibid.* at para. 58.
92   *Ibid.* at para. 61.

d) Costs

As indicated in section 3(b) above of this chapter, the OSC also has the authority, in certain circumstances, and following a hearing on the matter, to order a person or company who was the subject of an investigation to pay the costs of the investigation.[93]

C. STOCK EXCHANGES AND SELF-REGULATORY ORGANIZATIONS (SROs)

The OSC plays the primary role in the enforcement of securities laws. But, securities exchanges,[94] such as the Toronto Stock Exchange (TSE), and self-regulatory organizations,[95] such as the Investment Dealers Association of Canada (IDA) and Market Regulation Services Inc. (RS Inc.), also have an essential part to play in policing their members and others.

The TSE, for example, regulates the conduct of companies whose securities are listed on the TSE and participating organizations[96] (i.e., the securities firms that have access to the TSE trading system; prior to the April 2000 demutualization of the TSE, such firms would have been known as "Members" of the TSE).

The TSE has two principal enforcement tools with respect to listed companies: suspension of trading and delisting of an issuer's securities. The criteria used by the TSE in making suspension or delisting decisions are set out in the *Toronto Stock Exchange, Company Manual.*[97]

---

93   *OSA*, above note 2, s. 127.1.

94   A stock exchange may carry on business in Ontario only if it is recognized by the OSC (*OSA*, s. 21(1)).

95   A "self-regulatory organization" is defined in the *OSA* as "a person or company that represents registrants and is organized for the purpose of regulating the operations and the standards of practice and business conduct of its members and their representatives with a view to promoting the protection of investors and the public interest" (*OSA*, s. 1(1)). Such organizations must apply under the *OSA* for recognition by the OSC (*OSA*, s. 21.1).

96   "Participating Organization" is defined in s. 1-101 of *The Rules of the Toronto Stock Exchange.* Available online at <http://www.tse.ca/en/pdf/TSERules.pdf> (site accessed 2 May 2002) [TSE Rules].

97   *Toronto Stock Exchange, Company Manual,* ss. 708-717. Available online at <http://www.tse.ca/en/pdf/CompanyManual0202.pdf> (site accessed: 2 May 2002).

Many of these criteria relate to financial or other matters intended to ensure that listed companies meet the quality standards of the TSE. The TSE may suspend trading in, or delist, a company's securities where the company fails to comply with any of the requirements of the TSE[98] or with any disclosure requirements imposed by the TSE's own policies or the applicable securities law.[99]

With respect to participating organizations, the TSE has broad disciplinary powers, including the power, among other things, to impose any of the following:

- Reprimands
- Fines up to $1 million or three times the amount of any financial benefit accruing to a person committing a violation
- Suspension or termination of a person's status as a participating organization.[100]

As discussed in chapter 4, however, since 1997 the TSE essentially has delegated its regulation of participating organizations to other SROs, including the IDA. The IDA has similar powers to discipline its members and certain of its members' employees when such people violate securities laws. Penalties imposed by the IDA can include reprimands, monetary penalties (similar to those of the TSE described above), and termination of rights, or expulsion from the IDA.[101] The IDA is also authorized to negotiate settlement agreements.[102] Beginning in 2002, the TSE has also effectively delegated market regulation services to Market Regulation Services Inc. (RS Inc.), as discussed in chapter 4.

D. CONCLUSION

The courts, the stock exchanges, and the self-regulatory organizations all contribute to ensuring the integrity of Canada's capital markets. But, the OSC and its counterparts in other Canadian provinces and territories bear the principal responsibility for enforcing

---

98 *Ibid.* s. 713.
99 *Ibid.* s. 714.
100 TSE Rules, above note 96 at s. 7-106(2).
101 By-Law 20, s. 20.10 of the Investment Dealers Association of Canada, available online at: <http://www.ida.ca> (site accessed: 6 September 2001).
102 *Ibid.* s. 20.25.

Canadian securities laws and principles. The increasing complexity of Canadian capital markets and the growing sophistication of market participants continue to pose significant challenges for securities regulators. In the years ahead, it is not unreasonable to anticipate that ever greater resources will be directed towards enforcement activities and, perhaps, towards investor education to curb the proliferation of abusive market practices.

CHAPTER 12

RECENT DEVELOPMENTS AND CONCLUSION

A. RECENT DEVELOPMENTS

Since the material in the previous chapters was written, there have been a number of important recent developments in securities regulation. We will touch upon three of those developments in this chapter:

- The February 2002 British Columbia Securities Commission's Concept Paper entitled, "New Concepts for Securities Regulation"
- Approval of National Instruments 54-101 and 54-102, and the imminent rescission of National Policy No. 41
- The OSC's recently announced policy to give "credit" to those who cooperate with OSC investigations

1) British Columbia Securities Commission Concept Paper

In February 2002, the British Columbia Securities Commission published a concept paper entitled "New Concepts for Securities Regulation." Arising from the British Columbia Commission's deregulation project, the concept paper's deregulation goal is evident from the notice accompanying its release.

The paper discusses six central concepts:

- A proposed continuous market access system

- A simpler registration system
- A better mutual funds regime
- New trade disclosure (i.e., insider reporting, early warning, and control person) rules
- New securities commission enforcement and public interest powers
- New civil remedies

a) Continuous Market Access System

The proposed Continuous Market Access System (CMA) is the most ambitious issuer-based disclosure system yet advanced in Canada. It would represent a considerable advance even upon the proposed integrated disclosure system (IDS) discussed in chapter 9. The basic idea underlying the CMA is that a qualifying issuer would file an initial "entry document" that would contain mandated disclosure items. Thereafter, the issuer would be obliged to keep its public disclosure record up to date with periodic and timely disclosure filings. But whenever the issuer wished to access the capital markets, no special additional filings would be needed; nor would the issuer be required to deliver any prescribed disclosure document to prospective investors. The offering could be launched with a simple press release. An issuer would not be obliged to use any particular form of offering document; and, although any offering document the issuer chose to issue would need to be filed with securities regulators, that document would not be vetted in the way that prospectuses are today. (In order to preserve the availability of the MJDS for Canadian issuers seeking to access the U.S. market, which depends upon a prospectus review by Canadian regulators, an optional alternative system involving such a review would be preserved.) Backstopping such a system would be a new regime of statutory civil liability for misrepresentations in a CMA issuer's disclosure record and a more accessible securities class action regime discussed further below. Moreover, this CMA regime would eliminate the need for the closed system. Securities of a CMA issuer could thus be freely sold and resold, without hold periods or other restrictions. Unlike the IDS, which was envisioned to provide an optional alternative to the current prospectus regime, the British Columbia Commission has suggested making the new CMA system mandatory.

Under the CMA, issuers would be subdivided into three categories: listed, unlisted, and restricted. The term "listed issuers" refers to firms whose securities are listed or posted for trading on an organized market that performs both listing and trading regulation. A listed issuer would not be required to have an underwriter involved to perform due diligence at the time of its first public offering.

Unlisted issuers would be CMA issuers with no such exchange listing. Such issuers could, by complying with the CMA's disclosure rules, have access to the CMA system. However, unlike a listed issuer, an unlisted issuer would be required to engage an underwriter (or other appropriate due diligence provider.) The concept paper suggests that it is important to permit unlisted issuers to have access to the CMA system because, the report writers note, "we are entering an era of international competition among marketplaces, many of which will not offer issuer regulation or trading regulation. In this environment it seems doubtful that we will be able to sustain our current policies."

Finally, there may be issuers who do not wish to comply with the disclosure obligations of the CMA. Those issuers would therefore remain outside the CMA system and are dubbed "restricted issuers" in the concept paper. Securities of such restricted issuers could be sold only to a limited class of investors — essentially the same investors permitted to buy securities on an exempt basis under various existing and proposed British Columbia and Alberta prospectus exemptions.

The proposal would also accommodate foreign issuers in Canada by permitting such issuers, subject to credible regulation in their home jurisdiction, to become "approved foreign issuers," and so participate in the CMA system.

b) Simpler Registration System

In place of the current rule-based dealer registration system, the concept paper proposes a new principles-based code of conduct. The proposal also includes suggestions for a national "passport" registration system, based upon mutual recognition of, or mutual reliance upon, other provinces' registration requirements. (This proposal would go well beyond the currently proposed National Registration Database (NRD) discussed in chapter 4. Although the NRD provides for national registration, it makes no attempt to harmonize standards nationally or permit mutual recognition of differing provincial standards.) Finally, the paper introduces the possibility that only securities *firms* (rather than individuals) need be registered. (The onus would then fall upon the firm to ensure that its employees complied with all necessary standards.) Foreign registrants would also be permitted under certain circumstances to carry on business in Canada without registering, provided they did not solicit business from Canadians. SROs would be the principal guardians of registrant proficiency (although proficiency standards would be prescribed for any registrants that were not members of SROs.) Although the proposal would expand the latitude of firms to ensure the proficiency of their employees, it would also provide investors with additional avenues of redress, specifically new statutory rights of civil liability against registrants and their employees, and new Commission enforcement powers, including powers to order wayward firms to disgorge improperly earned profits.

c) Better Mutual Funds Regime

The "principles over rules" philosophy reflected in the registration proposals also underlies the paper's suggestion to replace the existing mutual fund regime of prescriptive rules with a principles-based code of conduct approach for mutual fund managers, portfolio managers, dealers, and distributors. The proposal also queries whether mutual fund prospectuses are, in fact, used by investors in making their investment decisions, and suggests conducting a survey of investors to determine whether the prospectus requirement could, in fact, be safely abolished. In its place, mutual funds would be required to provide continuous disclosure that would be accessible to investors via the Internet. The proposal also includes a suggestion that foreign mutual funds, subject to "credible" foreign regulation, could be permitted to offer funds in Canada using their home jurisdiction documents. These proposals, like others in the concept paper, would be buttressed by an expanded range of statutory civil liability remedies for aggrieved mutual fund investors.

d) Trade Disclosure

Special trade reporting rules applicable to insiders, control persons, and others holding significant blocks of a reporting issuer's shares, as discussed in chapters 8 and 9, are based on the assumption that such holders have access to information that is not necessarily available to other public investors. Accordingly, the signal provided when such holders trade is thought to be an important one for the markets. However, the concept paper notes that the current regulatory net may now be too broadly cast, requiring disclosure by persons who do not, in fact, have special informational access. The concept paper proposes two basic changes to the current regime. First, it suggests a functional classification for those required to file insider reports, rather than the current system based on the title and compensation of the individual. Second, with respect to significant shareholders, it suggests that the current early warning system, discussed in chapter 10, might be usefully modified in three respects. First, the reporting obligation should include significant sales (blocks of 2 percent or more) as well as purchases of that size. (The current regime applies only to purchases, of course, because it was intended to provide early takeover warning. But the British

Columbia Commission foresees that reporting by significant shareholders may convey useful information to the market for other purposes as
well.) The reporting obligation would also continue for major shareholders even after they have acquired a 20 percent interest. Again, this
would be a modification of the current early warning rules, as discussed
in chapter 10. Moreover, many of the duplicative reports would be eliminated and replaced by the requirement simply to file a press release.
The paper also introduces the concept of holding issuers responsible for
controlling insider trading in their securities. Improved civil remedies
in the case of breaches of insider trading rules are also proposed.

e) New Enforcement and Public Interest Powers

The proposal suggests that securities commissions (and not only the
courts) be empowered to order disgorgement and restitution in appropriate cases of unlawful profits gained through violation of securities
laws. Further, it is suggested that the commissions have more direct
power to discipline professionals (such as lawyers and accountants)
whose actions are thought to have an adverse effect on the capital markets. In Chapter 11, we discussed the controversial *Wilder*[1] case, in
which it was held that the OSC had the jurisdiction to reprimand a
lawyer. However, while a reprimand may have reputational impact, the
power to discipline envisioned by the B.C. proposal is much more significant and could include, for example, the power to prevent a professional from appearing before the commission, or even preparing
documents filed with it. In extreme cases, this could effectively prevent
a securities lawyer, for example, from carrying on her or his practice.
A second proposal involves permitting anyone to apply for a compliance or restraining order from the commission where a breach of securities law appears imminent. Abuse of such a mechanism, it is
suggested, could be dealt with by a provision requiring costs awards to
be levied against unsuccessful applicants. Finally, practices that are
unfair, yet fall short of constituting fraudulent conduct, would be
specifically prohibited by law, making punitive sanctions available to
deter such activities.

f) New Civil Remedies for Investors

Many of the earlier mentioned proposals would be supported and
enforced by an expanded regime of statutory civil remedies for
investors consisting of the following:

---

1   *Wilder v. Ontario (Securities Commission)* (2000), 47 O.R. (3d) 361 (Div. Ct.),
     aff'd (2001), 53 O.R. (3d) 519 (C.A.).

- All misrepresentations in continuous disclosure documents would be actionable, on a basis similar to that currently available under the statutory civil remedy that exists in the case of prospectus misrepresentations, although only damages, and not rescission, would be an available remedy.
- Dealers and their officers and directors would be liable for breaches of the dealer code of conduct, whether those breaches were committed by the dealer itself or its salespeople.
- Unlawful insider traders would be liable to all investors who traded at the same time as the insider trader (and not simply to those individual counterparties with whom they traded, as is now the case). Moreover, issuers themselves (who would have an expanded role in deterring insider trading) could also be held liable in such cases.
- Unfair trading practices by market participants (even those falling short of fraud) would attract statutory civil liability remedies.
- A new securities class action regime would be established.

These new statutory civil remedies would be in addition to all existing common law rights. The paper recognizes that these proposals represent a significant extension of the current statutory civil liability rules, and so also includes proposals for appropriate measures to protect defendants from frivolous or abusive actions, including liability caps in some cases. The other corollary to the expanded civil liability regime, is that the well-known two-day "withdrawal right" currently available in the case of purchases under a prospectus would be abandoned (except in the case of offerings by restricted issuers.)

g) Ideas, Not Proposals

The British Columbia Commission has emphasized the tentative nature of all of these concepts, by explaining in the release accompanying the paper that they are "ideas for discussion, not proposals." Undoubtedly, these ideas will generate significant discussion and debate in the coming months and, together with the results of Ontario's five-year review of securities laws, will play a significant role in the further evolution of the Canadian securities regulatory regime.

2) National Instruments 54-101 and 54-102

a) Overview

As discussed in chapter 9, most shareholders of Canadian corporations hold their shares not in their own names, but rather through their brokers whose share interests, in turn, are represented on the books of a depository, such as the Canadian Depository for Securities Limited (CDS). This book-based shareholding system facilitates the fast and efficient clearing and settlement of trades. However, corporate law has traditionally been premised on the notion that only registered shareholders have the right to receive notices and vote at meetings. Accordingly, securities regulators have struggled with the challenge of facilitating an efficient book-based shareholding system while ensuring that beneficial owners of shares are not disenfranchised.

On 26 March 2002, the OSC adopted two new national instruments as rules: National Instrument 54-101 and 54-102. Together these new national instruments, which are to come into force on 1 July 2002 (subject to some transitional provisions), will replace National Policy No. 41, which, as explained in Chapter 9, embodied a kind of issuer-depository-intermediary (broker) "relay" system (or "communication chain") for the delivery of proxy and other shareholder materials. The new rules continue this system, with some modifications including with respect to so-called "non-objecting beneficial owners" (NOBOs) of securities. Perhaps the clearest way to illustrate how the system operates is to set out a simple step-by-step example of how notice of a shareholders' meeting must be disseminated under National Instrument 54-101 when it comes into full effect.

b) Example

ABC Limited is a reporting issuer. The time is approaching for the calling of ABC's annual shareholders' meeting. The directors of ABC meet to decide upon a date for the meeting (as proposed by management). Because of the time requirements mandated by National Instrument 54-101, the date chosen for such a meeting will need to be at least fifty-five days in the future. The directors will need to set both a meeting date and an earlier record date. The record date refers to the date on which shareholders entitled to receive notice of the meeting will be determined. The record date must be considerably earlier than the meeting date, so that the company can settle the list of shareholders to whom they will deliver meeting notices and proxy materials. Shares in a public company change hands every day; so, unless a fixed record date is set, the list of shareholders would be a constantly moving target that would be impossible to finalize. The record date must be at least thirty, but not more than sixty, days before the meeting date. (NI 54-101, s. 2.1(b))

Once the record date and the meeting date have been determined, ABC must send a notice of these dates to depositories, any exchanges on which ABC securities are traded, and the securities regulators. That notice must be sent at least twenty-five days before the record date. (NI 54-101, s.2.2(1))

When ABC sends its notice to a depository (such as CDS), it will request the depository to provide ABC information essentially relating to the number of ABC securities the depository holds, and will also request a list of intermediaries and participants on whose behalf the depository is holding those ABC shares. (Participants would typically be securities brokerage firms.) ABC will also request the depository to complete and return to ABC an omnibus proxy in the form of Form 54-101F3. The depository is expected to return this form within two business days after receiving ABC's notice.

The purpose of the omnibus proxy is easily explained. Because the depository is the registered holder of ABC shares, in order for those shares to be voted at the meeting, the depository must either vote them itself, or provide a form of proxy permitting someone else to vote them. Of course, the depository has no beneficial interest in the shares whatsoever and so is forbidden from simply voting them. Indeed, the depository does not even know who the ultimate beneficial owners of the shares are. The only information available to the depository are the names of the participants and how many of the shares registered in the name of the depository are held on behalf of each participant. So, for example, suppose that CDS were the registered holder of 100,000 shares of ABC. CDS's own records might indicate that, of those 100,000 shares, 35,000 were held on behalf of BMO Nesbitt Burns, 40,000 were held on behalf of RBC Dominion Securities, and 25,000 were held on behalf of ScotiaMcLeod. The omnibus proxy signed by CDS would appoint each of those securities firms as CDS's proxyholder with respect to the respective number of ABC shares held by CDS on that firm's behalf. (It is this omnibus proxy form that will then permit the securities firms, in turn, to provide their clients — the beneficial owners of the shares — with the opportunity to vote those shares, as described below.)

The information about brokers and intermediaries provided to ABC by the depository now permits ABC to take the next step. ABC must now contact each of the intermediaries, at least twenty days before the record date, providing and requesting information as set out in Part 1 of Form 54-101F2. The purpose of this communication is, among other things, to determine how many beneficial owners of ABC shares each participant represents, so that an appropriate number of proxy material packages (containing the company's annual report, notice of meeting, and proxy information circular) need to be provided. In addition, ABC may request the names and contact information for any NOBOs (non-objecting beneficial owners) — that is, ABC shareholders who have previously indicated to the intermediary that they do not object to that intermediary disclosing their beneficial ownership information. (NI 54-101, s.2.5)

Within three business days of receiving the request described in the previous paragraph, the intermediaries must respond with the requested information in the form of Part 2 of Form 54-101F2. (NI 54-101, s. 4.1(1))

The proxy materials must then be delivered by ABC not only to its registered shareholders, but also (directly or indirectly) to the beneficial owners of its shares. In the case of NOBOs, ABC may send the proxy material directly at least twenty-one days before the meeting date. In the case of other beneficial owners — about whom ABC will have no information, not even their names — the proxy materials will be sent to the intermediaries who will, in turn, arrange for the materials to be sent to the beneficial owners. (To ensure that the intermediaries are in a position to send out materials at least twenty-one days before the meeting date, ABC will be obliged to send the appropriate number of proxy materials to the intermediaries three or four business days earlier — i.e., three or four business days before the date that is twenty-one days before the date set for the shareholders' meeting.)

Now, when the beneficial owners receive their meeting materials, they are, technically, in a position very different from that of a registered shareholder. If they wish their voice to be heard at the shareholders' meeting, they cannot, as a technical matter, simply attend the meeting and vote their shares. Only registered shareholders can do that. Nor can they deliver a form of proxy authorizing someone else to vote their shares on their behalf because, once again "their" shares are actually registered in someone else's name — usually in the name of the depository. However, NI 54-101 provides a mechanism by which these two voting alternatives are, functionally, made available to the beneficial owners as well. Thus, if the beneficial owner wishes to attend the meeting, she or he will be provided with a "legal proxy," signed by the registered holder, or by the intermediary that has itself been appointed as a proxyholder by the depository. (NI 54-101, s. 2.18) The effect of this legal proxy is this. The beneficial owner will, in effect, be appointed by the registered shareholder to act as the proxyholder in respect of those very shares which she or he owns beneficially. What this means, in practice, is that the beneficial owner may attend and vote at the shareholders' meeting just as if he or she were the registered shareholder. If, on the other hand, the beneficial owner does not wish to attend in person, he or she can, instead, provide "voting instructions" to the proxyholder (NI 54-101, s. 2.17), the effect of which, for all practical purposes, will be the same as if contained in instructions accompanying a form of proxy executed by a registered shareholder.

c) National Instrument 54-102

National Instrument 54-102, made by the OSC at the same time as National Instrument 54-101, provides an exemption to reporting issuers from what would otherwise be the requirement to send interim financial statements to all registered shareholders pursuant, in Ontario, to subsection 77(1) and section 79 of the OSA. To qualify for the exemption, a reporting issuer must (1) issue and file a news release summarizing the information contained in its interim financial statements; (2) file the interim financial statement with securities regulators and securities exchanges on which the issuer's securities are listed; and (3) send the statements to those registered and beneficial securityholders who have asked to have their names included on a "supplemental list" for the purpose of receiving such statements. Like National Instrument 54-101, National Instrument 54-102 is to come into force 1 July 2002.

3) Cooperation with Securities Regulators

On 9 April 2002, the OSC issued a press release announcing a "credit for cooperation" policy.[2] Where parties cooperate fully with OSC Staff during an investigation, the OSC may pursue matters in a more flexible or favourable manner. This policy echoes a similar approach articulated by the United States Securities and Exchange Commission (SEC) in October 2001 in connection with a cease and desist proceeding against Gisela de Leon-Meredith, a former officer of the subsidiary of a public company.[3] In the United States, the SEC's approach has generated some controversy relating, among other things, to delicate problems of attorney-client privilege in the context of a firm's internal investigation of suspected improprieties where the firm and individual officers and employees may be adverse in interest. Unlike the SEC's statement, however, which specifically refers to the possibility of cooperating firms wishing "to consider choosing not to assert the attorney-client privilege" in some cases,[4] the OSC's statement refers to more

---

2   Ontario Securities Commission, News Release, "OSC Announces Policy to Encourage Cooperation with Staff During Investigations" (9 April 2002). Available online at <http://www.osc.gov.on.ca> (site accessed: 10 April 2002).
3   See SEC, Release No. 34-44969 (23 October 2001).
4   *Ibid.*

innocuous elements of cooperation such as the fact that the party under investigation "has self-policed, self-reported, and self-corrected the problems."

B. CONCLUSION

Securities law comprises a vast body of rules and principles that cannot be fully canvassed in a book of this size or, indeed, in a book many times longer than this one. In the preceding chapters, we have tried to focus on those topics that we believe afford the best introduction to the essential principles and policies of Canadian securities regulation. But, we have made no attempt to survey every major issue with which securities law practitioners must regularly contend.

Although we endeavoured to discuss the most fundamental aspects of modern Canadian securities regulation in this book, it was possible to reveal only the uppermost tip of a vast regulatory iceberg. We do hope, however, that if the text has occasionally gone short on institutional and technical detail, it proves long enough in its review of basic principles that readers may continue a more detailed exploration of Canadian securities laws with a solid understanding of the basic foundation upon which those intricate laws were built.

TABLE OF CASES

INDEX